I always buy lots of notebooks whenever I go to a stationery store. When I see a blank notebook, I want to start doodling in it. I like to buy clothes and video games too, but buying notebooks is what makes me happiest.

—**Katsura Hoshino**

Shiga Prefecture native Katsura Hoshino's hit manga series *D.Gray-man* has been serialized in *Weekly Shonen Jump* since 2004. Katsura's debut manga, "Continue," appeared for the first time in *Weekly Shonen Jump* in 2003.

Katsura adores cats.

D.GRAY-MAN
VOL. 17
SHONEN JUMP ADVANCED
Manga Edition

STORY AND ART BY
KATSURA HOSHINO

English Adaptation/Lance Caselman
Translation/John Werry
Touch-up Art & Lettering/HudsonYards
Design/Matt Hinrichs
Editor/Gary Leach

VP, Production/Alvin Lu
VP, Sales & Product Marketing/Gonzalo Ferreyra
VP, Creative/Linda Espinosa
Publisher/Hyoe Narita

Printed in the U.S.A.

Published by VIZ Media, LLC
P.O. Box 77010
San Francisco, CA 94107

10 9 8 7 6 5 4 3 2 1
First printing, May 2010

www.viz.com

THE WORLD'S MOST
CUTTING-EDGE MANGA

SHONEN
JUMP
ADVANCED
www.shonenjump.com

SHONEN JUMP ADVANCED MANGA EDITION

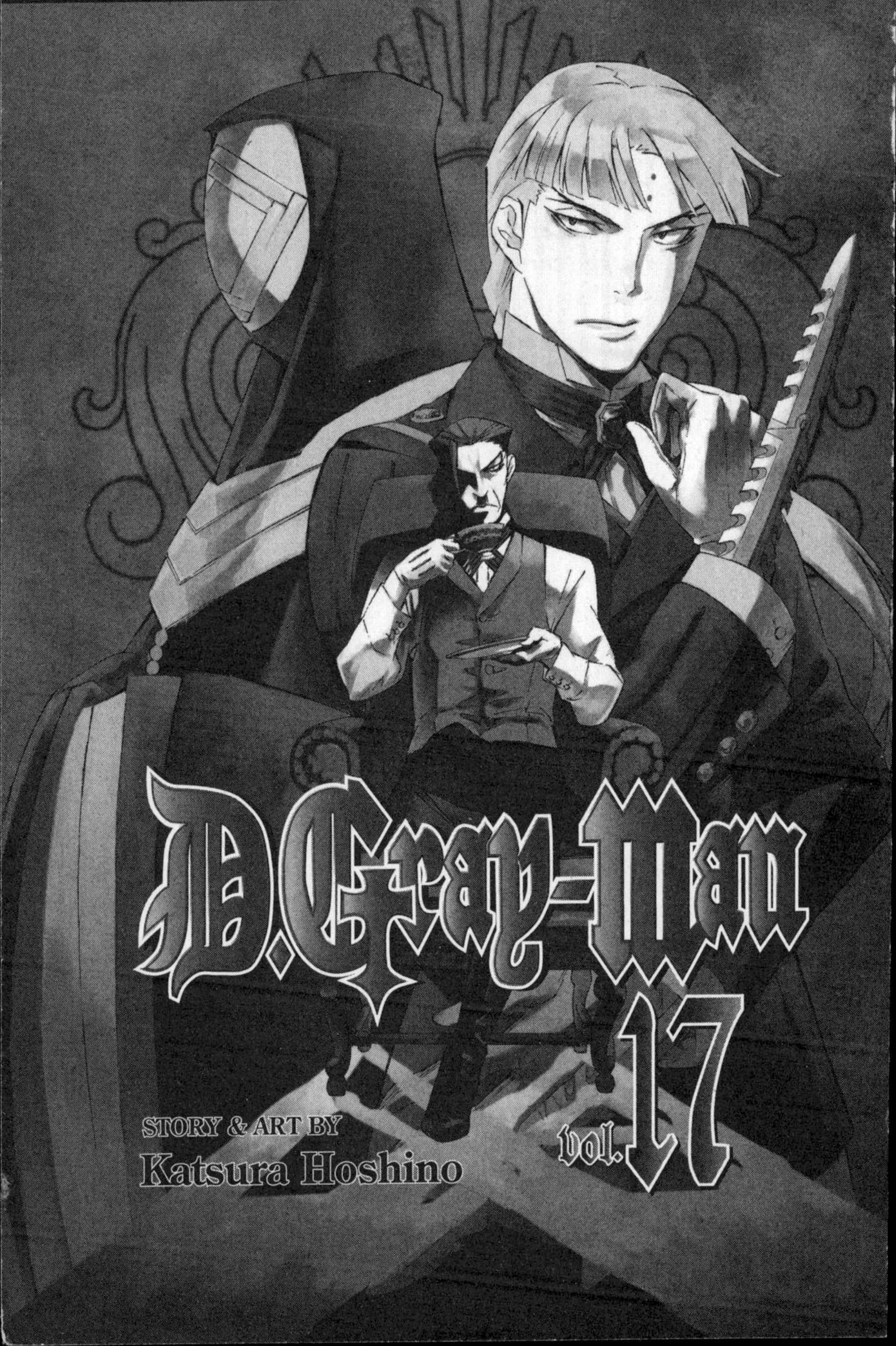
D.Gray-man
vol. 17
STORY & ART BY
Katsura Hoshino

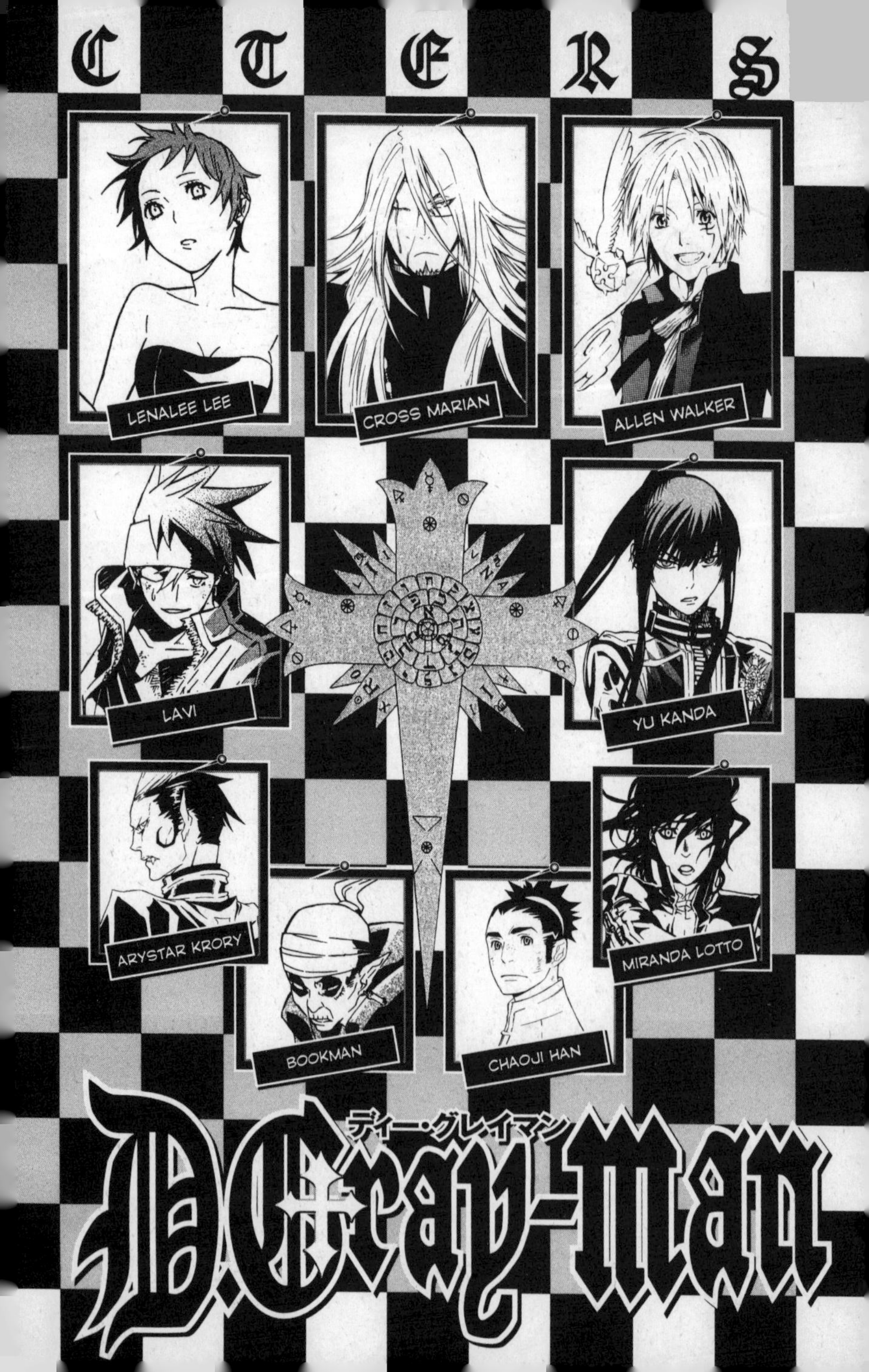
C T E R S
LENALEE LEE
CROSS MARIAN
ALLEN WALKER
LAVI
YU KANDA
ARYSTAR KRORY
MIRANDA LOTTO
BOOKMAN
CHAOJI HAN
ディー・グレイマン
D.Gray-man

C H A R A

JOHNNY GILL

BAK CHAN

KOMUI LEE

MILLENNIUM EARL

MALCOLM C. ROUVELIER

REEVER WENHAM

MANA WALKER

HOWARD LINK

S T O R Y

IT ALL BEGAN CENTURIES AGO WITH THE DISCOVERY OF A CUBE CONTAINING AN APOCALYPTIC PROPHECY FROM AN ANCIENT CIVILIZATION AND INSTRUCTIONS IN THE USE OF INNOCENCE, A CRYSTALLINE SUBSTANCE OF WONDROUS SUPERNATURAL POWER. THE CREATORS OF THE CUBE CLAIMED TO HAVE DEFEATED AN EVIL KNOWN AS THE MILLENNIUM EARL BY USING THE INNOCENCE. NEVERTHELESS, THE WORLD WAS DESTROYED BY THE GREAT FLOOD OF THE OLD TESTAMENT. NOW, TO AVERT A SECOND END OF THE WORLD, A GROUP OF EXORCISTS WIELDING WEAPONS MADE OF INNOCENCE MUST BATTLE THE MILLENNIUM EARL AND HIS TERRIBLE MINIONS, THE AKUMA.

FOLLOWING THE BATTLE ABOARD THE DISINTEGRATING ARK, CENTRAL AGENCY ASSIGNS A GUARD TO WATCH ALLEN'S EVERY MOVE. THEN LULU BELL AND A LEVEL 4 AKUMA ATTACK THE ORDER'S HEADQUARTERS, LEAVING IT IN RUINS. AS PREPARATIONS FOR A MOVE GET UNDERWAY, A MYSTERIOUS VIRUS INFECTS THE EXORCISTS, TURNING MOST OF THEM INTO ZOMBIES!

D.GRAY-MAN
Vol. 17

CONTENTS

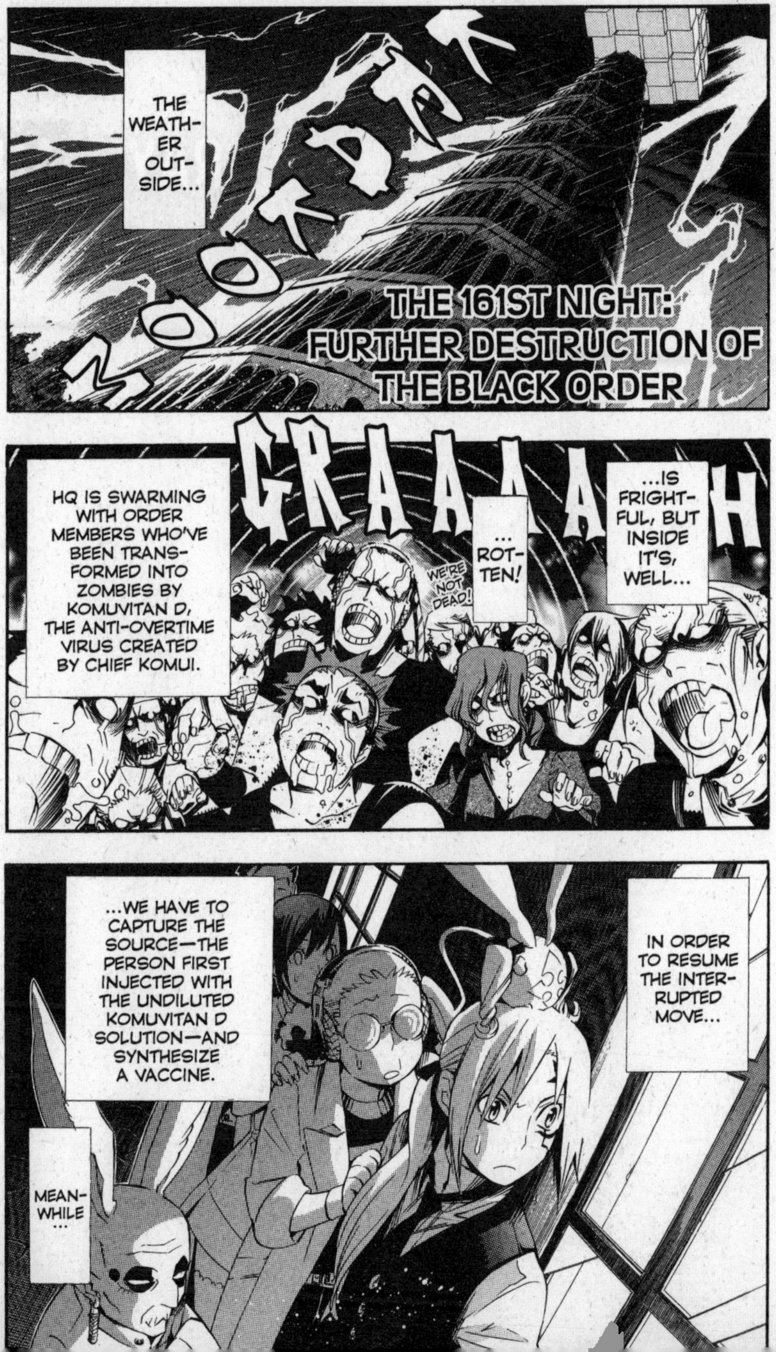
THE WEATHER OUTSIDE...
THE 161ST NIGHT: FURTHER DESTRUCTION OF THE BLACK ORDER
...IS FRIGHTFUL, BUT INSIDE IT'S, WELL...
...ROTTEN!
WE'RE NOT DEAD!
HQ IS SWARMING WITH ORDER MEMBERS WHO'VE BEEN TRANSFORMED INTO ZOMBIES BY KOMUVITAN D, THE ANTI-OVERTIME VIRUS CREATED BY CHIEF KOMUI.
IN ORDER TO RESUME THE INTERRUPTED MOVE...
...WE HAVE TO CAPTURE THE SOURCE—THE PERSON FIRST INJECTED WITH THE UNDILUTED KOMUVITAN D SOLUTION—AND SYNTHESIZE A VACCINE.
MEANWHILE...

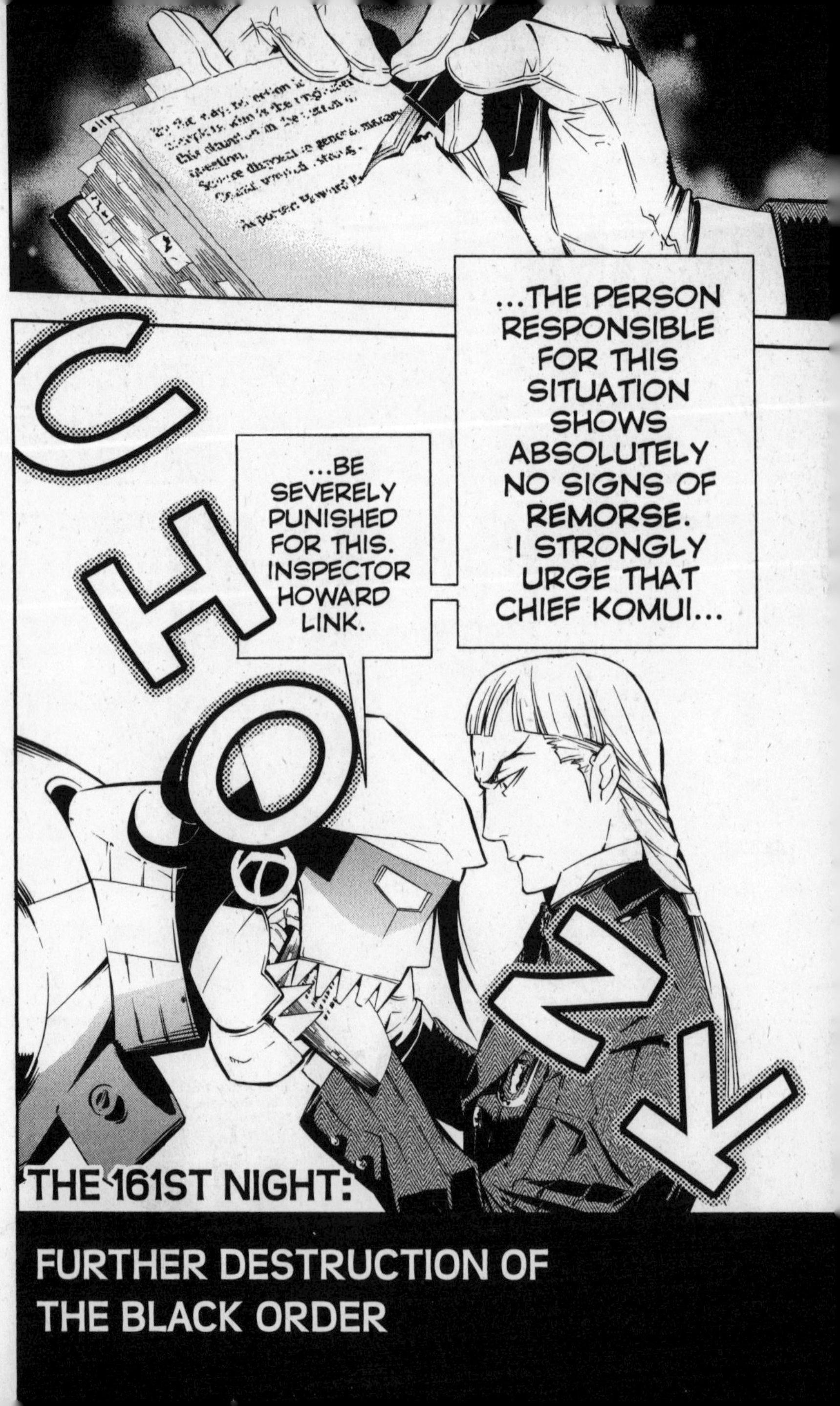
...THE PERSON RESPONSIBLE FOR THIS SITUATION SHOWS ABSOLUTELY NO SIGNS OF REMORSE. I STRONGLY URGE THAT CHIEF KOMUI...
...BE SEVERELY PUNISHED FOR THIS. INSPECTOR HOWARD LINK.
CHONK

THE 161ST NIGHT: FURTHER DESTRUCTION OF THE BLACK ORDER

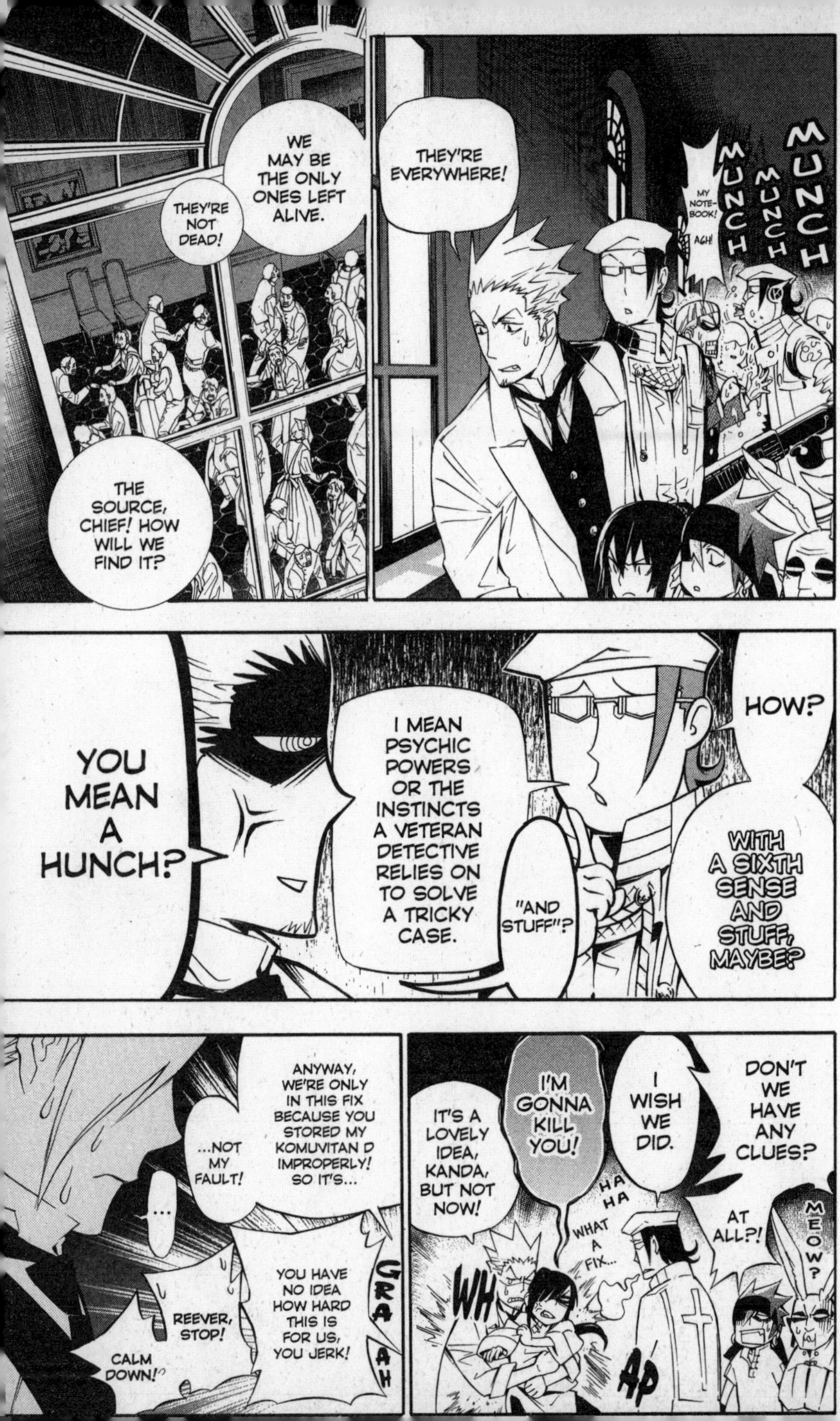
MUNCH
MUNCH
MUNCH
MY NOTE-BOOK!
AGH!
THEY'RE EVERYWHERE!
WE MAY BE THE ONLY ONES LEFT ALIVE.
THEY'RE NOT DEAD!
THE SOURCE, CHIEF! HOW WILL WE FIND IT?
HOW?
WITH A SIXTH SENSE AND STUFF, MAYBE?
"AND STUFF"?
I MEAN PSYCHIC POWERS OR THE INSTINCTS A VETERAN DETECTIVE RELIES ON TO SOLVE A TRICKY CASE.
YOU MEAN A HUNCH?
DON'T WE HAVE ANY CLUES?
AT ALL?!
MEOW?
I WISH WE DID.
I'M GONNA KILL YOU!
IT'S A LOVELY IDEA, KANDA, BUT NOT NOW!
HA HA
WHAT A FIX...
WHAP
ANYWAY, WE'RE ONLY IN THIS FIX BECAUSE YOU STORED MY KOMUVITAN D IMPROPERLY! SO IT'S...
...NOT MY FAULT!
GRAAH
YOU HAVE NO IDEA HOW HARD THIS IS FOR US, YOU JERK!
...
REEVER, STOP!
CALM DOWN!

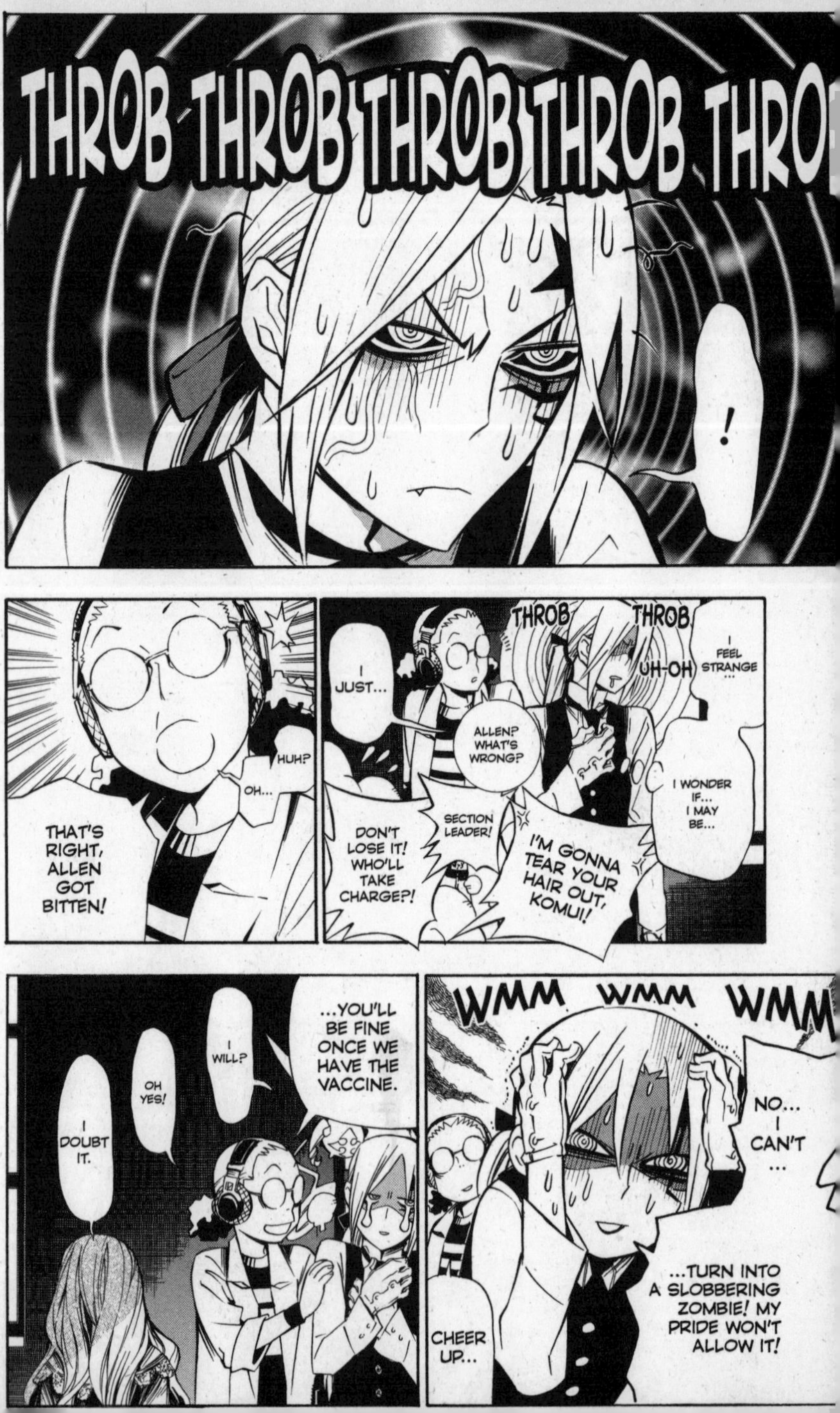
THROB THROB THROB THROB THRO
!
THROB THROB
UH-OH
I FEEL STRANGE...
I WONDER IF... I MAY BE...
I'M GONNA TEAR YOUR HAIR OUT, KOMUI!
SECTION LEADER!
ALLEN? WHAT'S WRONG?
I JUST...
DON'T LOSE IT! WHO'LL TAKE CHARGE?!
HUH?
OH...
THAT'S RIGHT, ALLEN GOT BITTEN!
WMM WMM WMM
NO... I CAN'T...
...TURN INTO A SLOBBERING ZOMBIE! MY PRIDE WON'T ALLOW IT!
CHEER UP...
...YOU'LL BE FINE ONCE WE HAVE THE VACCINE.
I WILL?
OH YES!
I DOUBT IT.

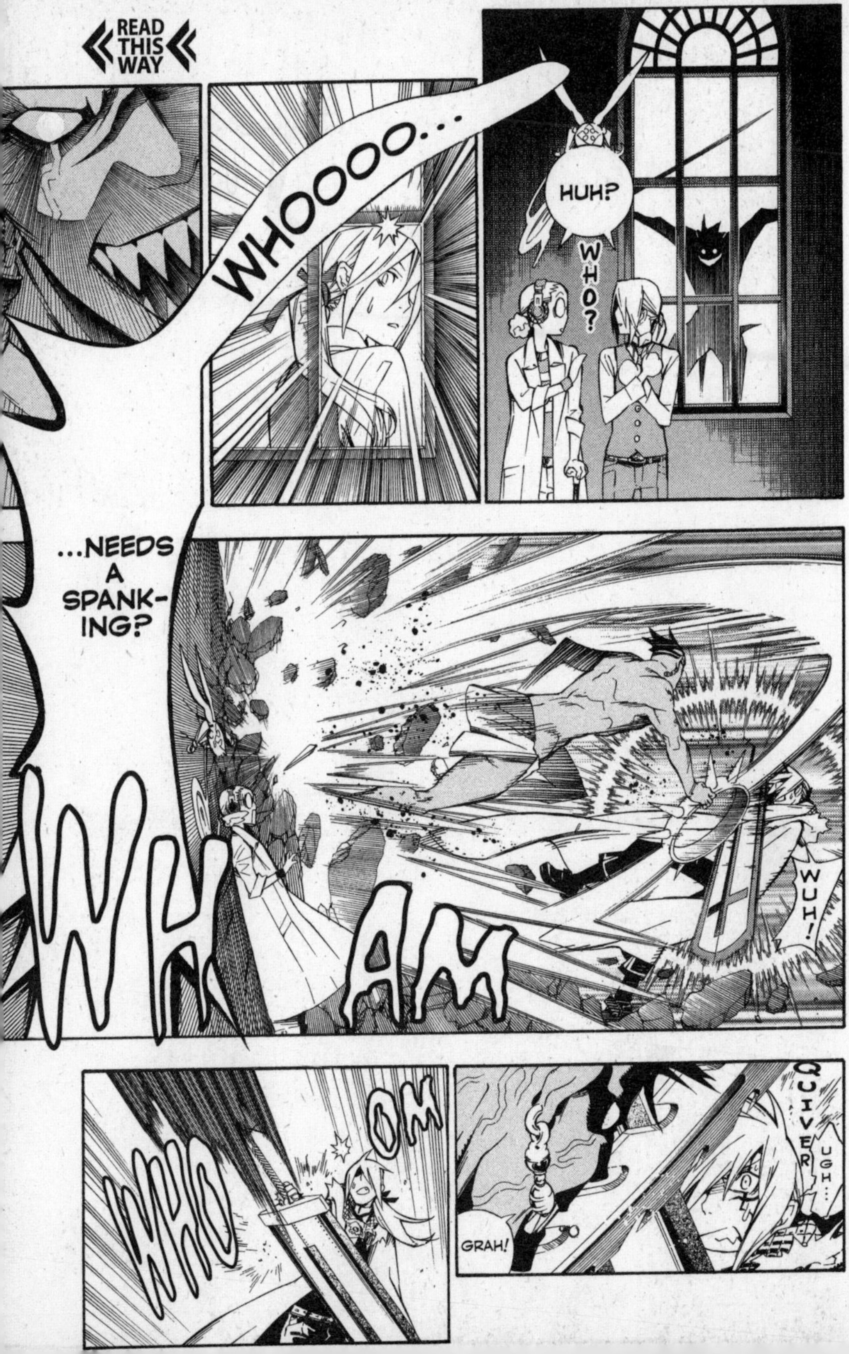
READ THIS WAY
HUH?
WHO?
WHOOOO...
...NEEDS A SPANK-ING?
WHAM
WUH!
QUIVER
UGH...
GRAH!
WHOOM

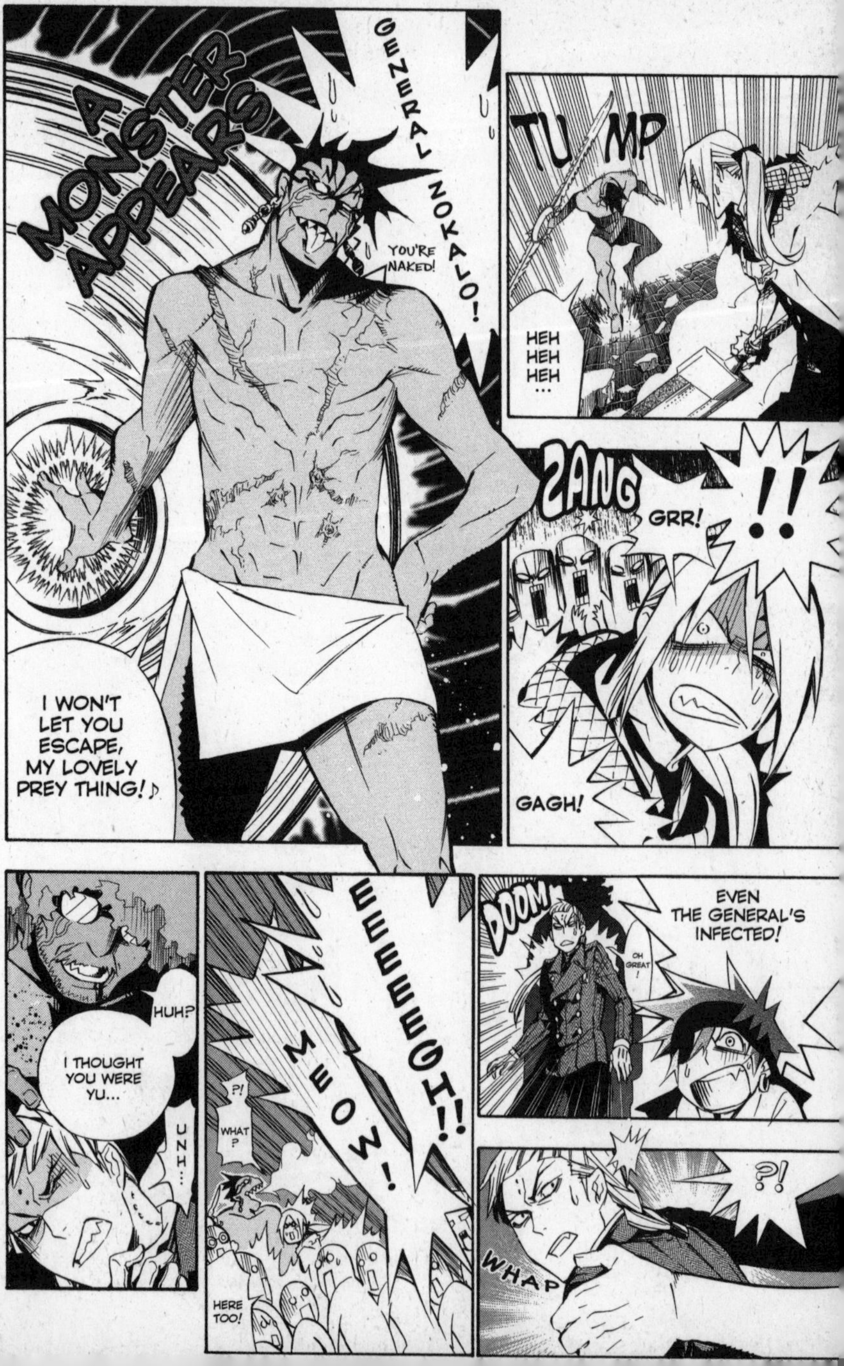
TUMP
HEH HEH HEH...
ZANG
GRR!
!!
GAGH!
GENERAL ZOKALO!
A MONSTER APPEARS
YOU'RE NAKED!
I WON'T LET YOU ESCAPE, MY LOVELY PREY THING!♪
EVEN THE GENERAL'S INFECTED!
DOOM
OH GREAT!
?!
WHAP
EEEEEEGH!!
MEOW!
?!
WHAT?
HERE TOO!
HUH?
I THOUGHT YOU WERE YU...
UNH...

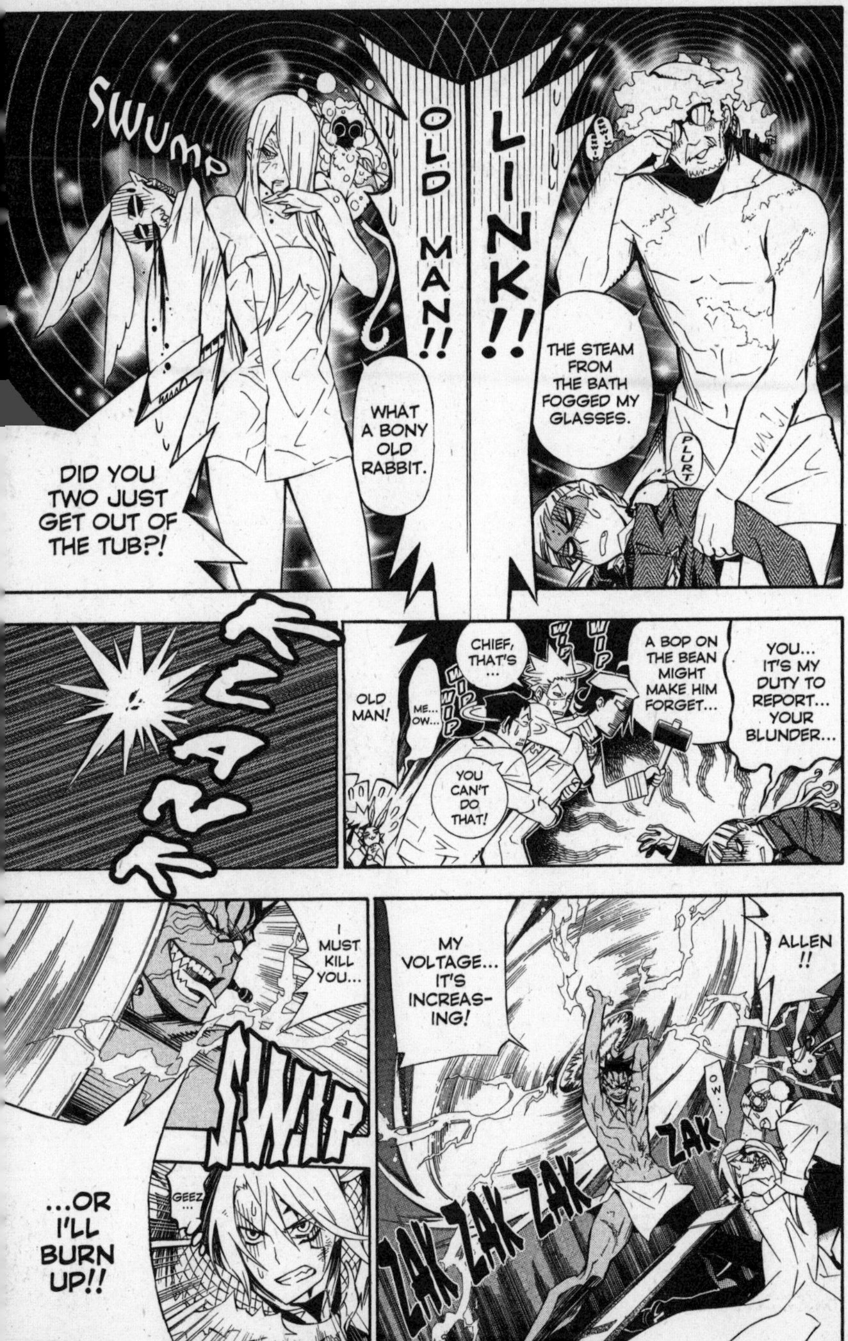
LINK!!
THE STEAM FROM THE BATH FOGGED MY GLASSES.
PLURT
OLD MAN!!
WHAT A BONY OLD RABBIT.
SWUMP
DID YOU TWO JUST GET OUT OF THE TUB?!
YOU... IT'S MY DUTY TO REPORT... YOUR BLUNDER...
A BOP ON THE BEAN MIGHT MAKE HIM FORGET...
WIP
WIP
CHIEF, THAT'S ...
WIP
WIP
ME... OW...
OLD MAN!
YOU CAN'T DO THAT!
ALLEN !!
OW...
MY VOLTAGE... IT'S INCREASING!
ZAK ZAK ZAK ZAK
I MUST KILL YOU...
SWIP
GEEZ ...
...OR I'LL BURN UP!!

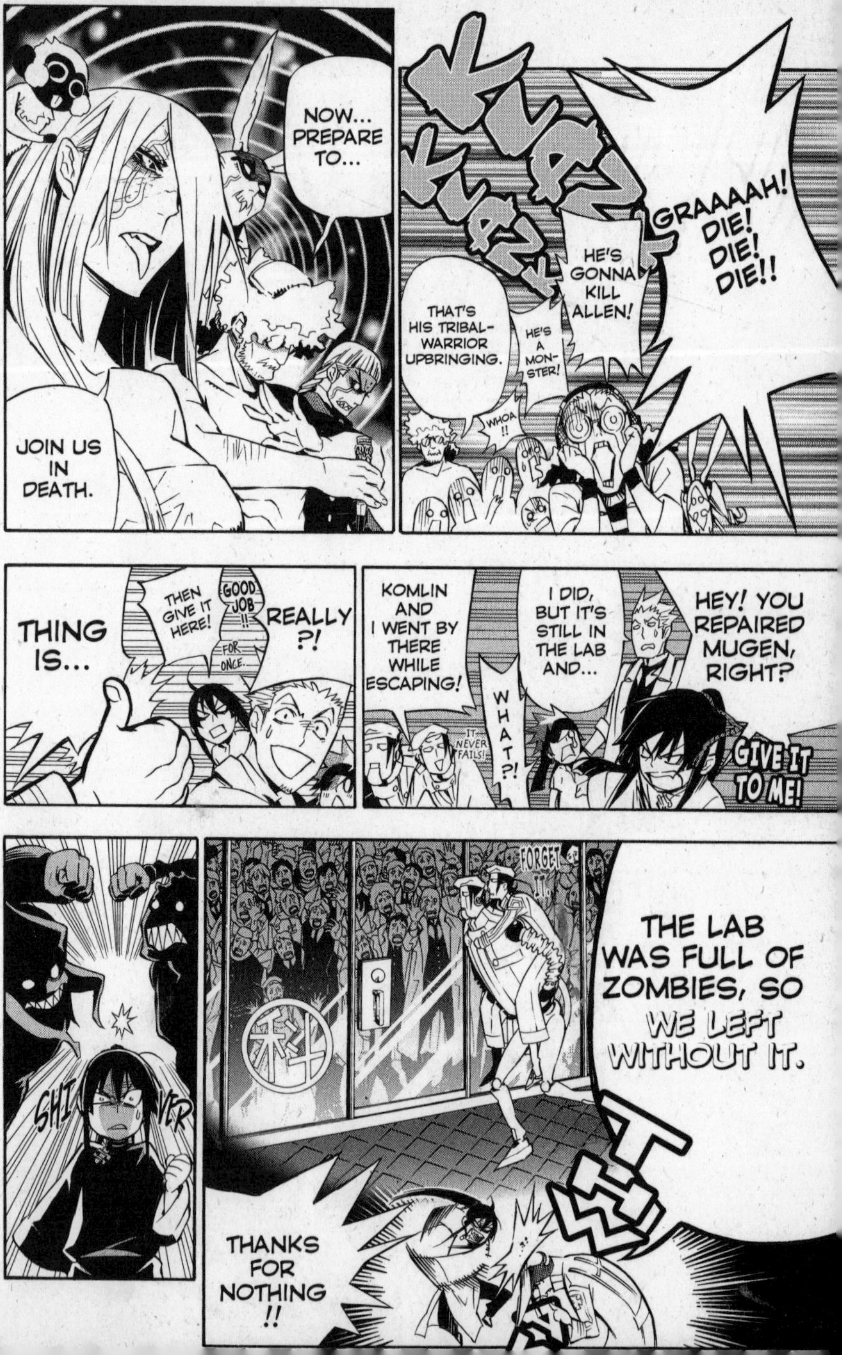
GRAAAAH! DIE! DIE! DIE!!
HE'S GONNA KILL ALLEN!
HE'S A MON-STER!
THAT'S HIS TRIBAL-WARRIOR UPBRINGING.
WHOA!!
NOW... PREPARE TO...
JOIN US IN DEATH.
HEY! YOU REPAIRED MUGEN, RIGHT?
GIVE IT TO ME!
I DID, BUT IT'S STILL IN THE LAB AND...
WHAT?!
KOMLIN AND I WENT BY THERE WHILE ESCAPING!
IT NEVER FAILS!
REALLY?!
GOOD JOB!!
FOR ONCE.
THEN GIVE IT HERE!
THING IS...
THE LAB WAS FULL OF ZOMBIES, SO WE LEFT WITHOUT IT.
FORGET IT.
THANKS FOR NOTHING!!
SHIVER

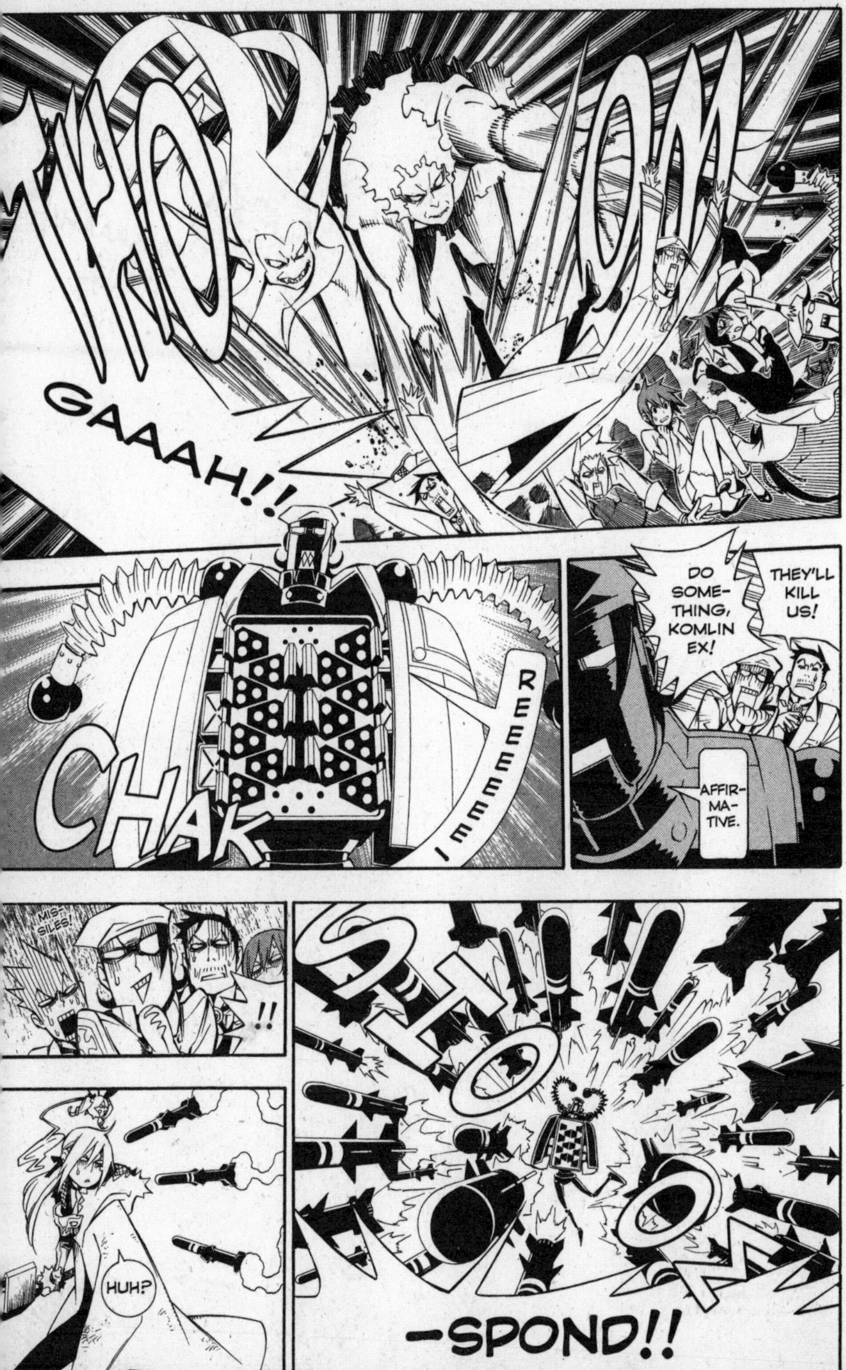
THOOOM
GAAAH!!
THEY'LL KILL US!
DO SOMETHING, KOMLIN EX!
AFFIRMATIVE.
REEEEEEEE!
CHAK
SHOOOM
-SPOND!!
MISSILES!
!!
HUH?

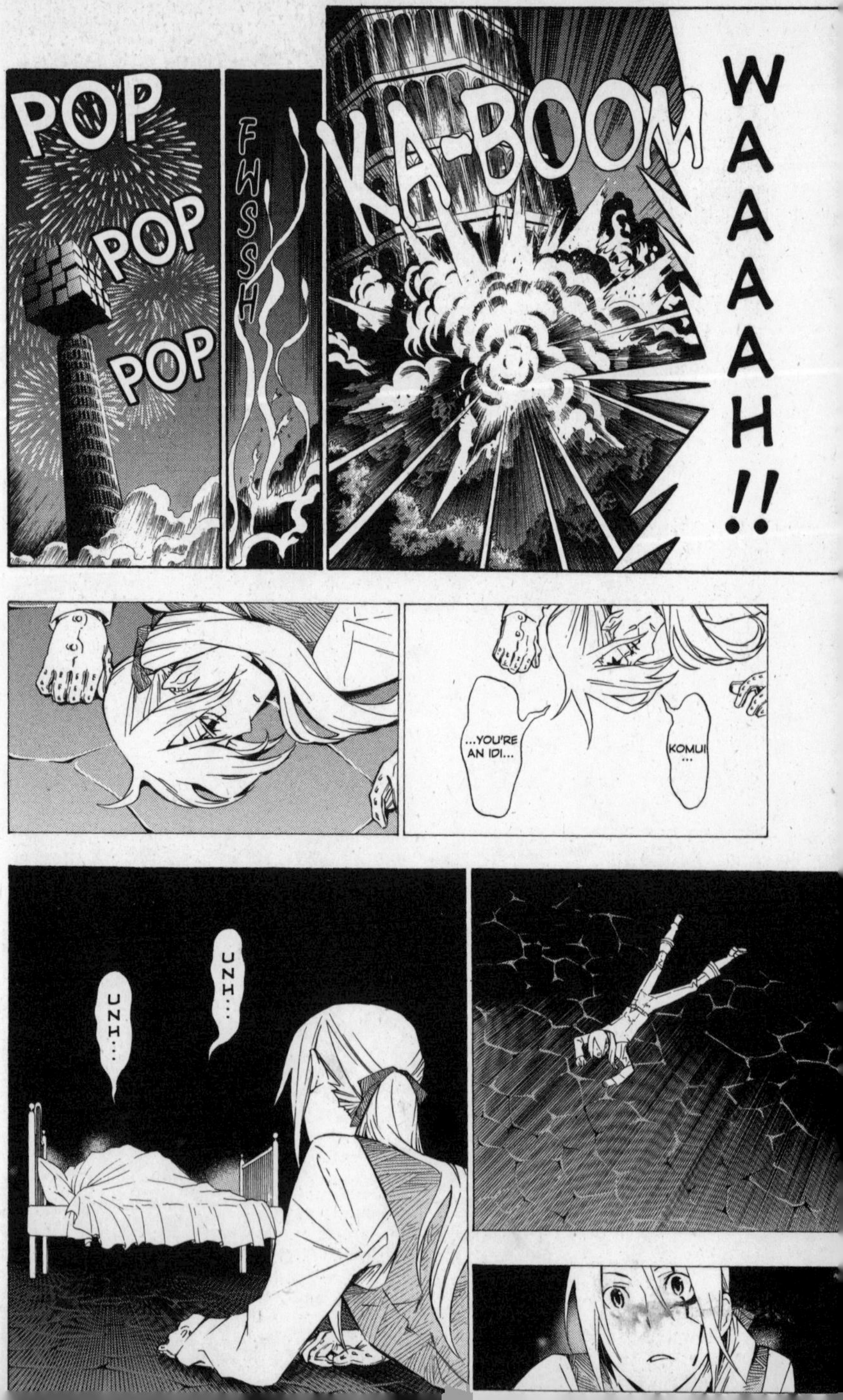
WAAAAH!!
KA-BOOM
FWSSH
POP
POP
POP
KOMUI ...
...YOU'RE AN IDI...
UNH...
UNH...

READ THIS WAY
THE PAIN...
UNH...
IT HURTS...
IT HURTS...
WHO IS THIS?
UNH...
UNH...

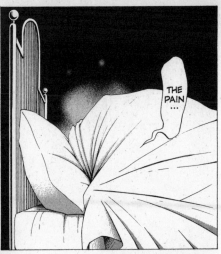

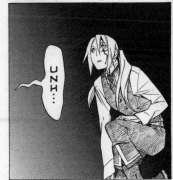

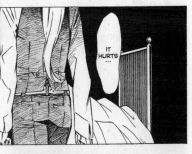

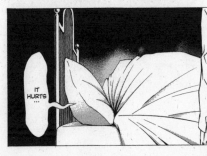

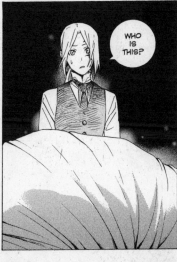

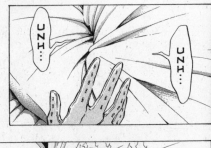

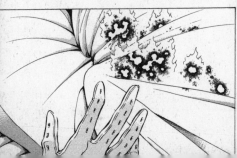

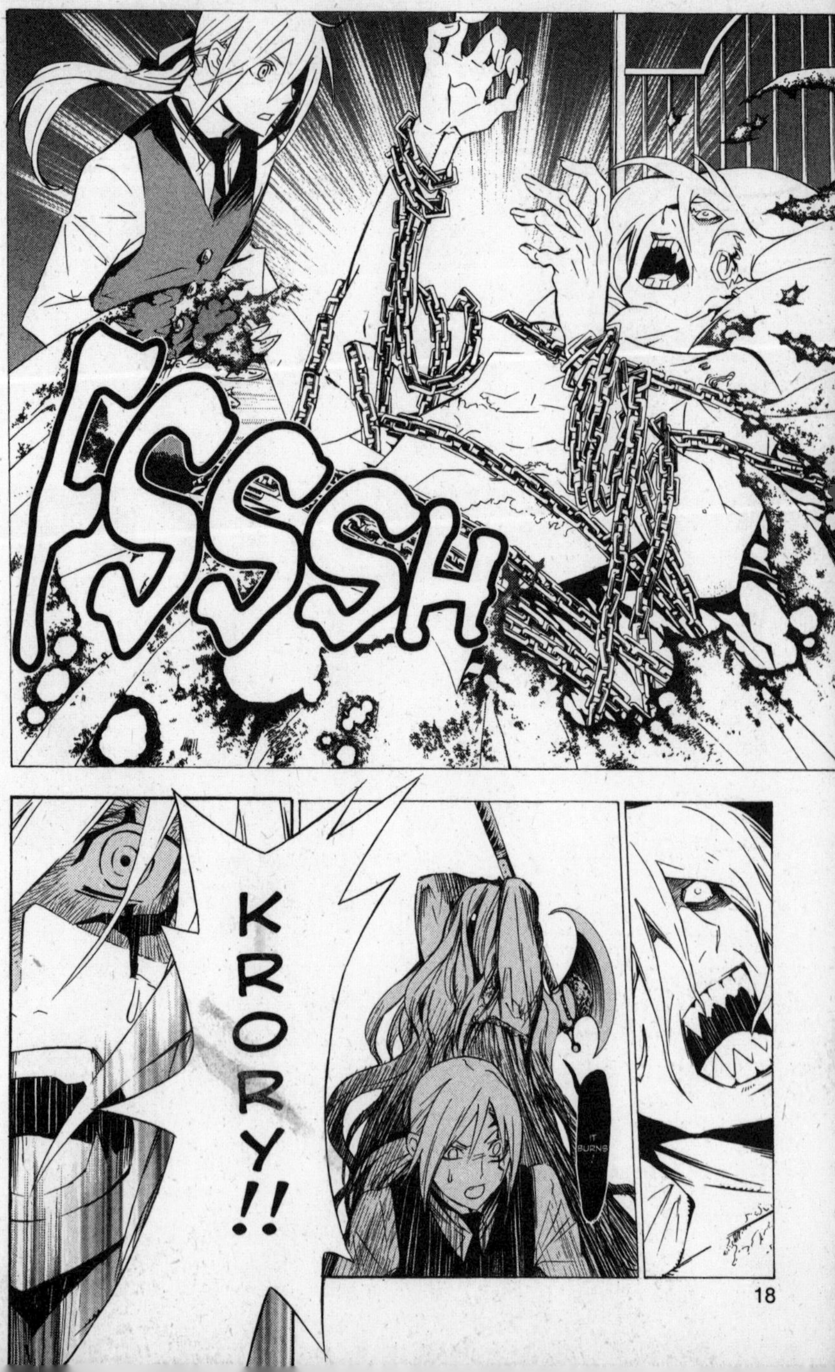
FSSSH
IT BURNS
KRORY!!

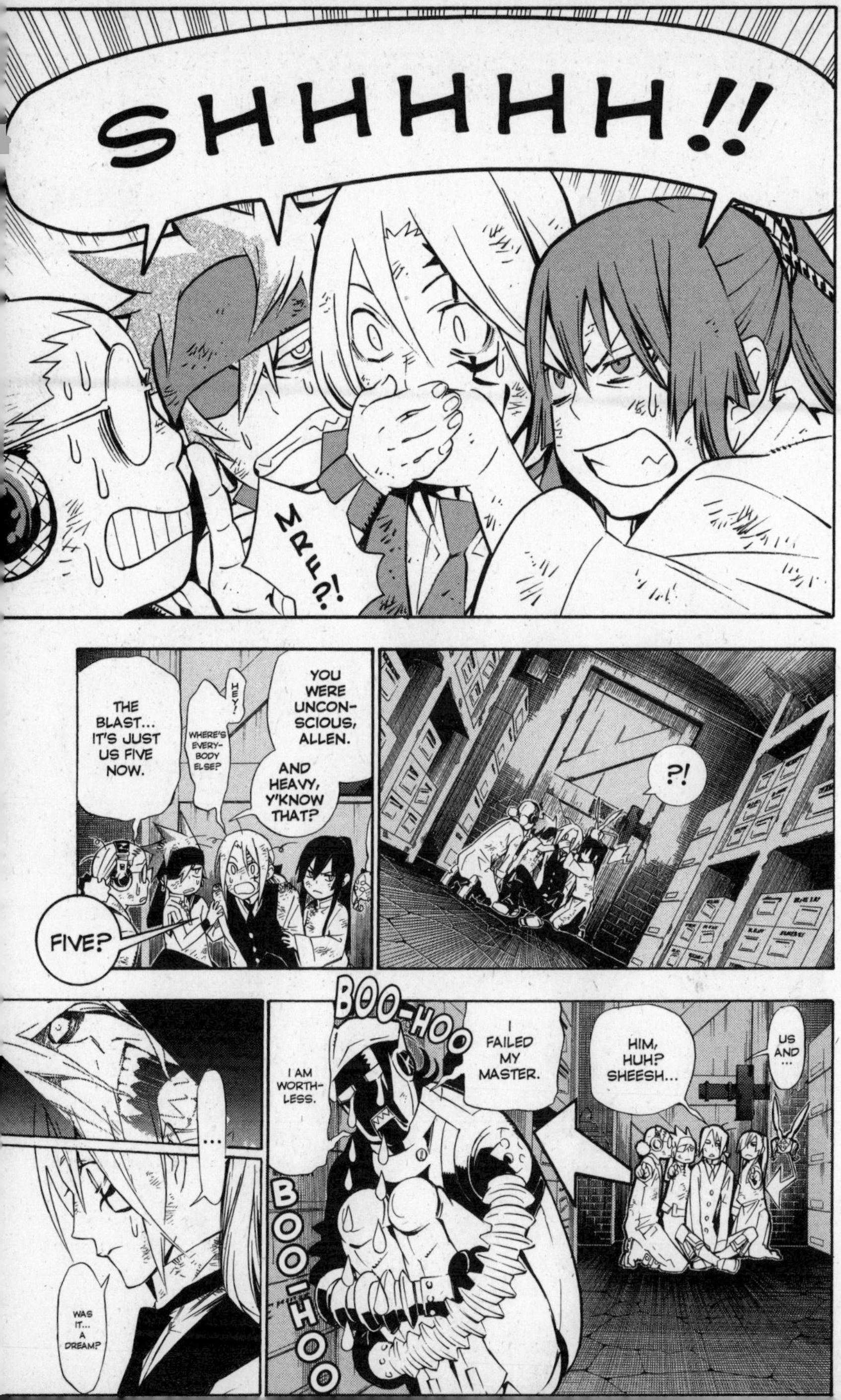
SHHHHH!!
MRF?!
?!
YOU WERE UNCONSCIOUS, ALLEN.
AND HEAVY, Y'KNOW THAT?
HEY!
WHERE'S EVERYBODY ELSE?
THE BLAST... IT'S JUST US FIVE NOW.
FIVE?
US AND ...
HIM, HUH? SHEESH...
I FAILED MY MASTER.
BOO-HOO
I AM WORTHLESS.
BOO-HOO
BOO-HOO
...
WAS IT... A DREAM?

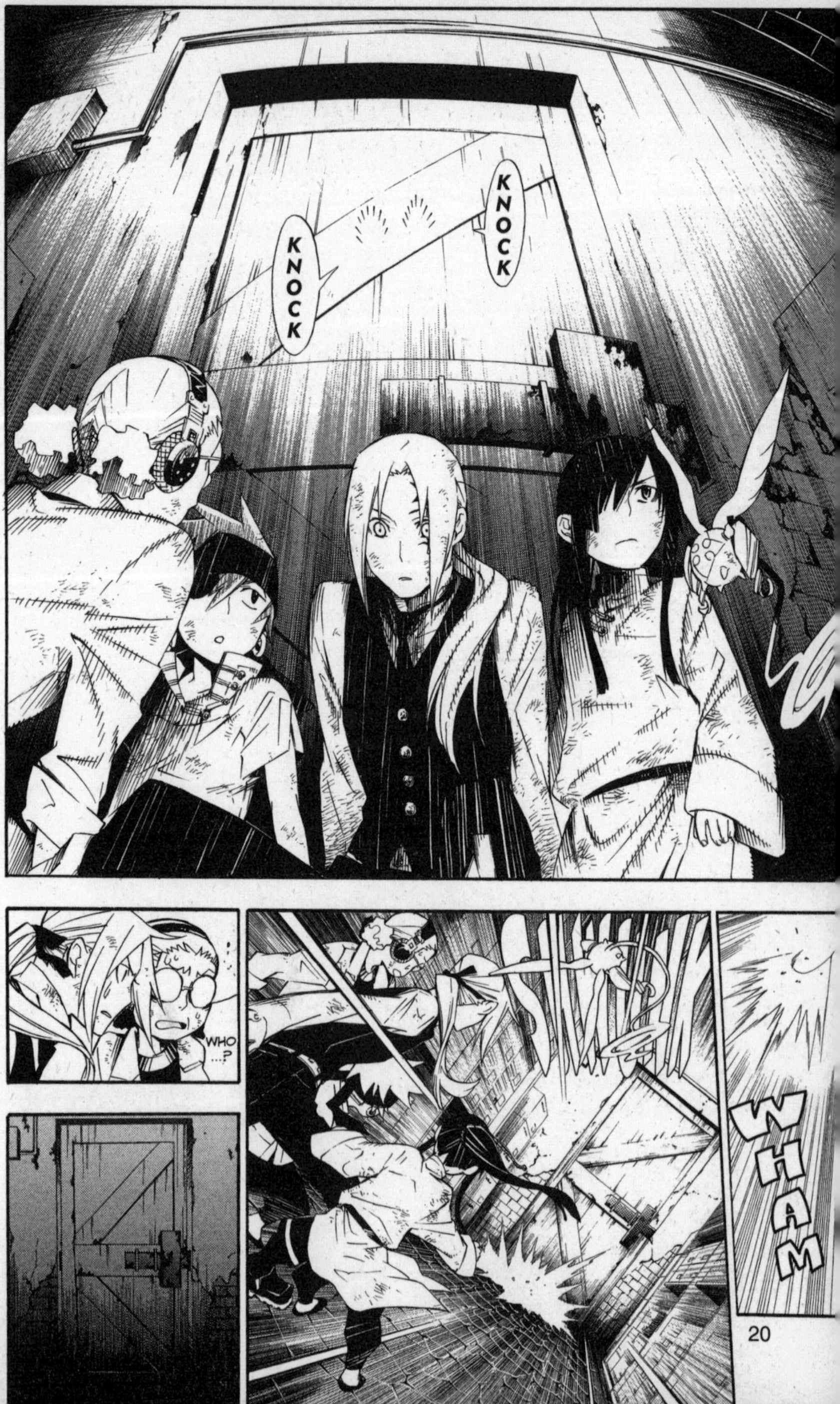
KNOCK
KNOCK
WHAM
WHO ...?

THAT VOICE ...

!!

IT IS I...

LAVI...

ALLEN...

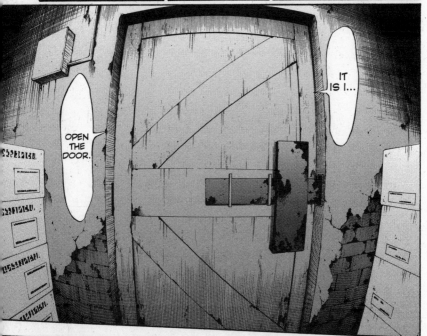

OPEN THE DOOR.

IT IS I...

KRORY?!

THE PEOPLE OF D.GRAY-HOUSE

SENSEI IS ONE OF THE FAMILY!

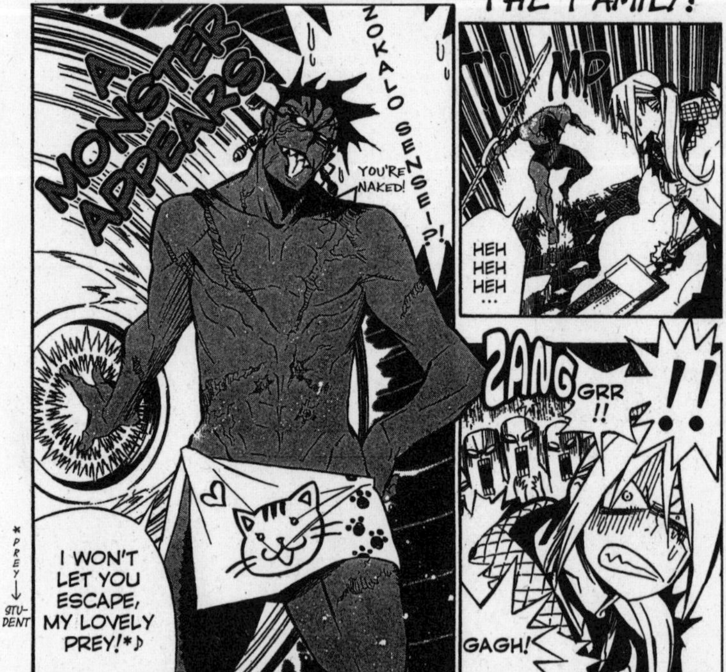
TUMP
HEH HEH HEH...
ZANG
GRR!!
!!
GAGH!
ZOKALO SENSEI?!
YOU'RE NAKED!
A MONSTER APPEARS
I WON'T LET YOU ESCAPE, MY LOVELY PREY!*♪
*PREY ↓ STUDENT
DOOM
THAT'S OUR SENSEI?! BUT WHY THE CAT?!
IT LOOKS LIKE CORO!
ICK!

LIVE-IN TUTOR ZOKALO SENSEI LIKES CATS.

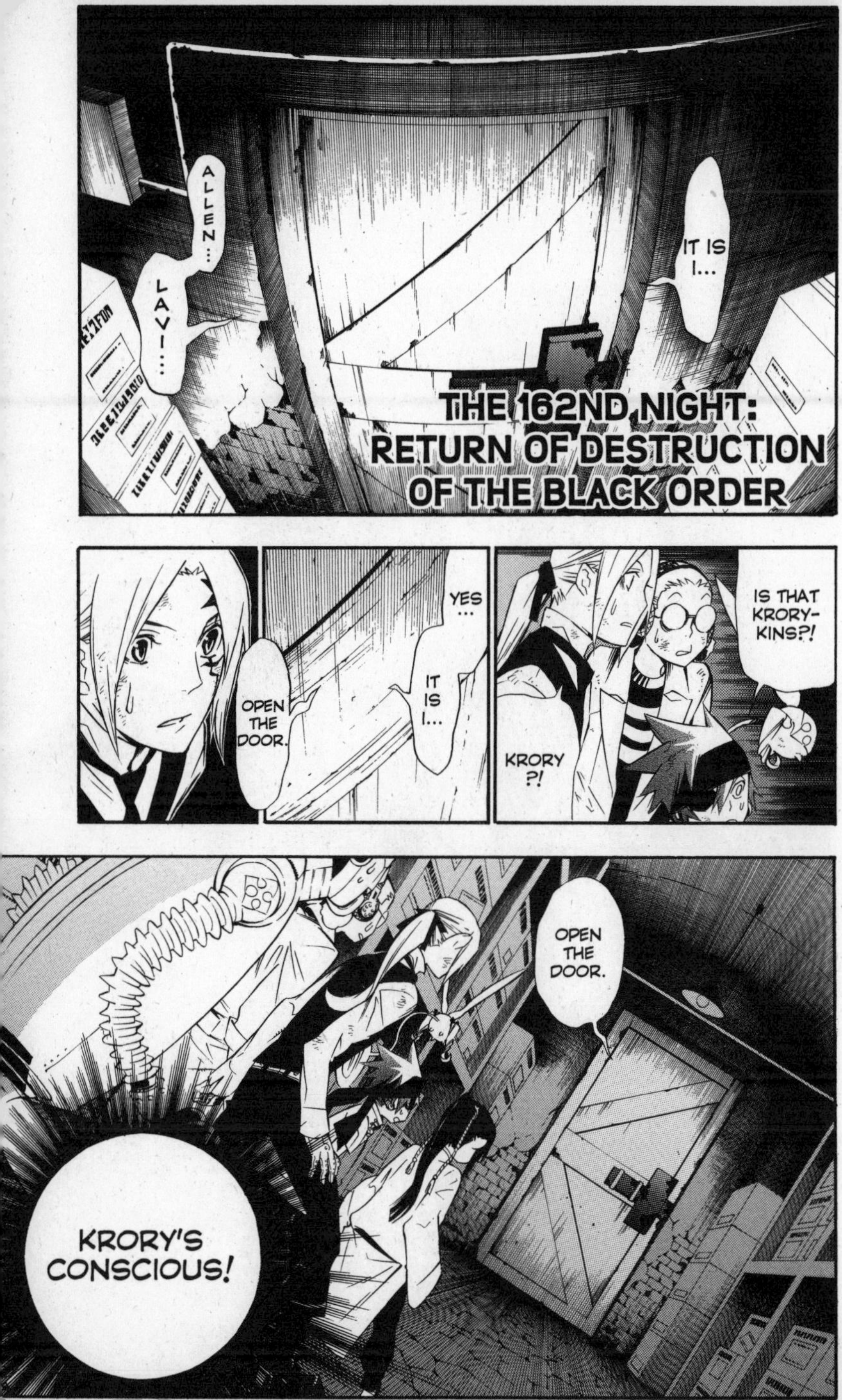
IT IS I...
ALLEN... LAVI...
THE 162ND NIGHT: RETURN OF DESTRUCTION OF THE BLACK ORDER
IS THAT KRORY-KINS?!
KRORY ?!
YES ...
IT IS I...
OPEN THE DOOR.
OPEN THE DOOR.
KRORY'S CONSCIOUS!

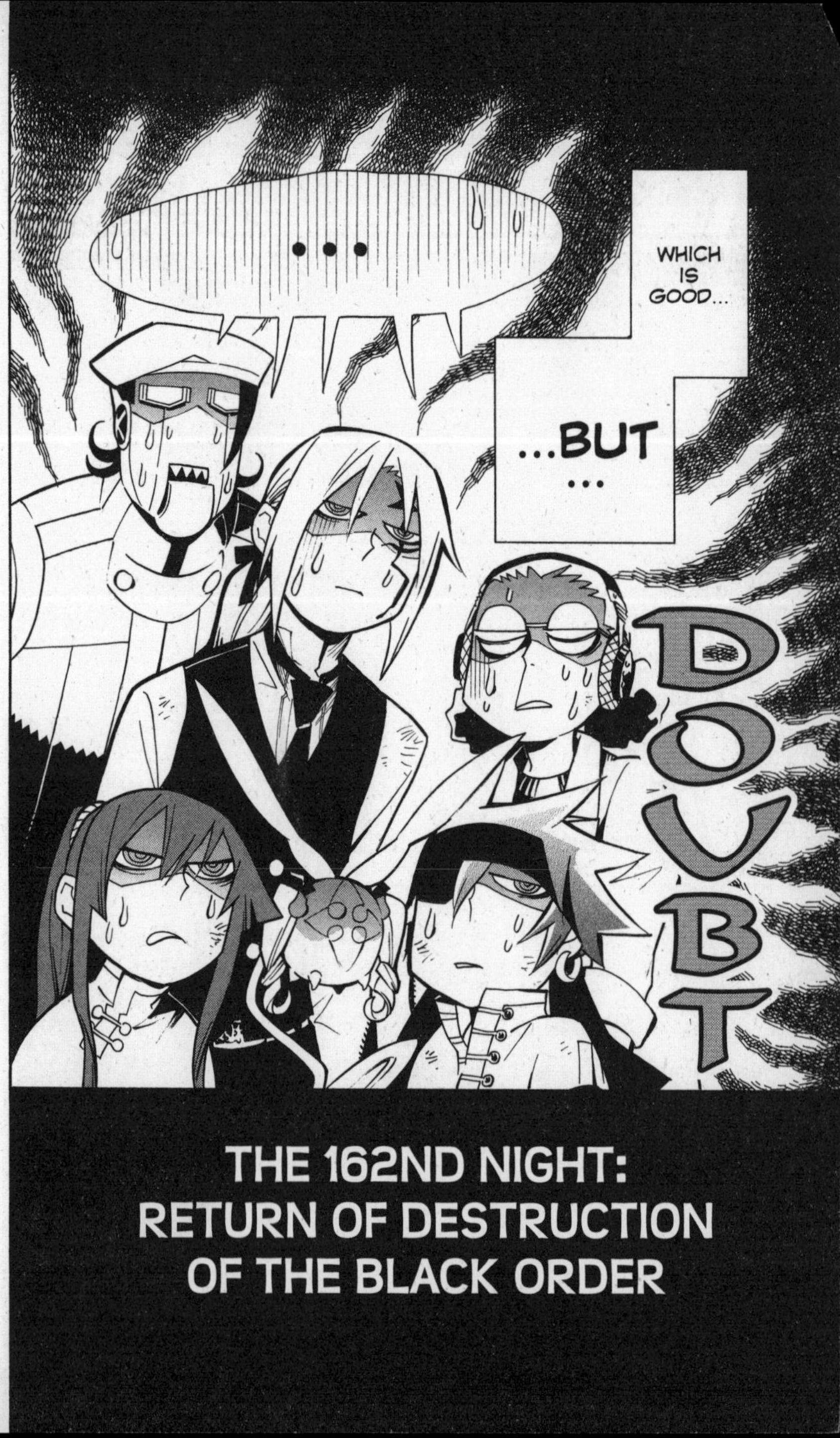
WHICH IS GOOD...
...BUT ...
...
DOUBT

THE 162ND NIGHT: RETURN OF DESTRUCTION OF THE BLACK ORDER

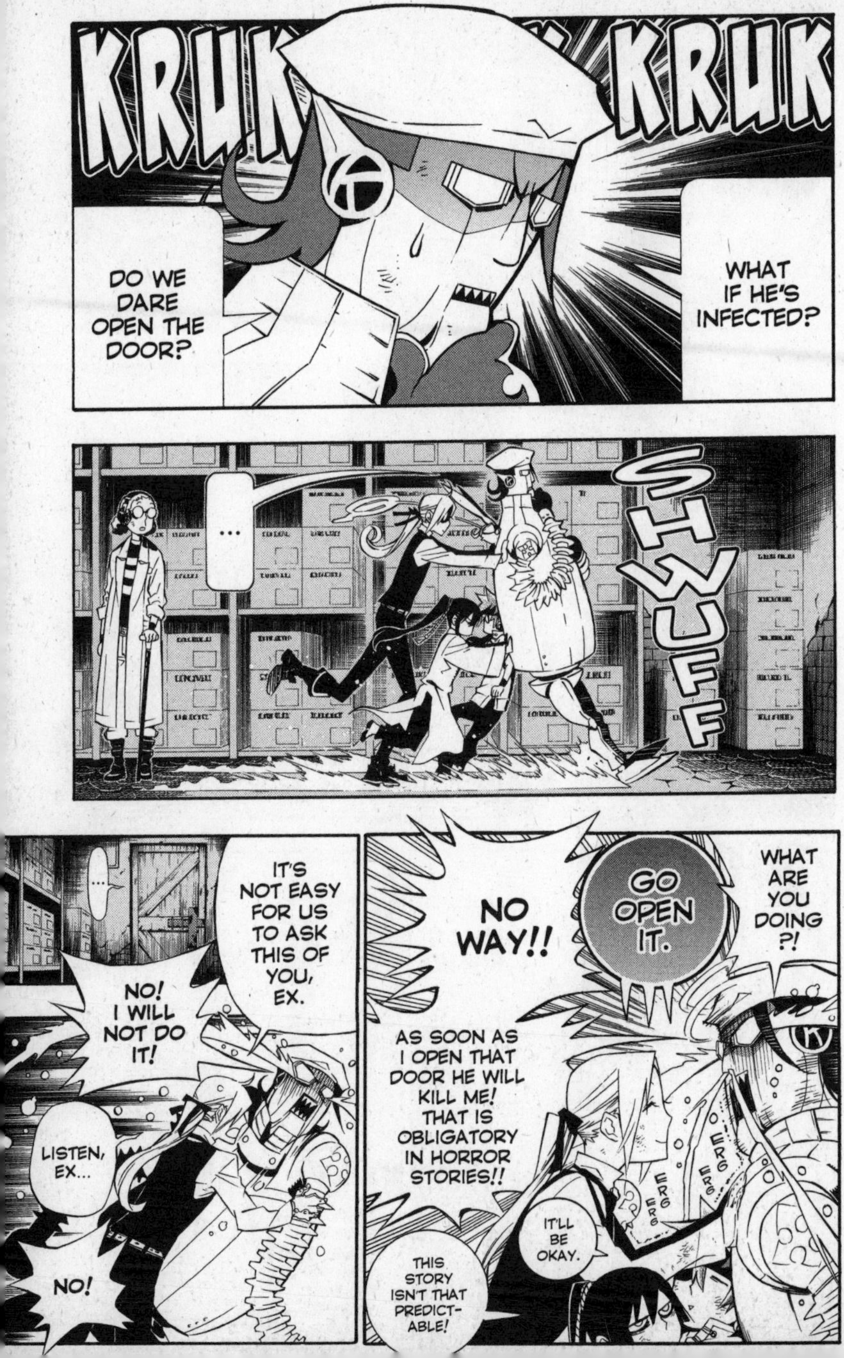
KRUK
WHAT IF HE'S INFECTED?
KRUK
DO WE DARE OPEN THE DOOR?
SHWUFF
...
WHAT ARE YOU DOING?!
GO OPEN IT.
NO WAY!!
AS SOON AS I OPEN THAT DOOR HE WILL KILL ME! THAT IS OBLIGATORY IN HORROR STORIES!!
ERG ERG
ERG ERG
IT'LL BE OKAY.
THIS STORY ISN'T THAT PREDICTABLE!
IT'S NOT EASY FOR US TO ASK THIS OF YOU, EX.
...
NO! I WILL NOT DO IT!
LISTEN, EX...
NO!

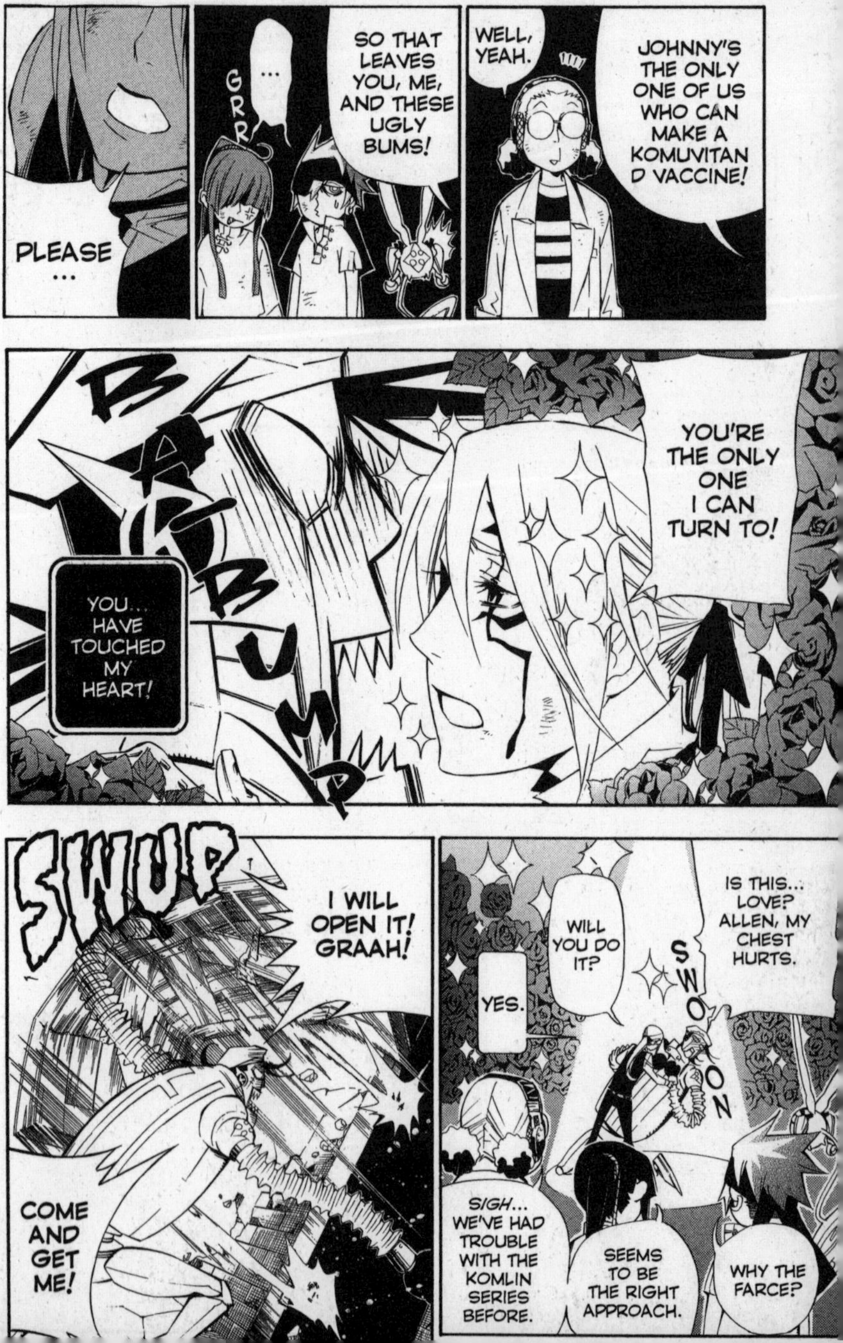
JOHNNY'S THE ONLY ONE OF US WHO CAN MAKE A KOMUVITAN D VACCINE!
WELL, YEAH.
SO THAT LEAVES YOU, ME, AND THESE UGLY BUMS!
...
GRR
PLEASE ...
YOU'RE THE ONLY ONE I CAN TURN TO!
YOU... HAVE TOUCHED MY HEART!
IS THIS... LOVE? ALLEN, MY CHEST HURTS.
SWOON
WILL YOU DO IT?
YES.
WHY THE FARCE?
SEEMS TO BE THE RIGHT APPROACH.
SIGH... WE'VE HAD TROUBLE WITH THE KOMLIN SERIES BEFORE.
I WILL OPEN IT! GRAAH!
SWUP
COME AND GET ME!

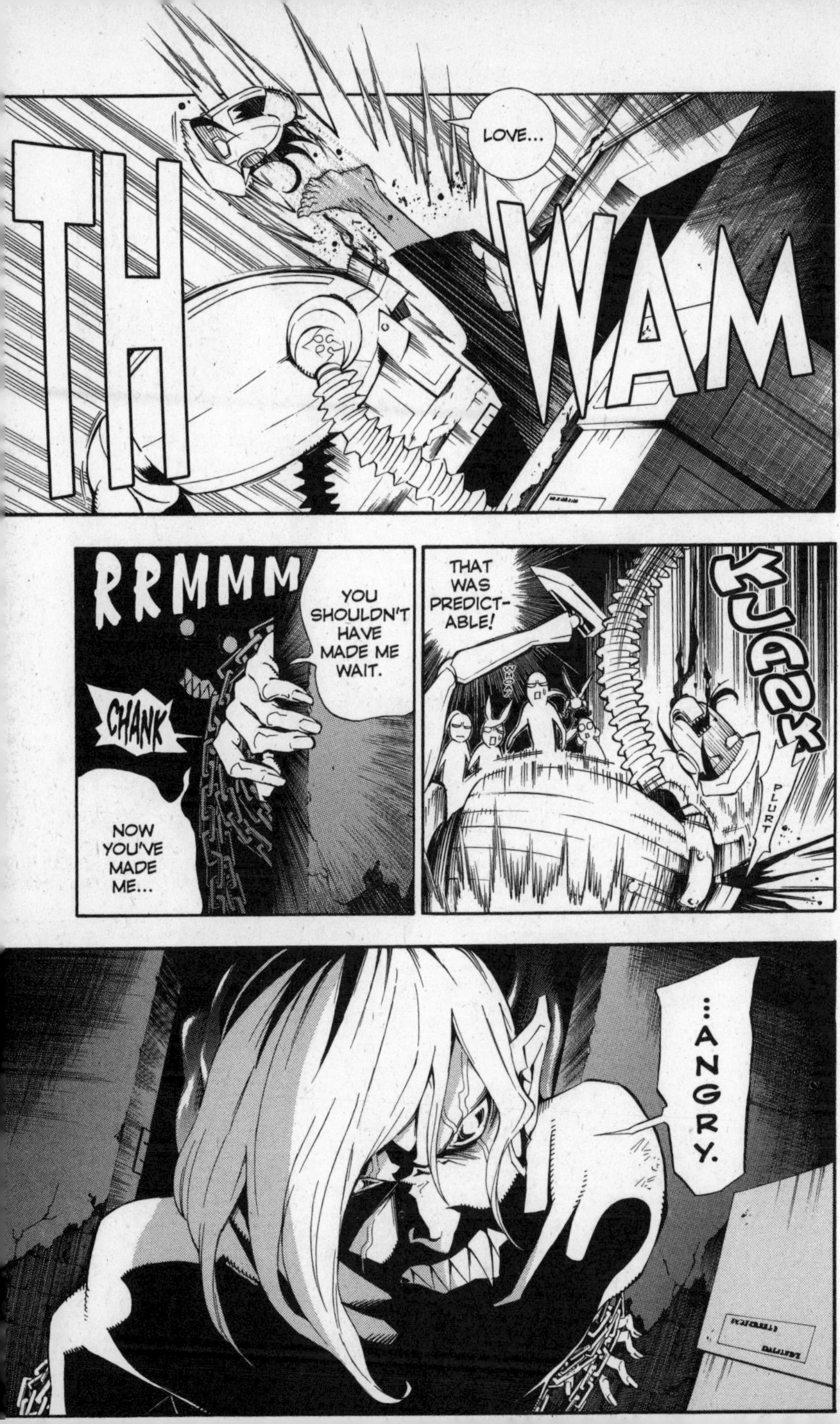
TH
WAM
LOVE...
KLACK
THAT WAS PREDICT-ABLE!
WHOA
PLURT
RRMMM
YOU SHOULDN'T HAVE MADE ME WAIT.
CHANK
NOW YOU'VE MADE ME...
...ANGRY.

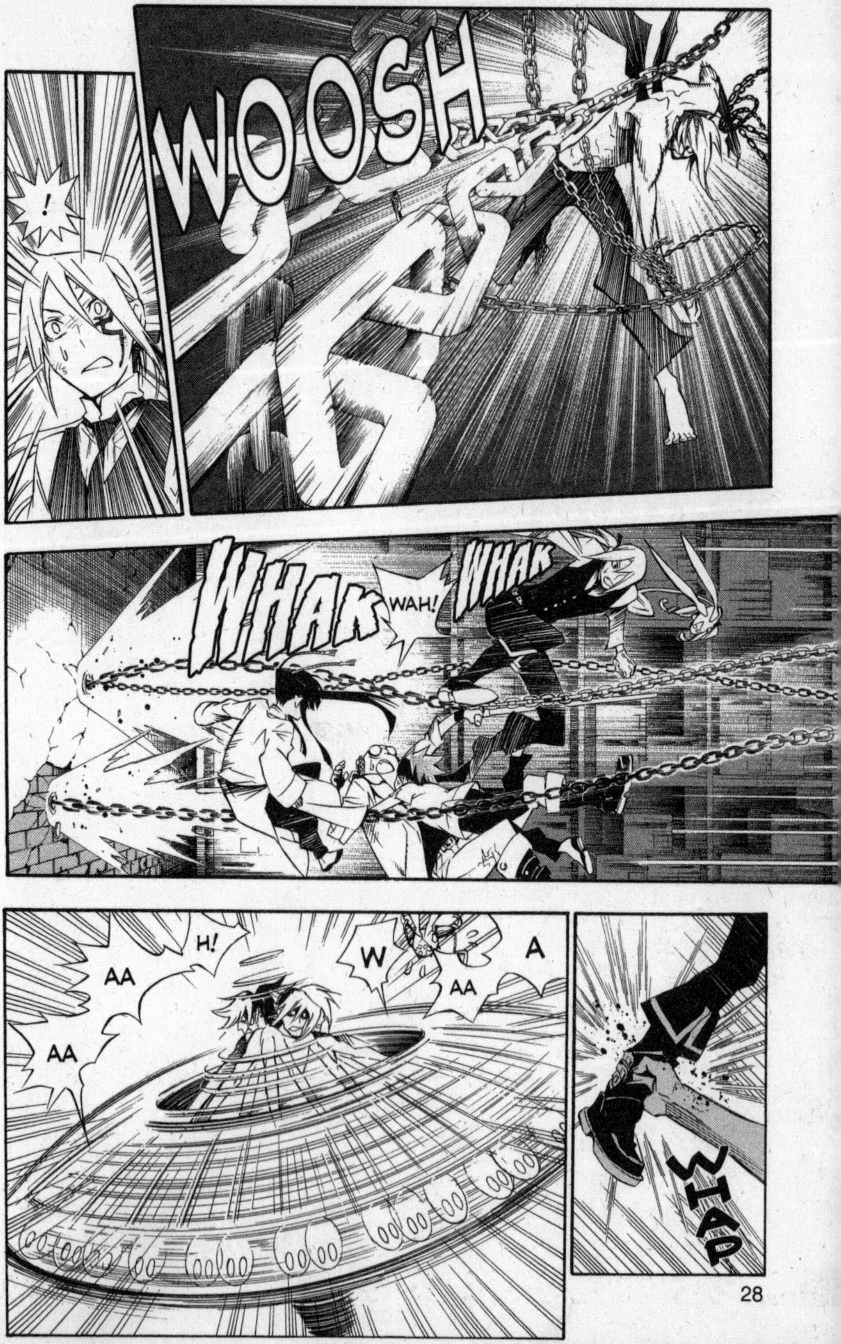
WOOSH
!
WHAK
WAH!
WHAK
WHAP
A
W
AA
H!
AA
AA

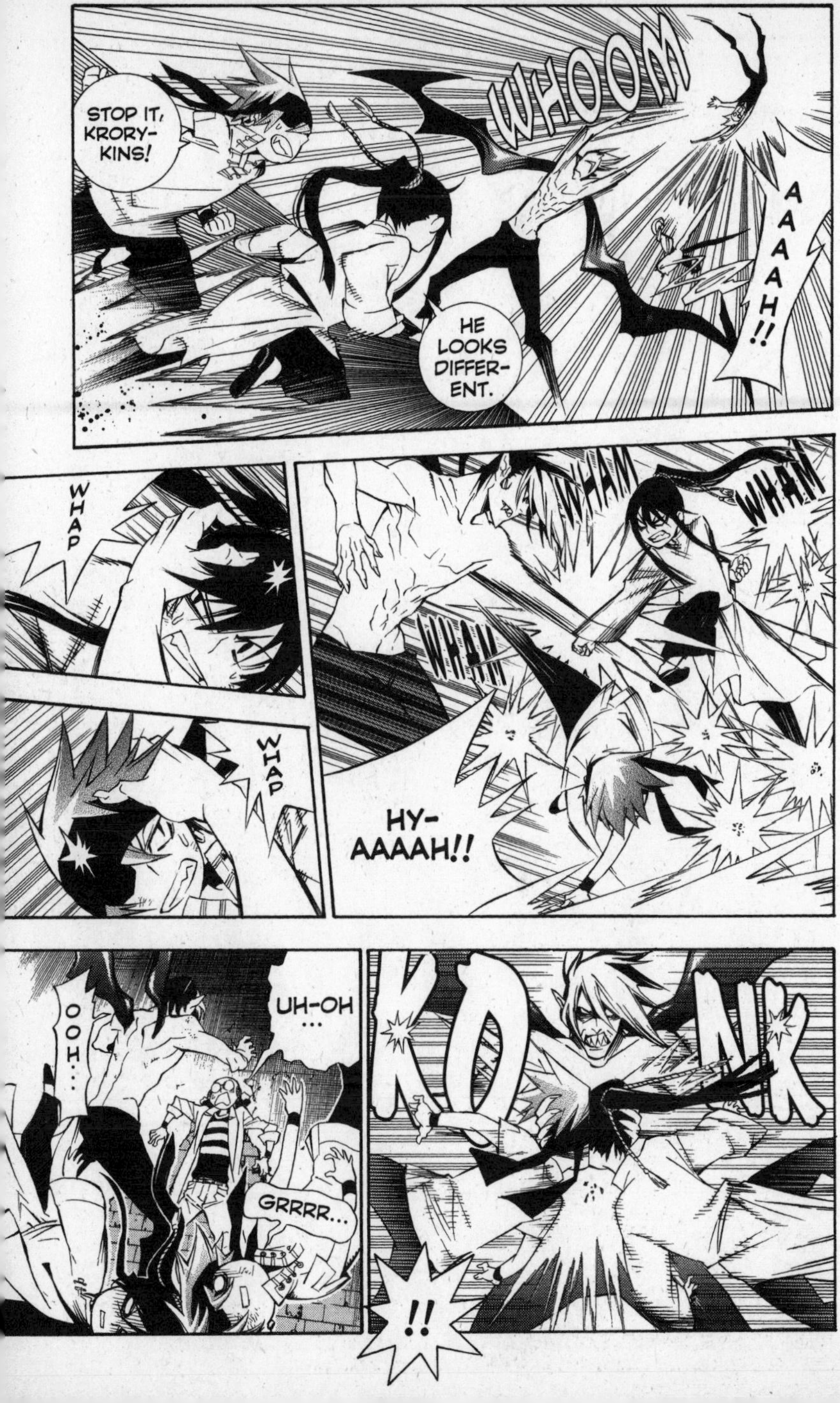
WHOOM
AAAAAH!!
STOP IT, KRORY-KINS!
HE LOOKS DIFFER-ENT.
WHAM
WHAM
WHAM
HY-AAAAH!!
WHAP
WHAP
KONK
!!
UH-OH...
OOH...
GRRRR...

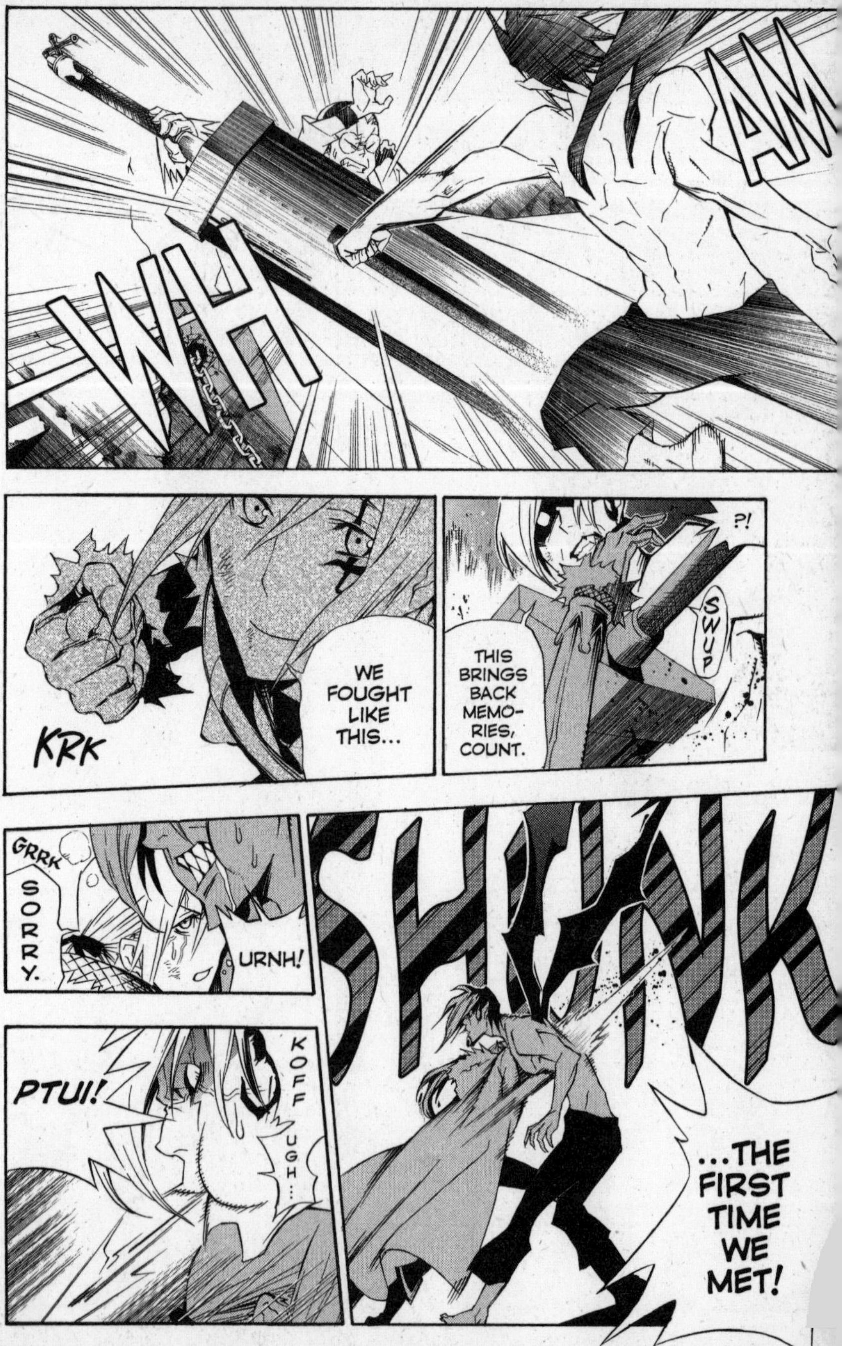
AM
WH
?!
SWUP
THIS BRINGS BACK MEMORIES, COUNT.
WE FOUGHT LIKE THIS...
KRK
SHINK
...THE FIRST TIME WE MET!
GRRK
SORRY.
URNH!
KOFF
UGH...
PTUI!

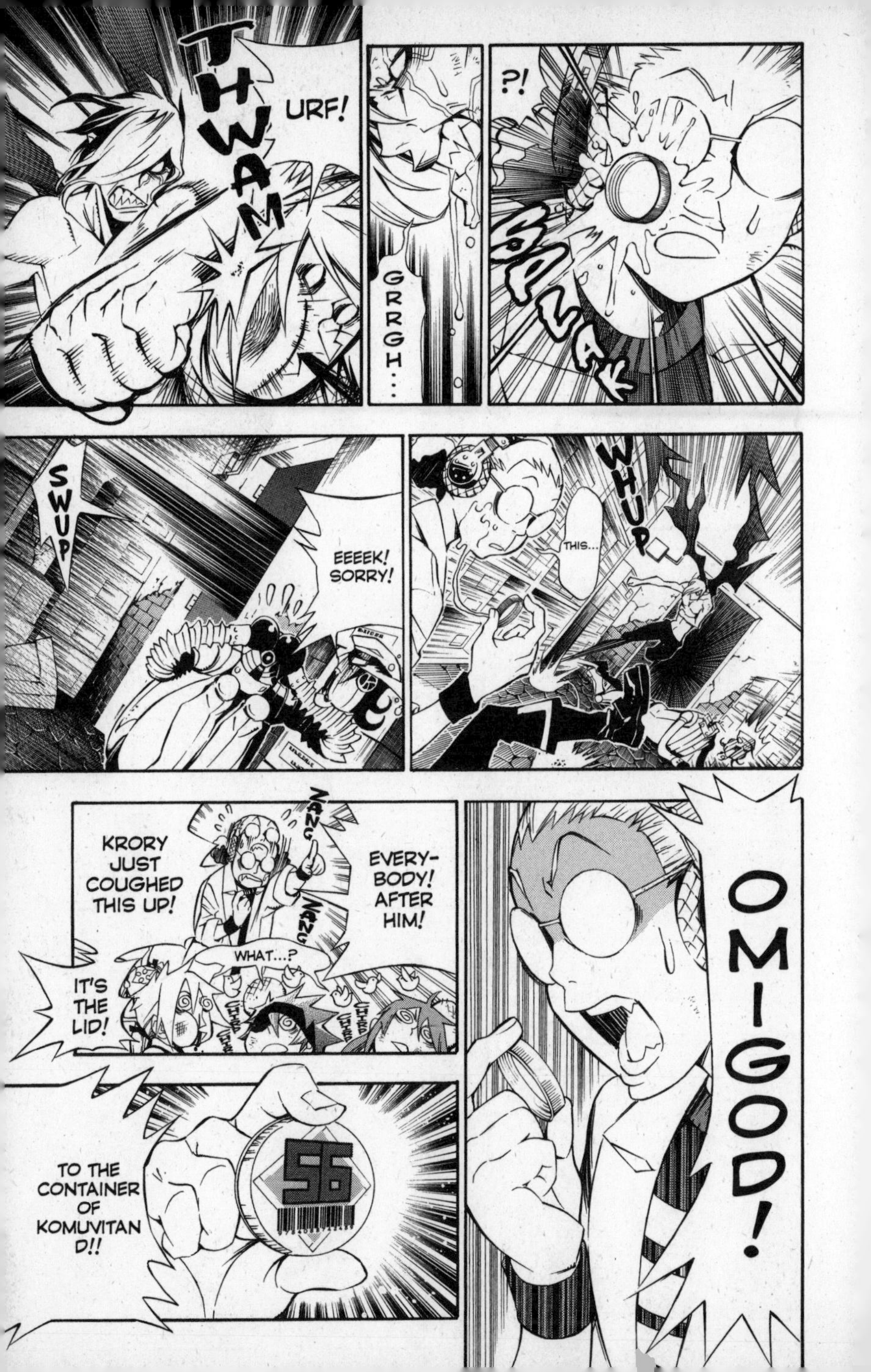
?!
SPLAK
GRRGH...
THWAM
URF!
WHUP
THIS...
SWUP
EEEEK! SORRY!
OMIGOD!
ZANG
EVERY-BODY! AFTER HIM!
ZANG
KRORY JUST COUGHED THIS UP!
WHAT...?
IT'S THE LID!
CHIRP CHIRP
TO THE CONTAINER OF KOMUVITAN D!!
56

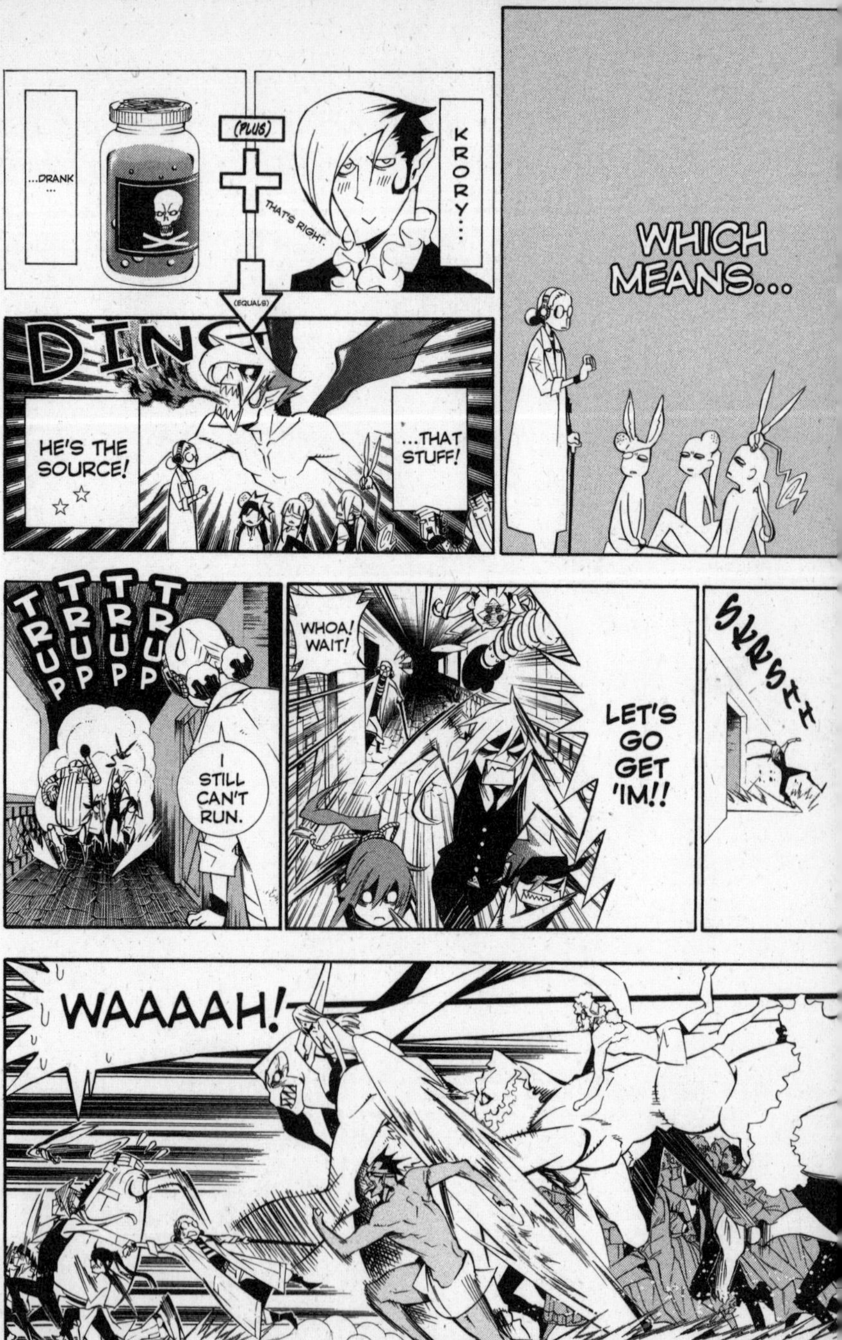
WHICH MEANS...
KRORY...
THAT'S RIGHT.
(PLUS)
...DRANK...
(EQUALS)
DING
...THAT STUFF!
HE'S THE SOURCE!
SKRSHH
LET'S GO GET 'IM!!
WHOA! WAIT!
TRUP TRUP TRUP TRUP TRUP
I STILL CAN'T RUN.
WAAAAH!

?

WHERE
...?

HEE
...

UNH
...

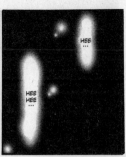

HEE
...

HEE
HEE
...

TU NK

OW!
OW!
OW!
OW!

S-
SORRY
...

I...I
CAN'T
...

HEY!
CUT IT
OUT!

LENALEE,
WHAT'S
GOING
ON?!

EH
?!

MMPH!
MMPH!

MMM
PH!

I'M NOT...IN
CONTROL...
OF MY
BODY...

REEVER
?!

WHAT
?!

SHAKE
SHAKE

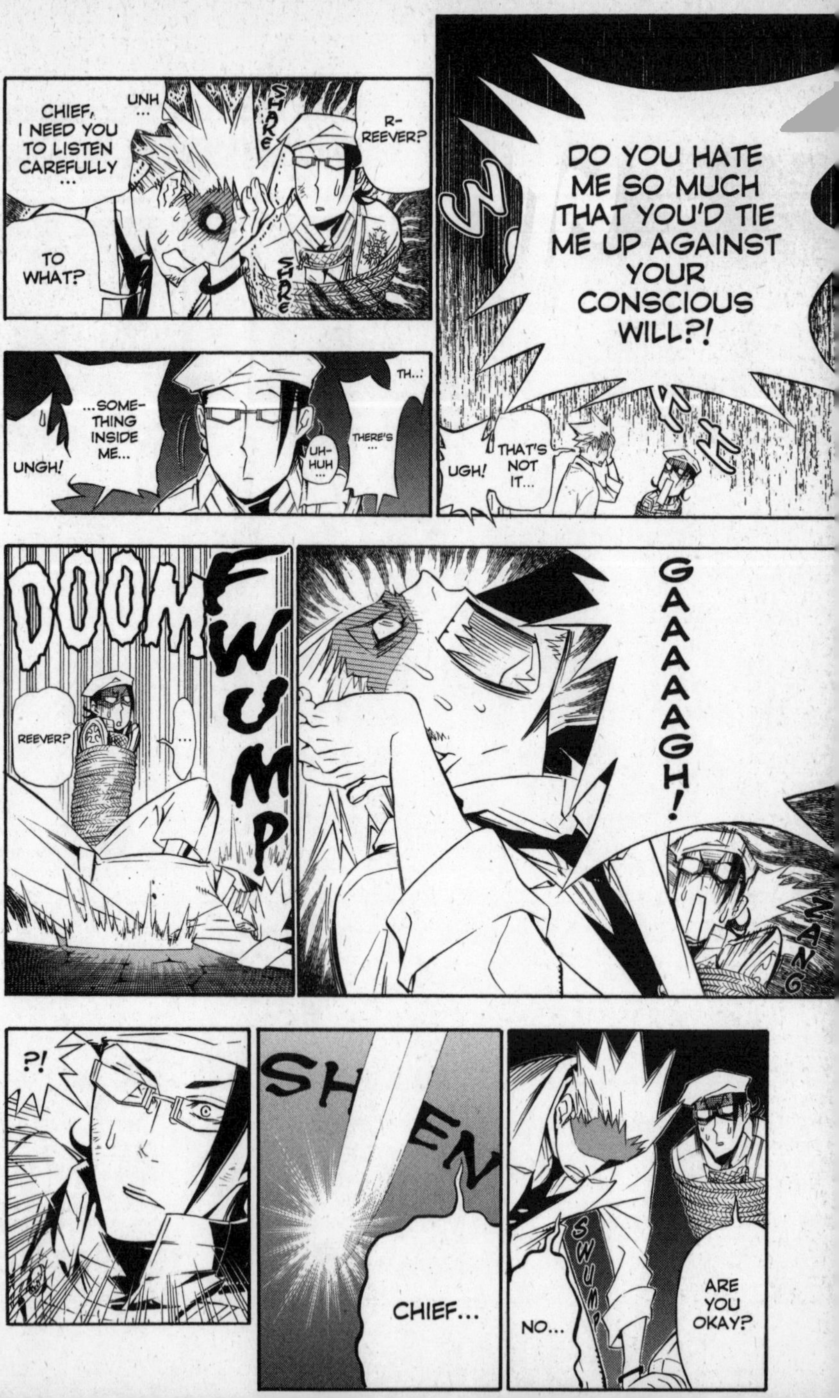
DO YOU HATE ME SO MUCH THAT YOU'D TIE ME UP AGAINST YOUR CONSCIOUS WILL?!
THAT'S NOT IT...
UGH!
R-REEVER?
SHAKE
UNH ...
CHIEF, I NEED YOU TO LISTEN CAREFULLY ...
SHAKE
TO WHAT?
TH...
THERE'S ...
UH-HUH ...
...SOMETHING INSIDE ME...
UNGH!
GAAAAAGH!
ZANG
FWUMP
DOOM
...
REEVER?
ARE YOU OKAY?
SWUMP
NO...
SHEEN
CHIEF...
?!

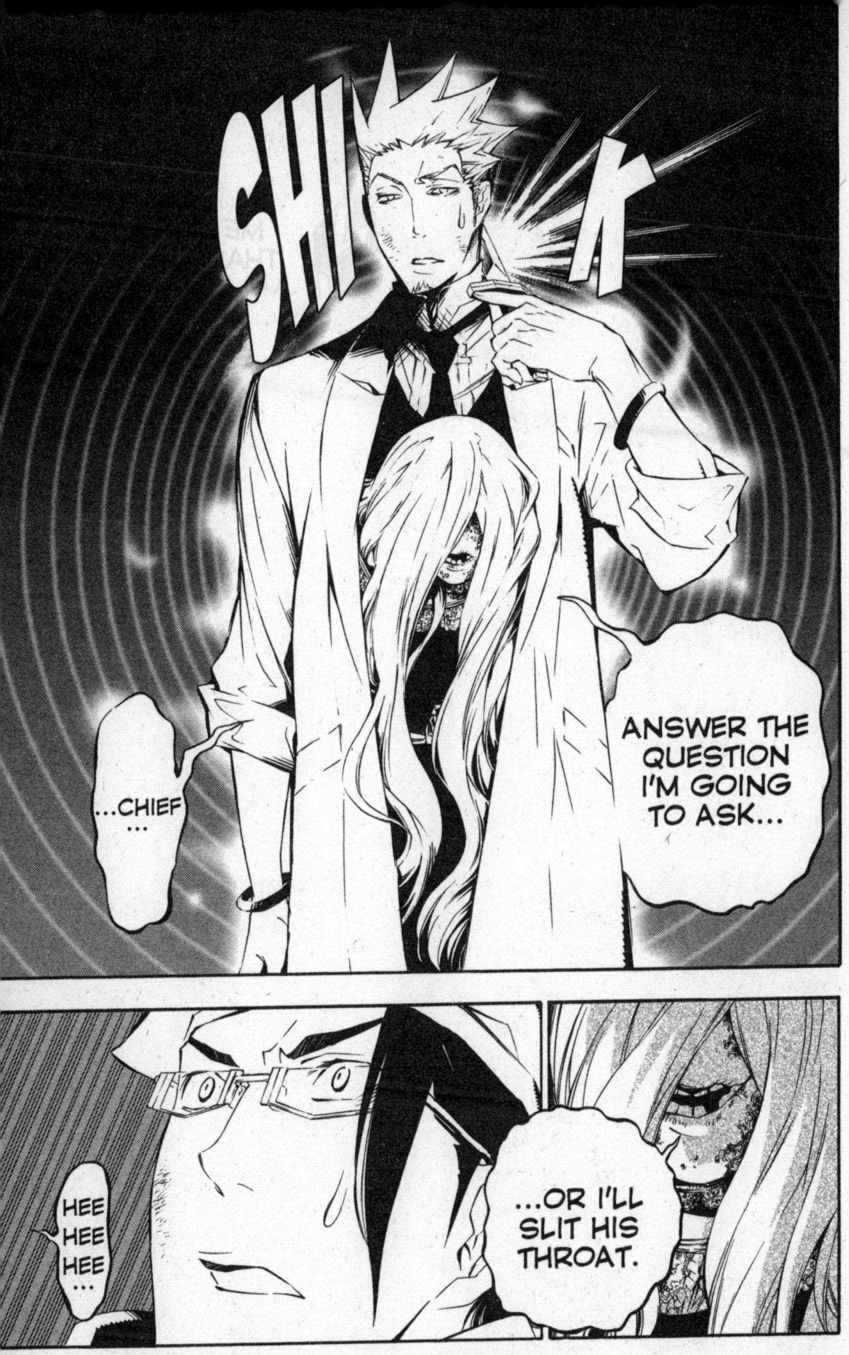
SHI K
ANSWER THE QUESTION I'M GOING TO ASK...
...CHIEF...
...OR I'LL SLIT HIS THROAT.
HEE HEE HEE...

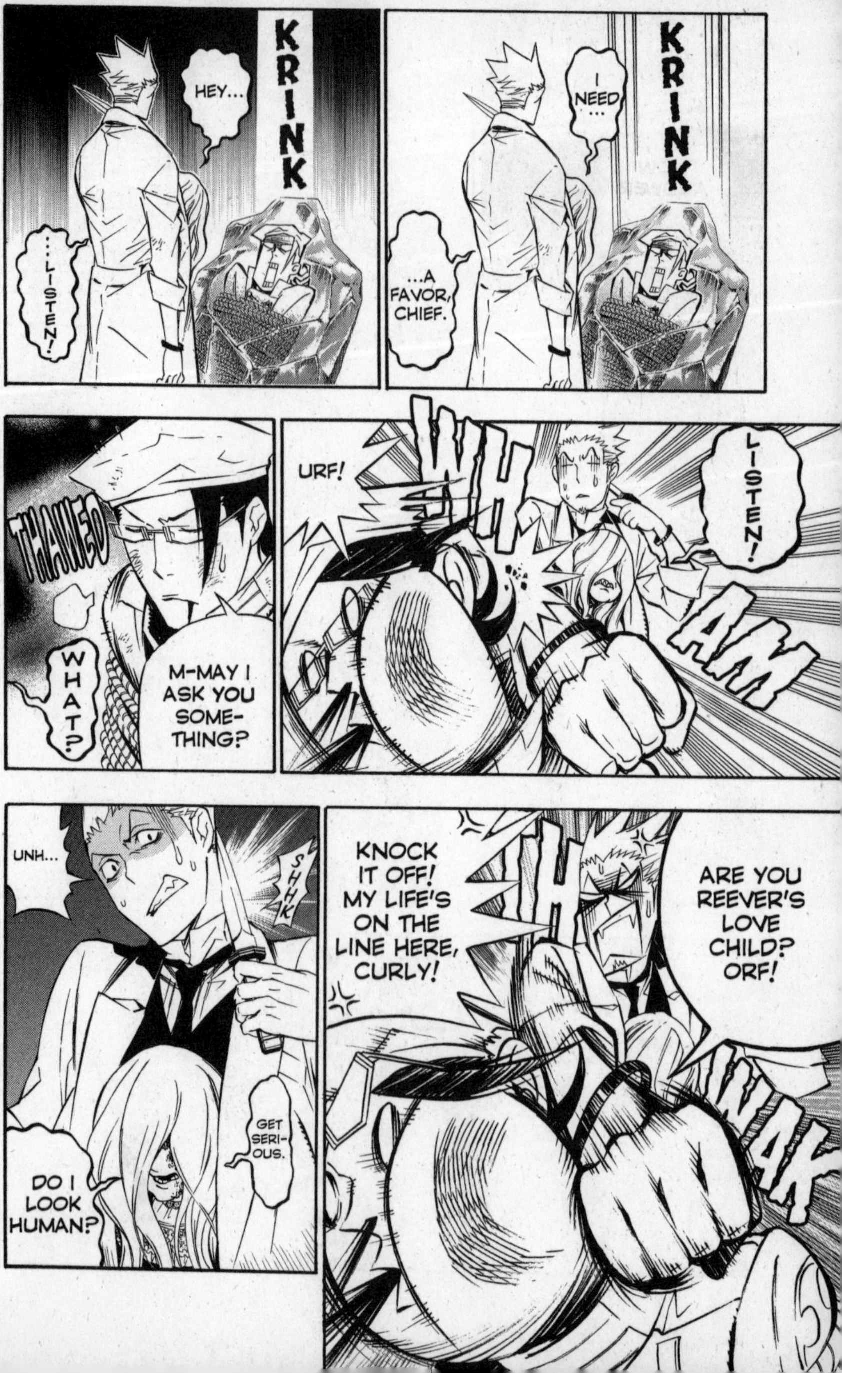
I NEED...
KRINK
...A FAVOR, CHIEF.
HEY...
KRINK
...LISTEN!
LISTEN!
WHAM
URF!
THAWED
M-MAY I ASK YOU SOMETHING?
WHAT?
ARE YOU REEVER'S LOVE CHILD? ORF!
KNOCK IT OFF! MY LIFE'S ON THE LINE HERE, CURLY!
SHHK
UNH...
GET SERI-OUS.
DO I LOOK HUMAN?

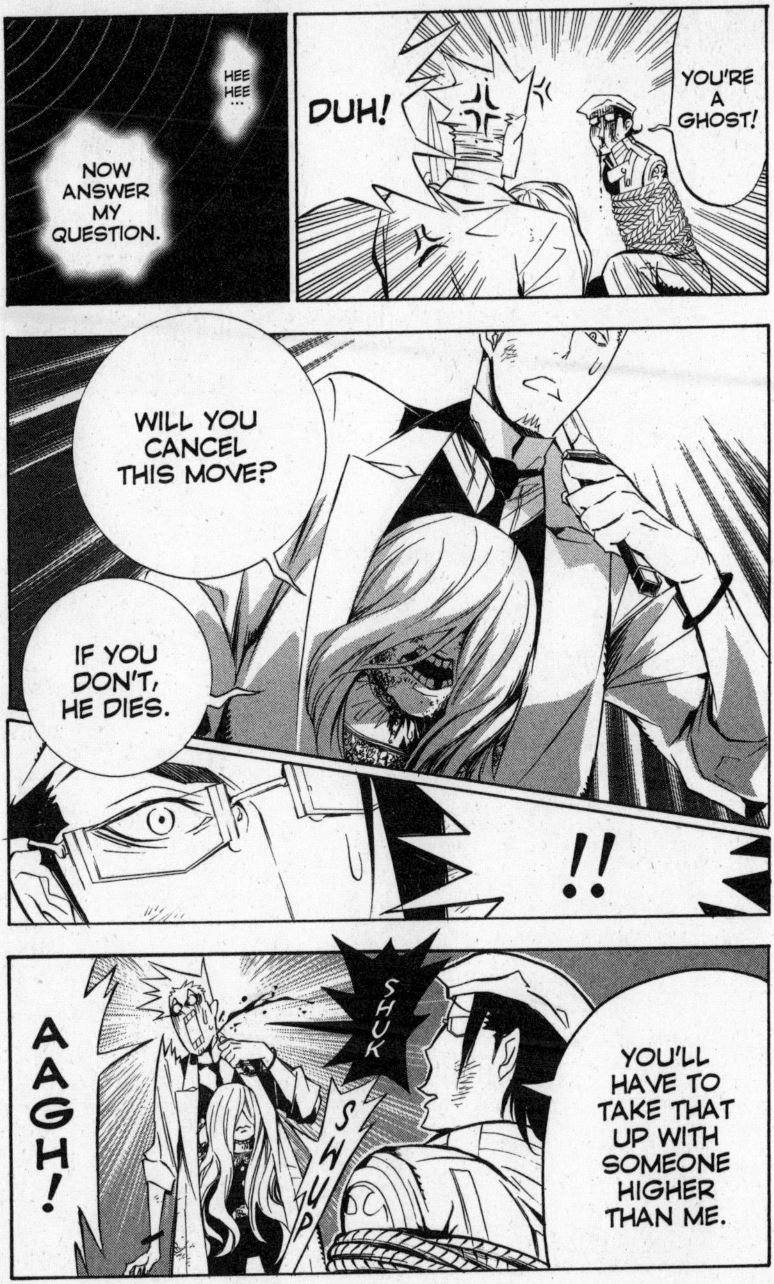
YOU'RE A GHOST!
DUH!
HEE HEE ...
NOW ANSWER MY QUESTION.
WILL YOU CANCEL THIS MOVE?
IF YOU DON'T, HE DIES.
!!
YOU'LL HAVE TO TAKE THAT UP WITH SOMEONE HIGHER THAN ME.
SHUK
SHWUP
AAGH!

GO FOR IT! YOU CAN DO IT, REEVER!!

THE PEOPLE OF D.GRAY-HOUSE: SIDE STORY

ZANG
HIROSHI
ARE WE THERE YET?
I'M HOT.
WHO'S THAT?
SURPRISE!

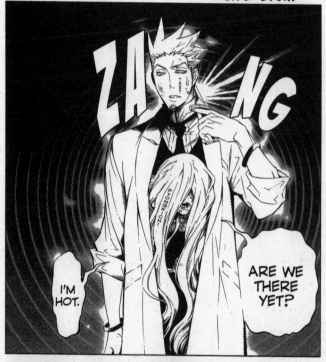

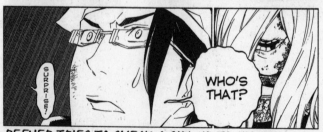

REEVER TRIES TO SNEAK A GIRL UP TO HIS ROOM.

THE 163RD NIGHT: SERIOUS DESTRUCTION OF THE BLACK ORDER

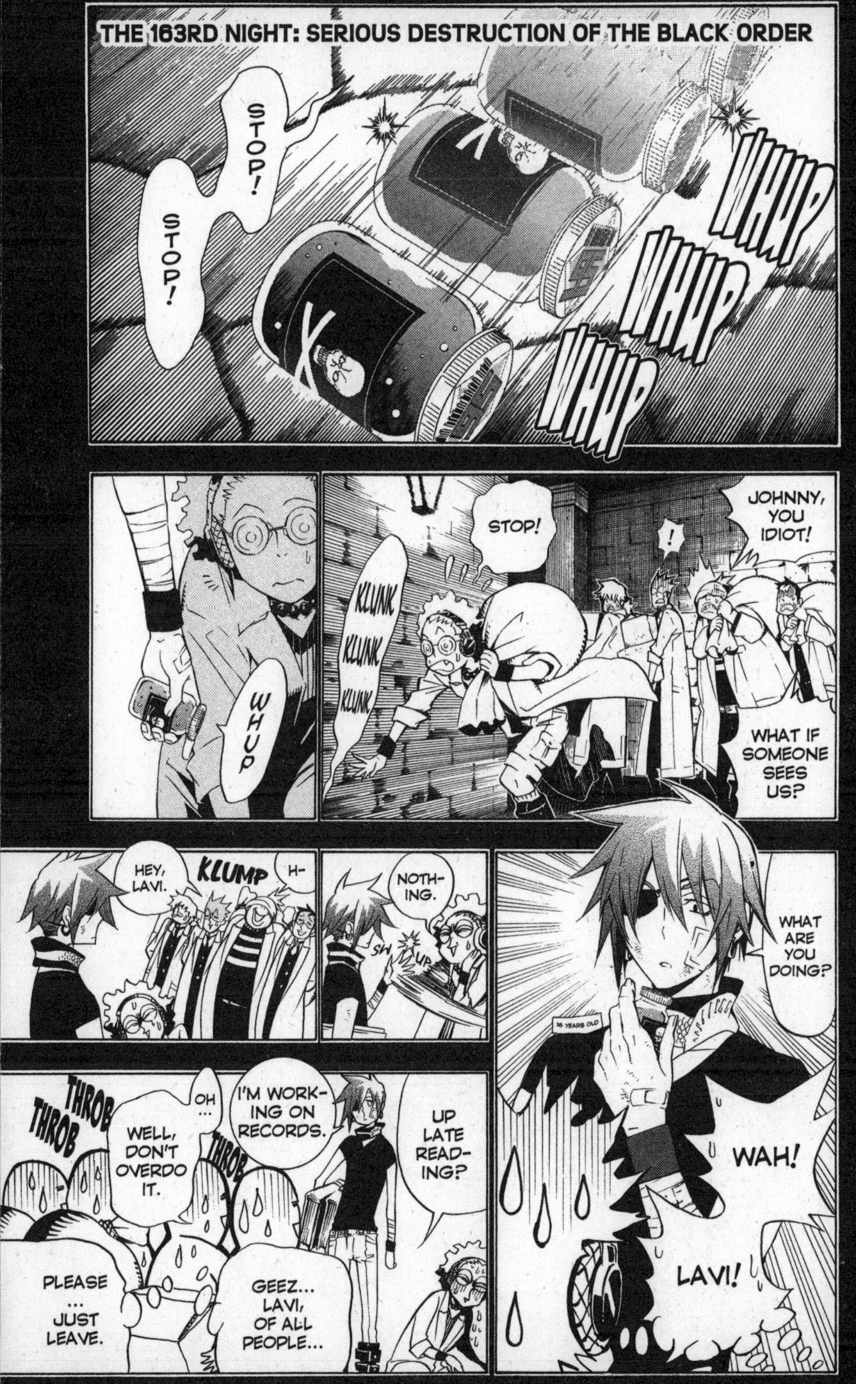
STOP!
STOP!
WHUP
WHUP
WHUP
JOHNNY, YOU IDIOT!
WHAT IF SOMEONE SEES US?
!
STOP!
KLUNK
KLUNK
KLUNK
WHUP
WHAT ARE YOU DOING?
16 YEARS OLD
WAH!
LAVI!
NOTH-ING.
SWUP
H-
KLUMP
HEY, LAVI.
UP LATE READ-ING?
I'M WORK-ING ON RECORDS.
OH ...
WELL, DON'T OVERDO IT.
THROB
THROB
THROB
GEEZ... LAVI, OF ALL PEOPLE...
PLEASE ... JUST LEAVE.

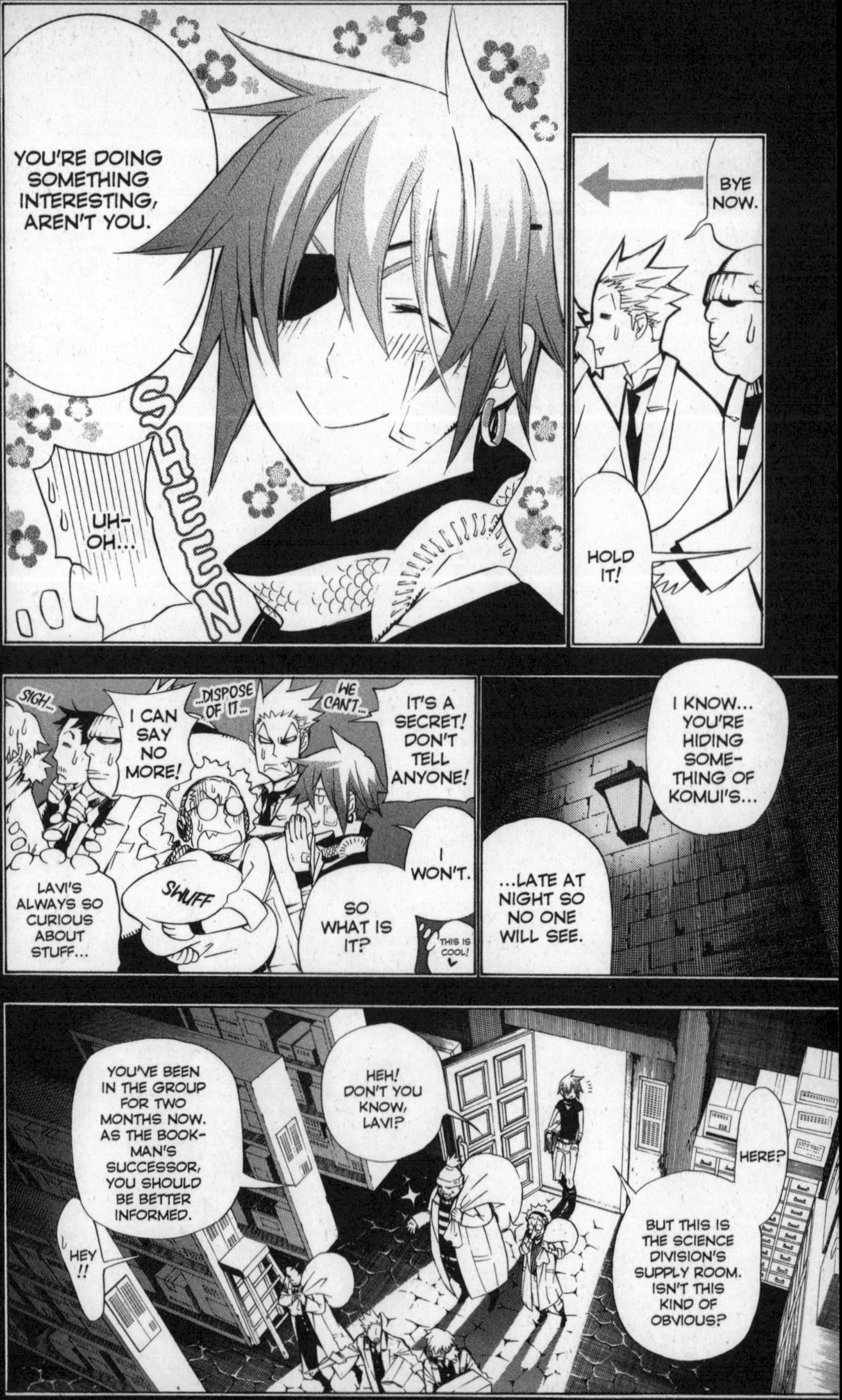
BYE NOW.
HOLD IT!
YOU'RE DOING SOMETHING INTERESTING, AREN'T YOU.
SHEEN
UH-OH...
I KNOW... YOU'RE HIDING SOME-THING OF KOMUI'S...
...LATE AT NIGHT SO NO ONE WILL SEE.
IT'S A SECRET! DON'T TELL ANYONE!
WE CAN'T...
...DISPOSE OF IT...
I CAN SAY NO MORE!
SIGH...
I WON'T.
SO WHAT IS IT?
THIS IS COOL!
SHUFF
LAVI'S ALWAYS SO CURIOUS ABOUT STUFF...
HERE?
BUT THIS IS THE SCIENCE DIVISION'S SUPPLY ROOM. ISN'T THIS KIND OF OBVIOUS?
HEH! DON'T YOU KNOW, LAVI?
YOU'VE BEEN IN THE GROUP FOR TWO MONTHS NOW. AS THE BOOK-MAN'S SUCCESSOR, YOU SHOULD BE BETTER INFORMED.
HEY!!

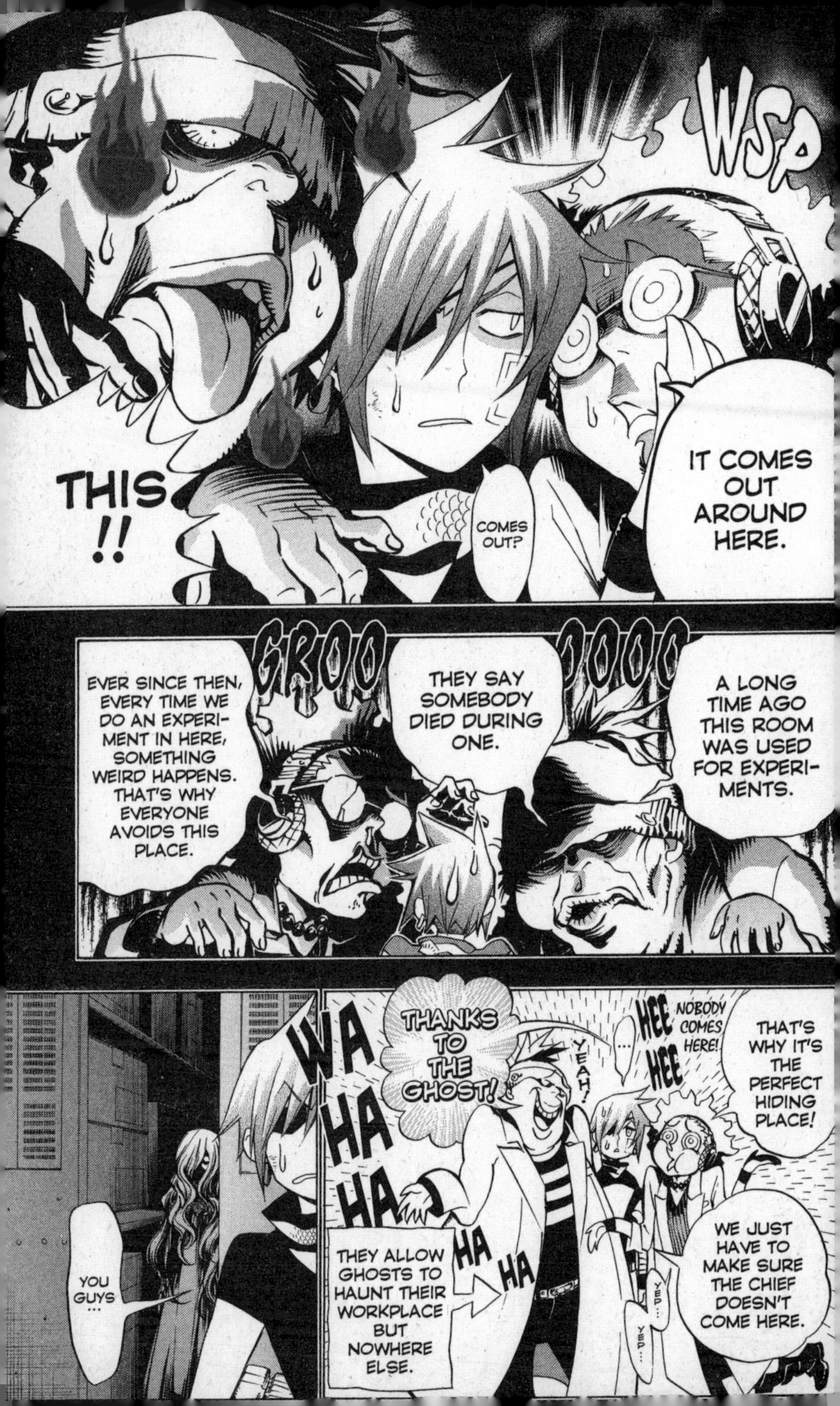
WSP
IT COMES OUT AROUND HERE.
COMES OUT?
THIS!!
A LONG TIME AGO THIS ROOM WAS USED FOR EXPERIMENTS.
GROOOOOOO
THEY SAY SOMEBODY DIED DURING ONE.
EVER SINCE THEN, EVERY TIME WE DO AN EXPERIMENT IN HERE, SOMETHING WEIRD HAPPENS. THAT'S WHY EVERYONE AVOIDS THIS PLACE.
THAT'S WHY IT'S THE PERFECT HIDING PLACE!
NOBODY COMES HERE!
HEE HEE
...
YEAH!
THANKS TO THE GHOST!
WA HA HA HA HA HA
WE JUST HAVE TO MAKE SURE THE CHIEF DOESN'T COME HERE.
YEP...
YEP...
THEY ALLOW GHOSTS TO HAUNT THEIR WORKPLACE BUT NOWHERE ELSE.
YOU GUYS...

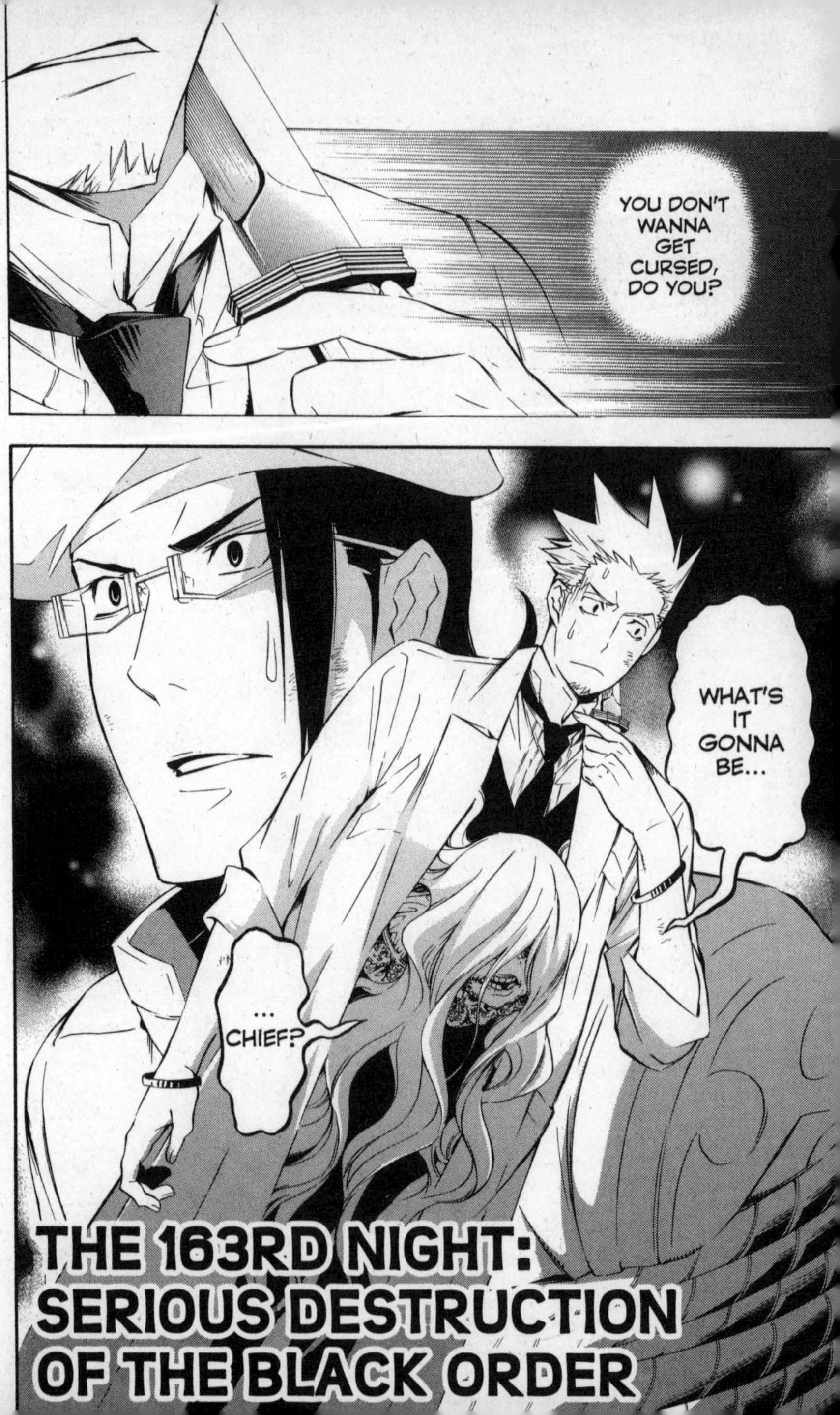
YOU DON'T WANNA GET CURSED, DO YOU?
WHAT'S IT GONNA BE...
... CHIEF?
THE 163RD NIGHT: SERIOUS DESTRUCTION OF THE BLACK ORDER

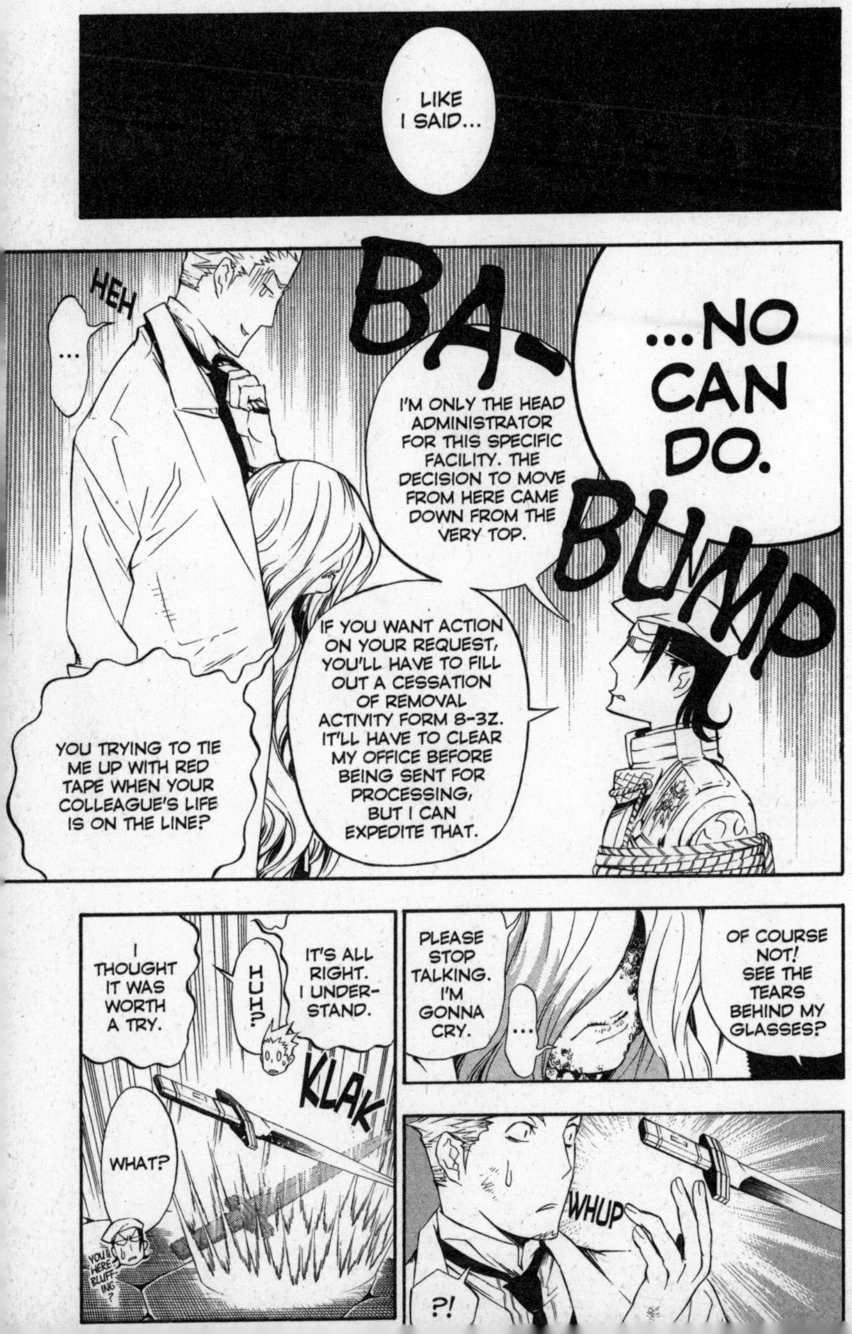
LIKE I SAID...
...NO CAN DO.
BA-BUMP
I'M ONLY THE HEAD ADMINISTRATOR FOR THIS SPECIFIC FACILITY. THE DECISION TO MOVE FROM HERE CAME DOWN FROM THE VERY TOP.
IF YOU WANT ACTION ON YOUR REQUEST, YOU'LL HAVE TO FILL OUT A CESSATION OF REMOVAL ACTIVITY FORM 8-3Z. IT'LL HAVE TO CLEAR MY OFFICE BEFORE BEING SENT FOR PROCESSING, BUT I CAN EXPEDITE THAT.
HEH
...
YOU TRYING TO TIE ME UP WITH RED TAPE WHEN YOUR COLLEAGUE'S LIFE IS ON THE LINE?
OF COURSE NOT! SEE THE TEARS BEHIND MY GLASSES?
...
PLEASE STOP TALKING. I'M GONNA CRY.
WHUP
?!
IT'S ALL RIGHT. I UNDER-STAND.
HUH?
I THOUGHT IT WAS WORTH A TRY.
KLAK
WHAT?
YOU WERE BLUFF-ING?

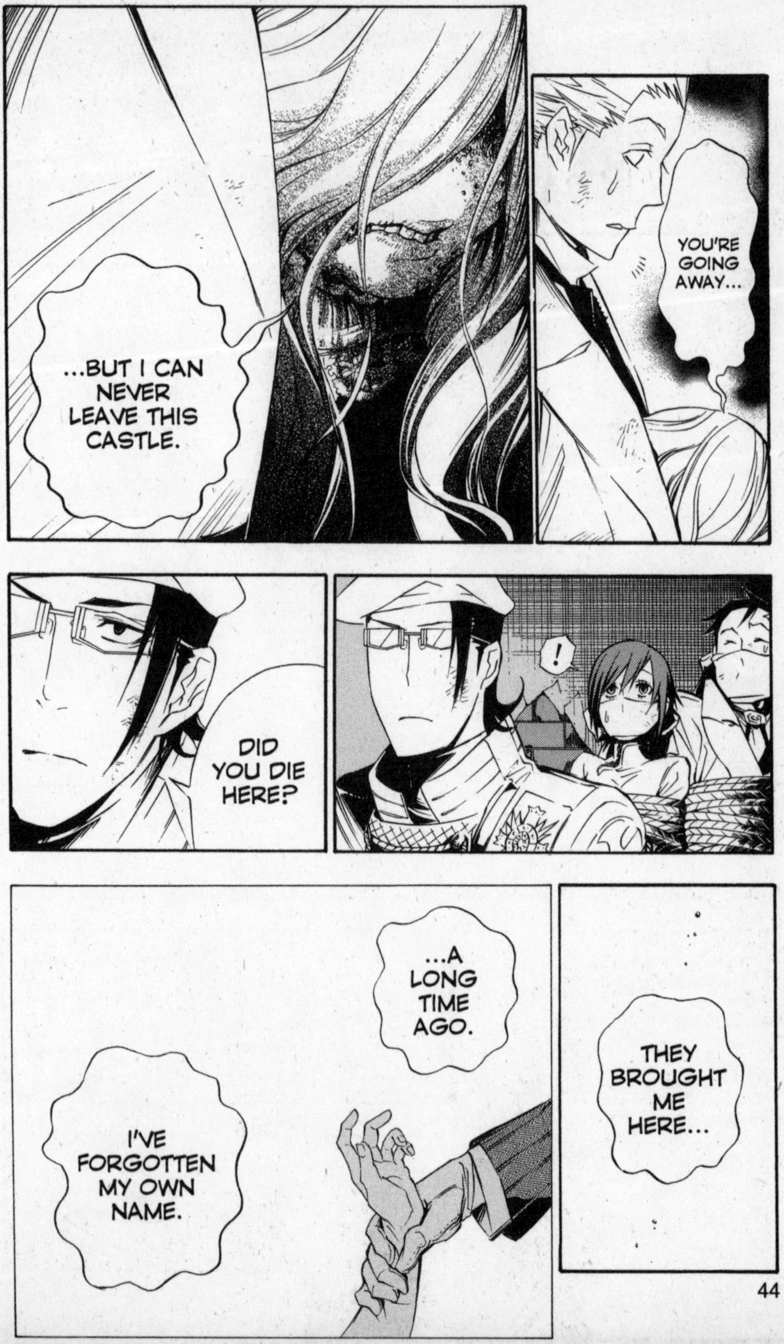
YOU'RE GOING AWAY...
...BUT I CAN NEVER LEAVE THIS CASTLE.
!
DID YOU DIE HERE?
THEY BROUGHT ME HERE...
...A LONG TIME AGO.
I'VE FORGOTTEN MY OWN NAME.

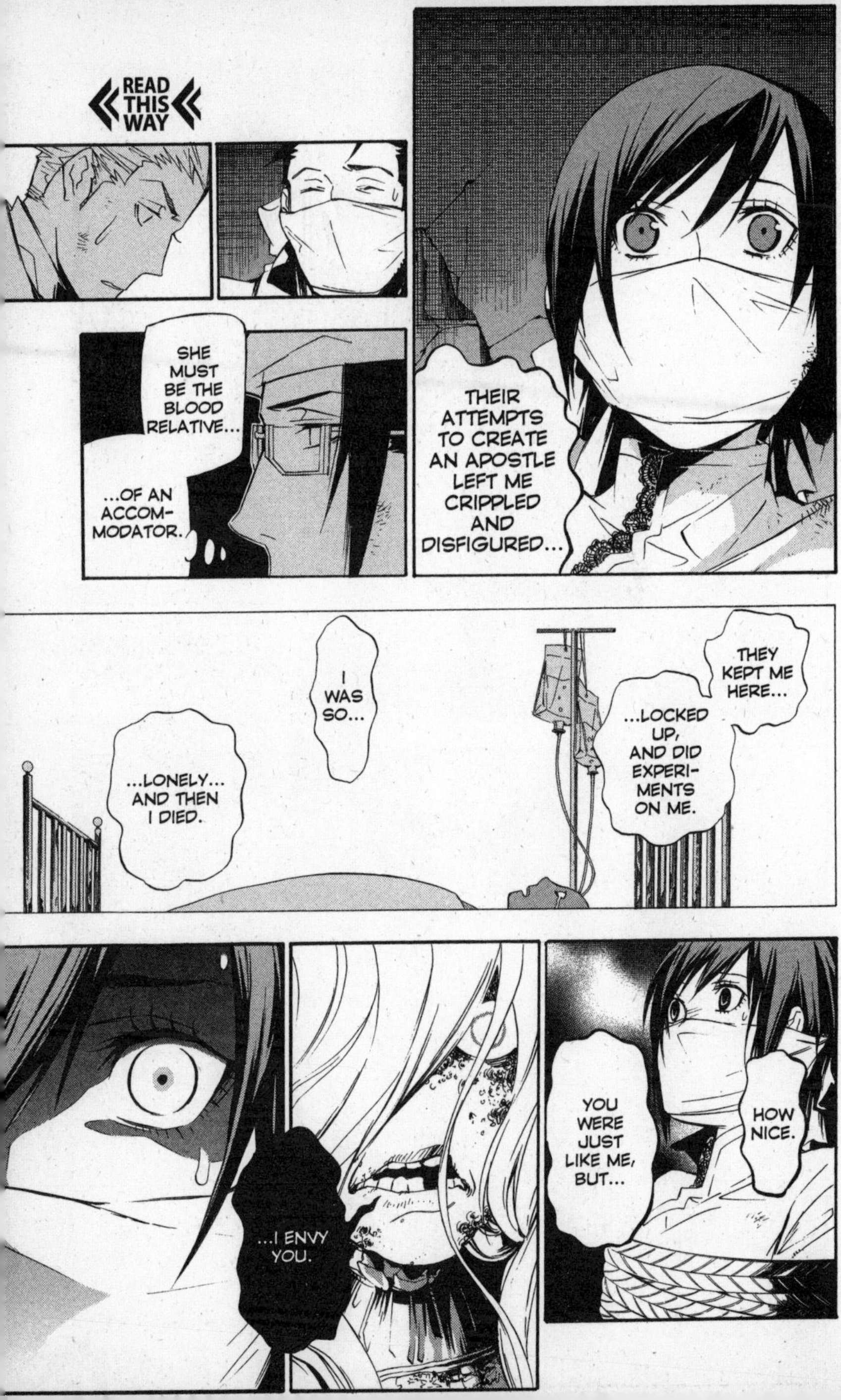
READ THIS WAY
THEIR ATTEMPTS TO CREATE AN APOSTLE LEFT ME CRIPPLED AND DISFIGURED...
SHE MUST BE THE BLOOD RELATIVE...
...OF AN ACCOMMODATOR.
THEY KEPT ME HERE...
...LOCKED UP, AND DID EXPERIMENTS ON ME.
I WAS SO...
...LONELY... AND THEN I DIED.
HOW NICE.
YOU WERE JUST LIKE ME, BUT...
...I ENVY YOU.

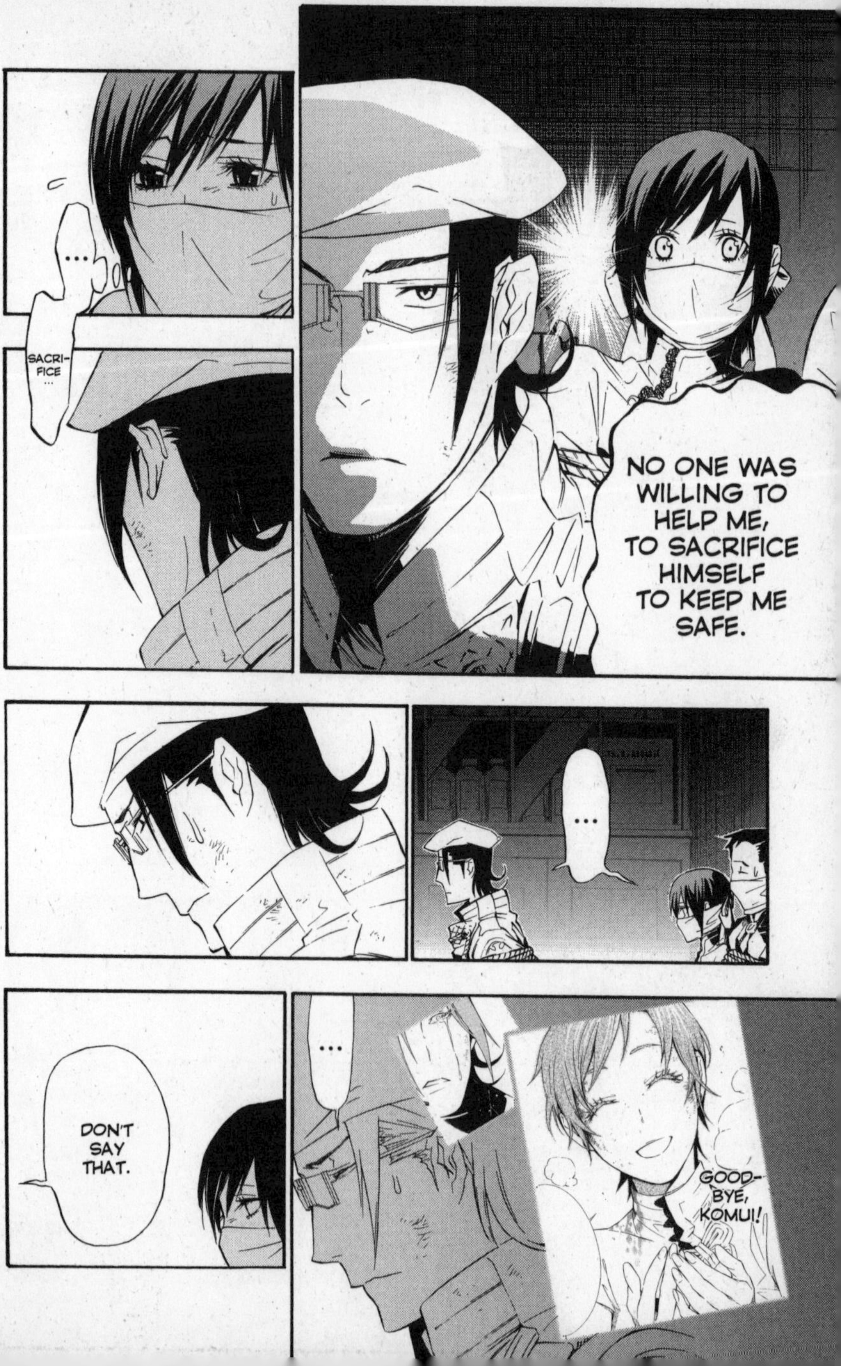
NO ONE WAS WILLING TO HELP ME, TO SACRIFICE HIMSELF TO KEEP ME SAFE.
...
SACRI-FICE ...
...
...
GOOD-BYE, KOMUI!
DON'T SAY THAT.

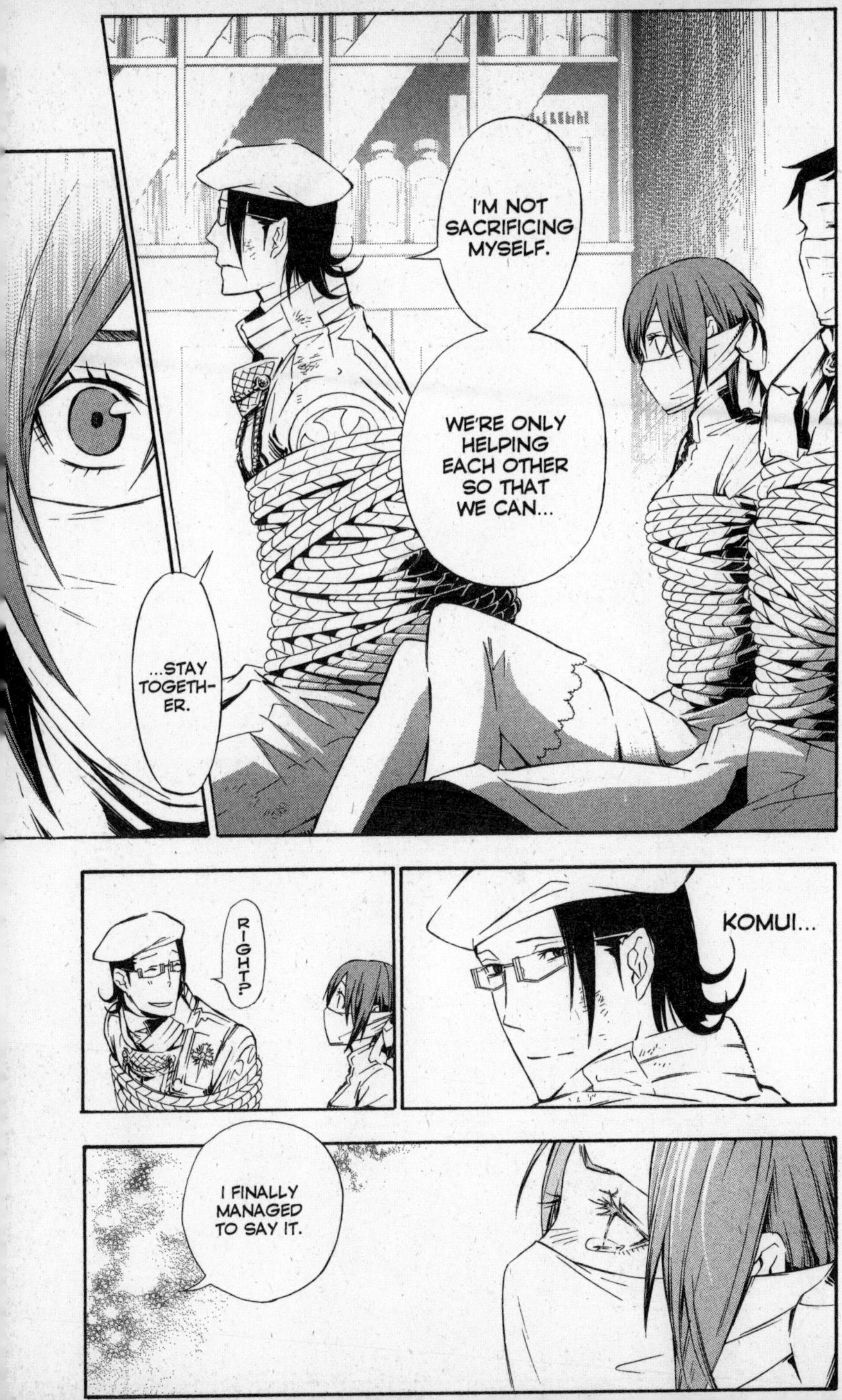
I'M NOT SACRIFICING MYSELF.
WE'RE ONLY HELPING EACH OTHER SO THAT WE CAN...
...STAY TOGETH-ER.
KOMUI...
RIGHT?
I FINALLY MANAGED TO SAY IT.

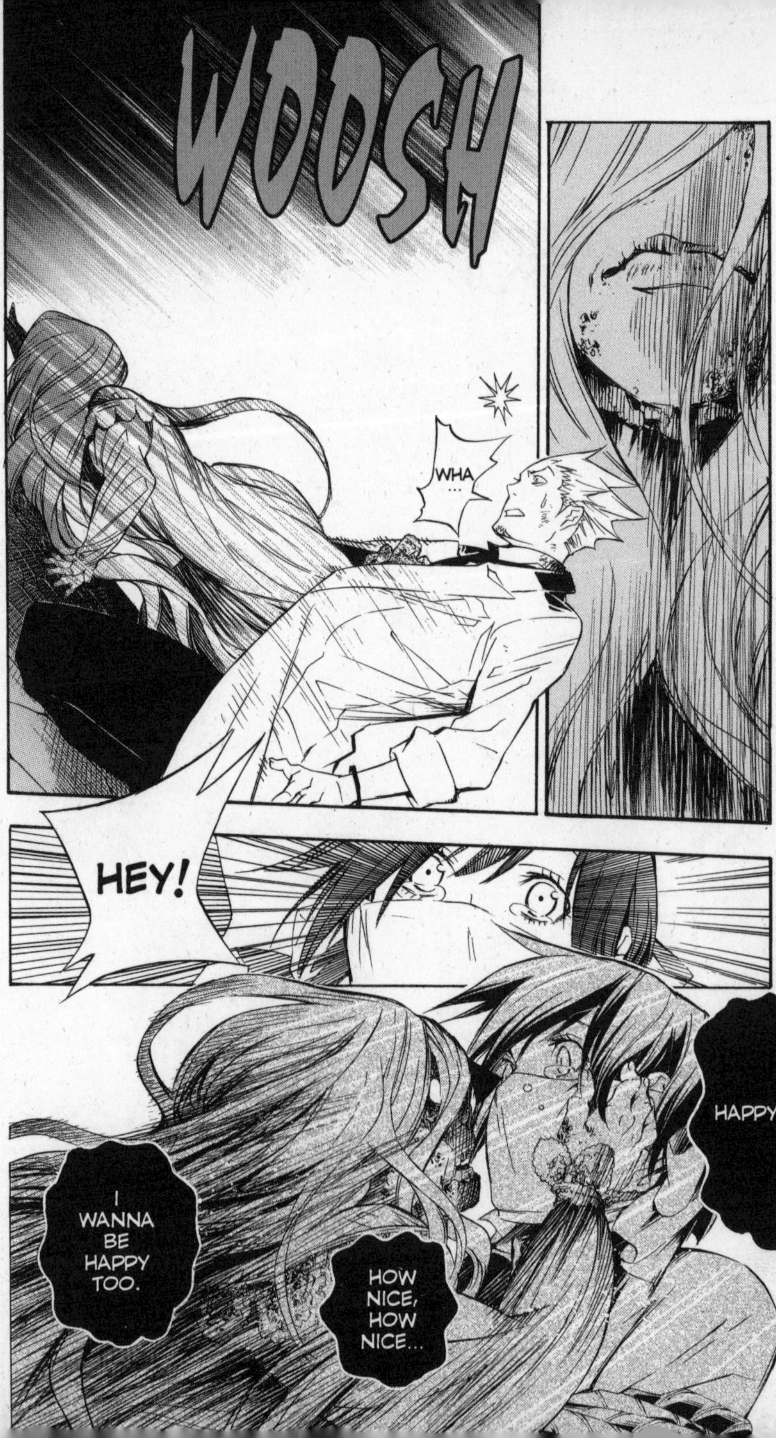
WOOSH
WHA...
HEY!
HAPPY?
HOW NICE, HOW NICE...
I WANNA BE HAPPY TOO.

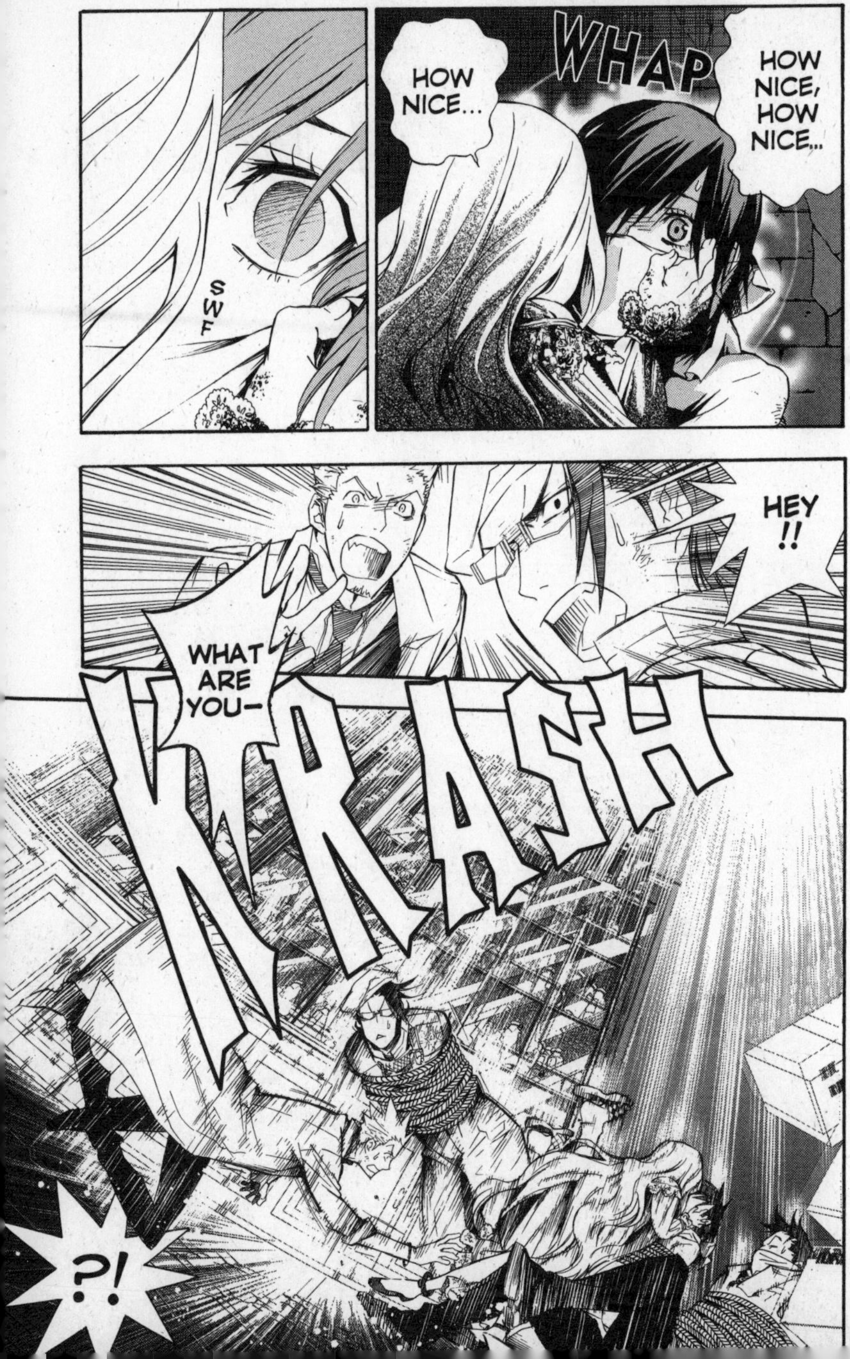
HOW NICE, HOW NICE, HOW NICE...
WHAP
HOW NICE...
SWF
HEY!!
WHAT ARE YOU—
KRASH
?!

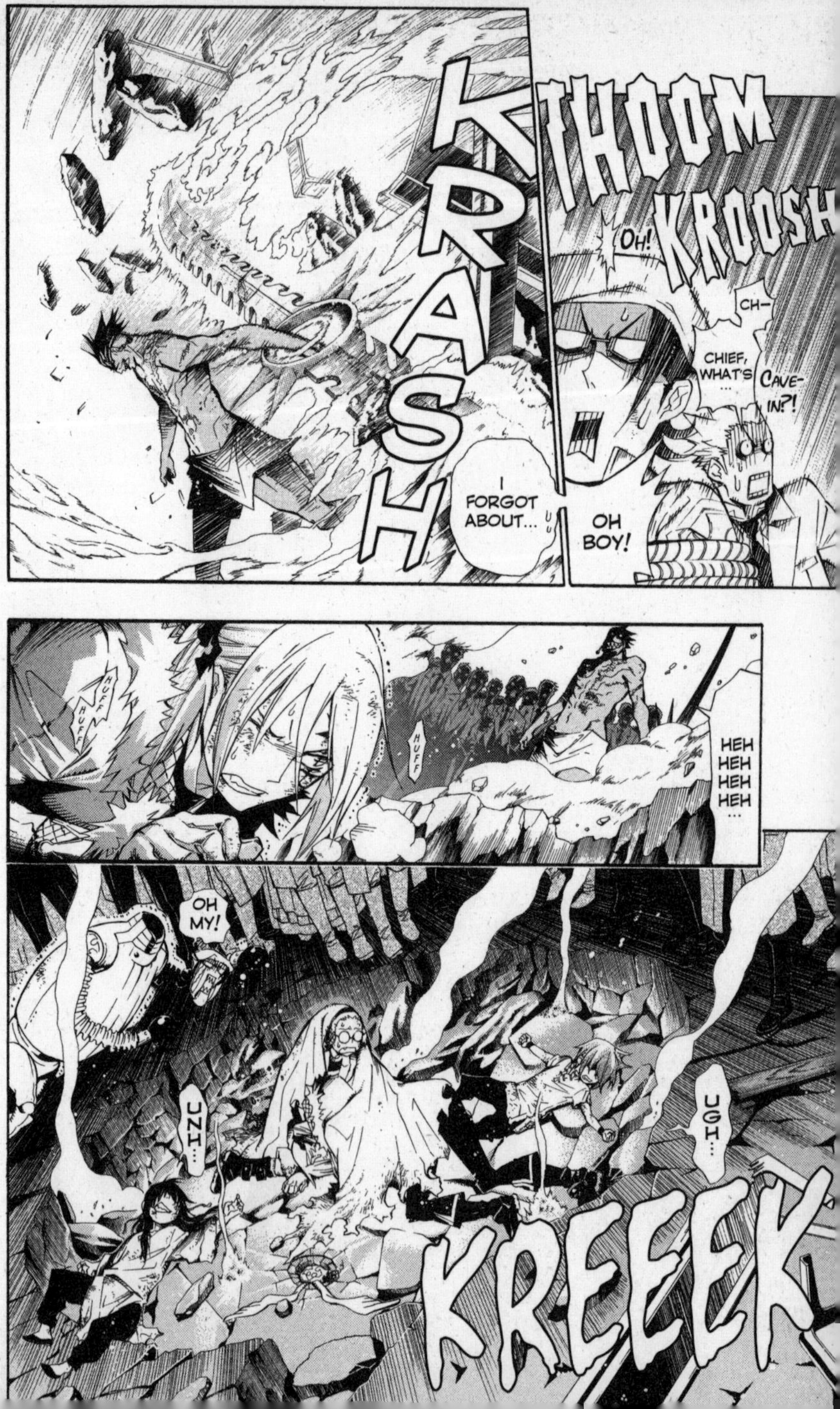
THOOM
OH!
KROOSH
CH-
CHIEF, WHAT'S ...
CAVE-IN?!
OH BOY!
KRASH
I FORGOT ABOUT...
HEH HEH HEH HEH ...
HUFF
HUFF HUFF
KREEEK
UGH...
UNH...
OH MY!

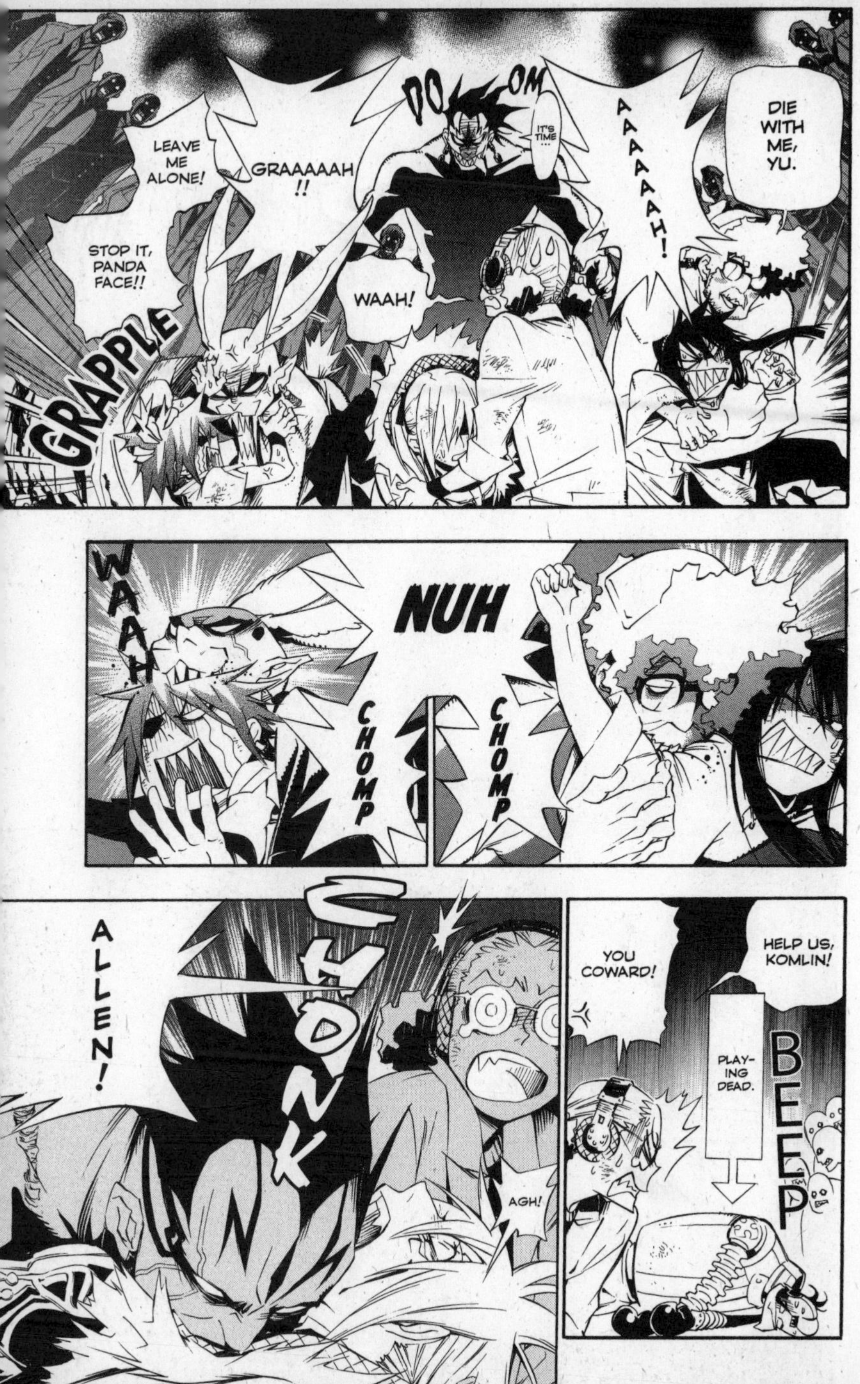
DIE WITH ME, YU.
AAAAAAH!
IT'S TIME...
DO-OM
GRAAAAAH!!
LEAVE ME ALONE!
WAAH!
STOP IT, PANDA FACE!!
GRAPPLE
NUH
CHOMP
CHOMP
WAAAH
HELP US, KOMLIN!
YOU COWARD!
PLAYING DEAD.
BEEP
CHONK
AGH!
ALLEN!

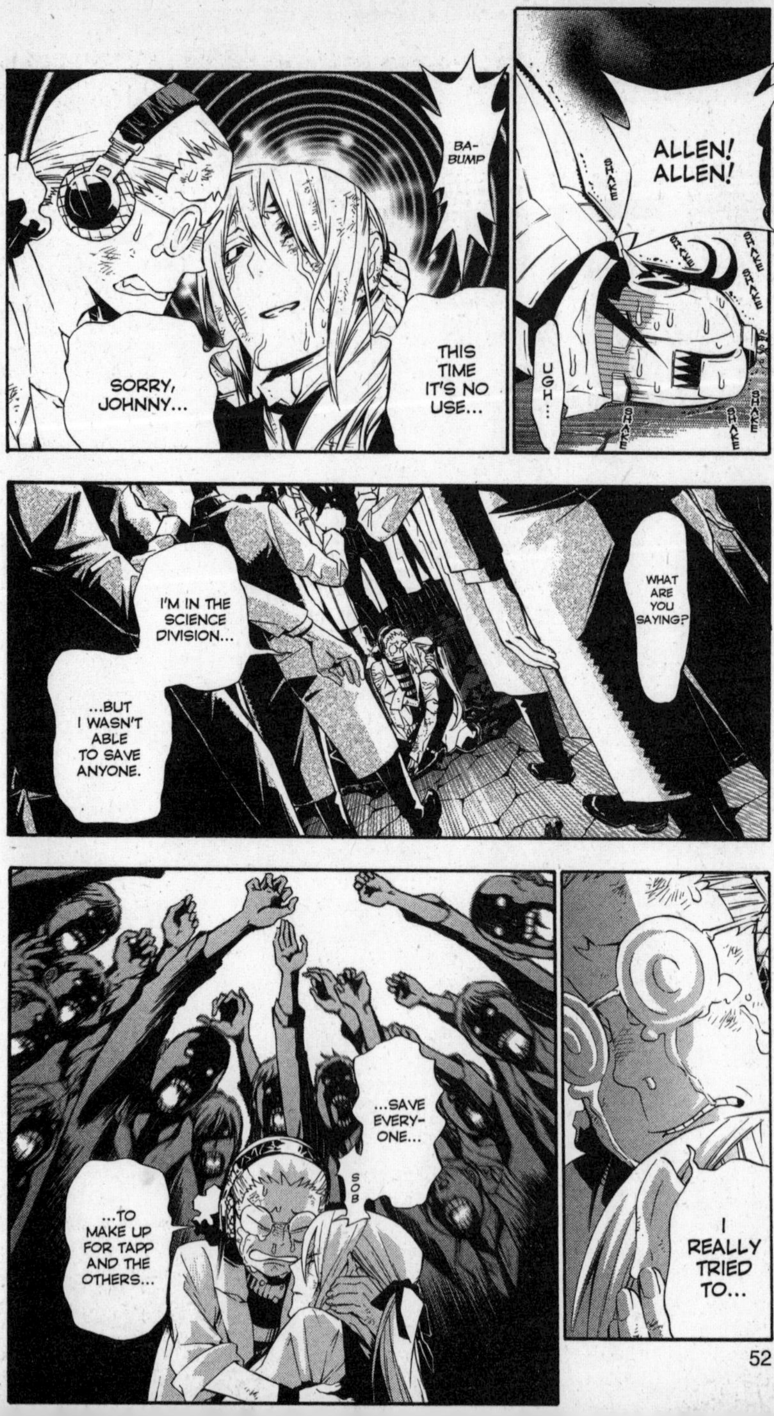
ALLEN! ALLEN!
SHAKE
SHAKE
SHAKE
SHAKE
SHAKE
SHAKE
UGH...
BA-BUMP
THIS TIME IT'S NO USE...
SORRY, JOHNNY...
WHAT ARE YOU SAYING?
I'M IN THE SCIENCE DIVISION...
...BUT I WASN'T ABLE TO SAVE ANYONE.
I REALLY TRIED TO...
...SAVE EVERY-ONE...
SOB
...TO MAKE UP FOR TAPP AND THE OTHERS...

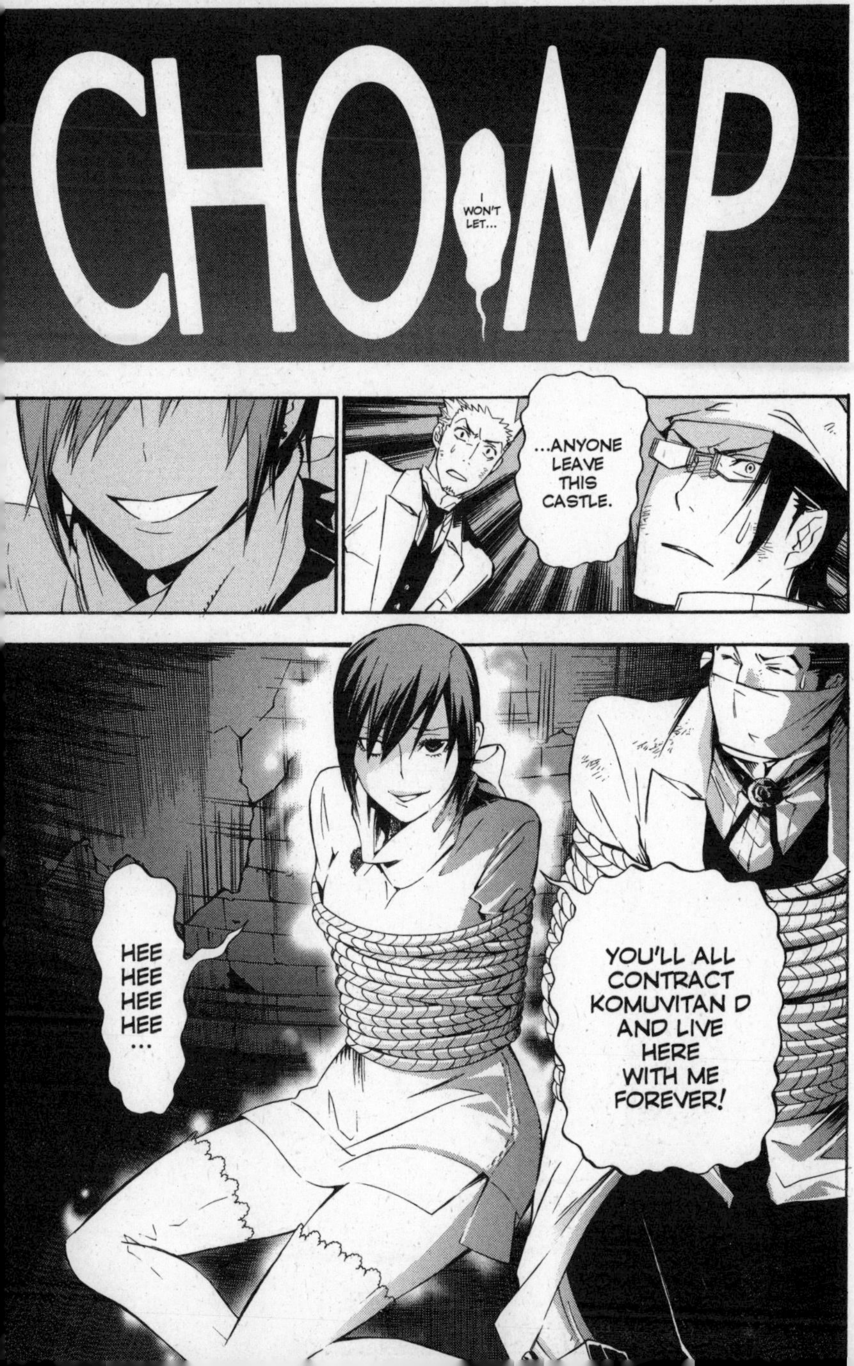
CHOMP
I WON'T LET...
...ANYONE LEAVE THIS CASTLE.
YOU'LL ALL CONTRACT KOMUVITAN D AND LIVE HERE WITH ME FOREVER!
HEE HEE HEE HEE ...

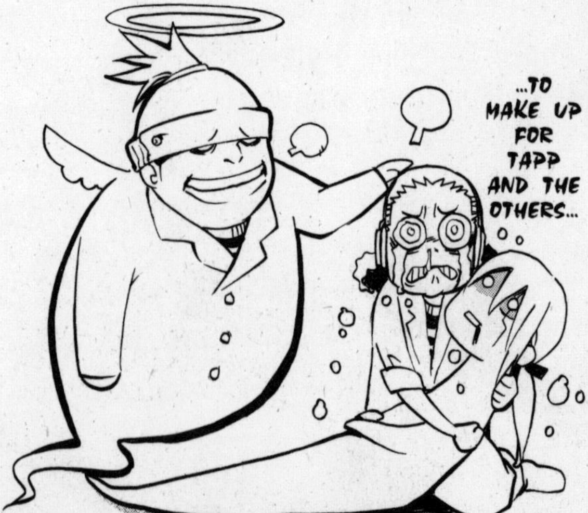
...TO MAKE UP FOR TAPP AND THE OTHERS...

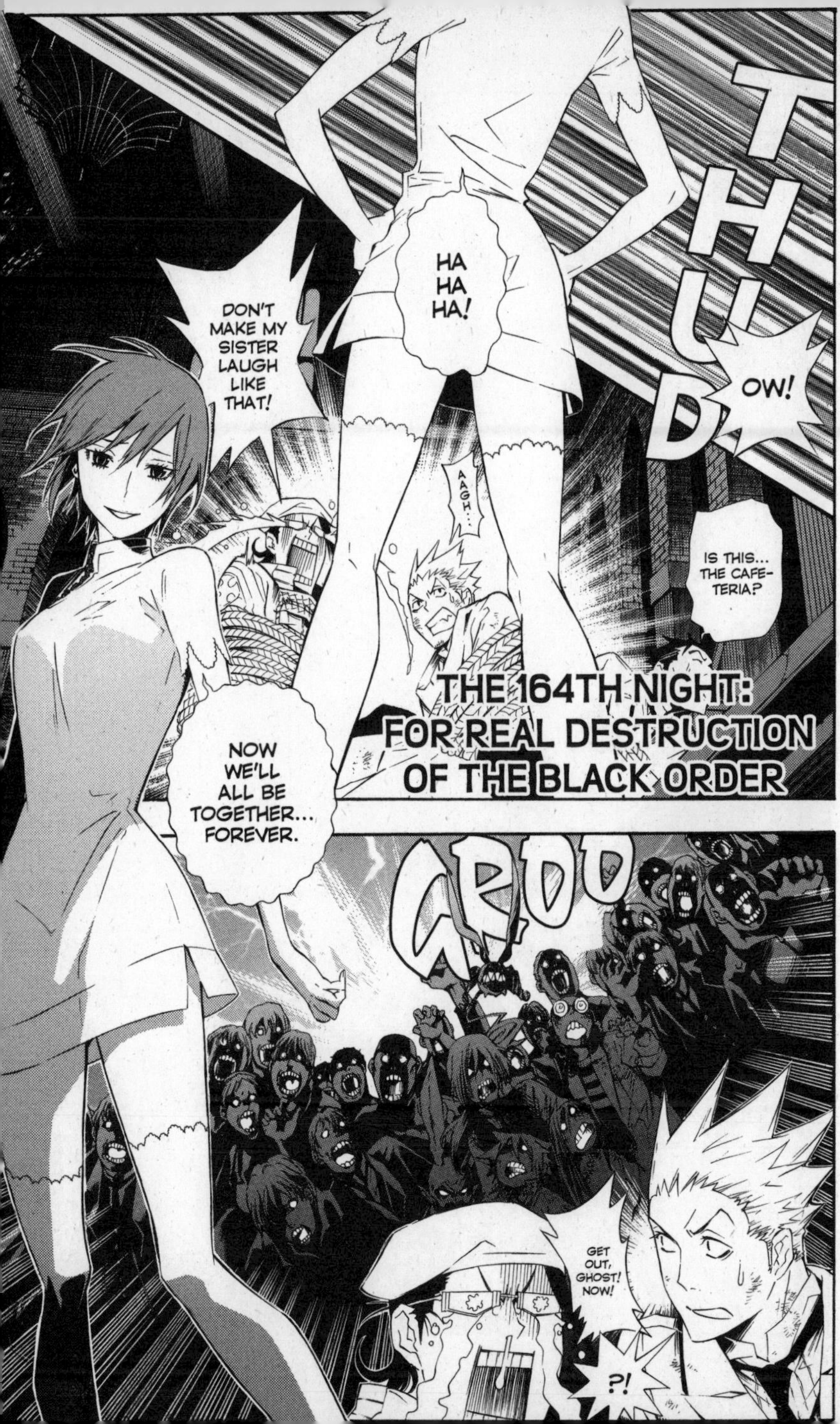
THUD
OW!
HA HA HA!
DON'T MAKE MY SISTER LAUGH LIKE THAT!
AAGH...
IS THIS... THE CAFE-TERIA?
THE 164TH NIGHT: FOR REAL DESTRUCTION OF THE BLACK ORDER
NOW WE'LL ALL BE TOGETHER... FOREVER.
GROO
GET OUT, GHOST! NOW!
?!

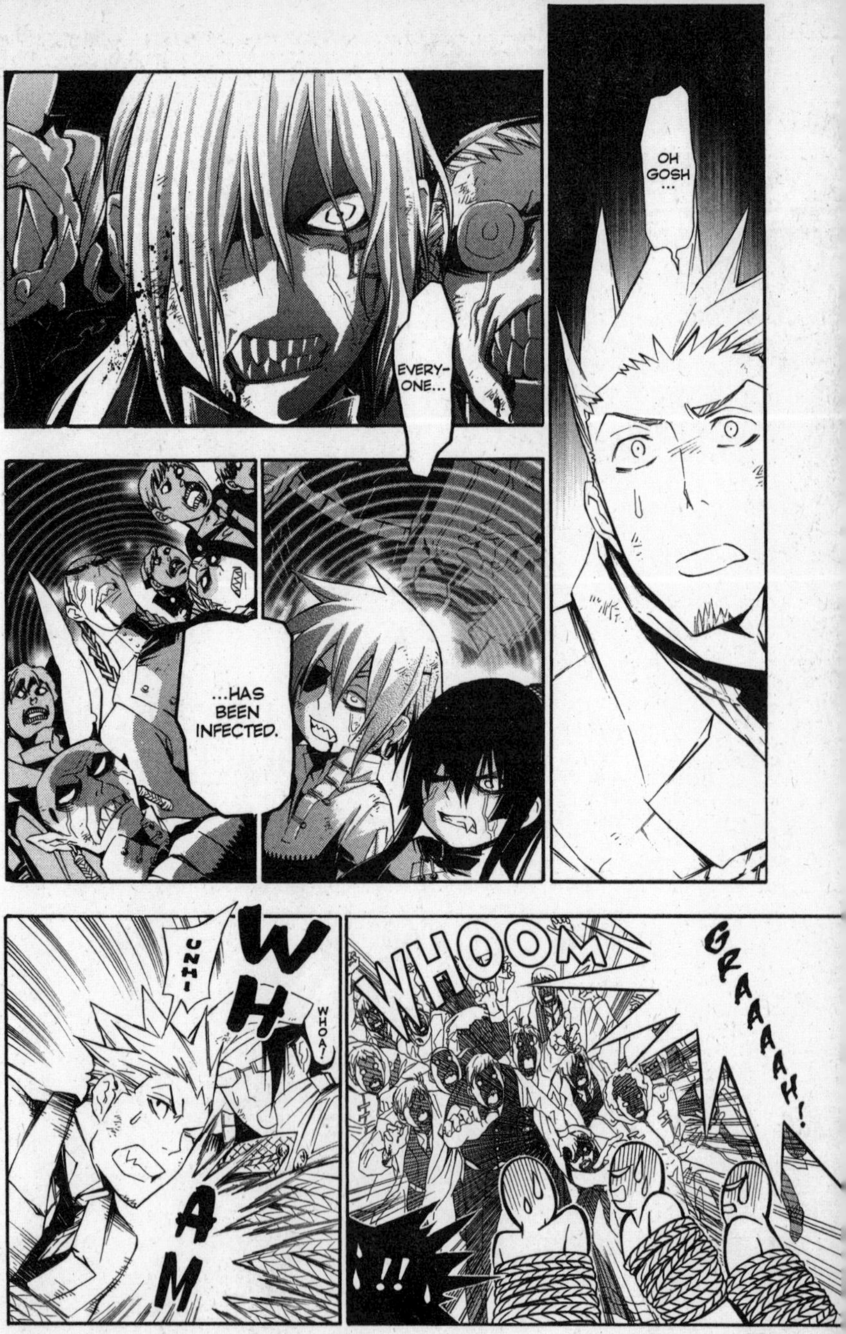

OH GOSH ...
EVERY-ONE...
...HAS BEEN INFECTED.
WHOOM
GRAAAAH!
!!
UNH!
WHAM
WHOA!

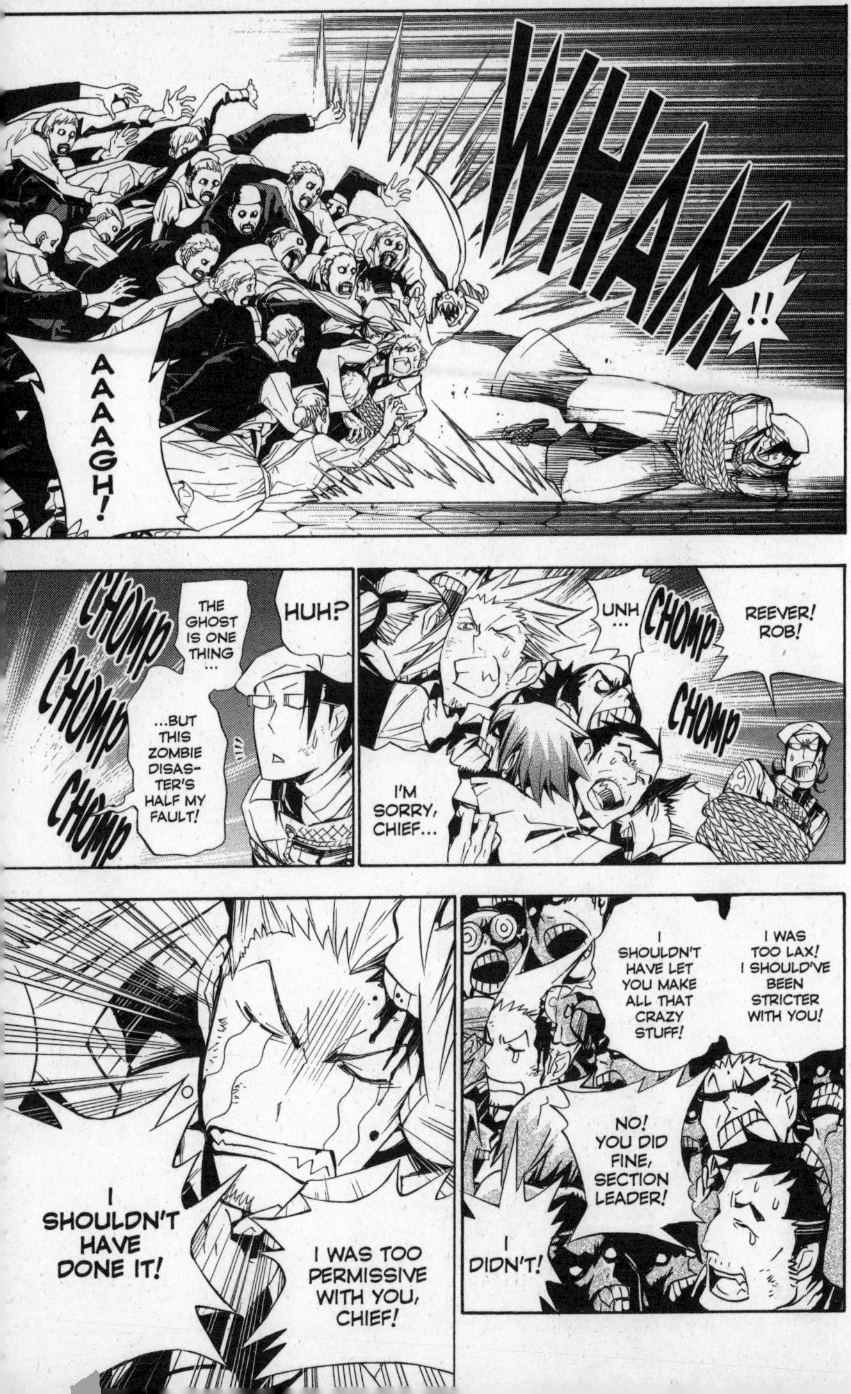
WHAM!!
AAAAGH!
REEVER! ROB!
CHOMP
UNH ...
CHOMP
I'M SORRY, CHIEF...
HUH?
THE GHOST IS ONE THING ...
CHOMP CHOMP CHOMP CHOMP
...BUT THIS ZOMBIE DISASTER'S HALF MY FAULT!
I WAS TOO LAX! I SHOULD'VE BEEN STRICTER WITH YOU!
I SHOULDN'T HAVE LET YOU MAKE ALL THAT CRAZY STUFF!
NO! YOU DID FINE, SECTION LEADER!
I DIDN'T!
I WAS TOO PERMISSIVE WITH YOU, CHIEF!
I SHOULDN'T HAVE DONE IT!

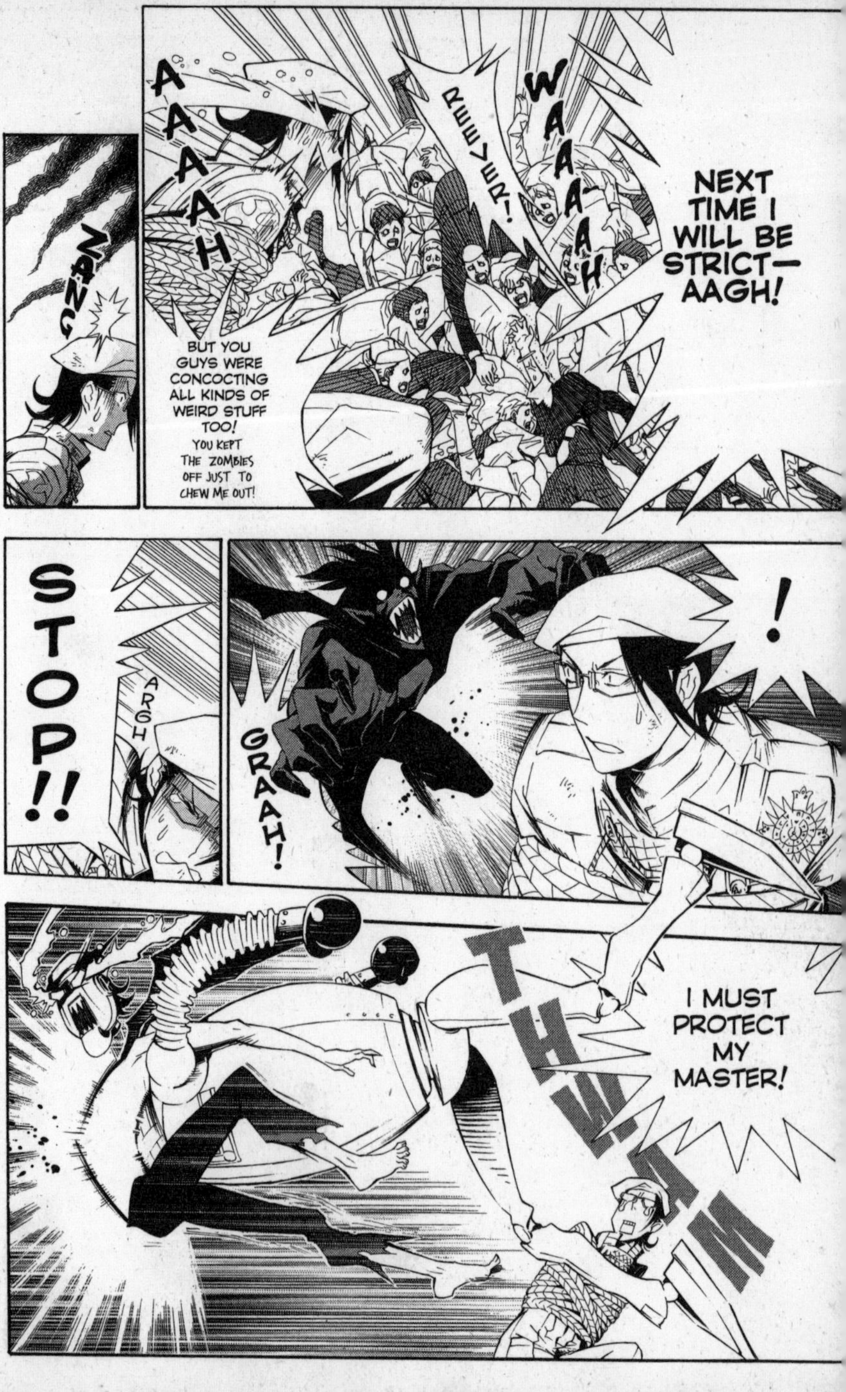
NEXT TIME I WILL BE STRICT—AAGH!
WAAAAAH
REEVER!
AAAAAH
BUT YOU GUYS WERE CONCOCTING ALL KINDS OF WEIRD STUFF TOO!
YOU KEPT THE ZOMBIES OFF JUST TO CHEW ME OUT!
ZANG
!
GRAAH!
STOP!!
ARGH
I MUST PROTECT MY MASTER!
THWAMM

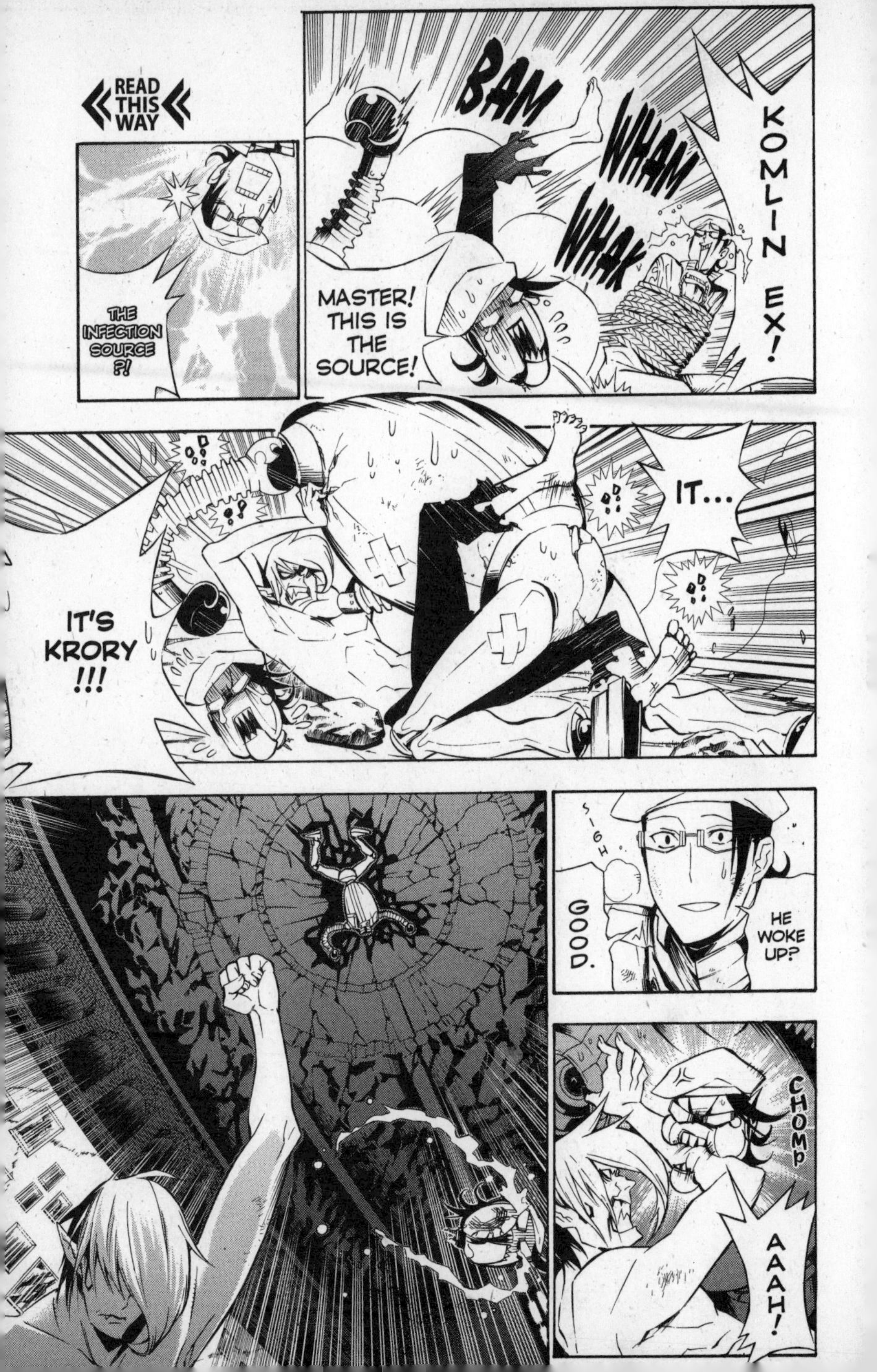
READ THIS WAY
BAM
WHAM
WHAK
KOMLIN EX!
MASTER! THIS IS THE SOURCE!
THE INFECTION SOURCE ?!
IT...
IT'S KRORY!!!
SIGH
HE WOKE UP?
GOOD.
CHOMP
AAAH!

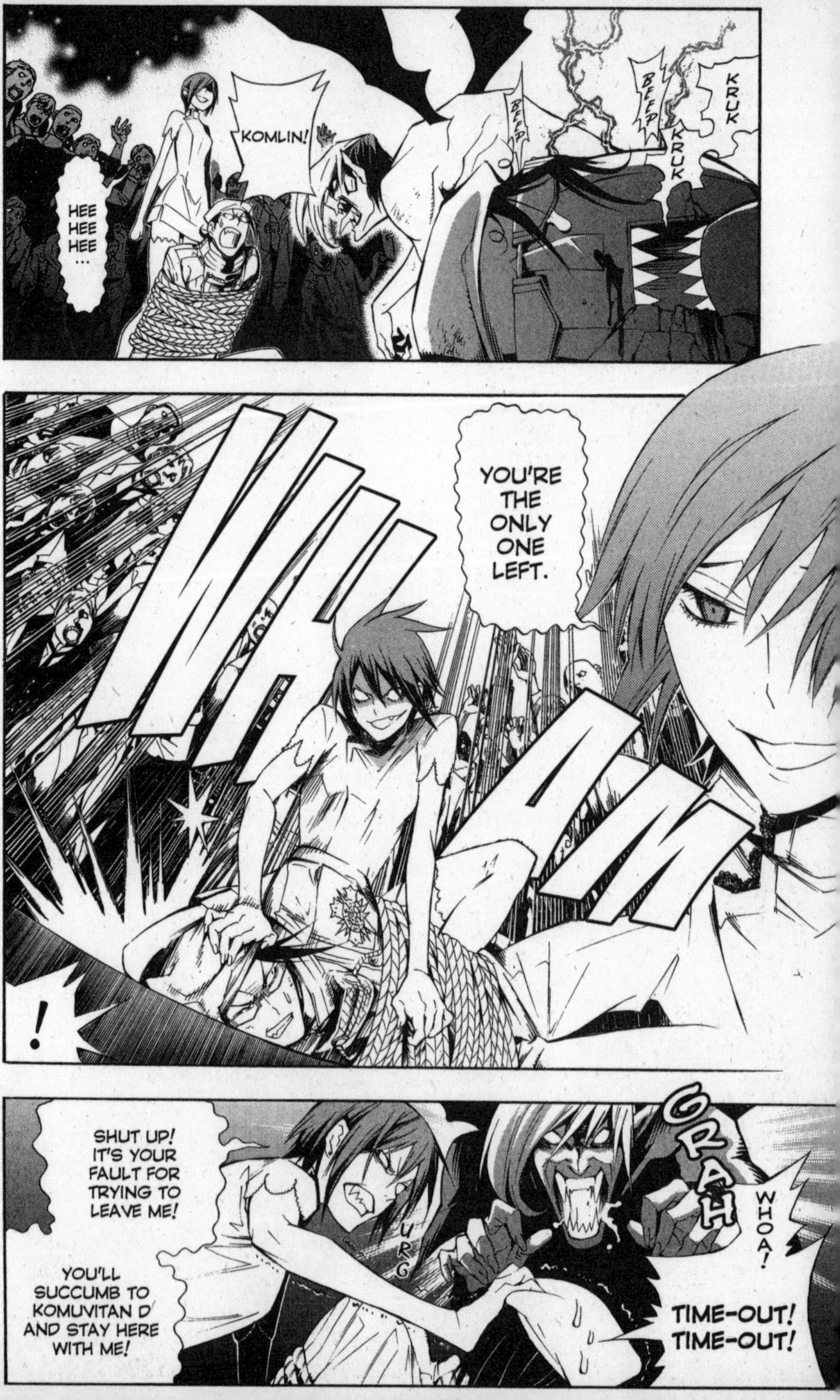
KRUK
BEEP
KRUK KRUK
BEEP
KOMLIN!
HEE HEE HEE...
YOU'RE THE ONLY ONE LEFT.
!
GRAH
WHOA!
TIME-OUT! TIME-OUT!
URG
SHUT UP! IT'S YOUR FAULT FOR TRYING TO LEAVE ME!
YOU'LL SUCCUMB TO KOMUVITAN D AND STAY HERE WITH ME!

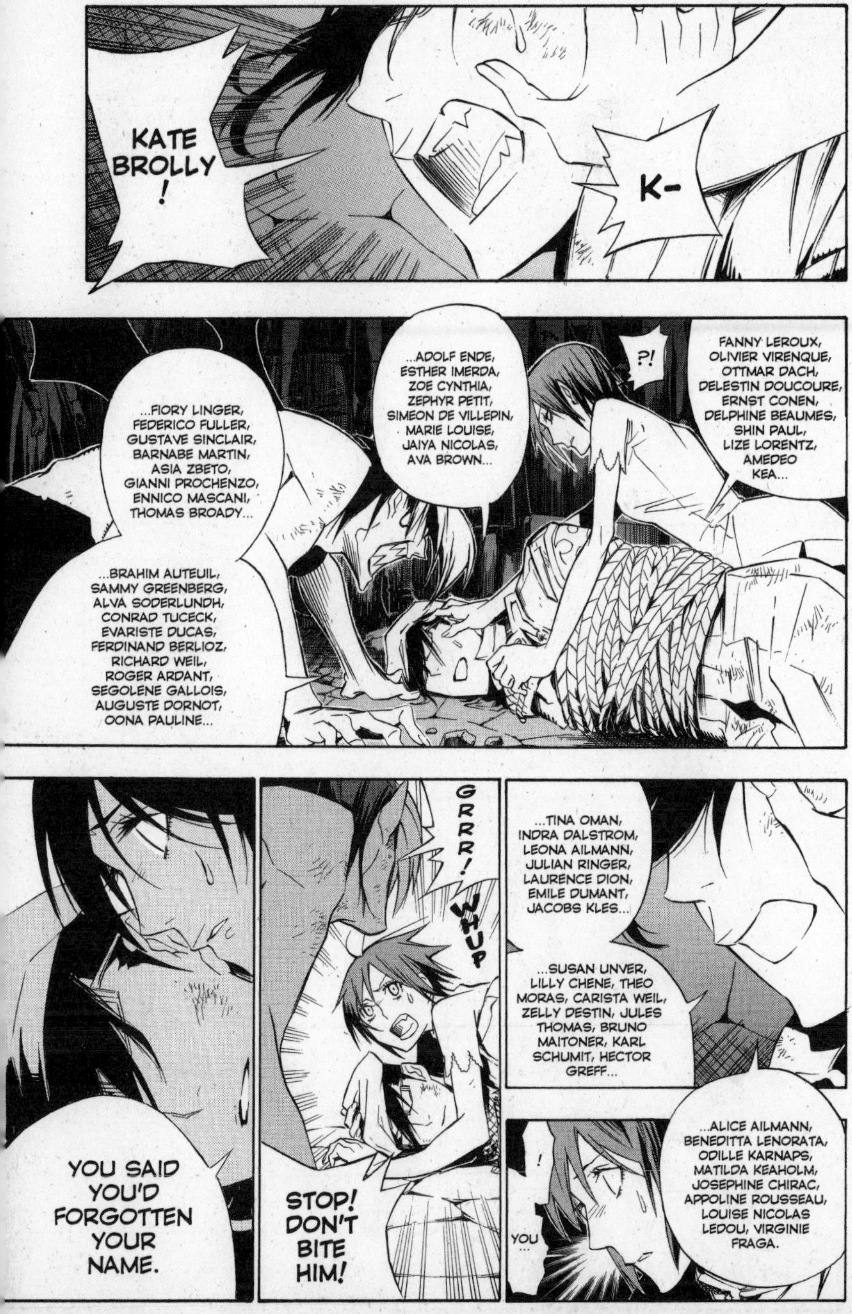
K-
KATE BROLLY !
FANNY LEROUX, OLIVIER VIRENQUE, OTTMAR DACH, DELESTIN DOUCOURE, ERNST CONEN, DELPHINE BEAUMES, SHIN PAUL, LIZE LORENTZ, AMEDEO KEA...
?!
...ADOLF ENDE, ESTHER IMERDA, ZOE CYNTHIA, ZEPHYR PETIT, SIMEON DE VILLEPIN, MARIE LOUISE, JAIYA NICOLAS, AVA BROWN...
...FIORY LINGER, FEDERICO FULLER, GUSTAVE SINCLAIR, BARNABE MARTIN, ASIA ZBETO, GIANNI PROCHENZO, ENNICO MASCANI, THOMAS BROADY...
...BRAHIM AUTEUIL, SAMMY GREENBERG, ALVA SODERLUNDH, CONRAD TUCECK, EVARISTE DUCAS, FERDINAND BERLIOZ, RICHARD WEIL, ROGER ARDANT, SEGOLENE GALLOIS, AUGUSTE DORNOT, OONA PAULINE...
...TINA OMAN, INDRA DALSTROM, LEONA AILMANN, JULIAN RINGER, LAURENCE DION, EMILE DUMANT, JACOBS KLES...
...SUSAN UNVER, LILLY CHENE, THEO MORAS, CARISTA WEIL, ZELLY DESTIN, JULES THOMAS, BRUNO MAITONER, KARL SCHUMIT, HECTOR GREFF...
...ALICE AILMANN, BENEDITTA LENORATA, ODILLE KARNAPS, MATILDA KEAHOLM, JOSEPHINE CHIRAC, APPOLINE ROUSSEAU, LOUISE NICOLAS LEDOU, VIRGINIE FRAGA.
!
YOU ...
GRRR!
WHUP
STOP! DON'T BITE HIM!
YOU SAID YOU'D FORGOTTEN YOUR NAME.

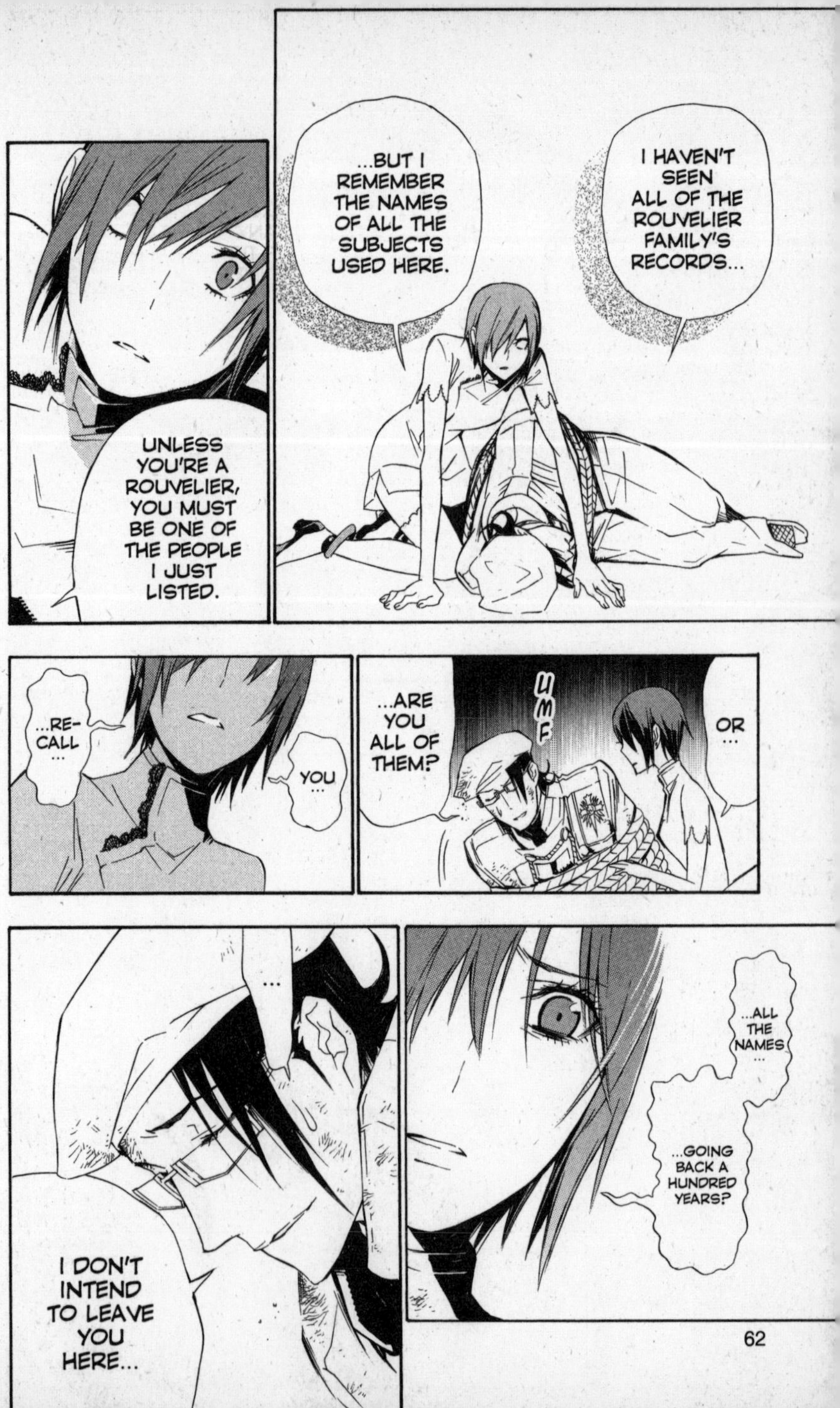
I HAVEN'T SEEN ALL OF THE ROUVELIER FAMILY'S RECORDS...
...BUT I REMEMBER THE NAMES OF ALL THE SUBJECTS USED HERE.
UNLESS YOU'RE A ROUVELIER, YOU MUST BE ONE OF THE PEOPLE I JUST LISTED.
OR ...
UMF
...ARE YOU ALL OF THEM?
YOU ...
...RE-CALL ...
...ALL THE NAMES ...
...GOING BACK A HUNDRED YEARS?
...
I DON'T INTEND TO LEAVE YOU HERE...

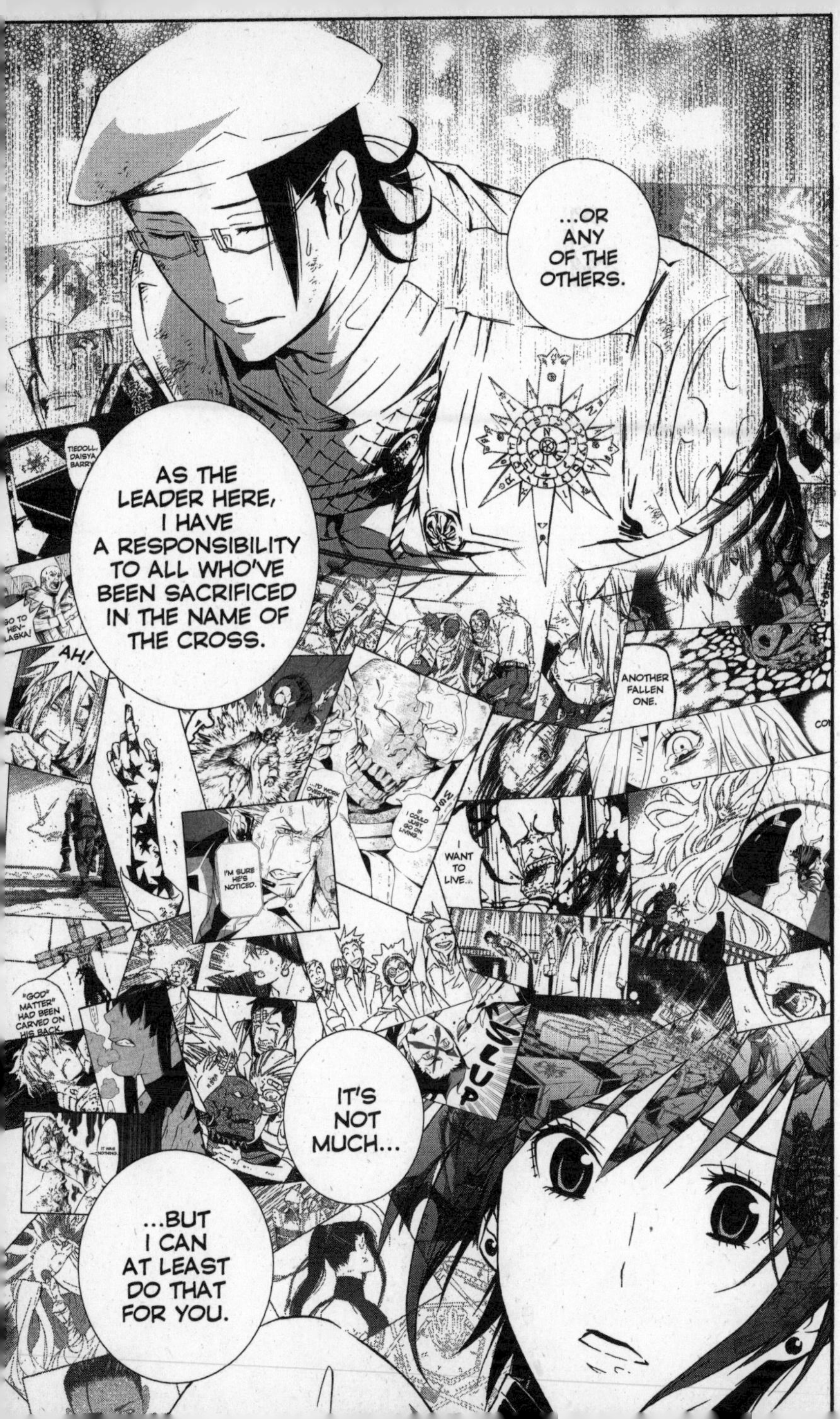
...OR ANY OF THE OTHERS.
AS THE LEADER HERE, I HAVE A RESPONSIBILITY TO ALL WHO'VE BEEN SACRIFICED IN THE NAME OF THE CROSS.
TIEDOLL, DAISYA BARRY
GO TO HEVLASKA!
ANOTHER FALLEN ONE.
AH!
I WANT TO LIVE...
IF I COULD JUST GO ON LIVING...
I'M SURE HE'S NOTICED.
"GOD" MATTER" HAD BEEN CARVED ON HIS BACK.
SLUP
IT'S NOT MUCH...
...BUT I CAN AT LEAST DO THAT FOR YOU.

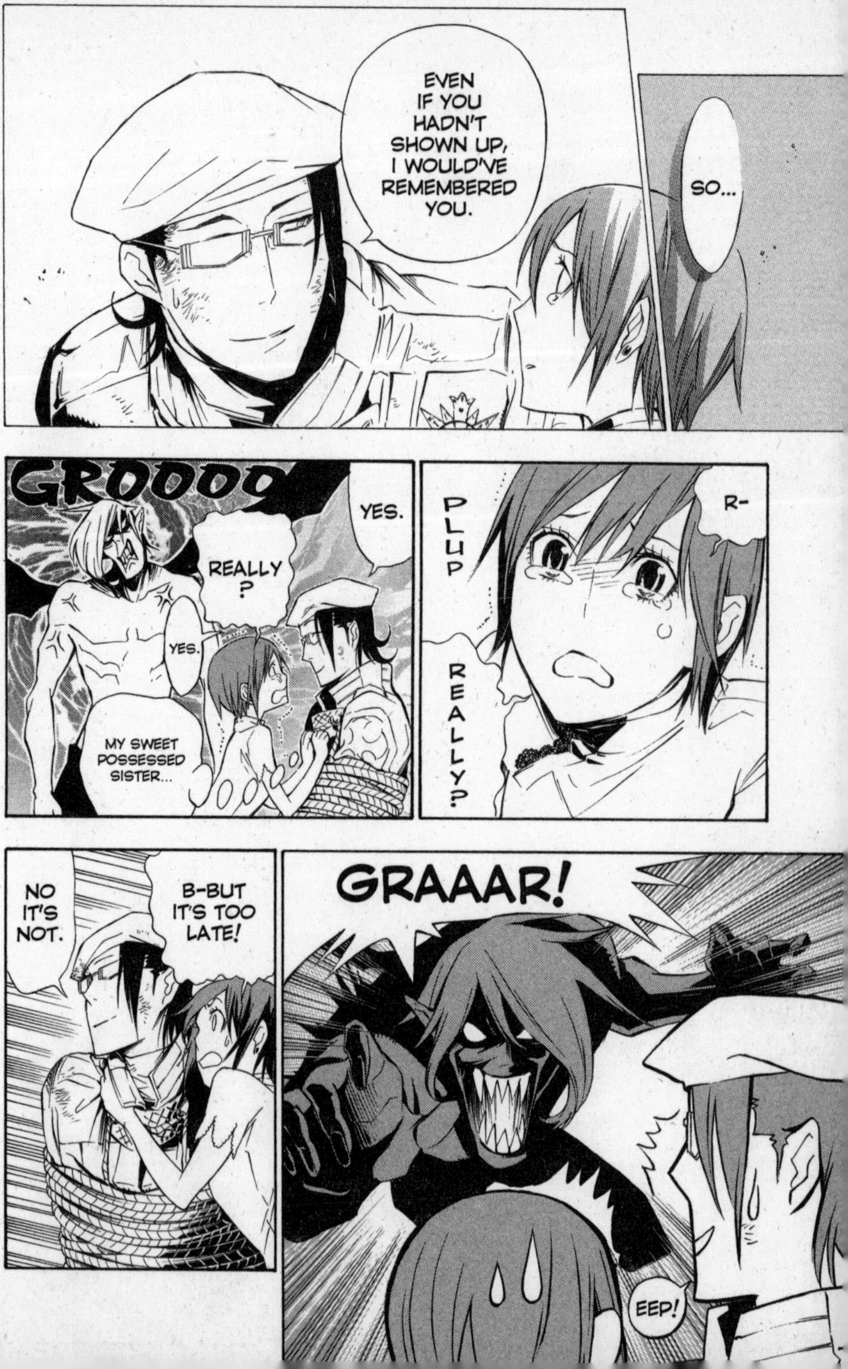
SO...
EVEN IF YOU HADN'T SHOWN UP, I WOULD'VE REMEMBERED YOU.
R-
PLUP
REALLY?
GROOOOO
YES.
REALLY?
YES.
MY SWEET POSSESSED SISTER...
GRAAAR!
EEP!
B-BUT IT'S TOO LATE!
NO IT'S NOT.

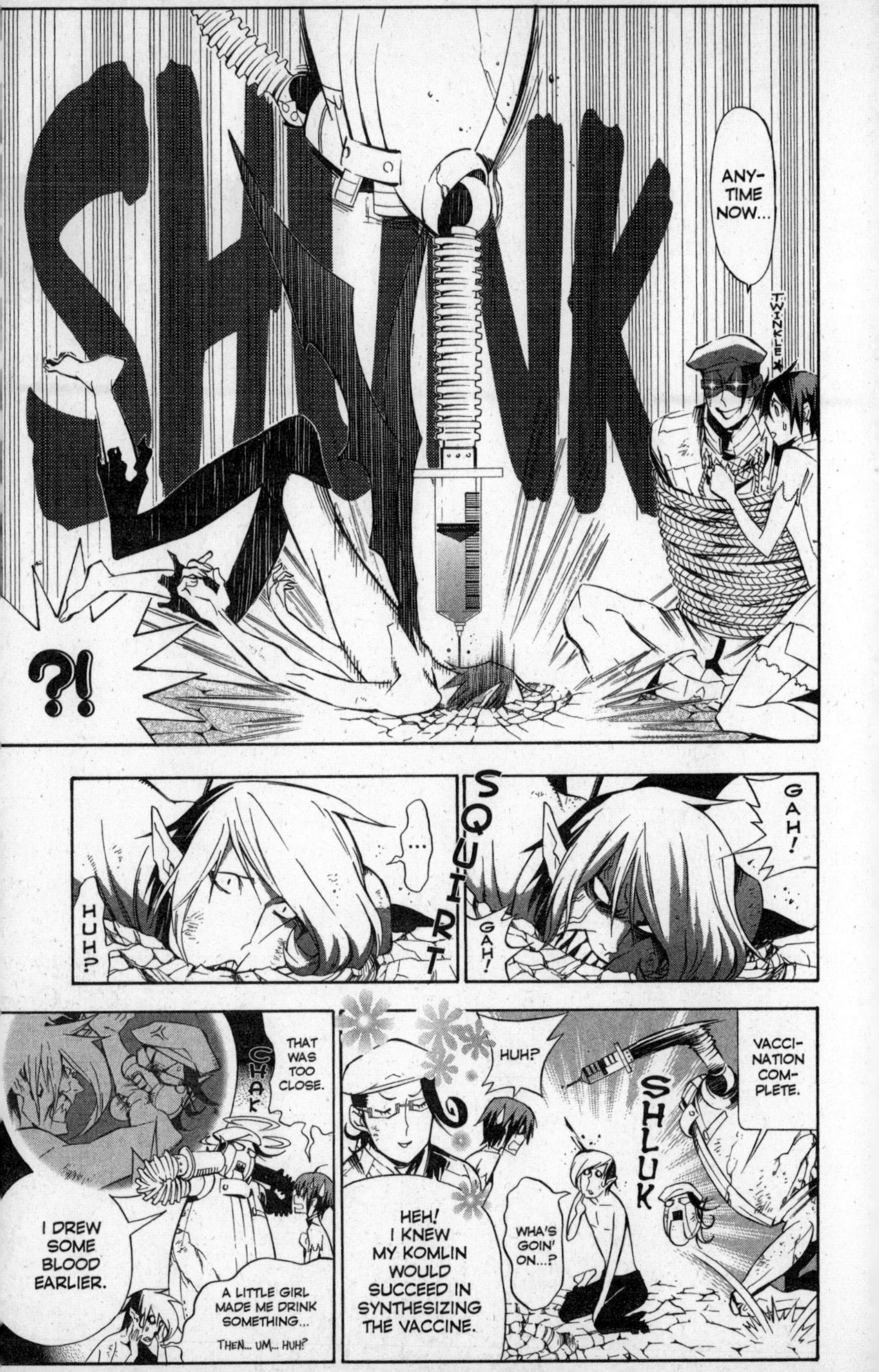
ANY-TIME NOW...
TWINKLE
?!
GAH!
GAH!
SQUIRT
...
HUH?
VACCI-NATION COM-PLETE.
SHLUK
HUH?
WHA'S GOIN' ON...?
HEH! I KNEW MY KOMLIN WOULD SUCCEED IN SYNTHESIZING THE VACCINE.
THAT WAS TOO CLOSE.
CHAK
I DREW SOME BLOOD EARLIER.
A LITTLE GIRL MADE ME DRINK SOMETHING...
THEN... UM... HUH?

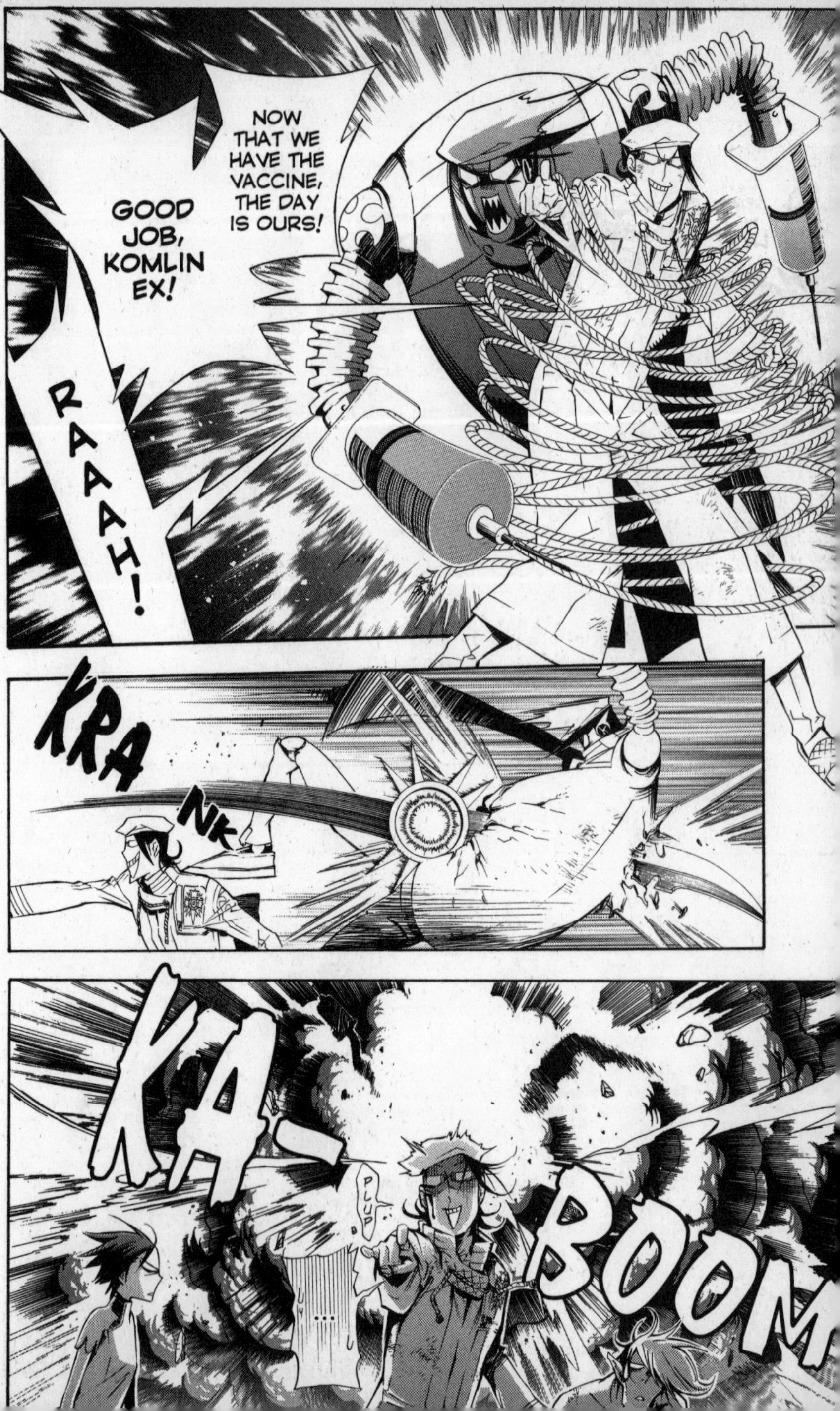
NOW THAT WE HAVE THE VACCINE, THE DAY IS OURS!
GOOD JOB, KOMLIN EX!
RAAAH!
KRANK
KA-BOOM
PLUP
...

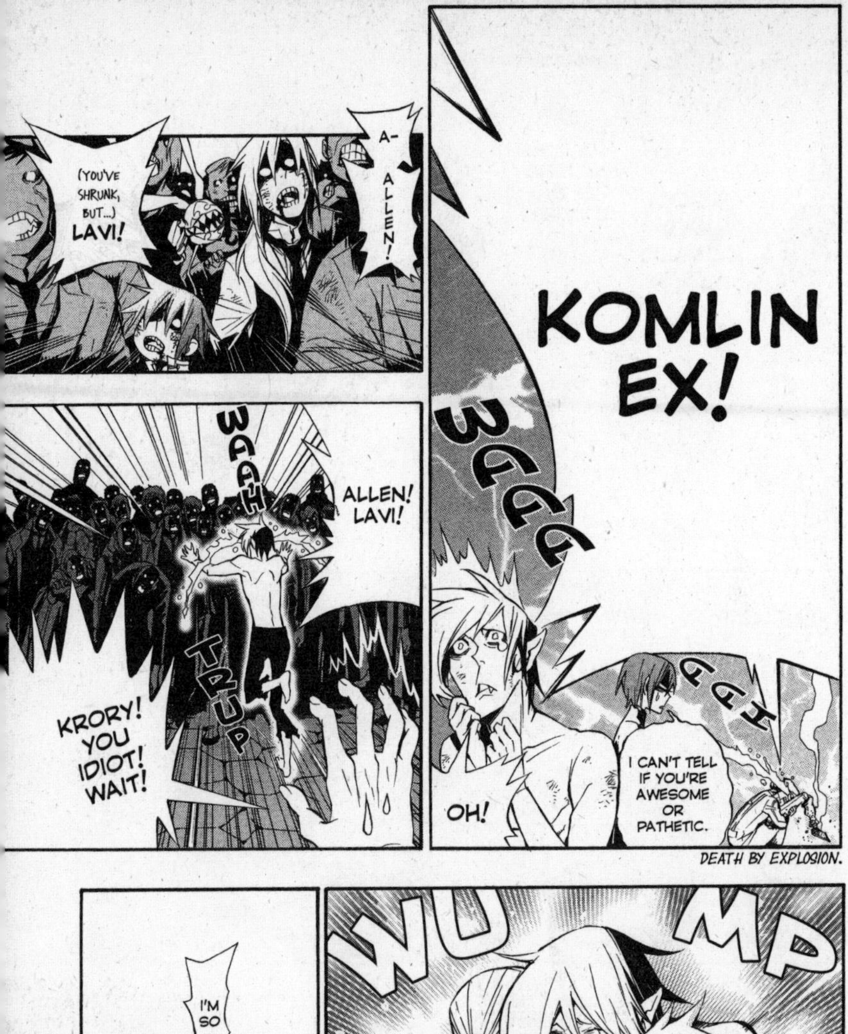
KOMLIN EX!
WAAAA
GGH
OH!
I CAN'T TELL IF YOU'RE AWESOME OR PATHETIC.
A- ALLEN!
(YOU'VE SHRUNK, BUT...) LAVI!
WAAH
ALLEN! LAVI!
TRUP
KRORY! YOU IDIOT! WAIT!

DEATH BY EXPLOSION.

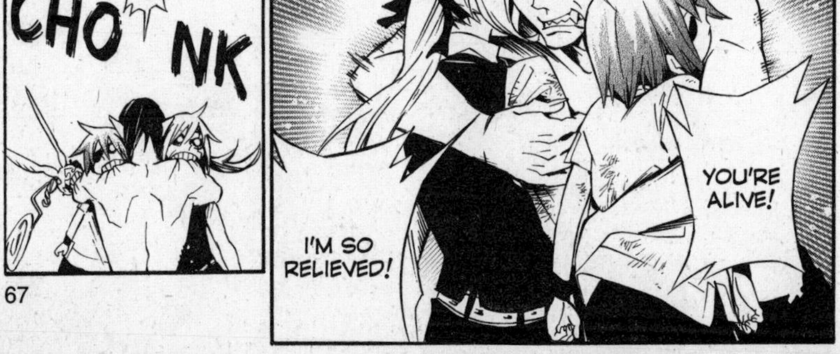
WUMP
YOU'RE ALIVE!
I'M SO RELIEVED!
I'M SO ...
CHONK

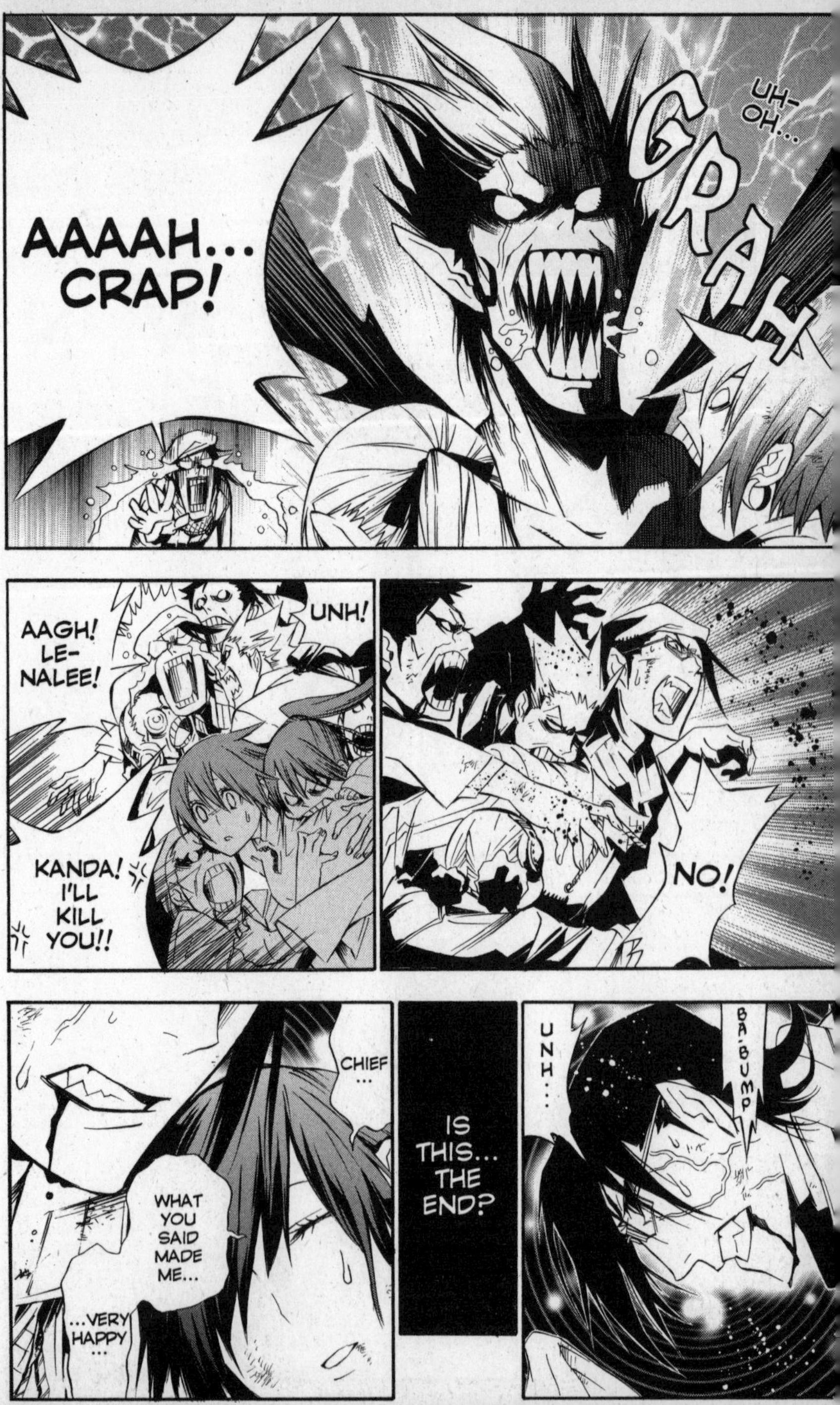
UH-OH...
GRAH
AAAAH... CRAP!
NO!
UNH!
AAGH! LE-NALEE!
KANDA! I'LL KILL YOU!!
BA-BUMP
UNH...
IS THIS... THE END?
CHIEF...
WHAT YOU SAID MADE ME...
...VERY HAPPY...

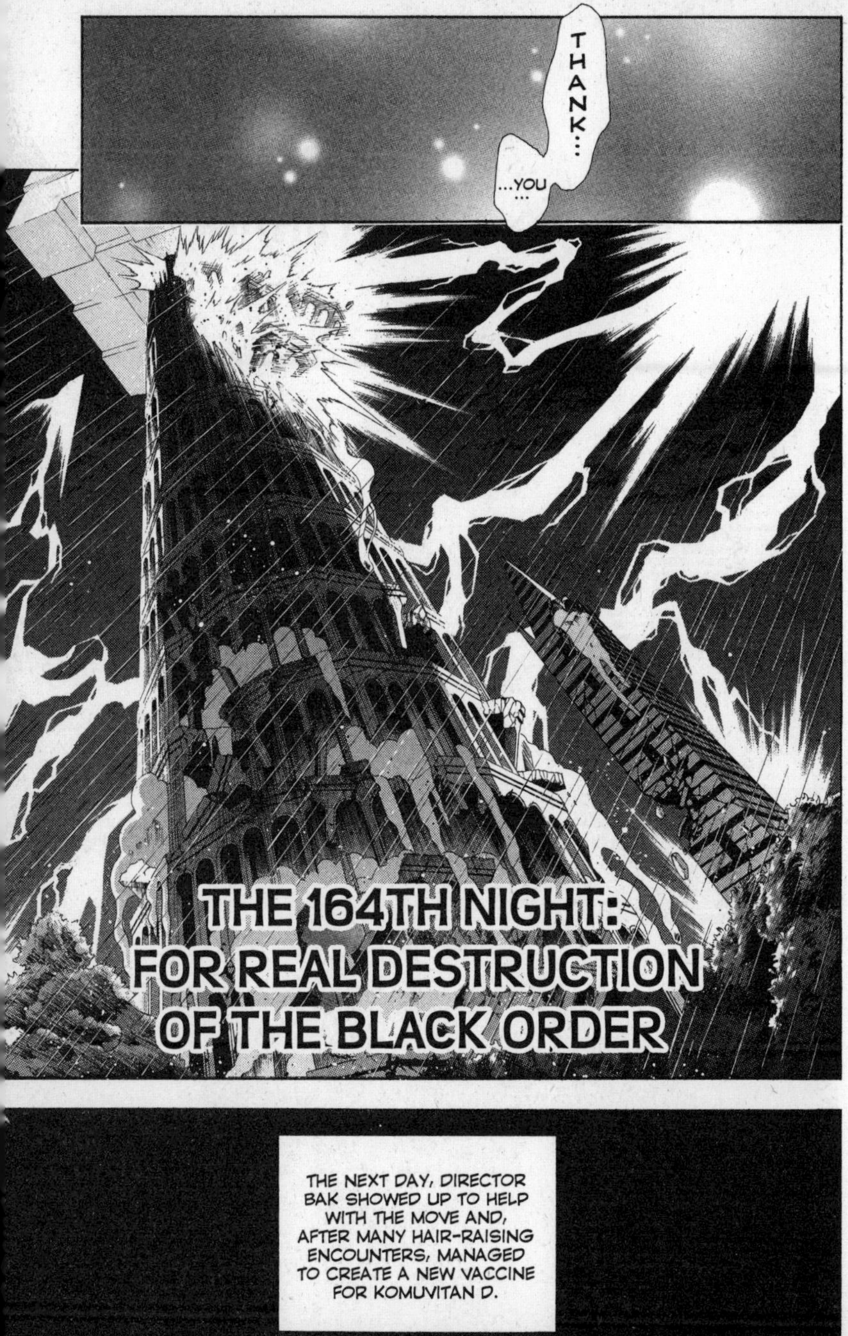
THANK...
...YOU...
THE 164TH NIGHT: FOR REAL DESTRUCTION OF THE BLACK ORDER
THE NEXT DAY, DIRECTOR BAK SHOWED UP TO HELP WITH THE MOVE AND, AFTER MANY HAIR-RAISING ENCOUNTERS, MANAGED TO CREATE A NEW VACCINE FOR KOMUVITAN D.

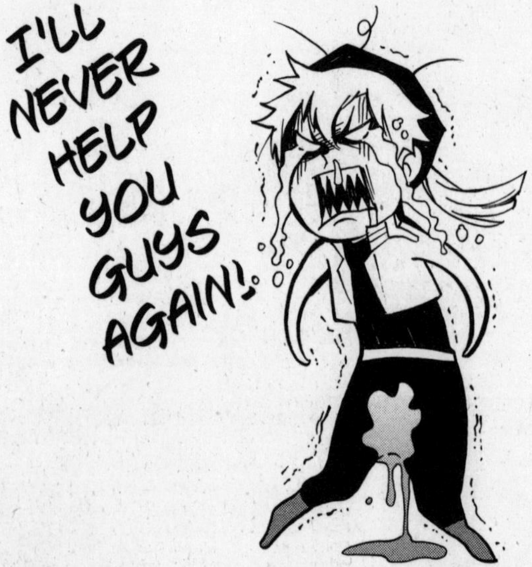
I'LL NEVER HELP YOU GUYS AGAIN!!

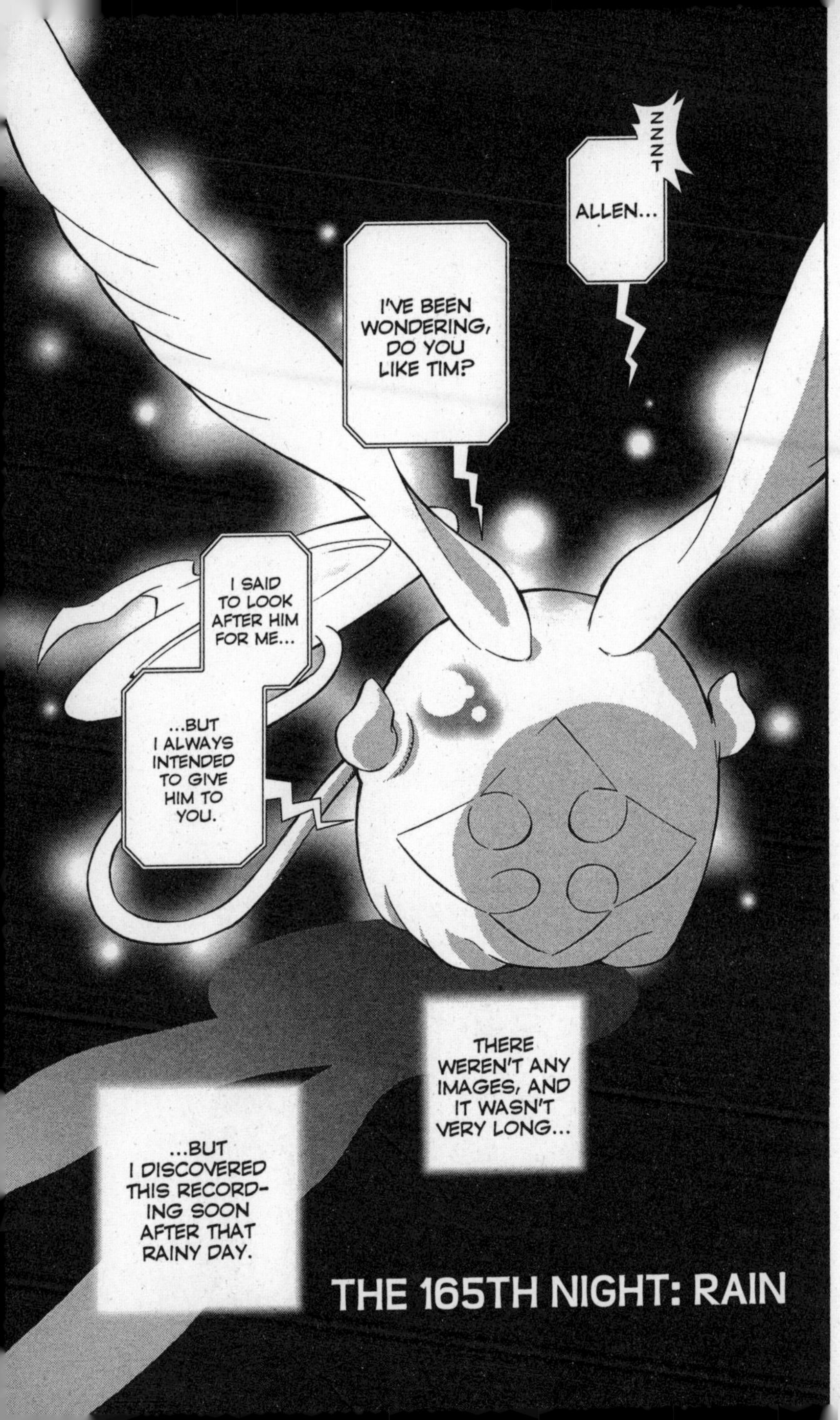
ZZZT
ALLEN...
I'VE BEEN WONDERING, DO YOU LIKE TIM?
I SAID TO LOOK AFTER HIM FOR ME...
...BUT I ALWAYS INTENDED TO GIVE HIM TO YOU.
THERE WEREN'T ANY IMAGES, AND IT WASN'T VERY LONG...
...BUT I DISCOVERED THIS RECORD-ING SOON AFTER THAT RAINY DAY.
THE 165TH NIGHT: RAIN

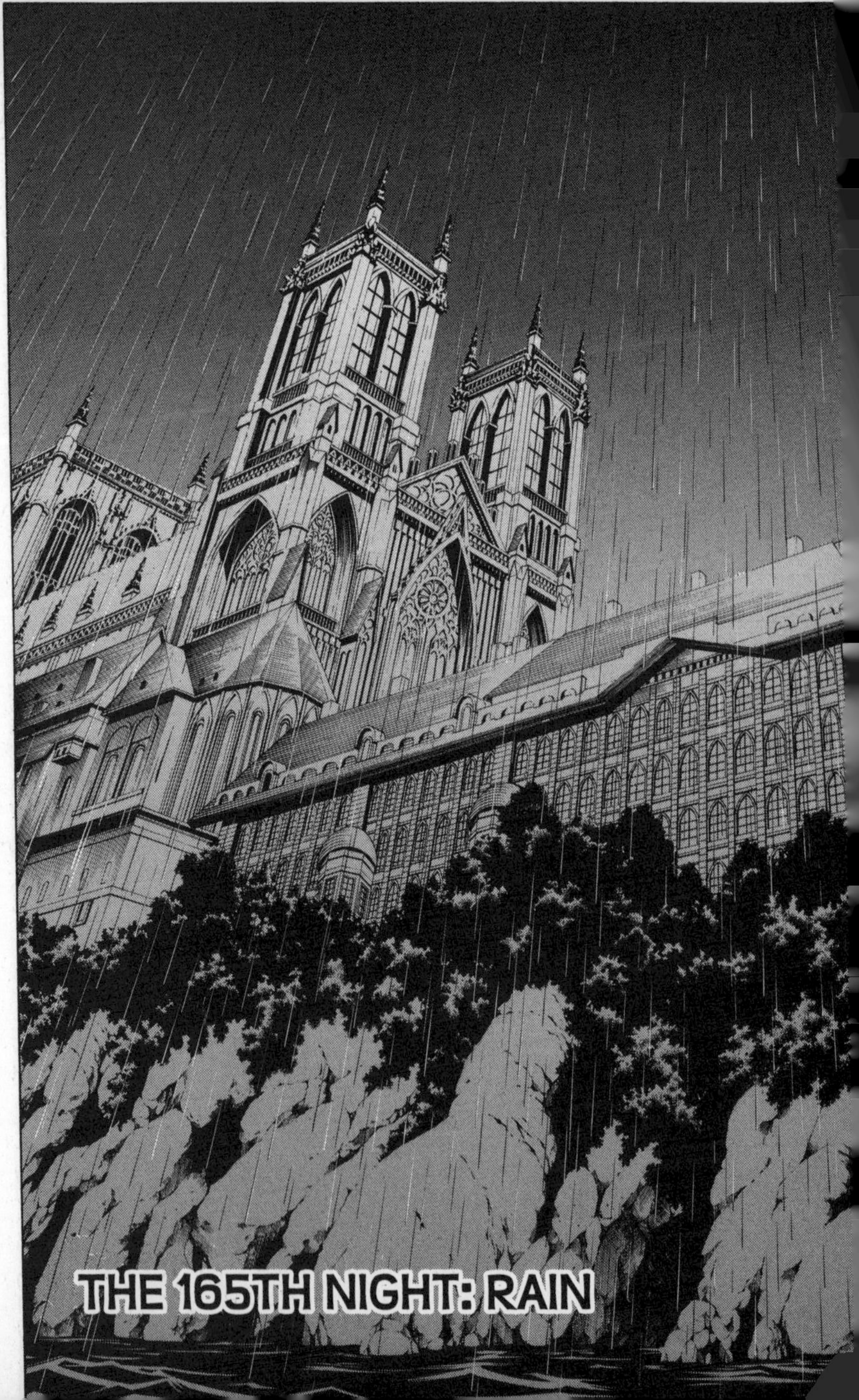
THE 165TH NIGHT: RAIN

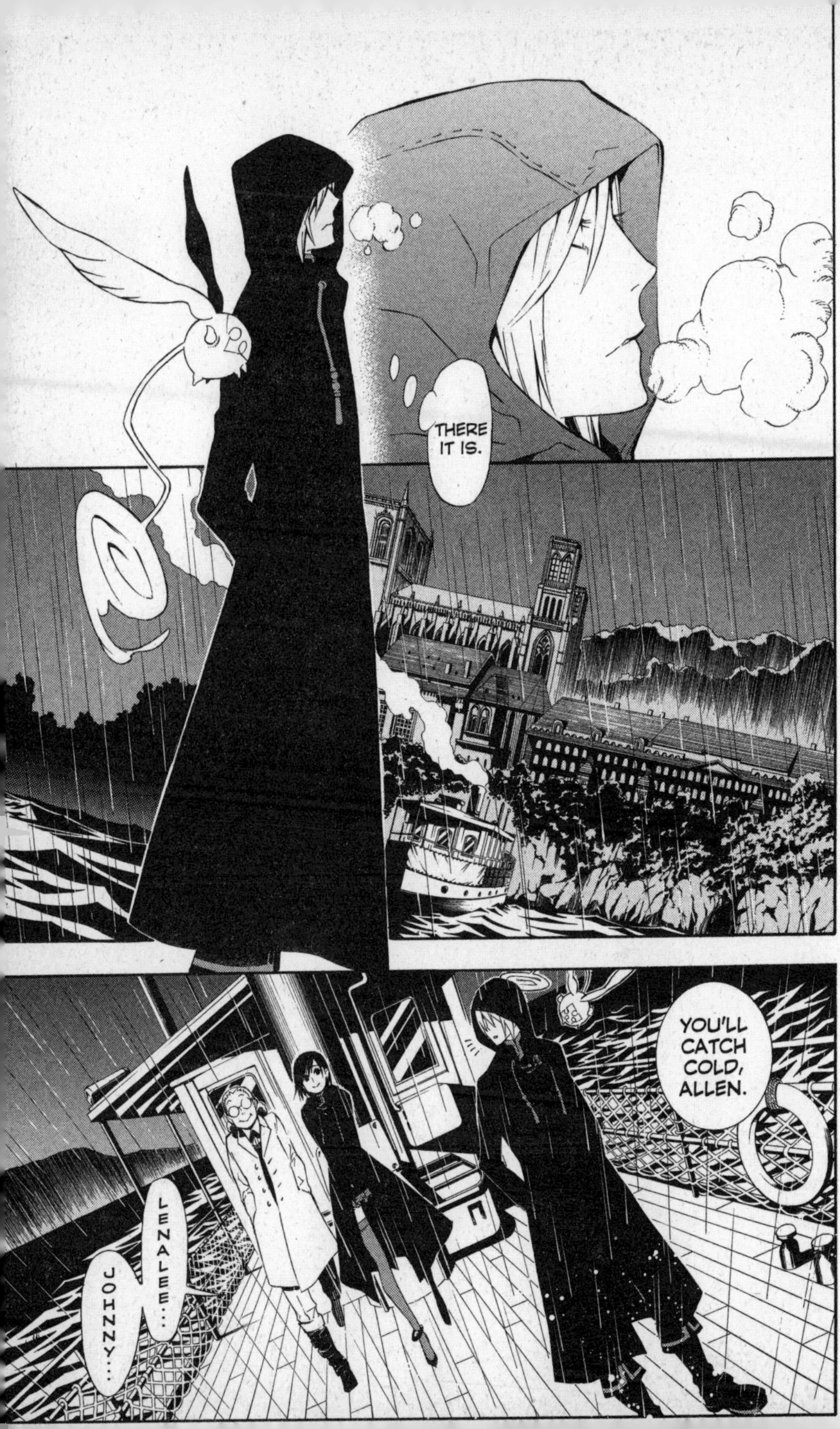
THERE IT IS.
YOU'LL CATCH COLD, ALLEN.
LENALEE...
JOHNNY...

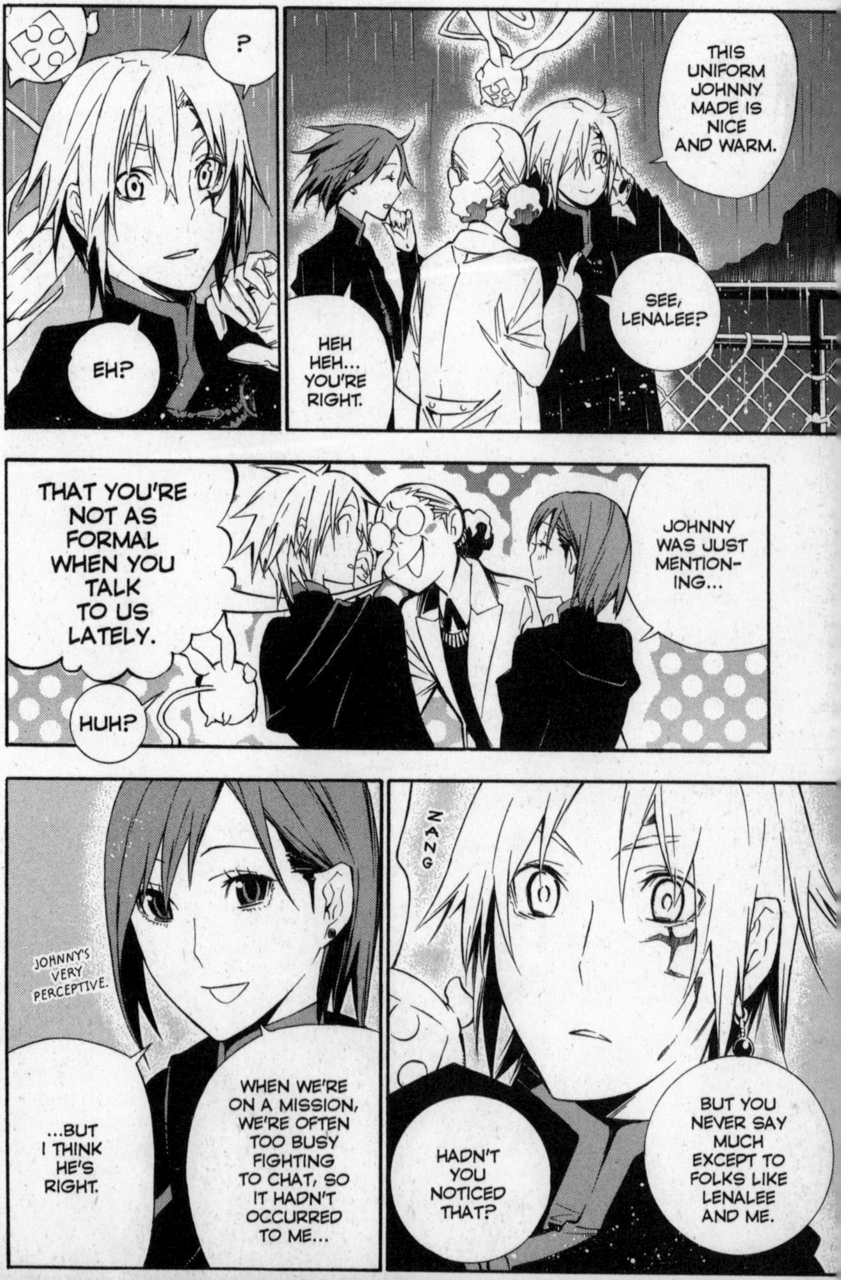
THIS UNIFORM JOHNNY MADE IS NICE AND WARM.
SEE, LENALEE?
HEH HEH... YOU'RE RIGHT.
?
EH?
JOHNNY WAS JUST MENTION-ING...
THAT YOU'RE NOT AS FORMAL WHEN YOU TALK TO US LATELY.
HUH?
ZANG
BUT YOU NEVER SAY MUCH EXCEPT TO FOLKS LIKE LENALEE AND ME.
HADN'T YOU NOTICED THAT?
JOHNNY'S VERY PERCEPTIVE.
WHEN WE'RE ON A MISSION, WE'RE OFTEN TOO BUSY FIGHTING TO CHAT, SO IT HADN'T OCCURRED TO ME...
...BUT I THINK HE'S RIGHT.

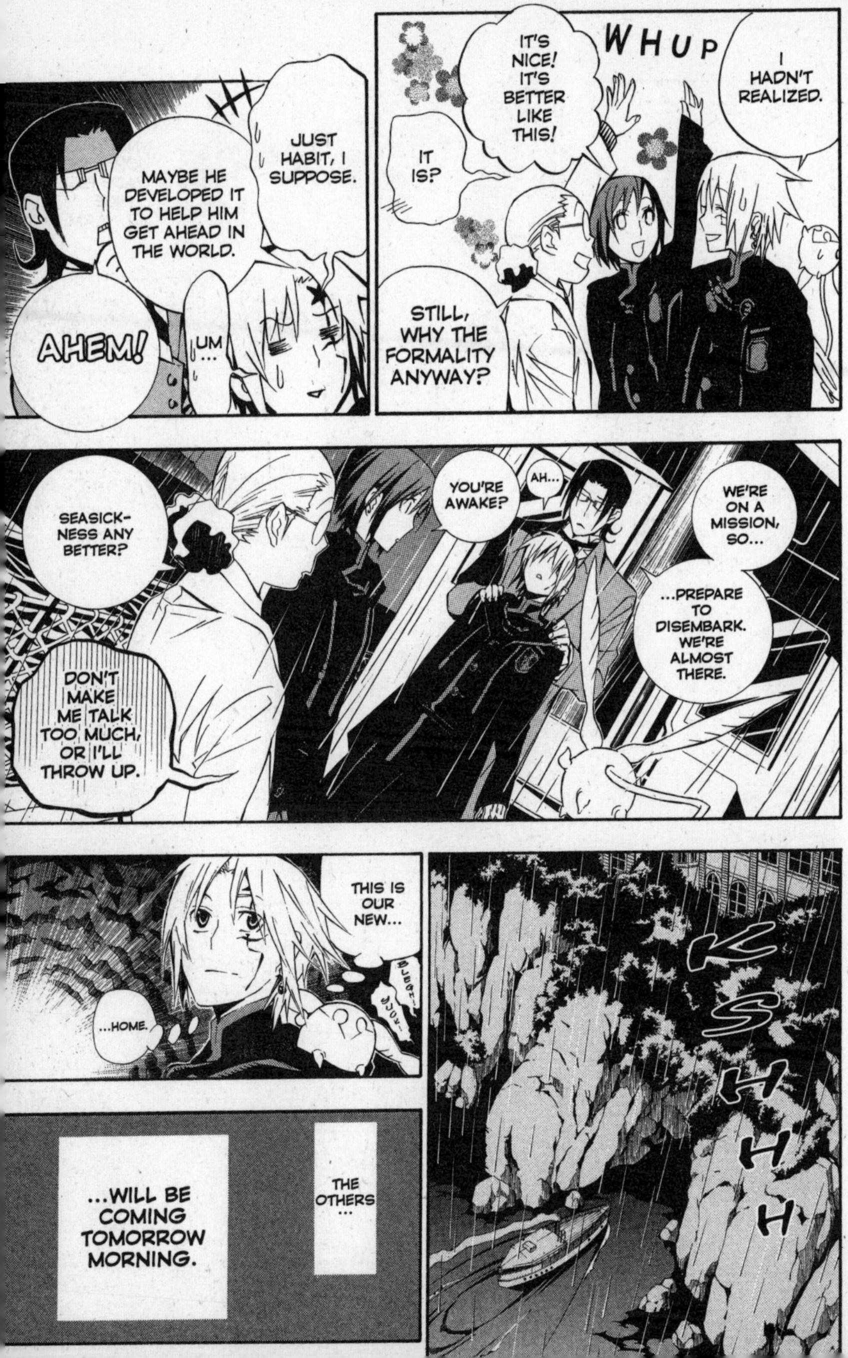
I HADN'T REALIZED.
WHUP
IT'S NICE! IT'S BETTER LIKE THIS!
IT IS?
STILL, WHY THE FORMALITY ANYWAY?
JUST HABIT, I SUPPOSE.
MAYBE HE DEVELOPED IT TO HELP HIM GET AHEAD IN THE WORLD.
UM...
AHEM!
WE'RE ON A MISSION, SO...
...PREPARE TO DISEMBARK. WE'RE ALMOST THERE.
AH...
YOU'RE AWAKE?
SEASICK-NESS ANY BETTER?
DON'T MAKE ME TALK TOO MUCH, OR I'LL THROW UP.
KSHHHH
THIS IS OUR NEW...
BLEGH!!
...HOME.
THE OTHERS...
...WILL BE COMING TOMORROW MORNING.

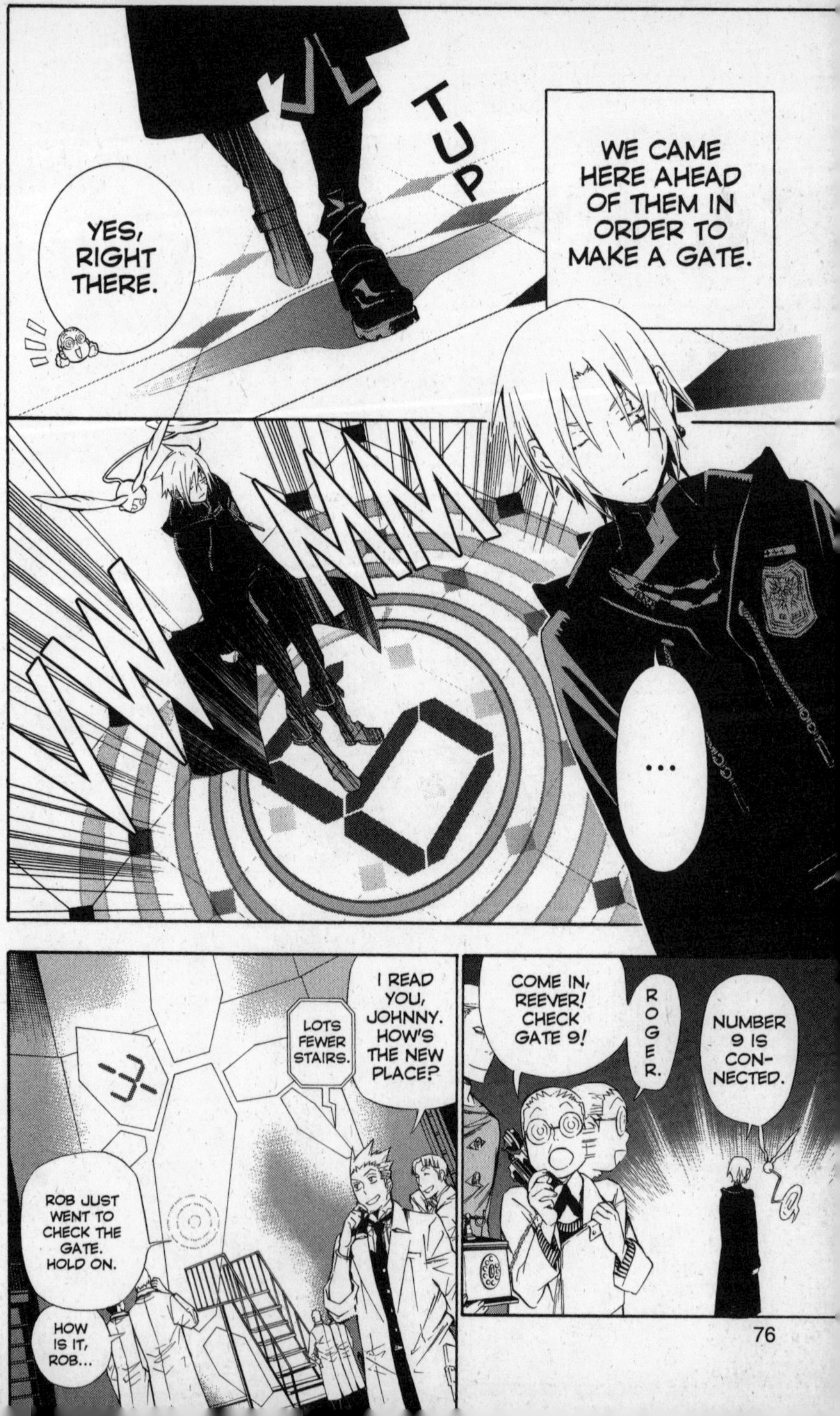
WE CAME HERE AHEAD OF THEM IN ORDER TO MAKE A GATE.
TUP
YES, RIGHT THERE.
...
NUMBER 9 IS CON-NECTED.
ROGER.
COME IN, REEVER! CHECK GATE 9!
I READ YOU, JOHNNY. HOW'S THE NEW PLACE?
LOTS FEWER STAIRS.
ROB JUST WENT TO CHECK THE GATE. HOLD ON.
HOW IS IT, ROB...

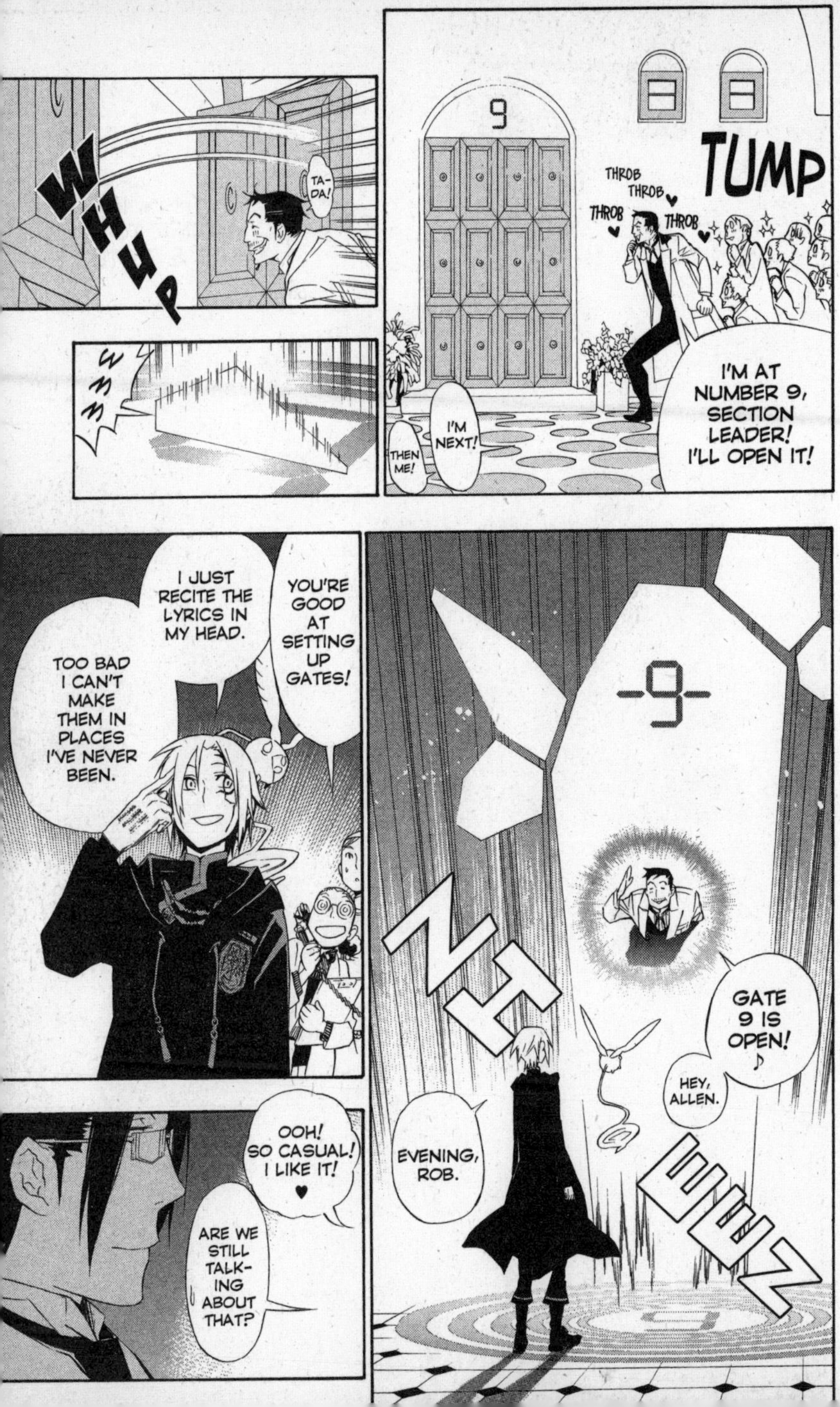
9
TUMP
THROB THROB THROB THROB
I'M AT NUMBER 9, SECTION LEADER! I'LL OPEN IT!
I'M NEXT!
THEN ME!
WHUP
TA-DA!
9
GATE 9 IS OPEN! ♪
HEY, ALLEN.
EVENING, ROB.
YOU'RE GOOD AT SETTING UP GATES!
I JUST RECITE THE LYRICS IN MY HEAD.
TOO BAD I CAN'T MAKE THEM IN PLACES I'VE NEVER BEEN.
OOH! SO CASUAL! I LIKE IT! ♥
ARE WE STILL TALKING ABOUT THAT?

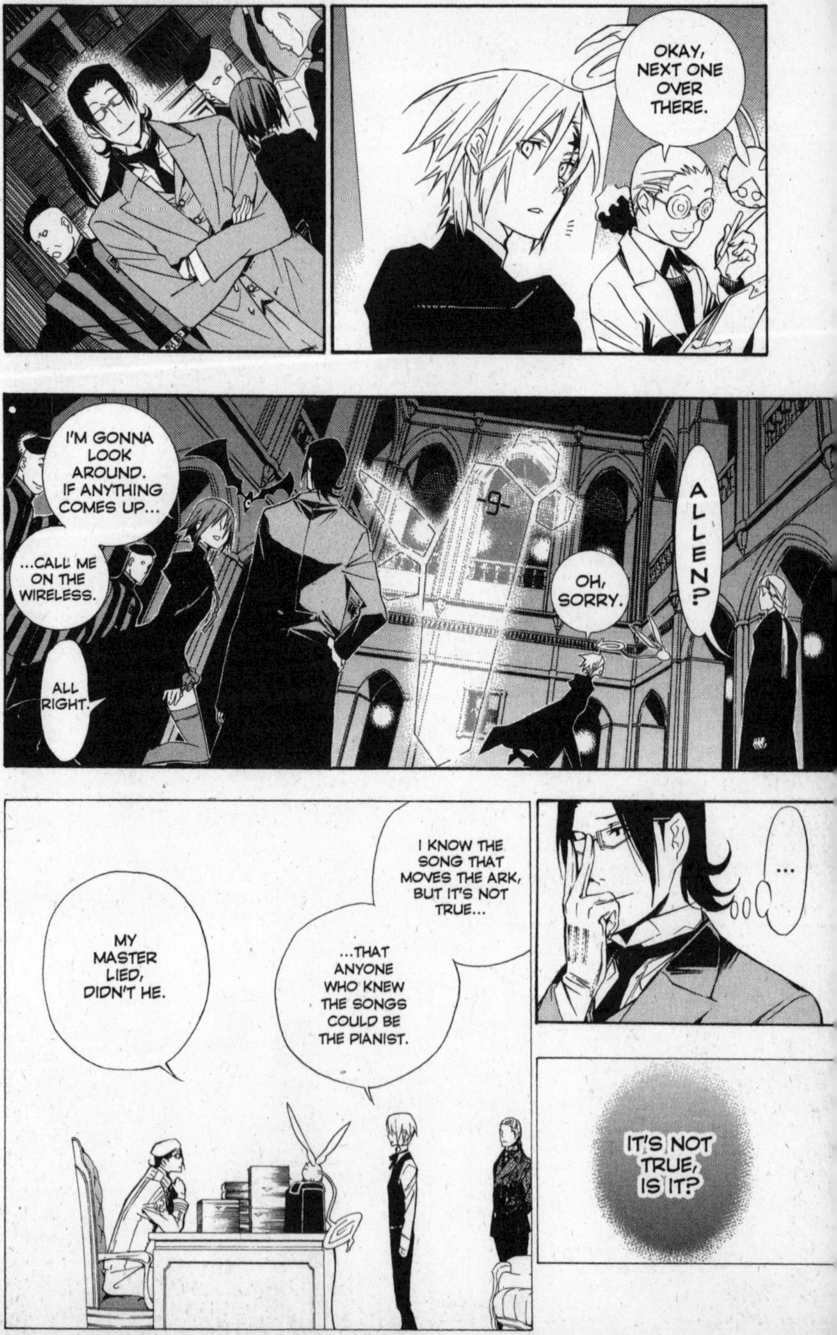
OKAY, NEXT ONE OVER THERE.
ALLEN?
OH, SORRY.
I'M GONNA LOOK AROUND. IF ANYTHING COMES UP...
...CALL ME ON THE WIRELESS.
ALL RIGHT.
...
IT'S NOT TRUE, IS IT?
I KNOW THE SONG THAT MOVES THE ARK, BUT IT'S NOT TRUE...
...THAT ANYONE WHO KNEW THE SONGS COULD BE THE PIANIST.
MY MASTER LIED, DIDN'T HE.

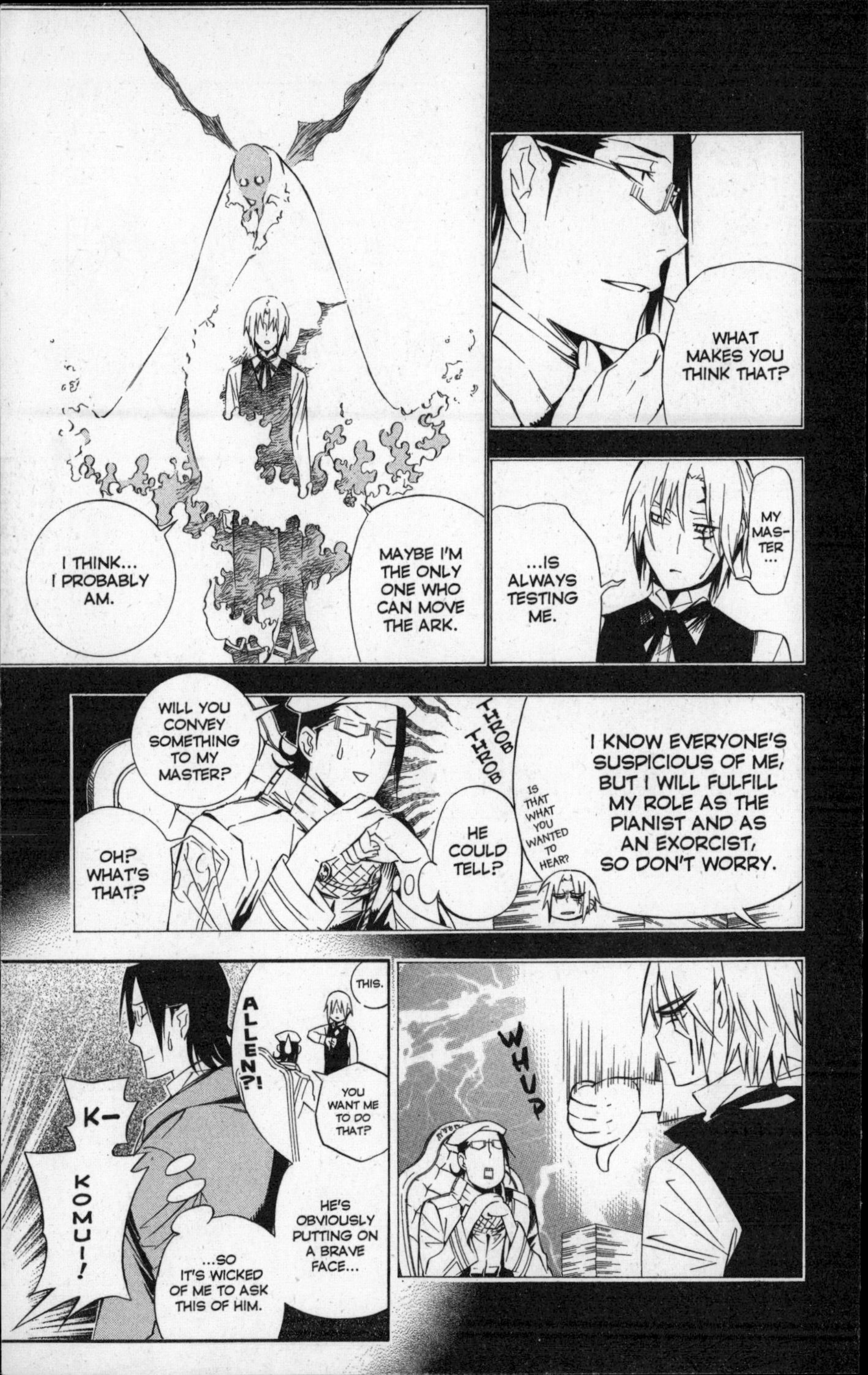
WHAT MAKES YOU THINK THAT?
MY MASTER...
...IS ALWAYS TESTING ME.
MAYBE I'M THE ONLY ONE WHO CAN MOVE THE ARK.
I THINK... I PROBABLY AM.
I KNOW EVERYONE'S SUSPICIOUS OF ME, BUT I WILL FULFILL MY ROLE AS THE PIANIST AND AS AN EXORCIST, SO DON'T WORRY.
IS THAT WHAT YOU WANTED TO HEAR?
THROB THROB
HE COULD TELL?
WILL YOU CONVEY SOMETHING TO MY MASTER?
OH? WHAT'S THAT?
WHUP
THIS.
YOU WANT ME TO DO THAT?
ALLEN?!
HE'S OBVIOUSLY PUTTING ON A BRAVE FACE...
...SO IT'S WICKED OF ME TO ASK THIS OF HIM.
K—
KOMUI!

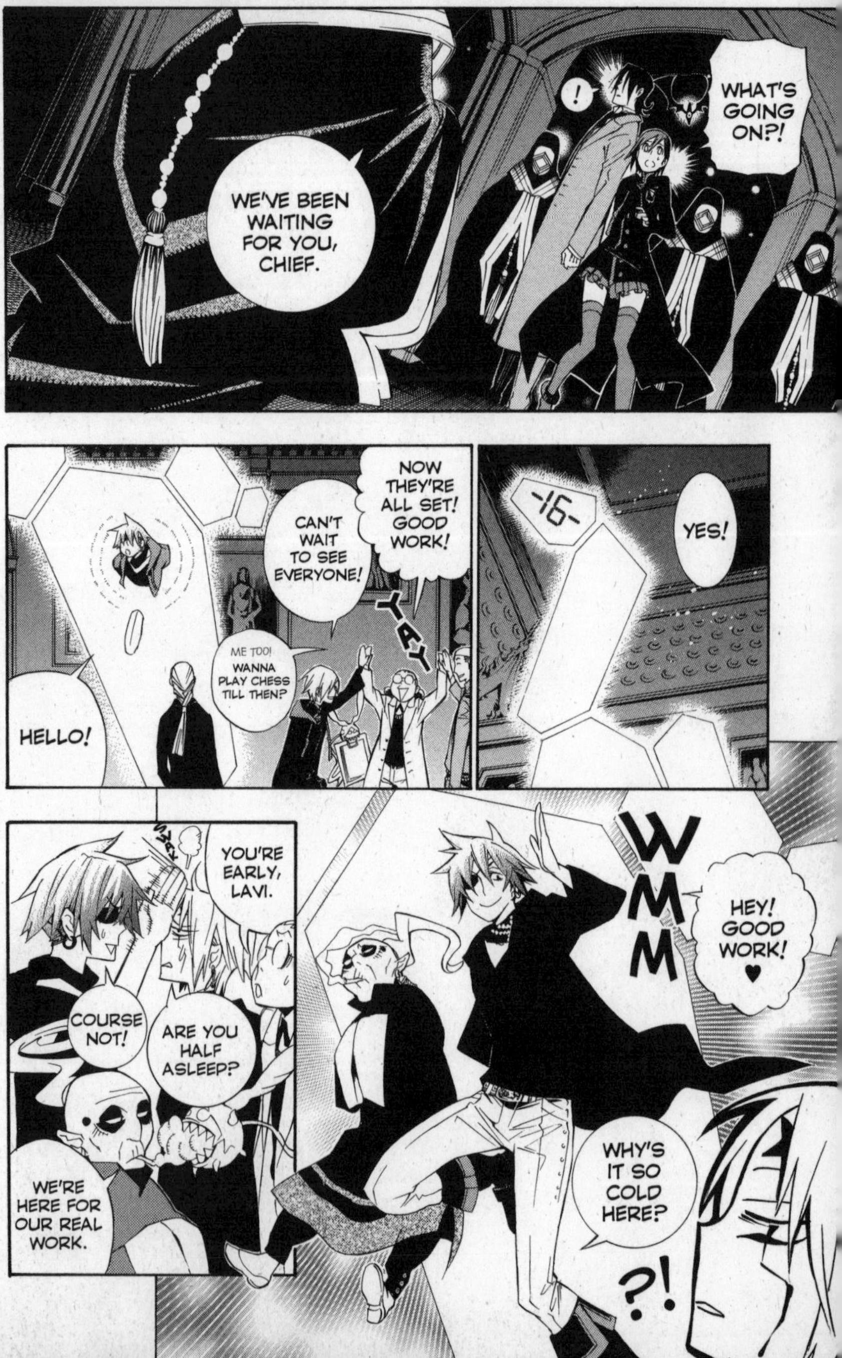
WHAT'S GOING ON?!
!
WE'VE BEEN WAITING FOR YOU, CHIEF.
-16-
YES!
NOW THEY'RE ALL SET! GOOD WORK!
YAY
CAN'T WAIT TO SEE EVERYONE!
ME TOO! WANNA PLAY CHESS TILL THEN?
HELLO!
WMM
HEY! GOOD WORK! ♥
WHY'S IT SO COLD HERE?
?!
YOU'RE EARLY, LAVI.
SWAY
ARE YOU HALF ASLEEP?
COURSE NOT!
WE'RE HERE FOR OUR REAL WORK.

READ THIS WAY

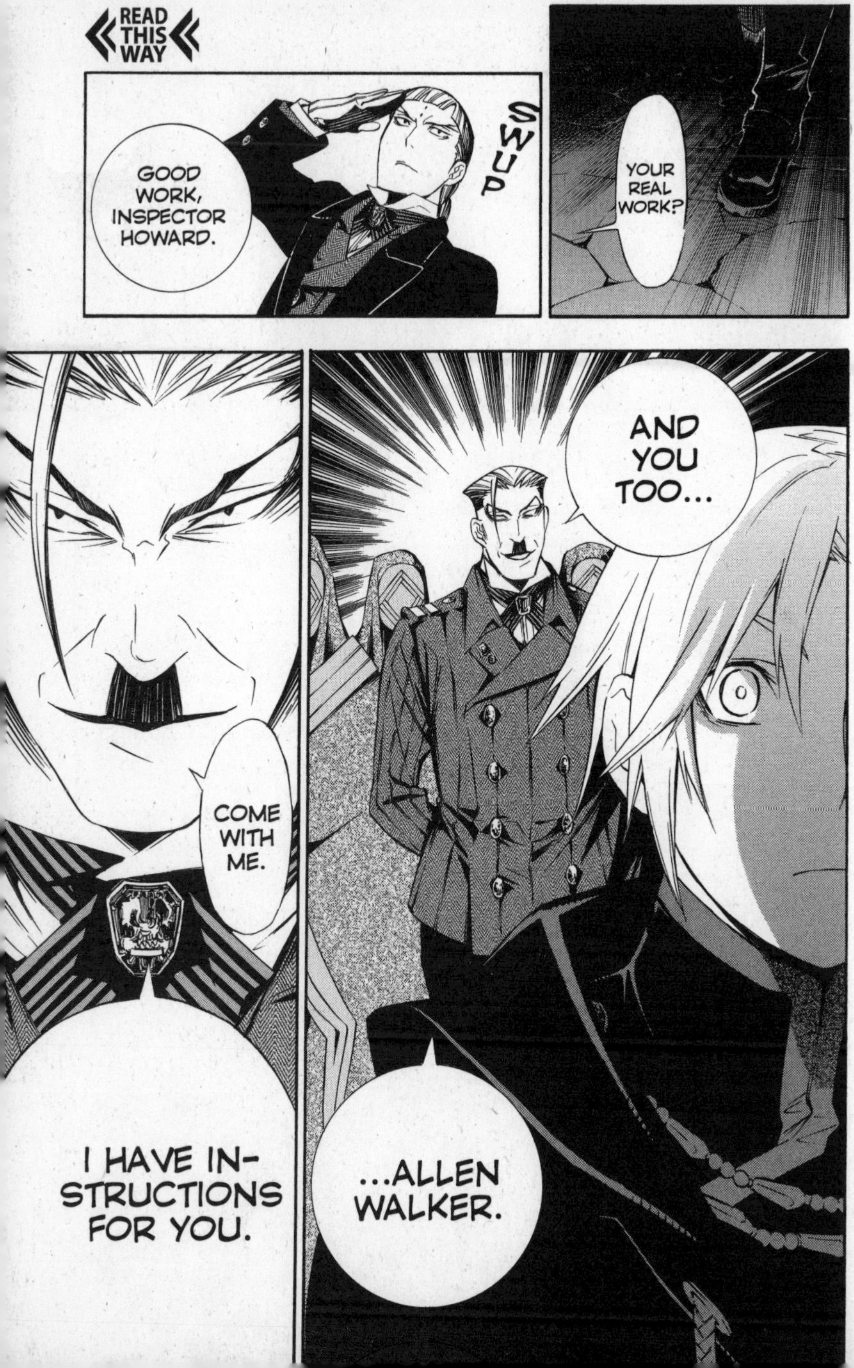
YOUR REAL WORK?
GOOD WORK, INSPECTOR HOWARD.
SWUP
AND YOU TOO...
...ALLEN WALKER.
COME WITH ME.
I HAVE IN-STRUCTIONS FOR YOU.

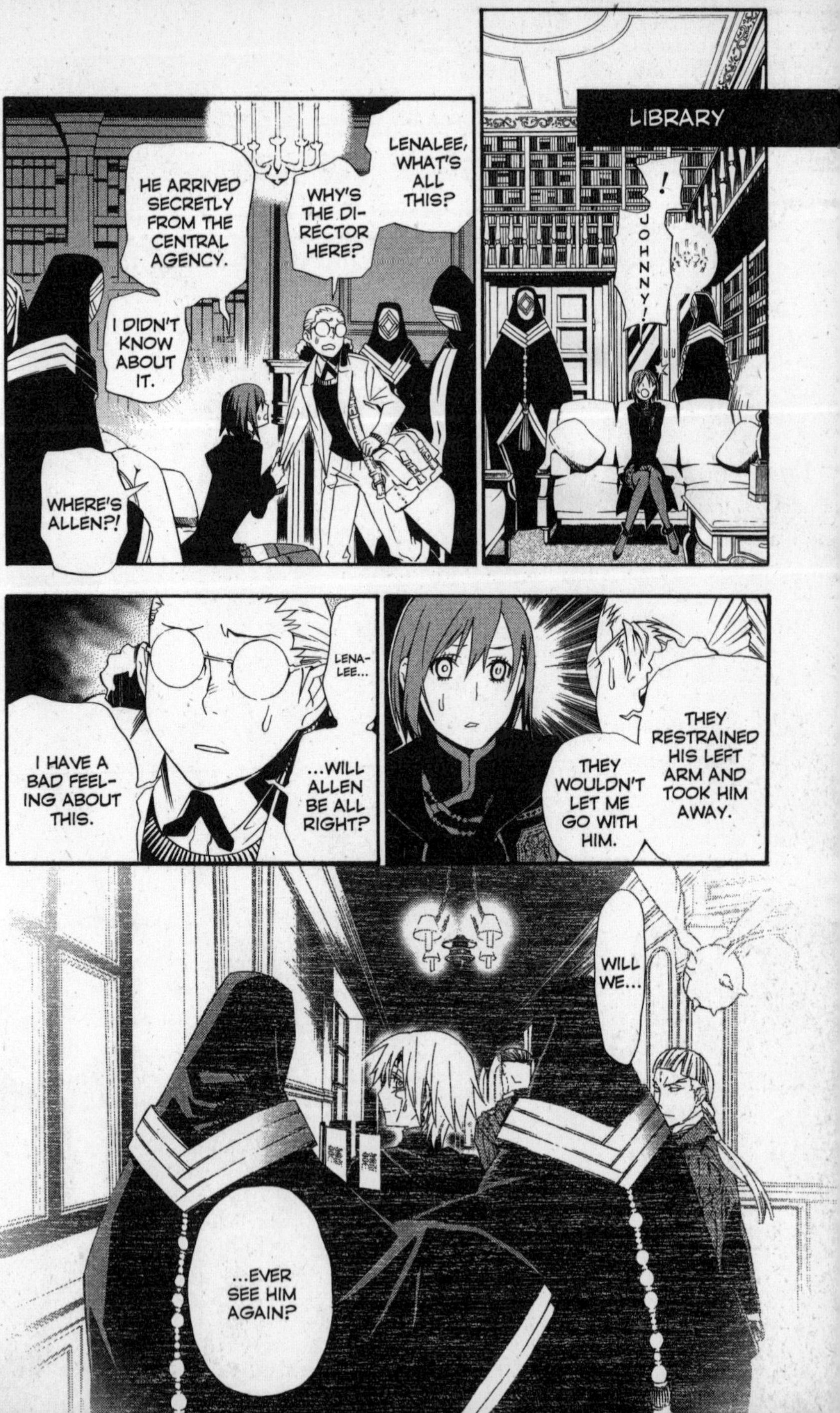
LIBRARY
!
JOHNNY!
LENALEE, WHAT'S ALL THIS?
WHY'S THE DIRECTOR HERE?
HE ARRIVED SECRETLY FROM THE CENTRAL AGENCY.
I DIDN'T KNOW ABOUT IT.
WHERE'S ALLEN?!
THEY RESTRAINED HIS LEFT ARM AND TOOK HIM AWAY.
THEY WOULDN'T LET ME GO WITH HIM.
LENALEE...
...WILL ALLEN BE ALL RIGHT?
I HAVE A BAD FEELING ABOUT THIS.
WILL WE...
...EVER SEE HIM AGAIN?

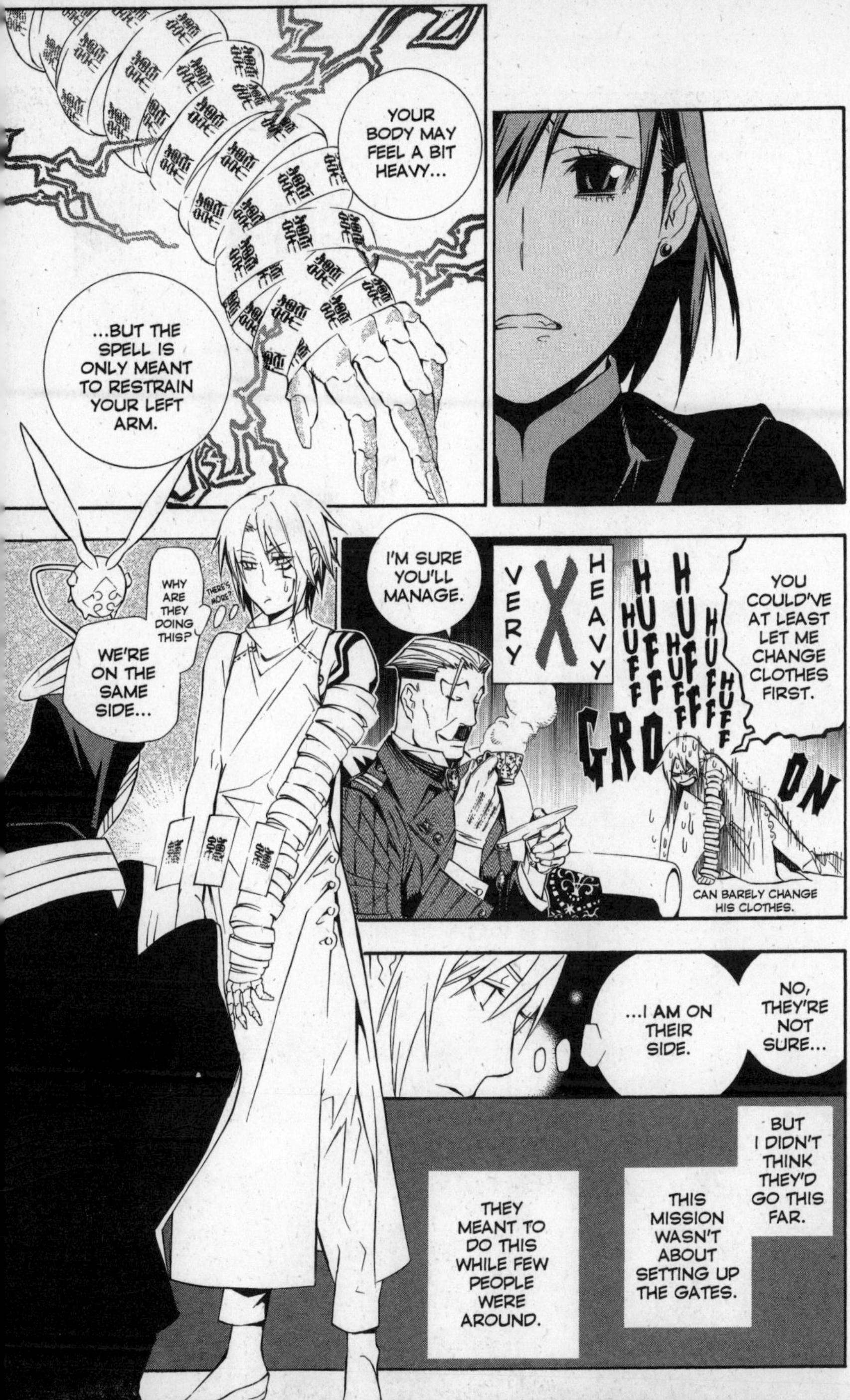
YOUR BODY MAY FEEL A BIT HEAVY...
...BUT THE SPELL IS ONLY MEANT TO RESTRAIN YOUR LEFT ARM.
YOU COULD'VE AT LEAST LET ME CHANGE CLOTHES FIRST.
HUFF HUFF HUFF HUFF HUFF HUFF
VERY HEAVY
I'M SURE YOU'LL MANAGE.
GRO ON
CAN BARELY CHANGE HIS CLOTHES.
NO, THEY'RE NOT SURE...
...I AM ON THEIR SIDE.
BUT I DIDN'T THINK THEY'D GO THIS FAR.
THIS MISSION WASN'T ABOUT SETTING UP THE GATES.
THEY MEANT TO DO THIS WHILE FEW PEOPLE WERE AROUND.
WHY ARE THEY DOING THIS?
THERE'S MORE?
WE'RE ON THE SAME SIDE...

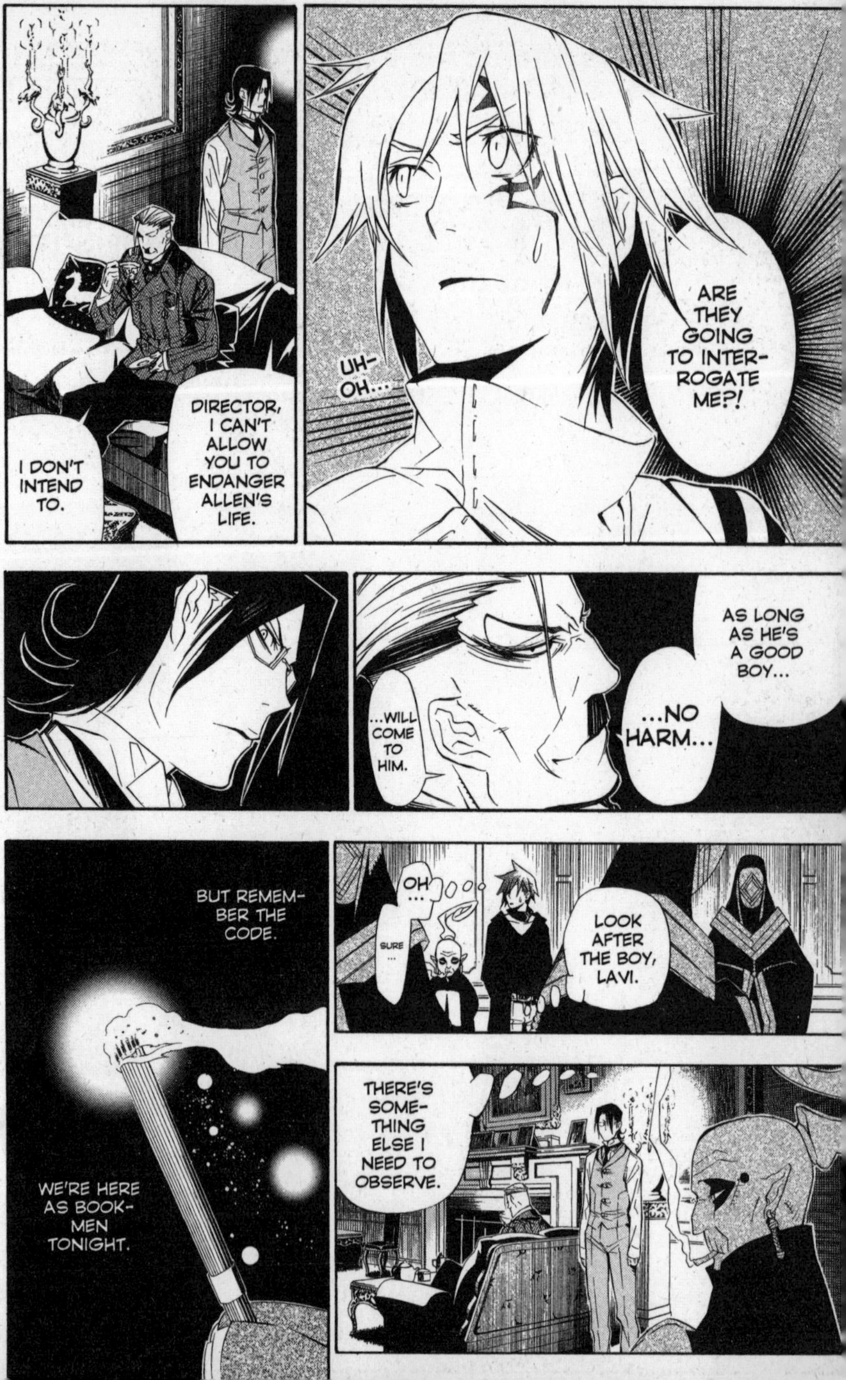
ARE THEY GOING TO INTER-ROGATE ME?!
UH-OH...
DIRECTOR, I CAN'T ALLOW YOU TO ENDANGER ALLEN'S LIFE.
I DON'T INTEND TO.
AS LONG AS HE'S A GOOD BOY...
...NO HARM...
...WILL COME TO HIM.
LOOK AFTER THE BOY, LAVI.
OH...
SURE...
THERE'S SOME-THING ELSE I NEED TO OBSERVE.
BUT REMEM-BER THE CODE.
WE'RE HERE AS BOOK-MEN TONIGHT.

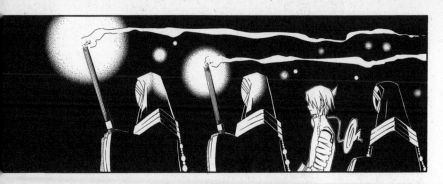

GENERAL CROSS MARIAN IS ON THE OTHER SIDE OF THIS DOOR.

ENTER.

!!!

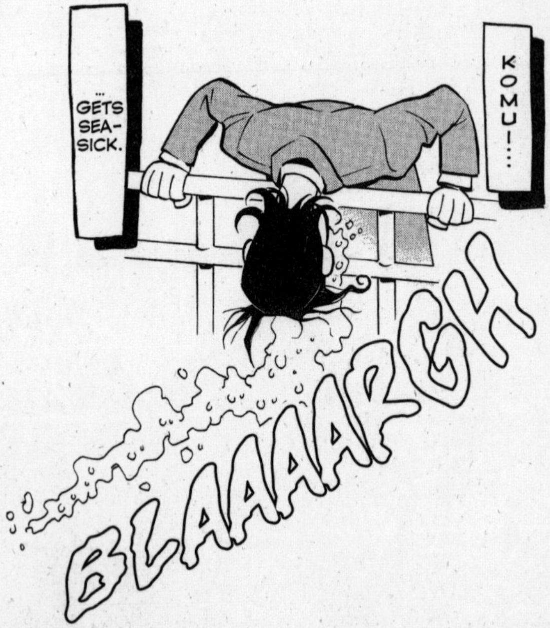
KOMUI...
...GETS SEA-SICK.
BLAAAARGH

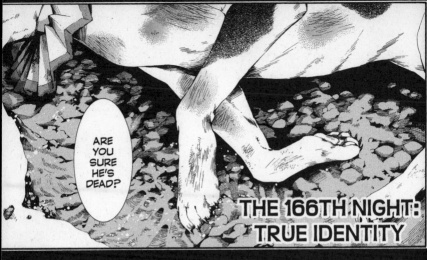

ARE YOU SURE HE'S DEAD?

THE 166TH NIGHT: TRUE IDENTITY

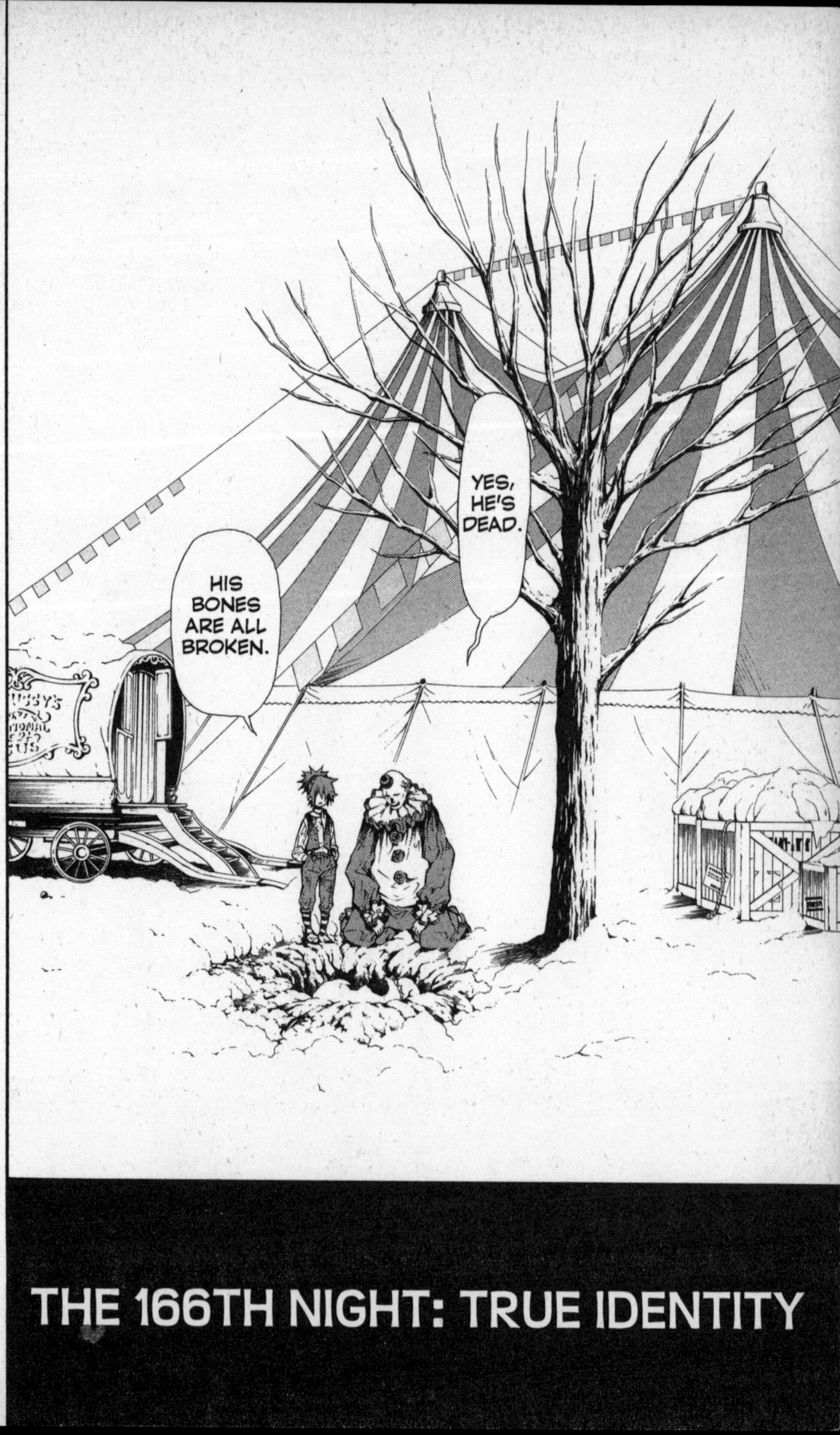
YES, HE'S DEAD.
HIS BONES ARE ALL BROKEN.

THE 166TH NIGHT: TRUE IDENTITY

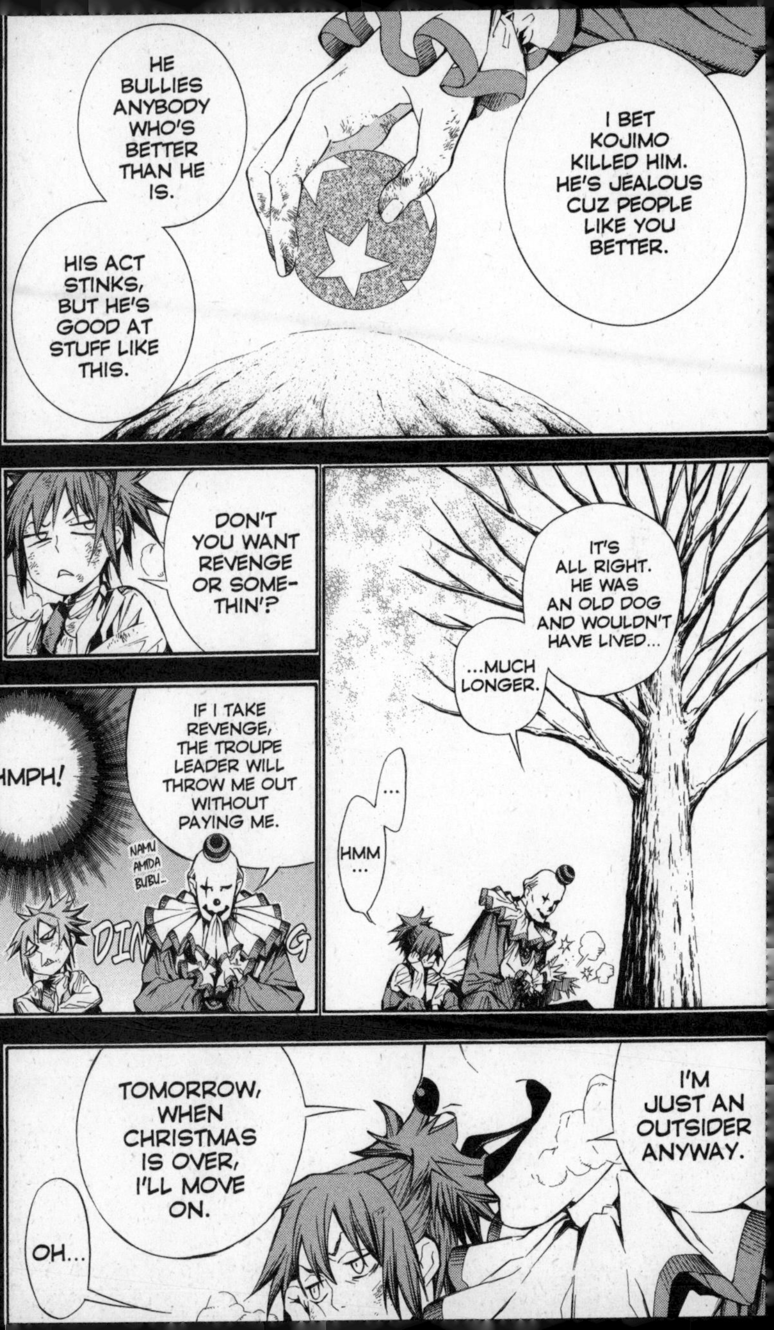
I BET KOJIMO KILLED HIM. HE'S JEALOUS CUZ PEOPLE LIKE YOU BETTER.
HE BULLIES ANYBODY WHO'S BETTER THAN HE IS.
HIS ACT STINKS, BUT HE'S GOOD AT STUFF LIKE THIS.
IT'S ALL RIGHT. HE WAS AN OLD DOG AND WOULDN'T HAVE LIVED...
...MUCH LONGER.
...
HMM ...
DON'T YOU WANT REVENGE OR SOME-THIN'?
IF I TAKE REVENGE, THE TROUPE LEADER WILL THROW ME OUT WITHOUT PAYING ME.
HMPH!
NAMU AMIDA BUBU...
DING
I'M JUST AN OUTSIDER ANYWAY.
TOMORROW, WHEN CHRISTMAS IS OVER, I'LL MOVE ON.
OH...

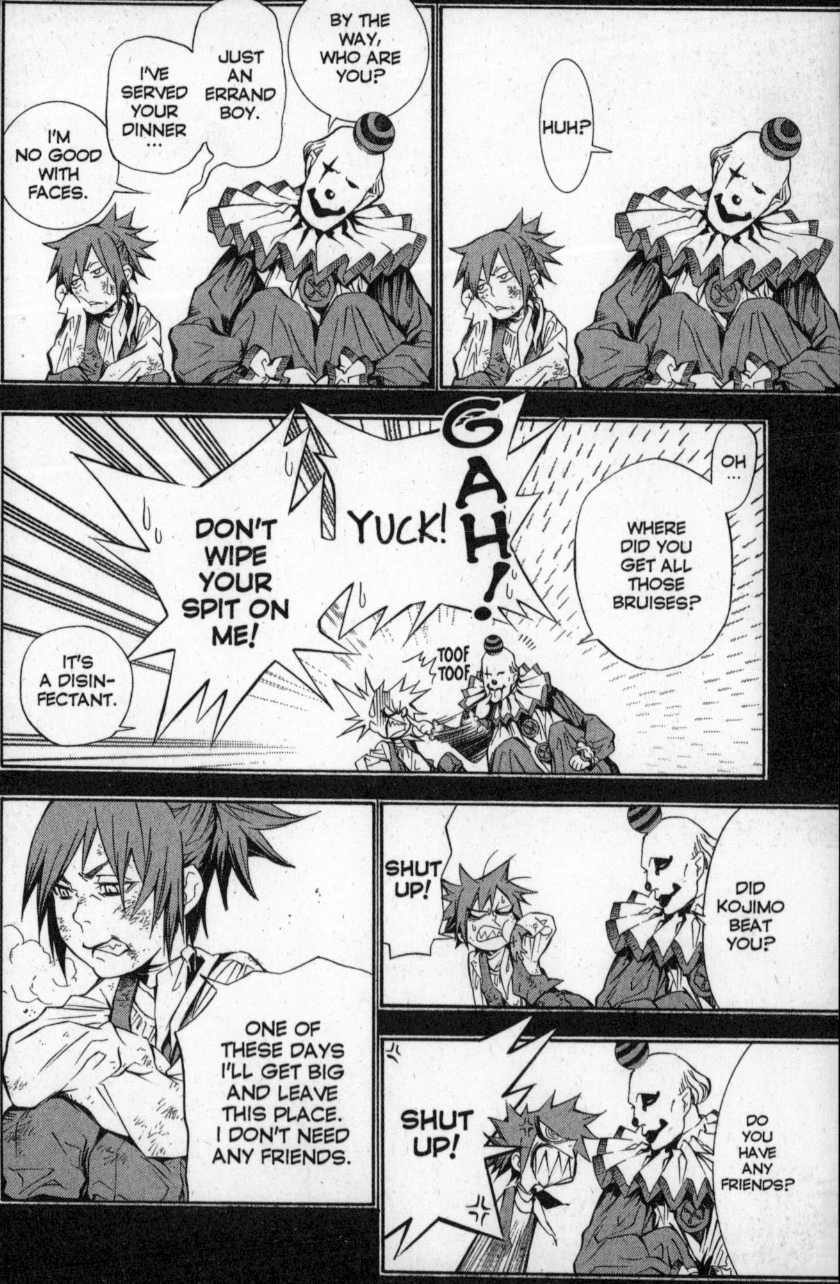
HUH?
BY THE WAY, WHO ARE YOU?
JUST AN ERRAND BOY.
I'VE SERVED YOUR DINNER ...
I'M NO GOOD WITH FACES.
OH ...
WHERE DID YOU GET ALL THOSE BRUISES?
GAH!
YUCK!
TOOF TOOF
DON'T WIPE YOUR SPIT ON ME!
IT'S A DISIN-FECTANT.
DID KOJIMO BEAT YOU?
SHUT UP!
DO YOU HAVE ANY FRIENDS?
SHUT UP!
ONE OF THESE DAYS I'LL GET BIG AND LEAVE THIS PLACE. I DON'T NEED ANY FRIENDS.

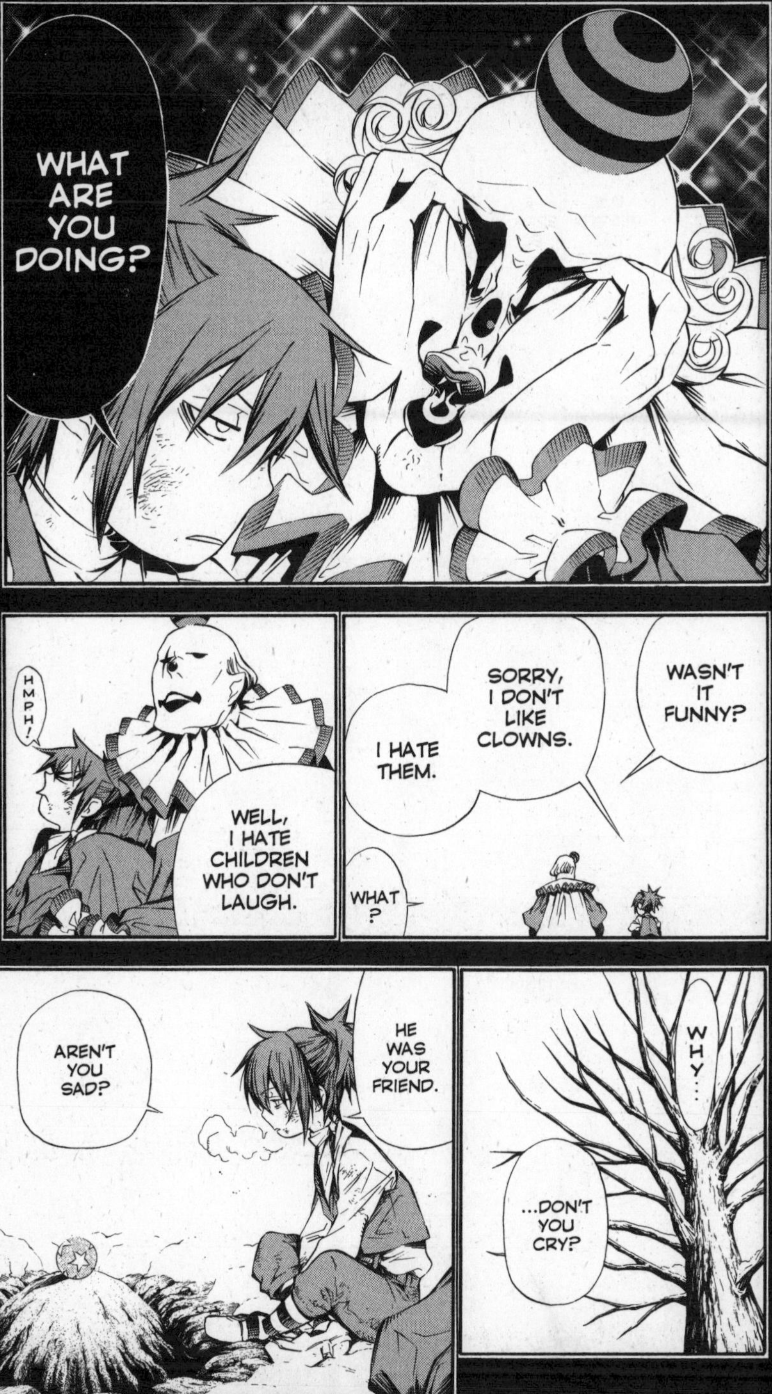
WHAT ARE YOU DOING?
WASN'T IT FUNNY?
SORRY, I DON'T LIKE CLOWNS.
I HATE THEM.
WHAT?
WELL, I HATE CHILDREN WHO DON'T LAUGH.
HMPH!
WHY...
...DON'T YOU CRY?
HE WAS YOUR FRIEND.
AREN'T YOU SAD?

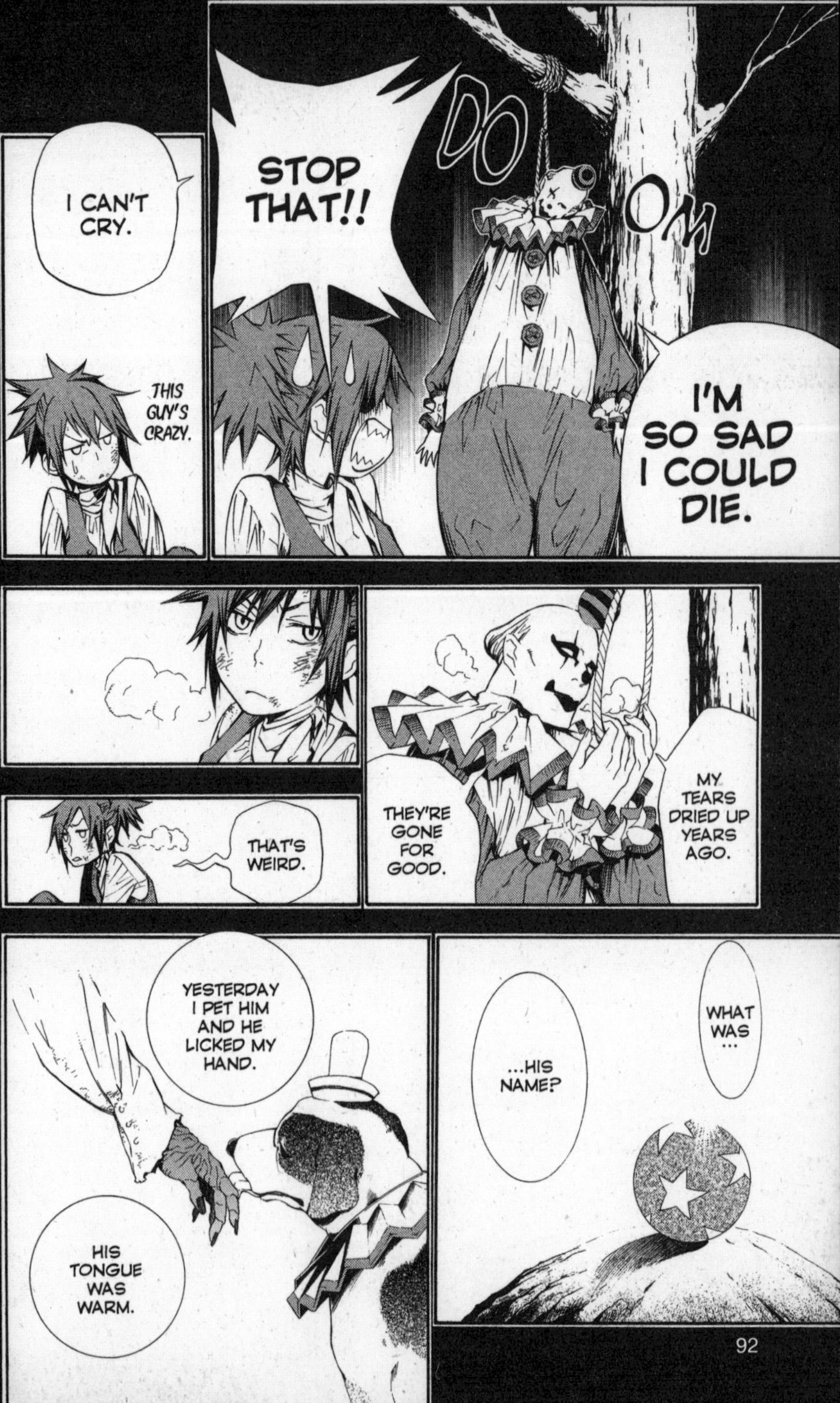
DOOM
I'M SO SAD I COULD DIE.
STOP THAT!!
I CAN'T CRY.
THIS GUY'S CRAZY.
MY TEARS DRIED UP YEARS AGO.
THEY'RE GONE FOR GOOD.
THAT'S WEIRD.
WHAT WAS...
...HIS NAME?
YESTERDAY I PET HIM AND HE LICKED MY HAND.
HIS TONGUE WAS WARM.

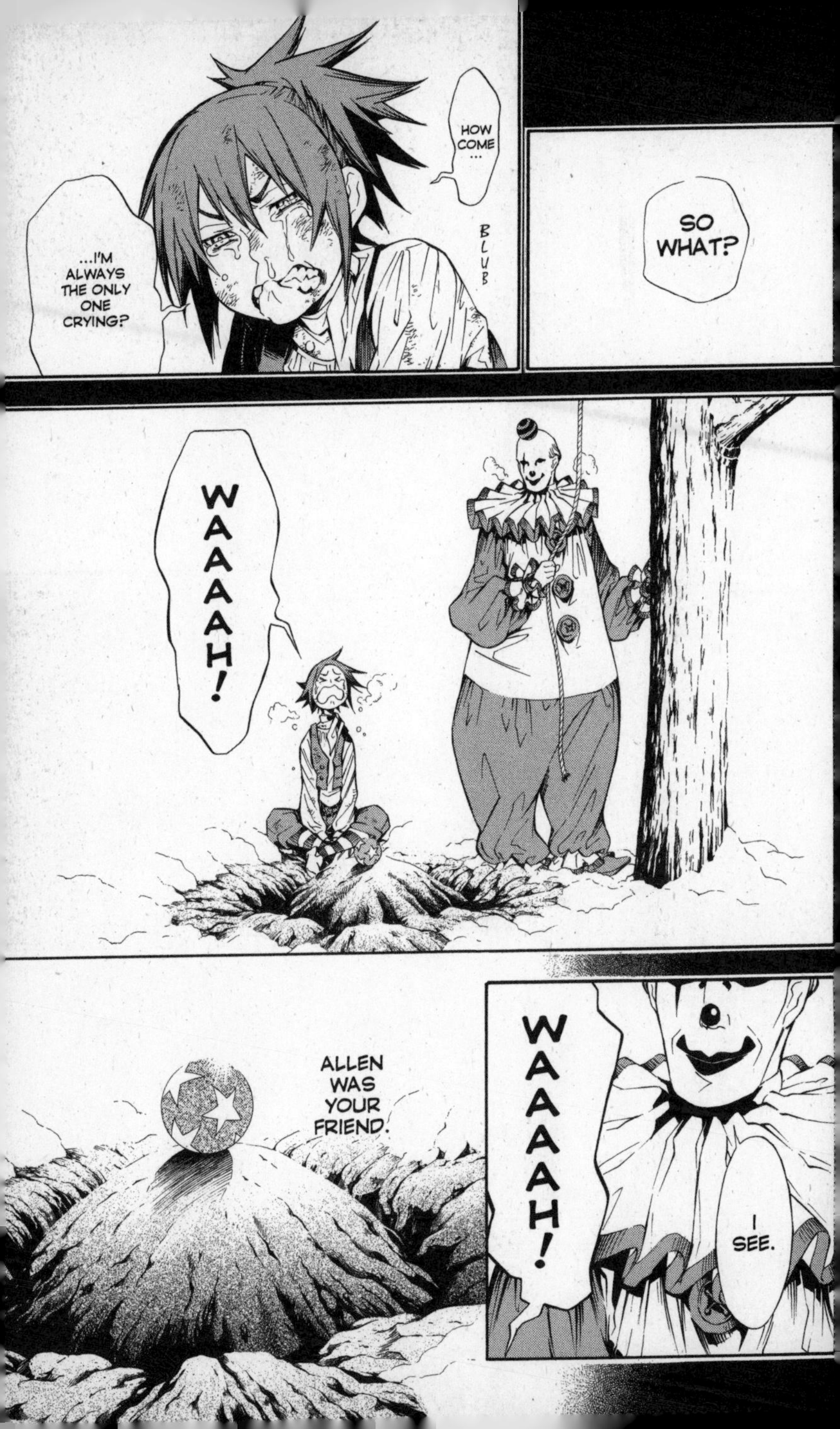
SO WHAT?
HOW COME...
...I'M ALWAYS THE ONLY ONE CRYING?
BLUB
WAAAAAH!
WAAAAAH!
I SEE.
ALLEN WAS YOUR FRIEND.

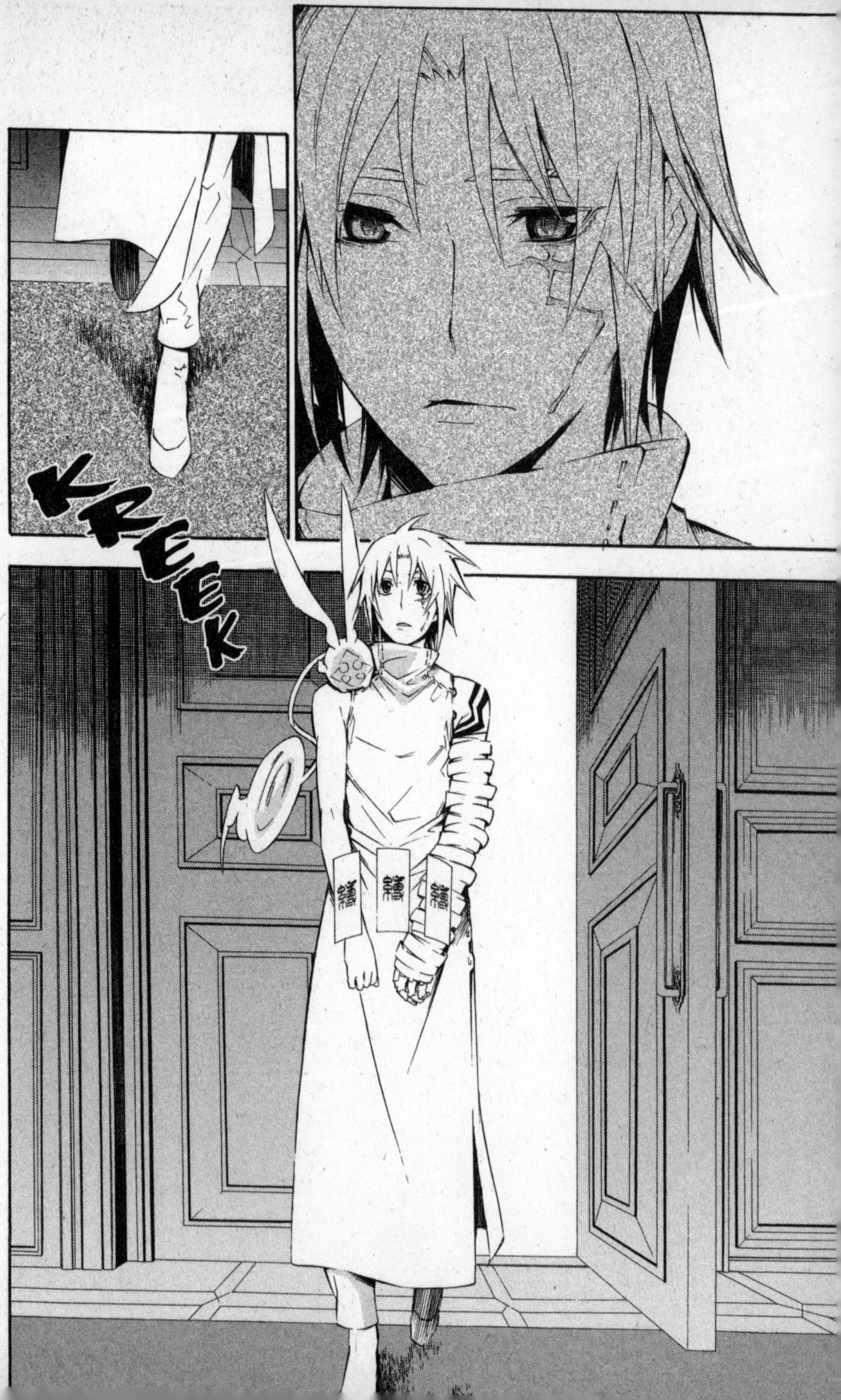
KREEK

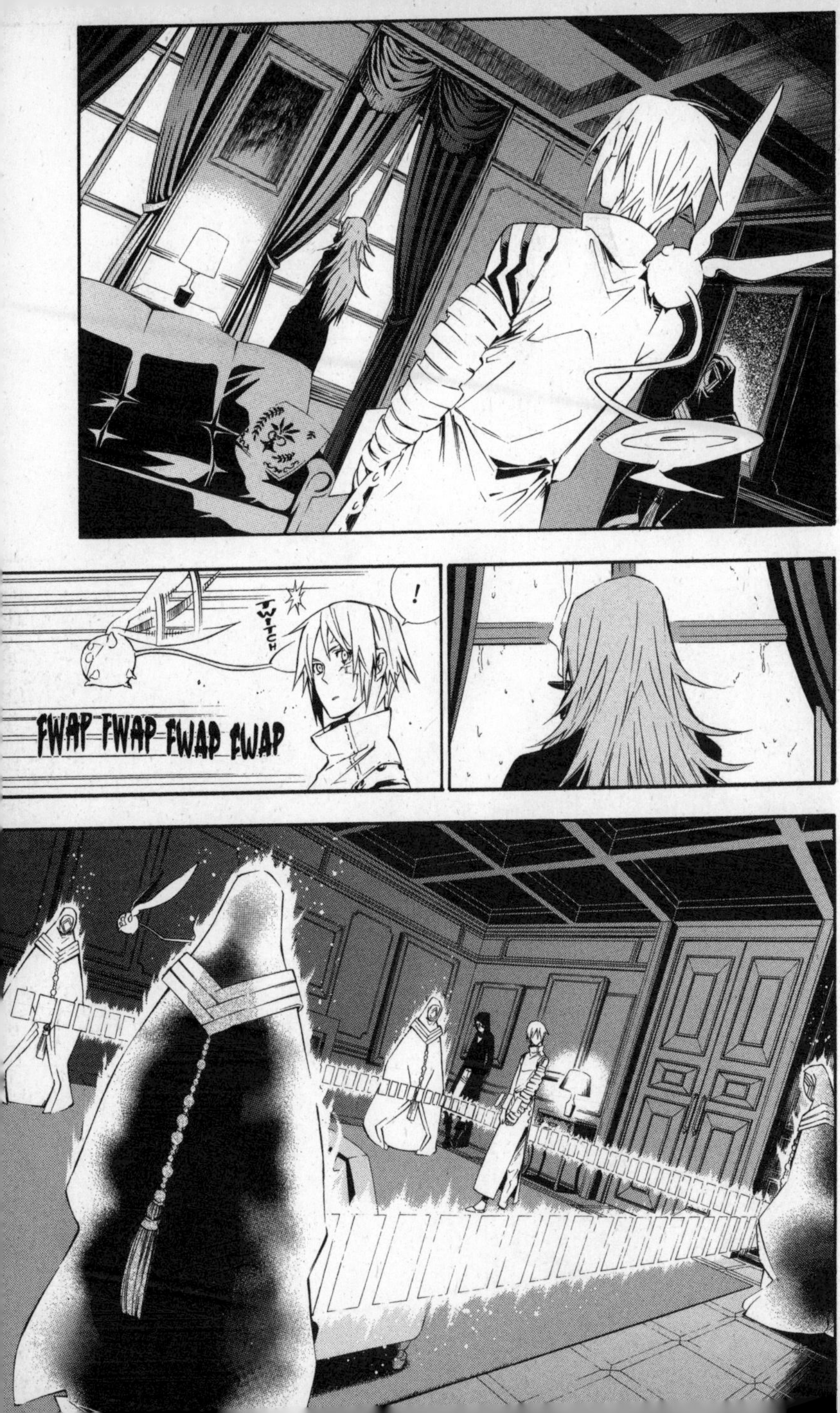
!
TWITCH
FWAP FWAP FWAP FWAP

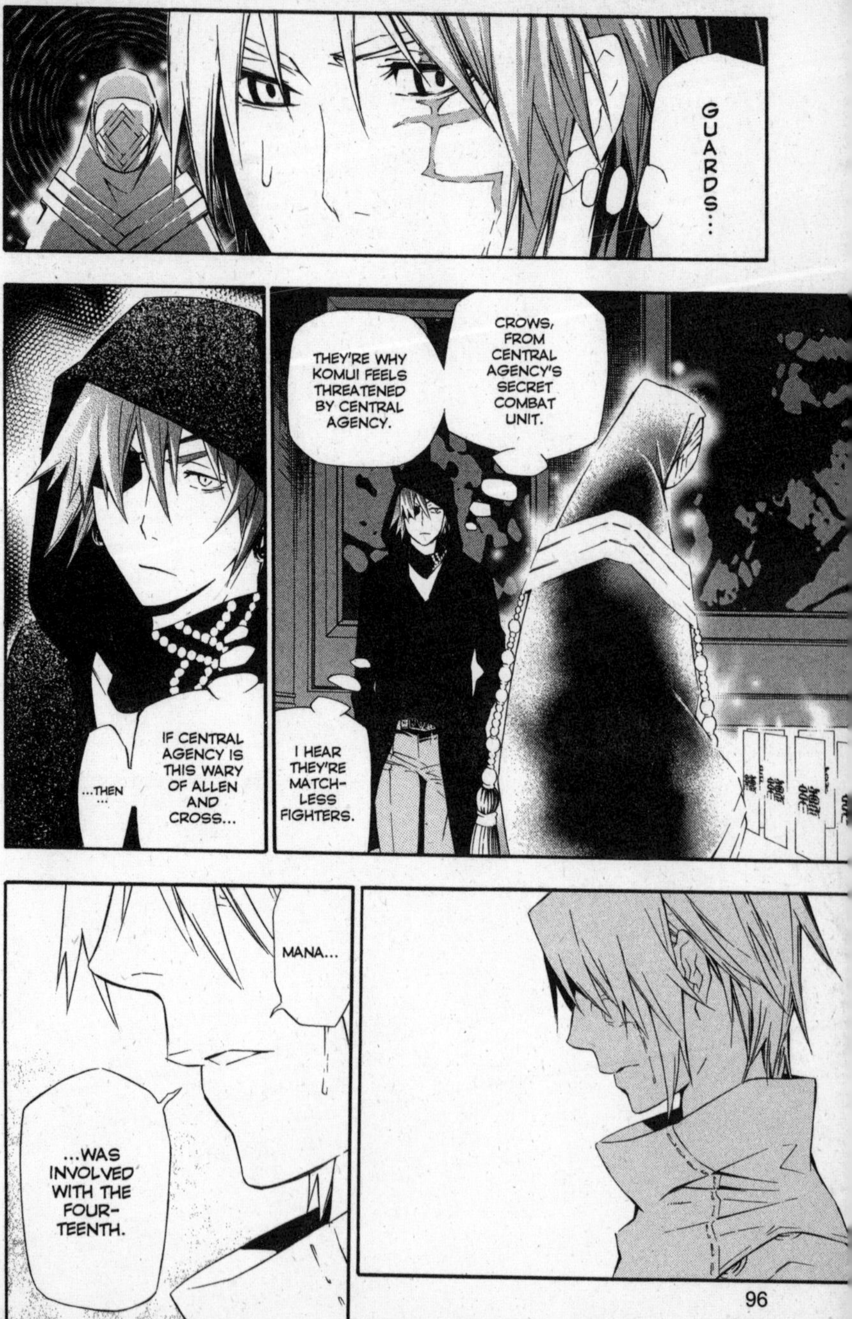
GUARDS...
CROWS, FROM CENTRAL AGENCY'S SECRET COMBAT UNIT.
THEY'RE WHY KOMUI FEELS THREATENED BY CENTRAL AGENCY.
I HEAR THEY'RE MATCH-LESS FIGHTERS.
IF CENTRAL AGENCY IS THIS WARY OF ALLEN AND CROSS...
...THEN ...
MANA...
...WAS INVOLVED WITH THE FOUR-TEENTH.

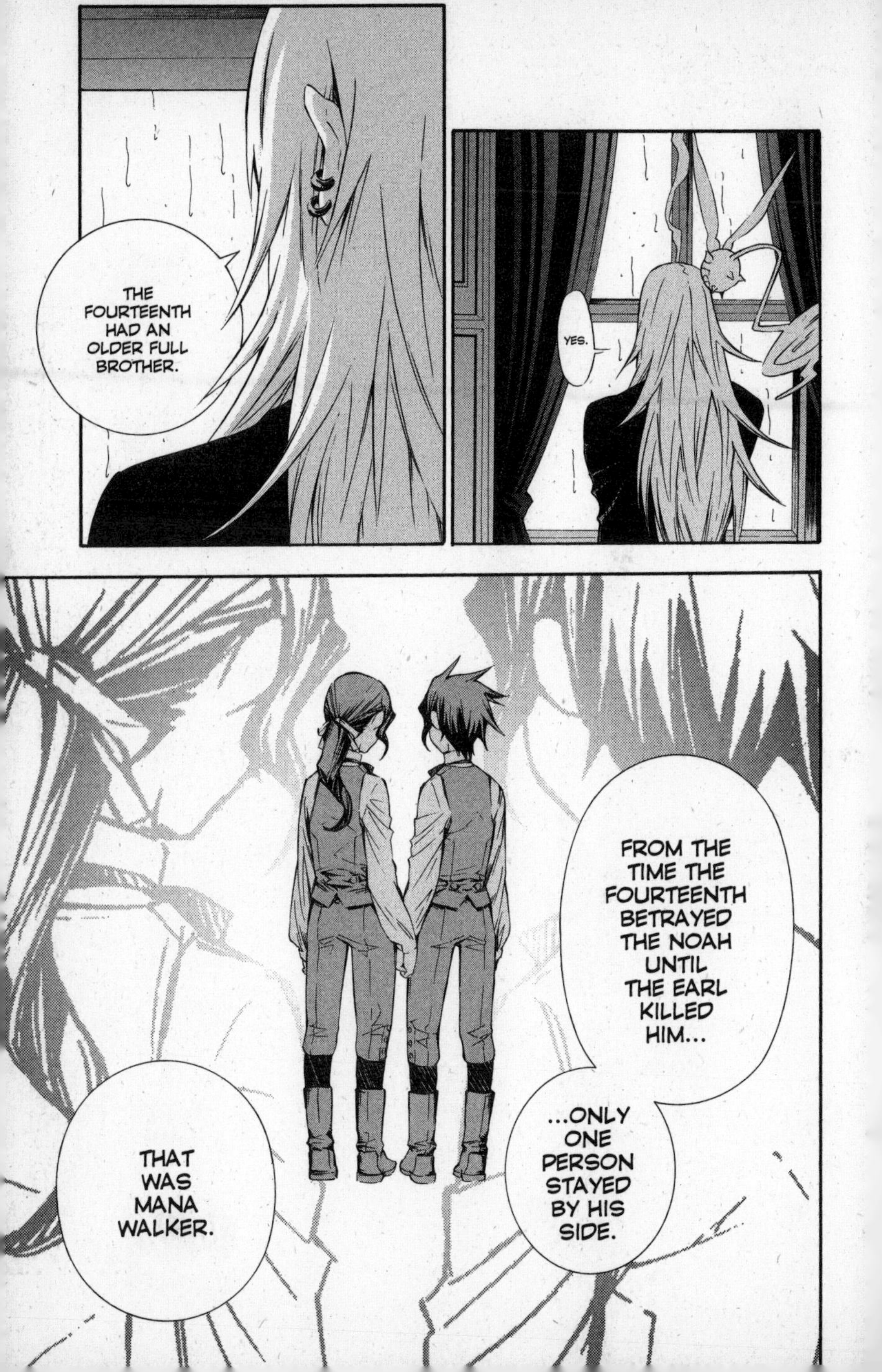
YES.
THE FOURTEENTH HAD AN OLDER FULL BROTHER.
FROM THE TIME THE FOURTEENTH BETRAYED THE NOAH UNTIL THE EARL KILLED HIM...
...ONLY ONE PERSON STAYED BY HIS SIDE.
THAT WAS MANA WALKER.

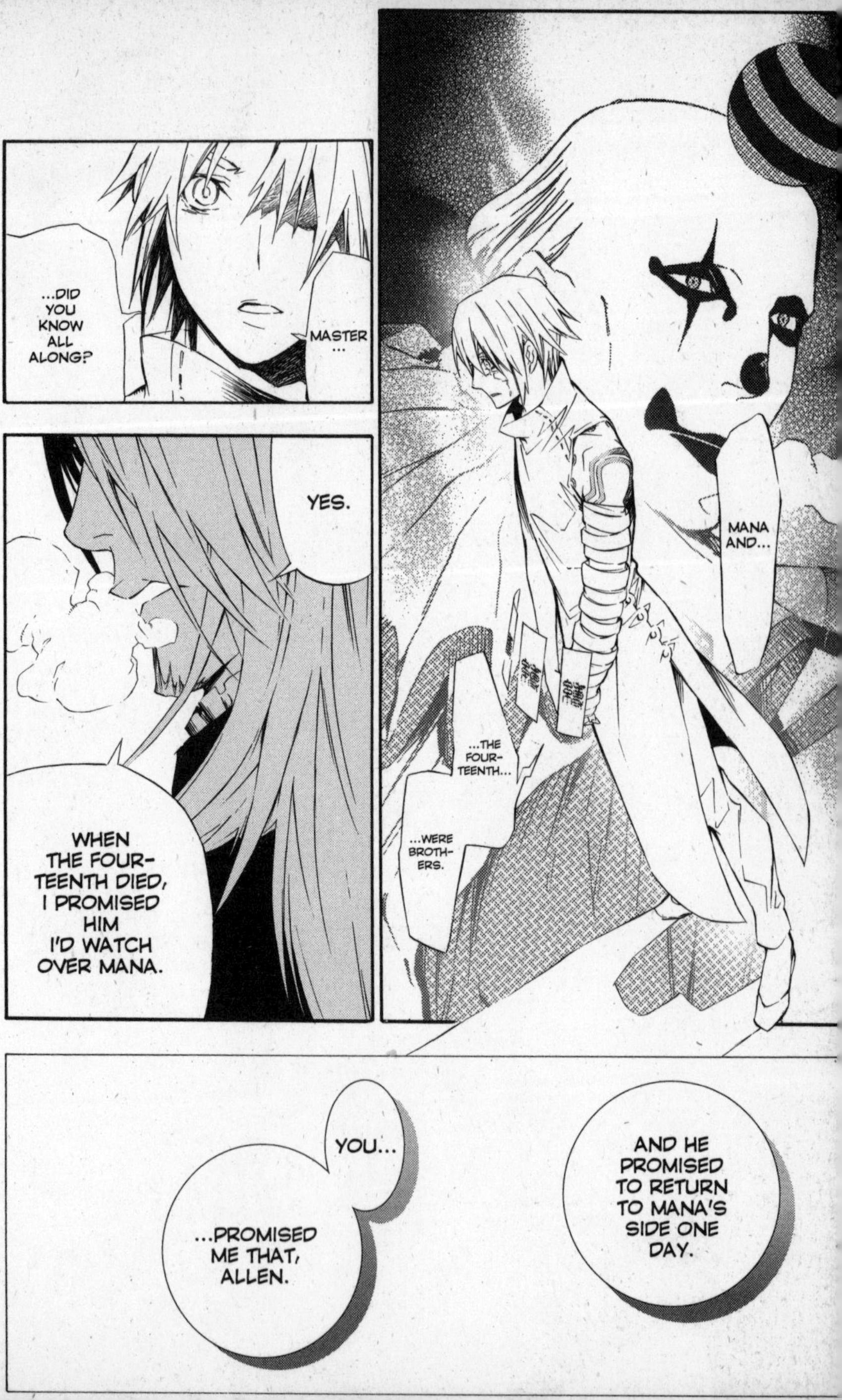
MANA AND...
...THE FOURTEENTH...
...WERE BROTHERS.
MASTER...
...DID YOU KNOW ALL ALONG?
YES.
WHEN THE FOURTEENTH DIED, I PROMISED HIM I'D WATCH OVER MANA.
AND HE PROMISED TO RETURN TO MANA'S SIDE ONE DAY.
YOU...
...PROMISED ME THAT, ALLEN.

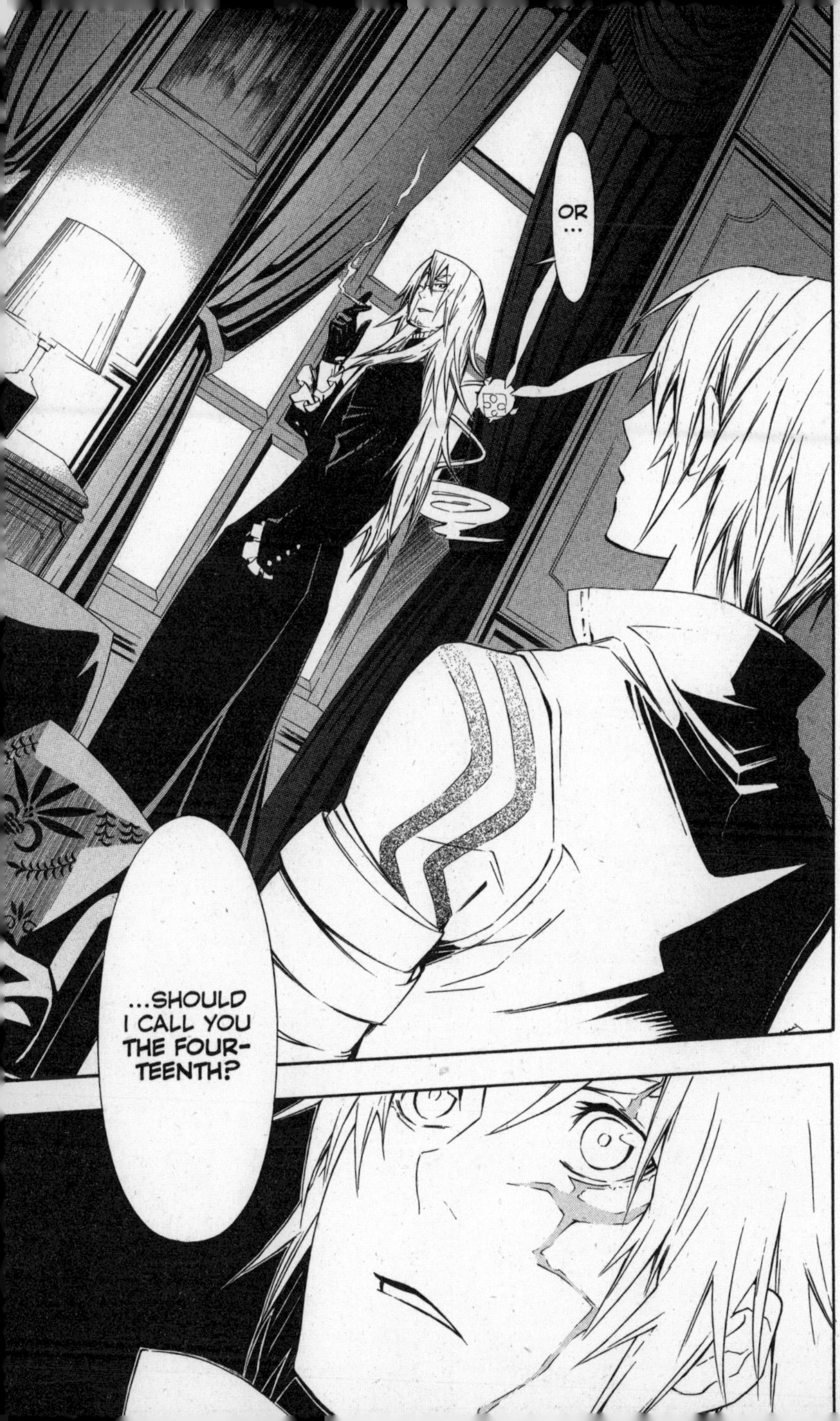
OR ...
...SHOULD I CALL YOU THE FOUR-TEENTH?

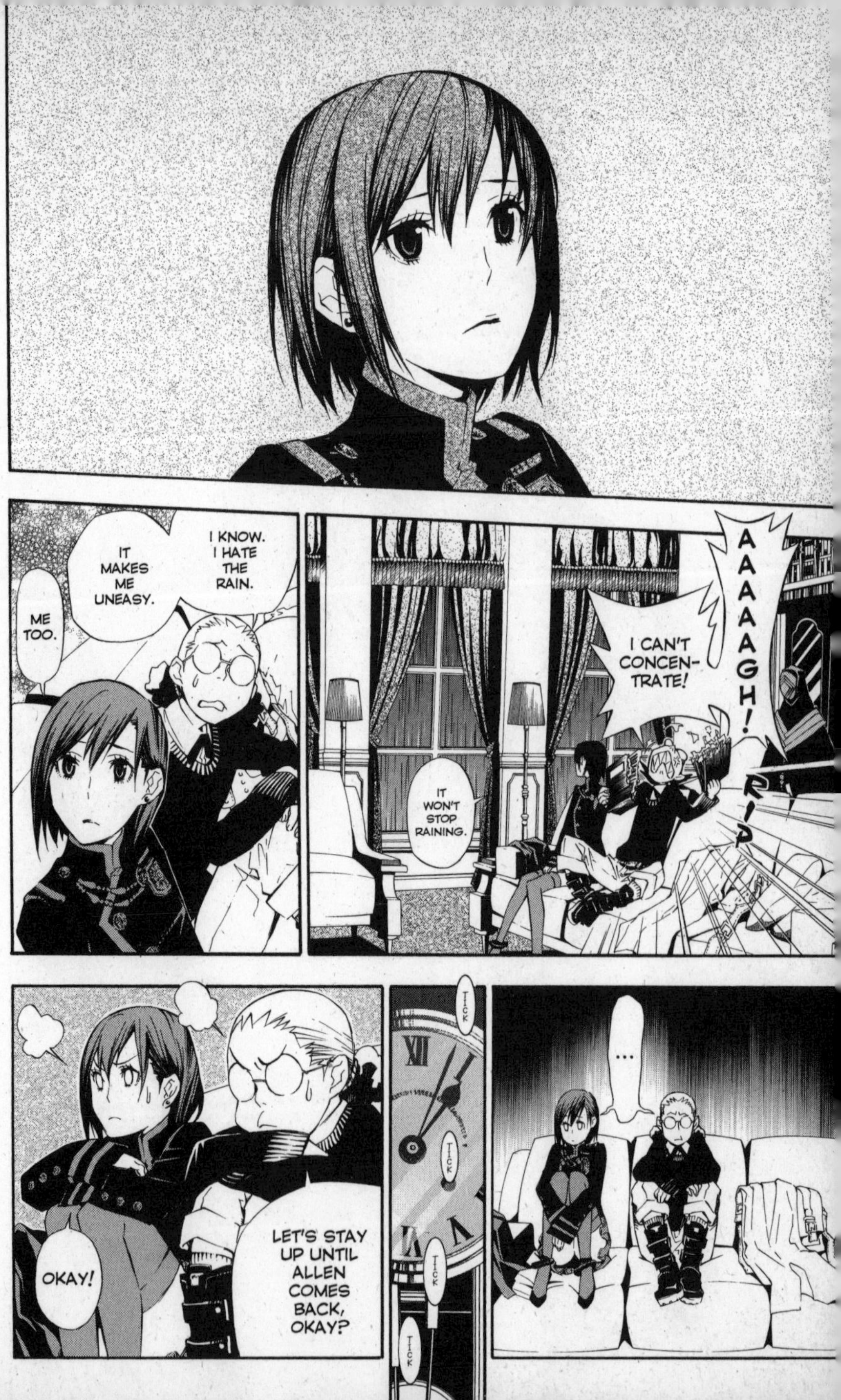
AAAAAGH!
I CAN'T CONCENTRATE!
RIP
IT WON'T STOP RAINING.
I KNOW. I HATE THE RAIN.
IT MAKES ME UNEASY.
ME TOO.
...
TICK
TICK
TICK
TICK
LET'S STAY UP UNTIL ALLEN COMES BACK, OKAY?
OKAY!

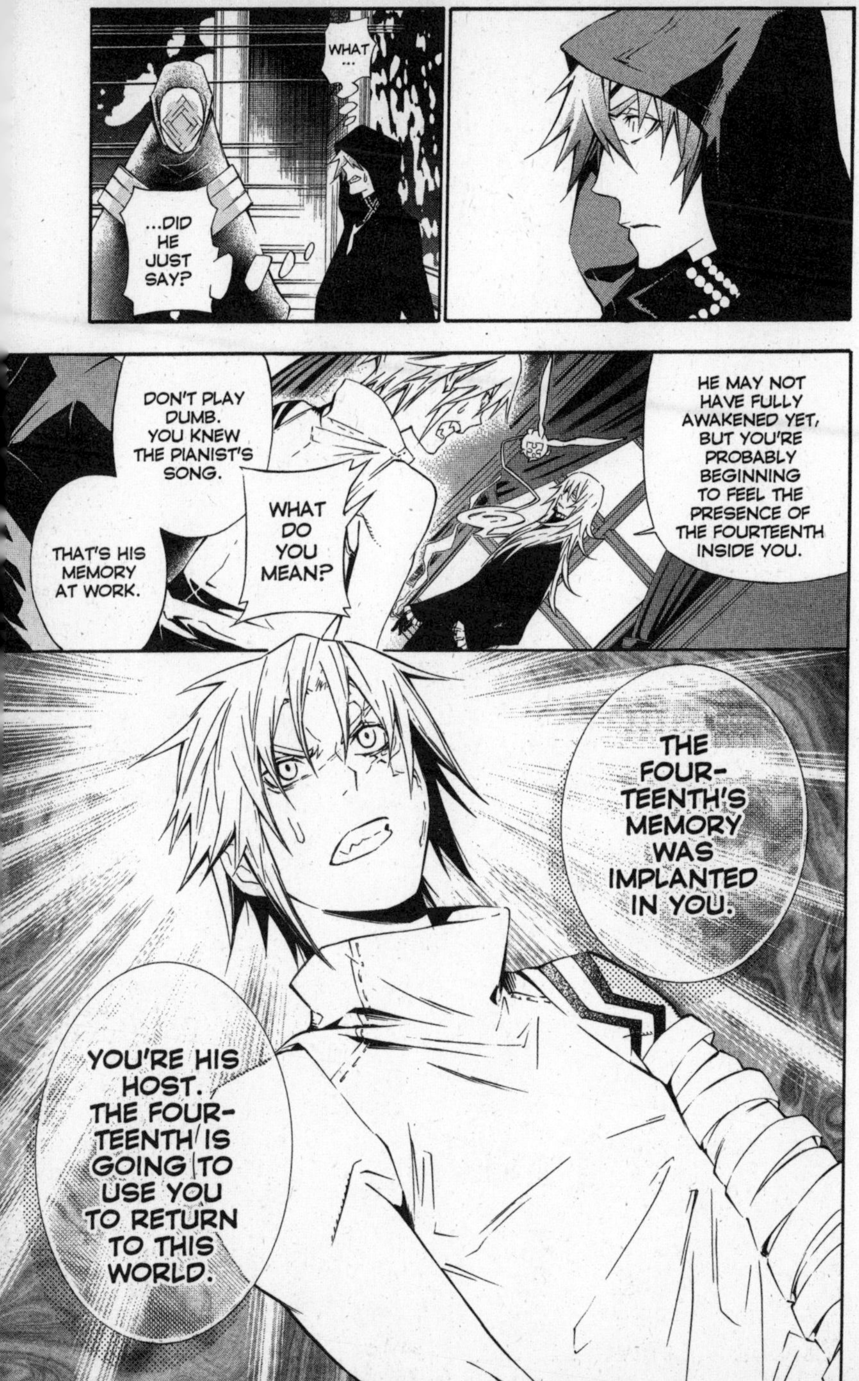
WHAT ...
...DID HE JUST SAY?
HE MAY NOT HAVE FULLY AWAKENED YET, BUT YOU'RE PROBABLY BEGINNING TO FEEL THE PRESENCE OF THE FOURTEENTH INSIDE YOU.
WHAT DO YOU MEAN?
DON'T PLAY DUMB. YOU KNEW THE PIANIST'S SONG.
THAT'S HIS MEMORY AT WORK.
THE FOUR-TEENTH'S MEMORY WAS IMPLANTED IN YOU.
YOU'RE HIS HOST. THE FOUR-TEENTH IS GOING TO USE YOU TO RETURN TO THIS WORLD.

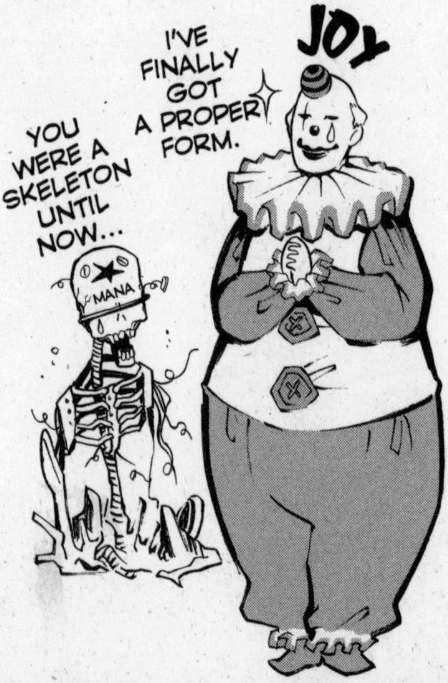
JOY
I'VE FINALLY GOT A PROPER FORM.
YOU WERE A SKELETON UNTIL NOW...
MANA

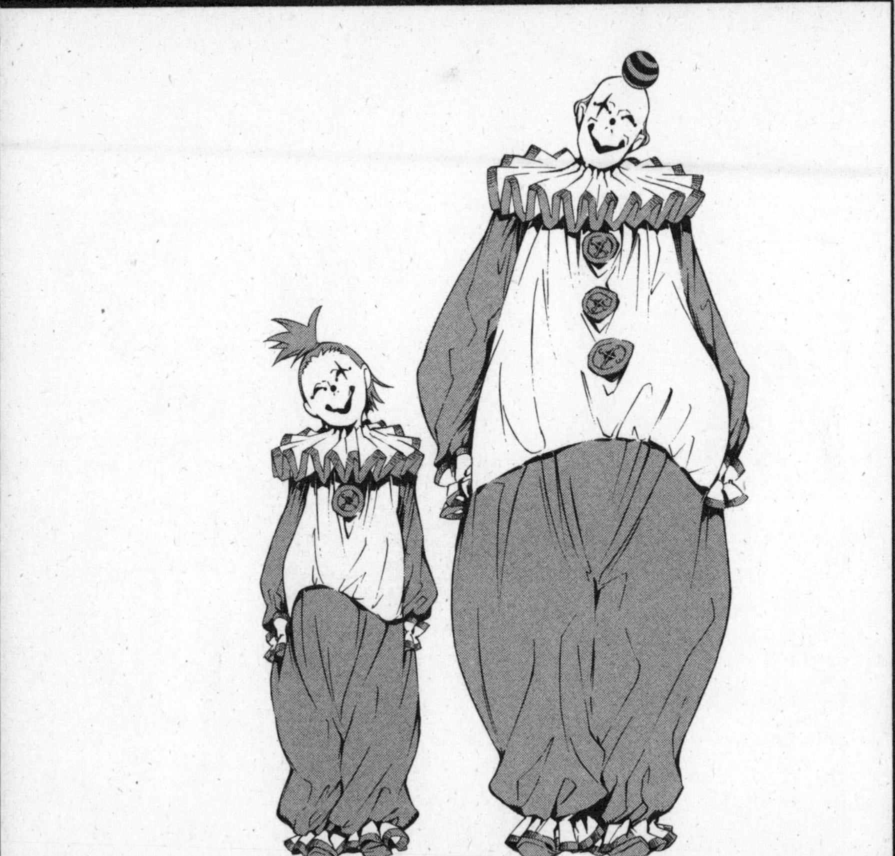

THE 167TH NIGHT: CLUES

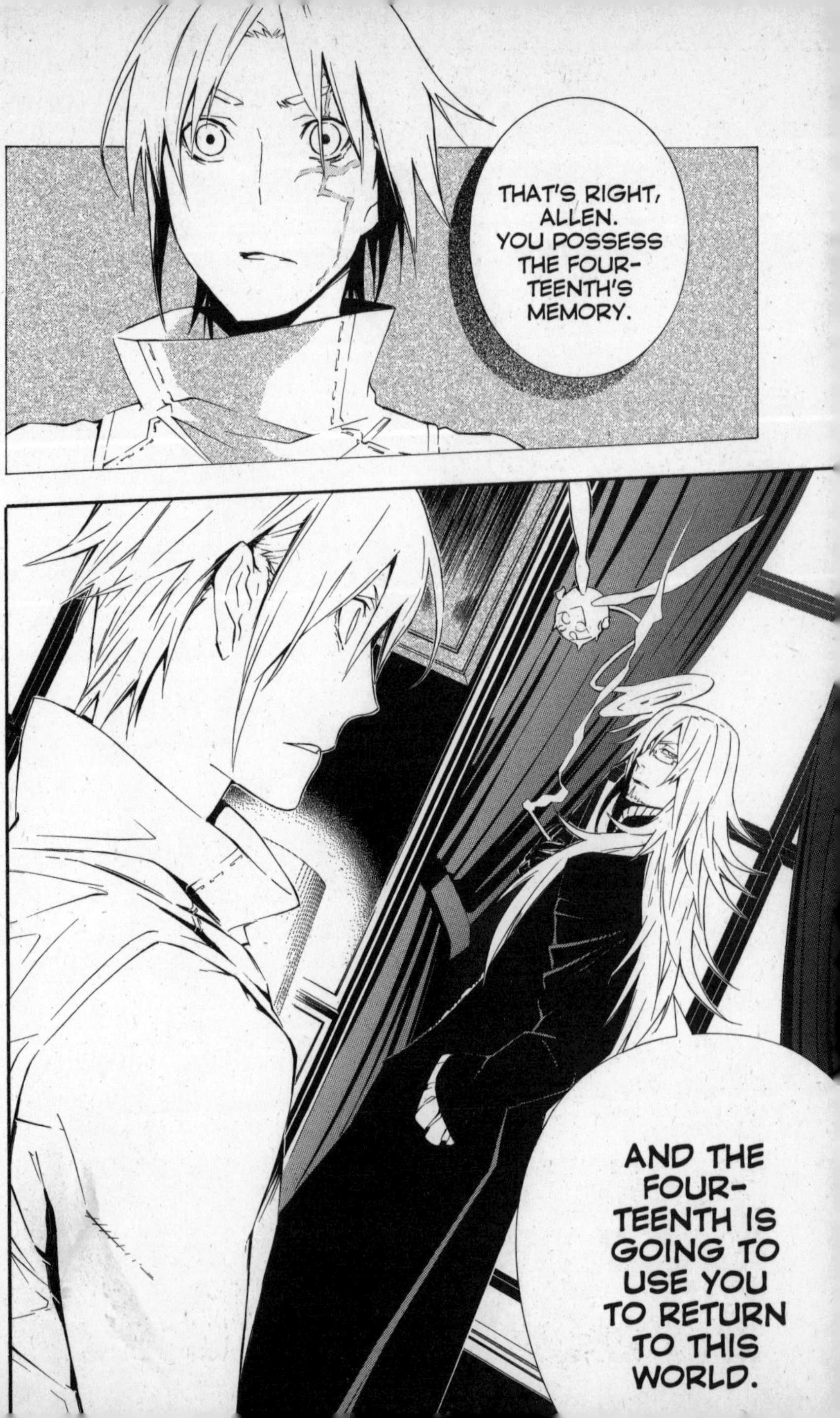
THAT'S RIGHT, ALLEN. YOU POSSESS THE FOUR-TEENTH'S MEMORY.
AND THE FOUR-TEENTH IS GOING TO USE YOU TO RETURN TO THIS WORLD.

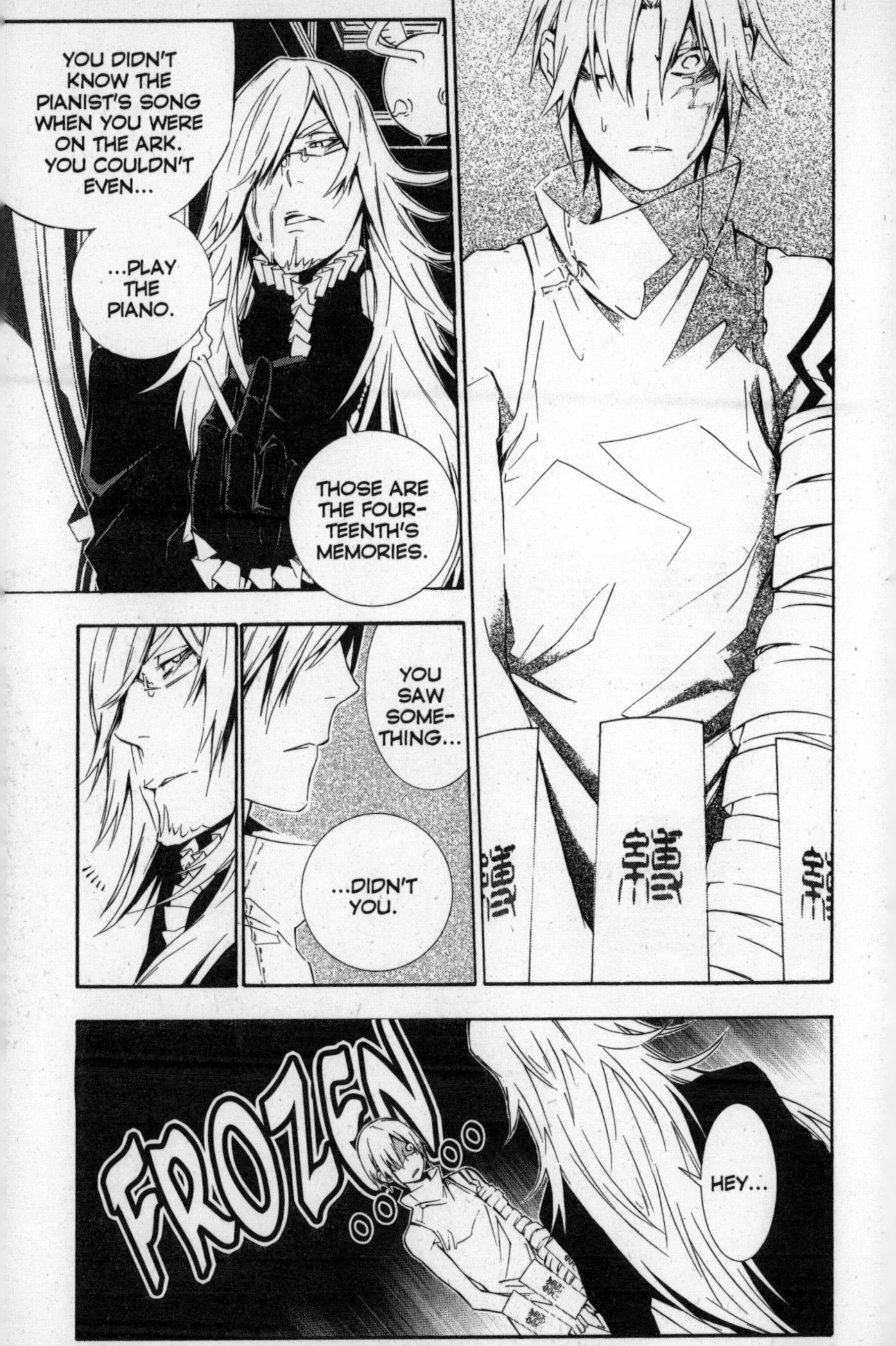

YOU DIDN'T KNOW THE PIANIST'S SONG WHEN YOU WERE ON THE ARK. YOU COULDN'T EVEN...
...PLAY THE PIANO.
THOSE ARE THE FOUR-TEENTH'S MEMORIES.
YOU SAW SOME-THING...
...DIDN'T YOU.
HEY...
FROZEN...

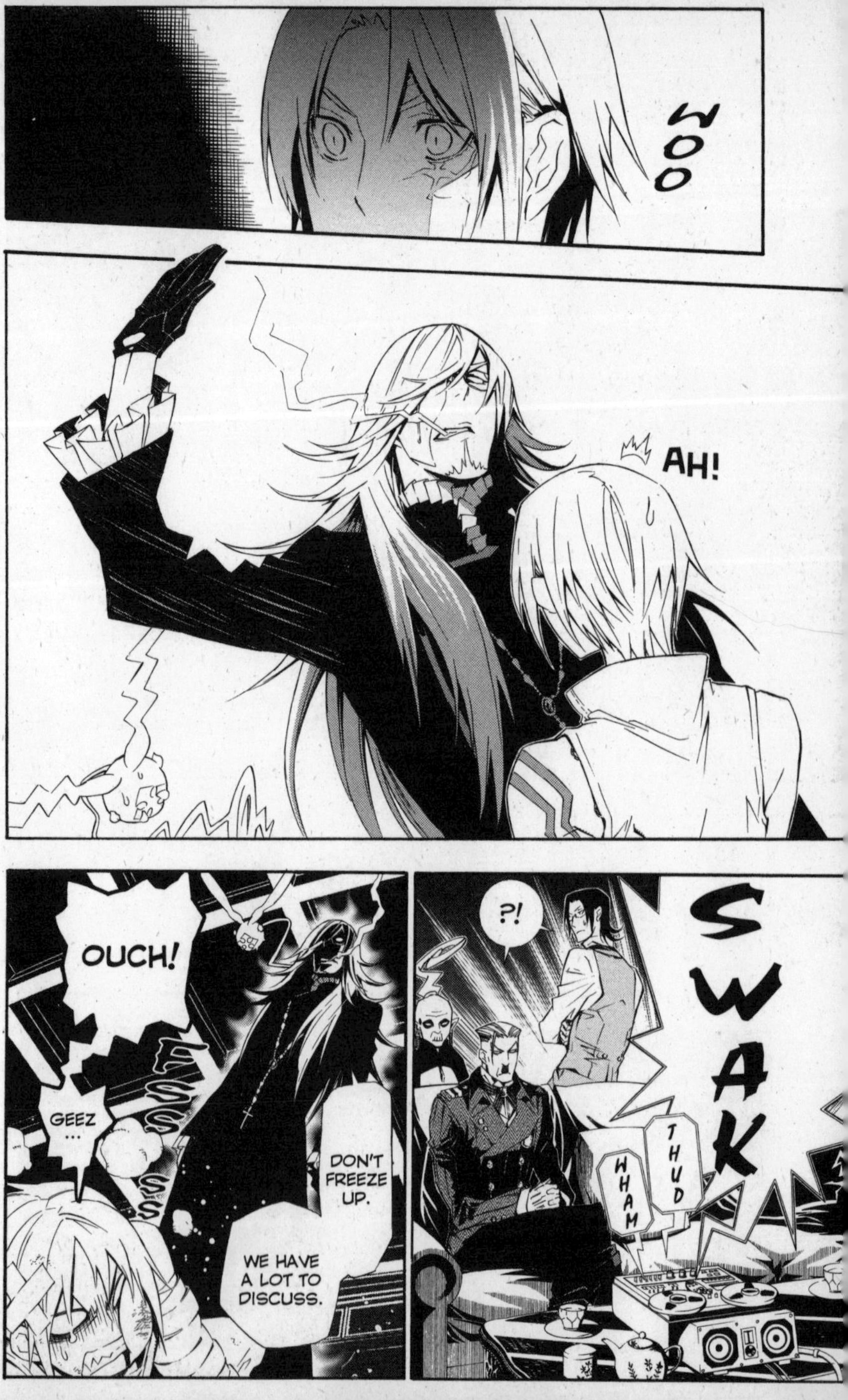
WOO
AH!
?!
SWAK
THUD
WHAM
OUCH!
FSSSS
GEEZ...
DON'T FREEZE UP.
WE HAVE A LOT TO DISCUSS.

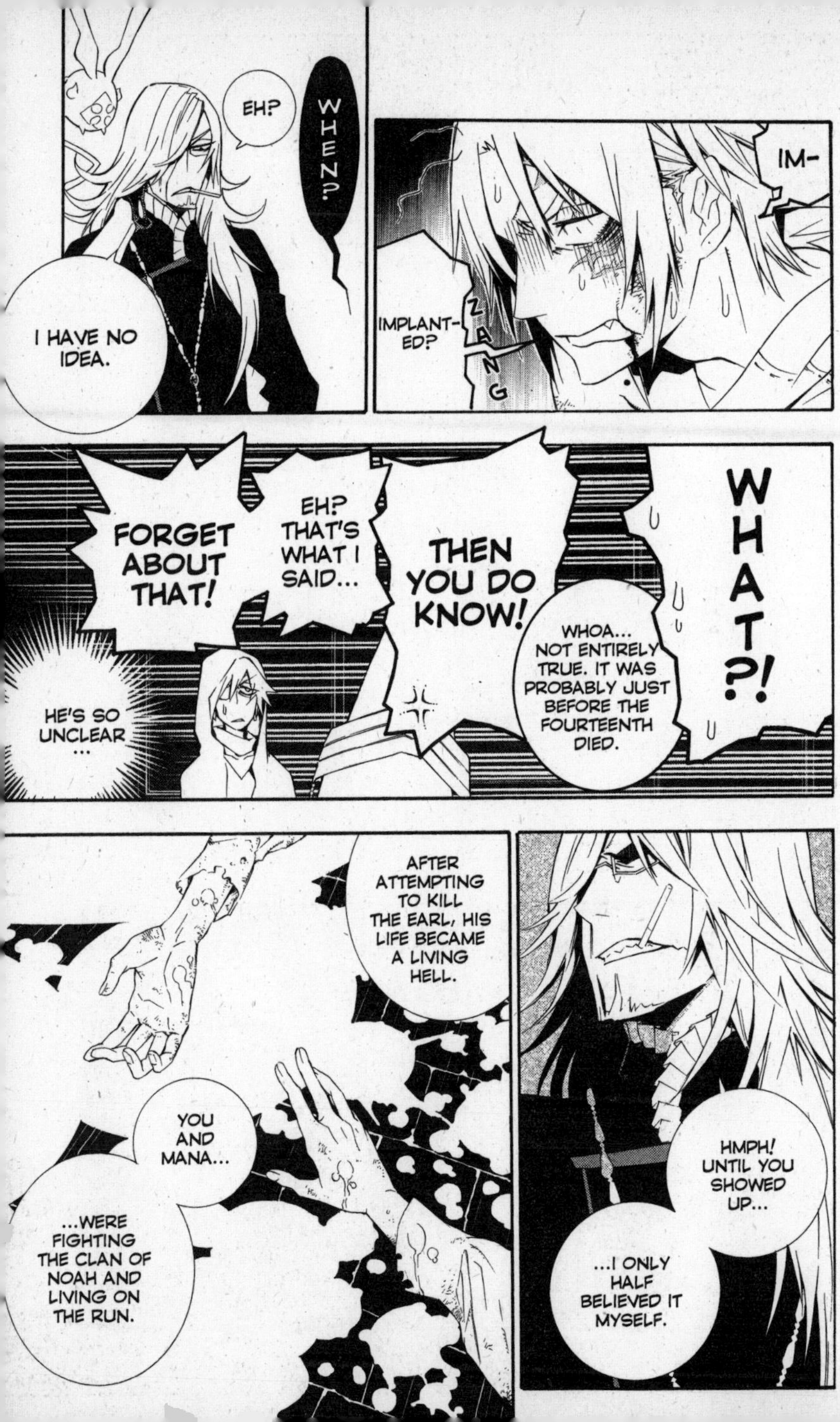
IM-
IMPLANT-ED?
ZANG
EH?
WHEN?!
I HAVE NO IDEA.
WHAT?!
WHOA... NOT ENTIRELY TRUE. IT WAS PROBABLY JUST BEFORE THE FOURTEENTH DIED.
THEN YOU DO KNOW!
EH? THAT'S WHAT I SAID...
FORGET ABOUT THAT!
HE'S SO UNCLEAR...
HMPH! UNTIL YOU SHOWED UP...
...I ONLY HALF BELIEVED IT MYSELF.
AFTER ATTEMPTING TO KILL THE EARL, HIS LIFE BECAME A LIVING HELL.
YOU AND MANA...
...WERE FIGHTING THE CLAN OF NOAH AND LIVING ON THE RUN.

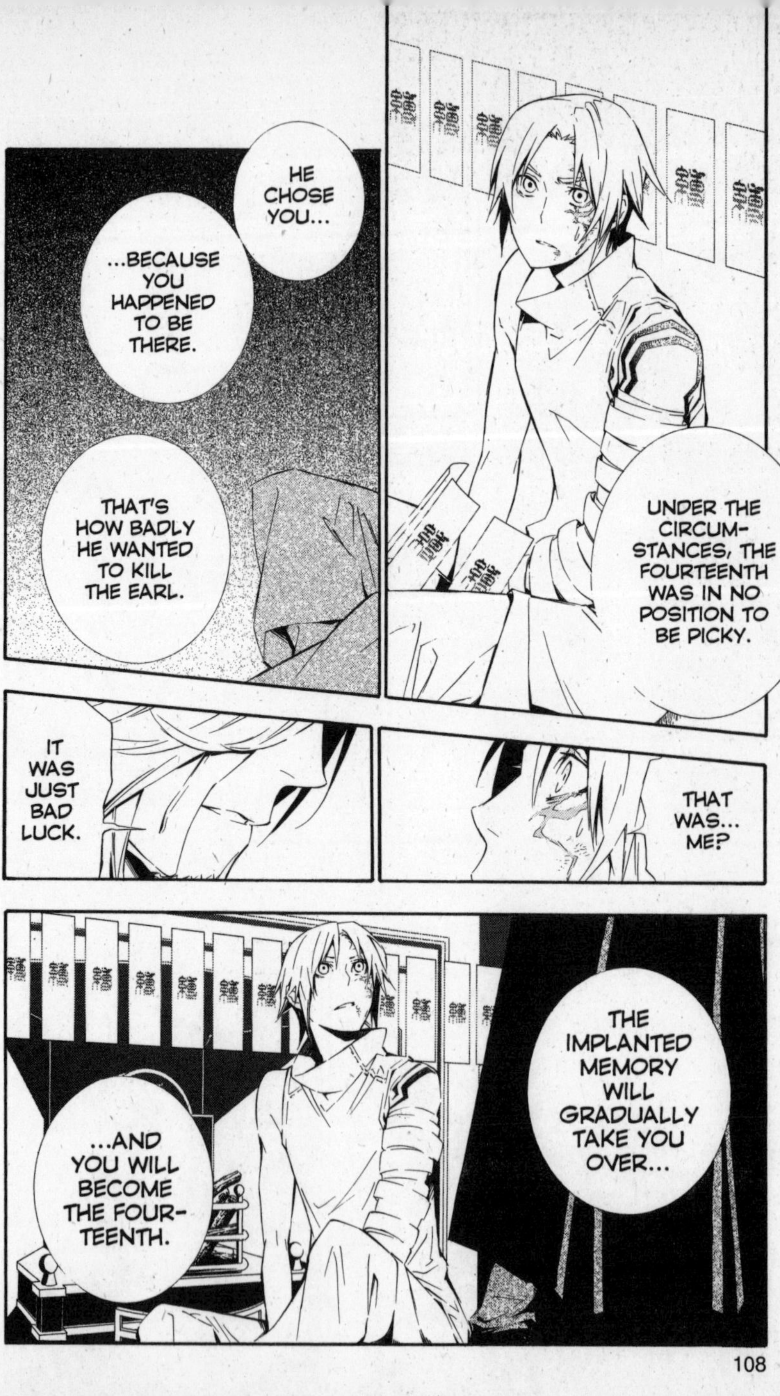
UNDER THE CIRCUM-STANCES, THE FOURTEENTH WAS IN NO POSITION TO BE PICKY.
HE CHOSE YOU...
...BECAUSE YOU HAPPENED TO BE THERE.
THAT'S HOW BADLY HE WANTED TO KILL THE EARL.
THAT WAS... ME?
IT WAS JUST BAD LUCK.
THE IMPLANTED MEMORY WILL GRADUALLY TAKE YOU OVER...
...AND YOU WILL BECOME THE FOUR-TEENTH.

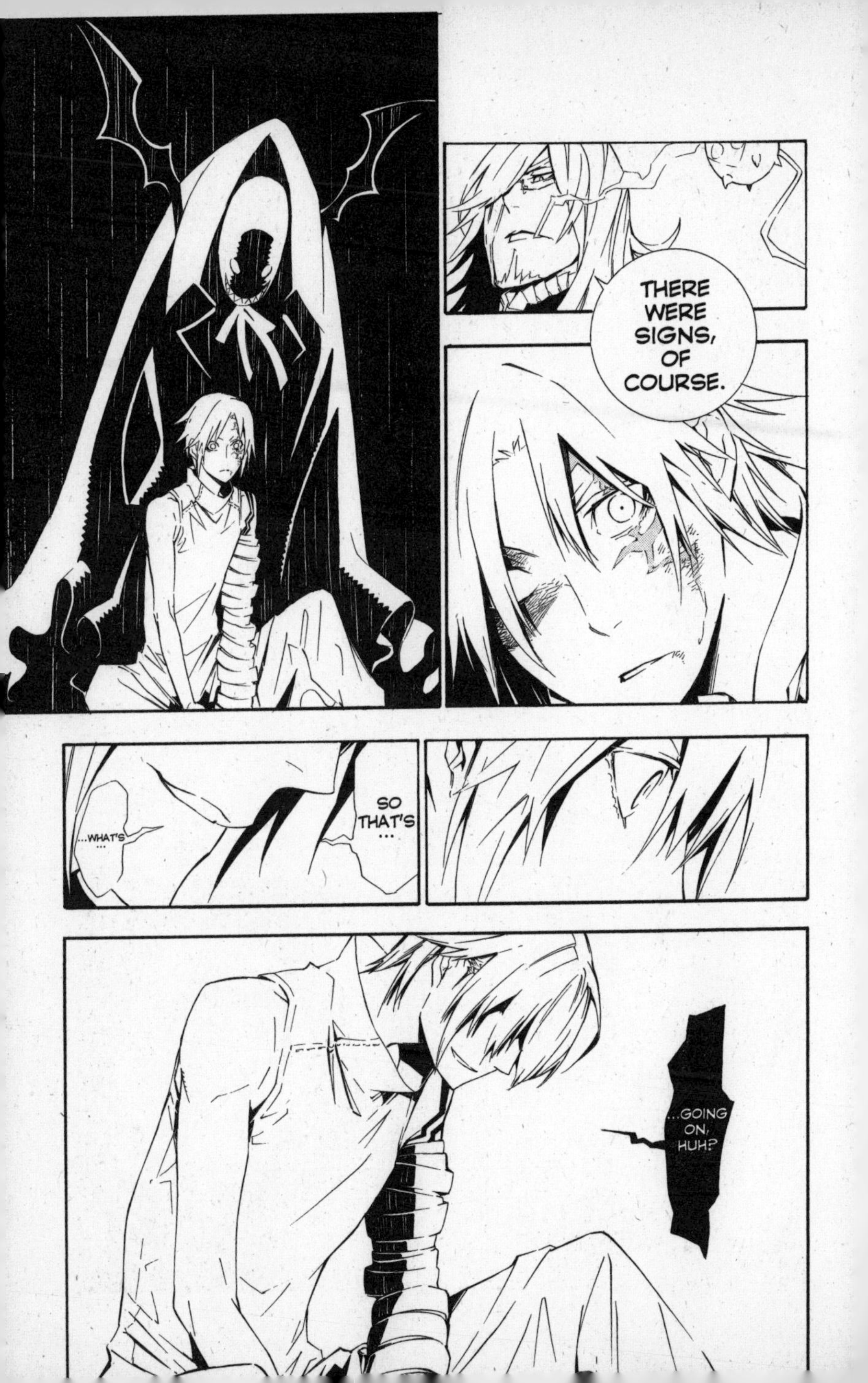
THERE WERE SIGNS, OF COURSE.
SO THAT'S ...
...WHAT'S ...
...GOING ON, HUH?

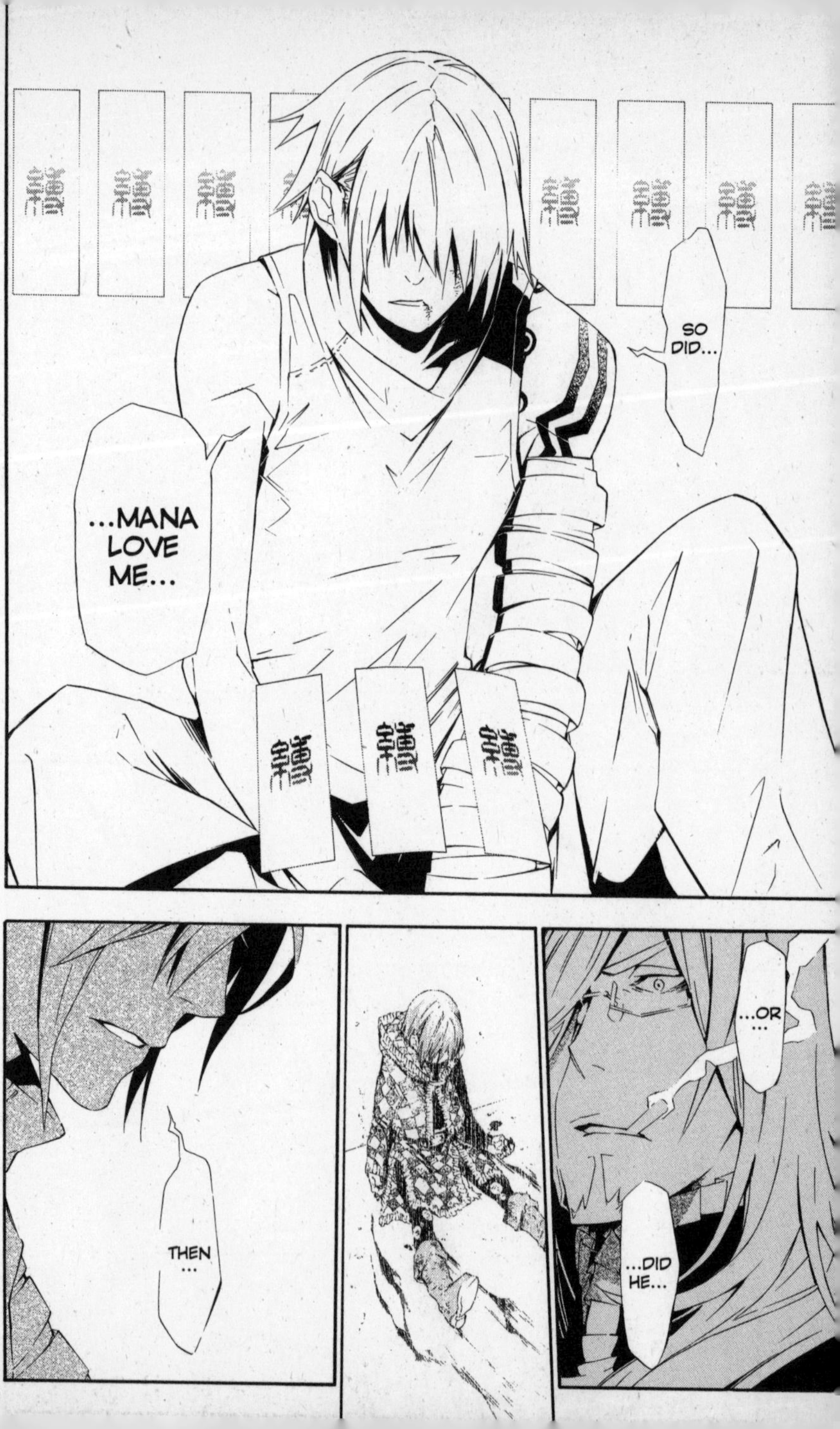
SO DID...
...MANA LOVE ME...
...OR ...
...DID HE...
THEN ...

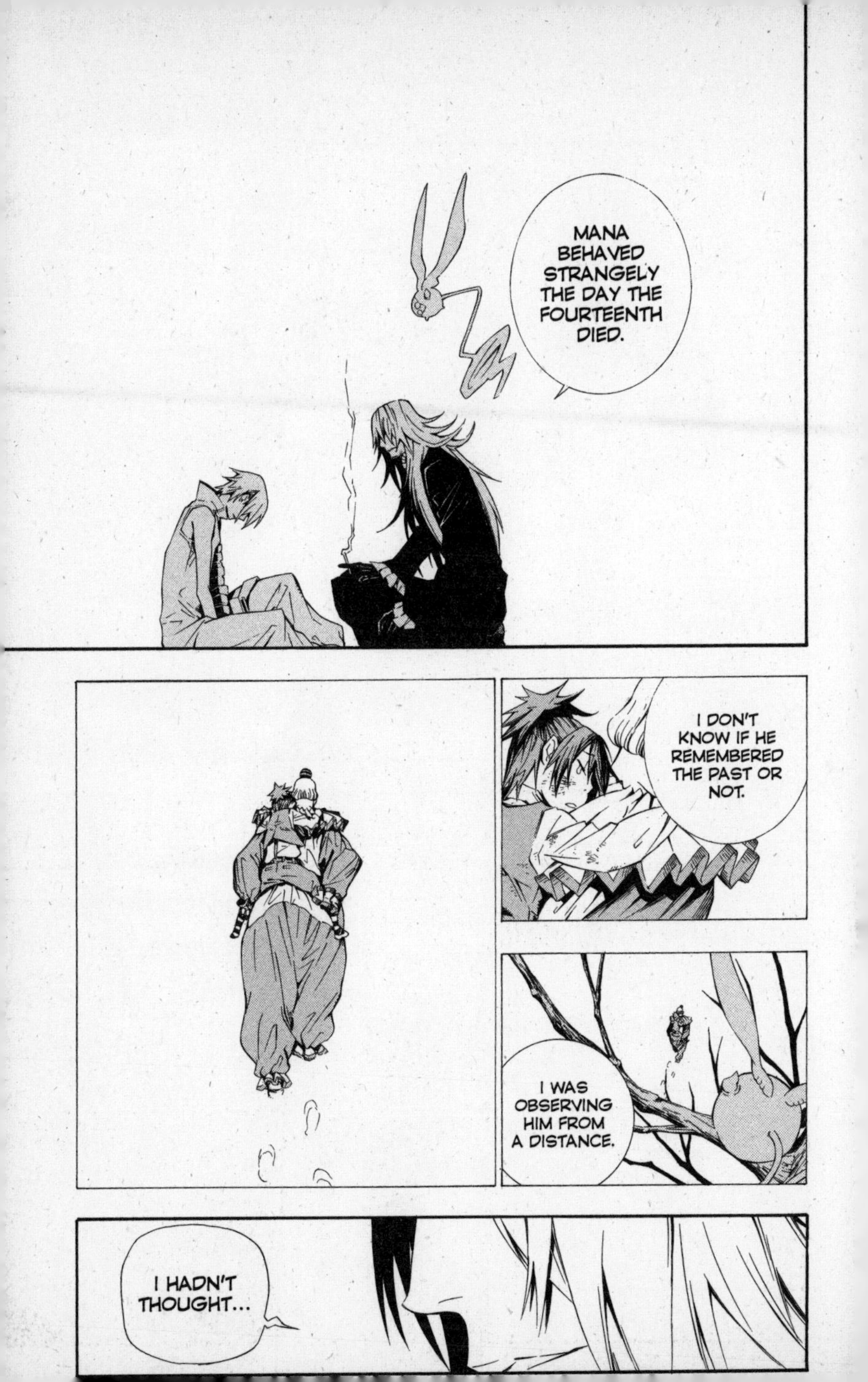
MANA BEHAVED STRANGELY THE DAY THE FOURTEENTH DIED.
I DON'T KNOW IF HE REMEMBERED THE PAST OR NOT.
I WAS OBSERVING HIM FROM A DISTANCE.
I HADN'T THOUGHT...

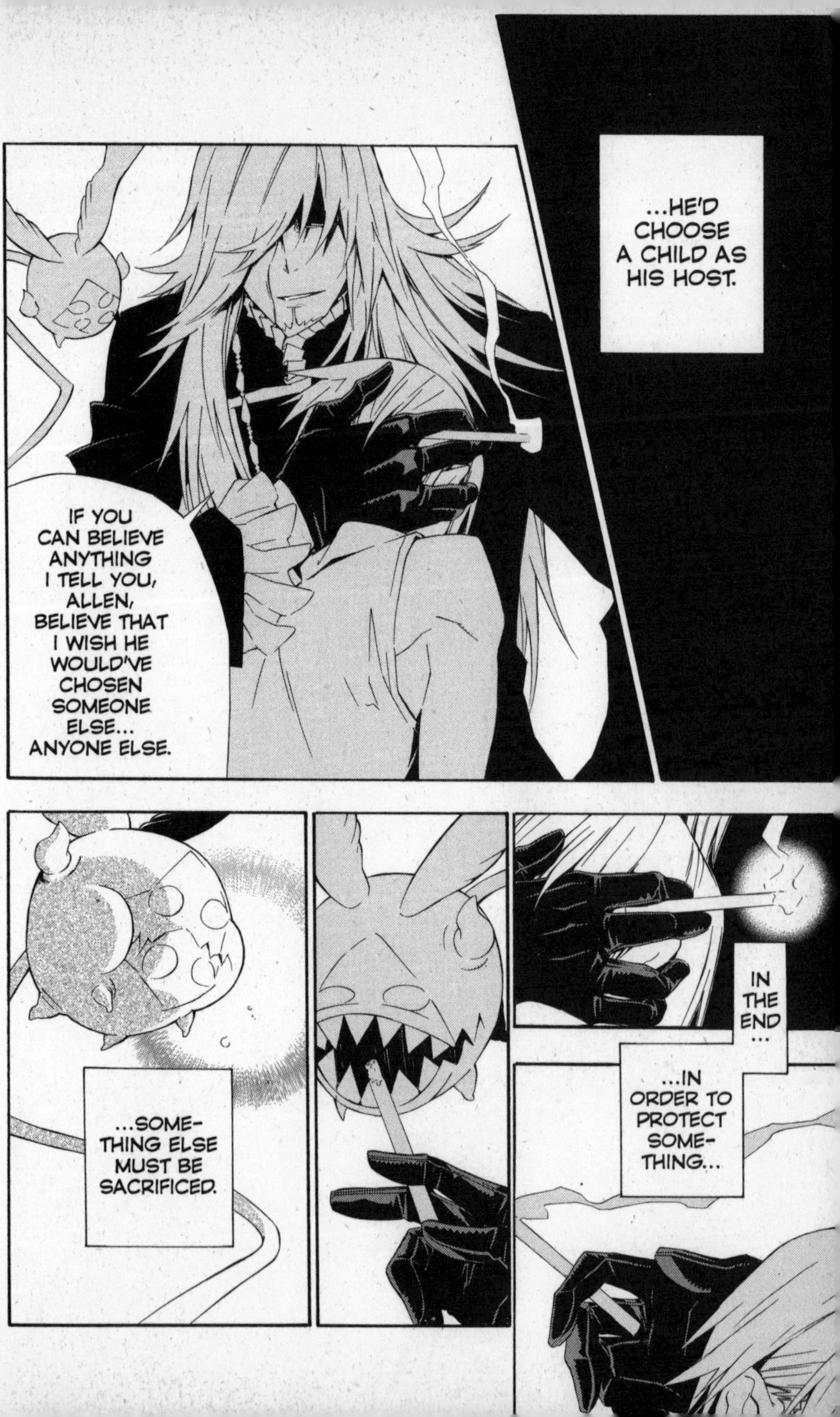
...HE'D CHOOSE A CHILD AS HIS HOST.
IF YOU CAN BELIEVE ANYTHING I TELL YOU, ALLEN, BELIEVE THAT I WISH HE WOULD'VE CHOSEN SOMEONE ELSE... ANYONE ELSE.
IN THE END...
...IN ORDER TO PROTECT SOME-THING...
...SOME-THING ELSE MUST BE SACRIFICED.

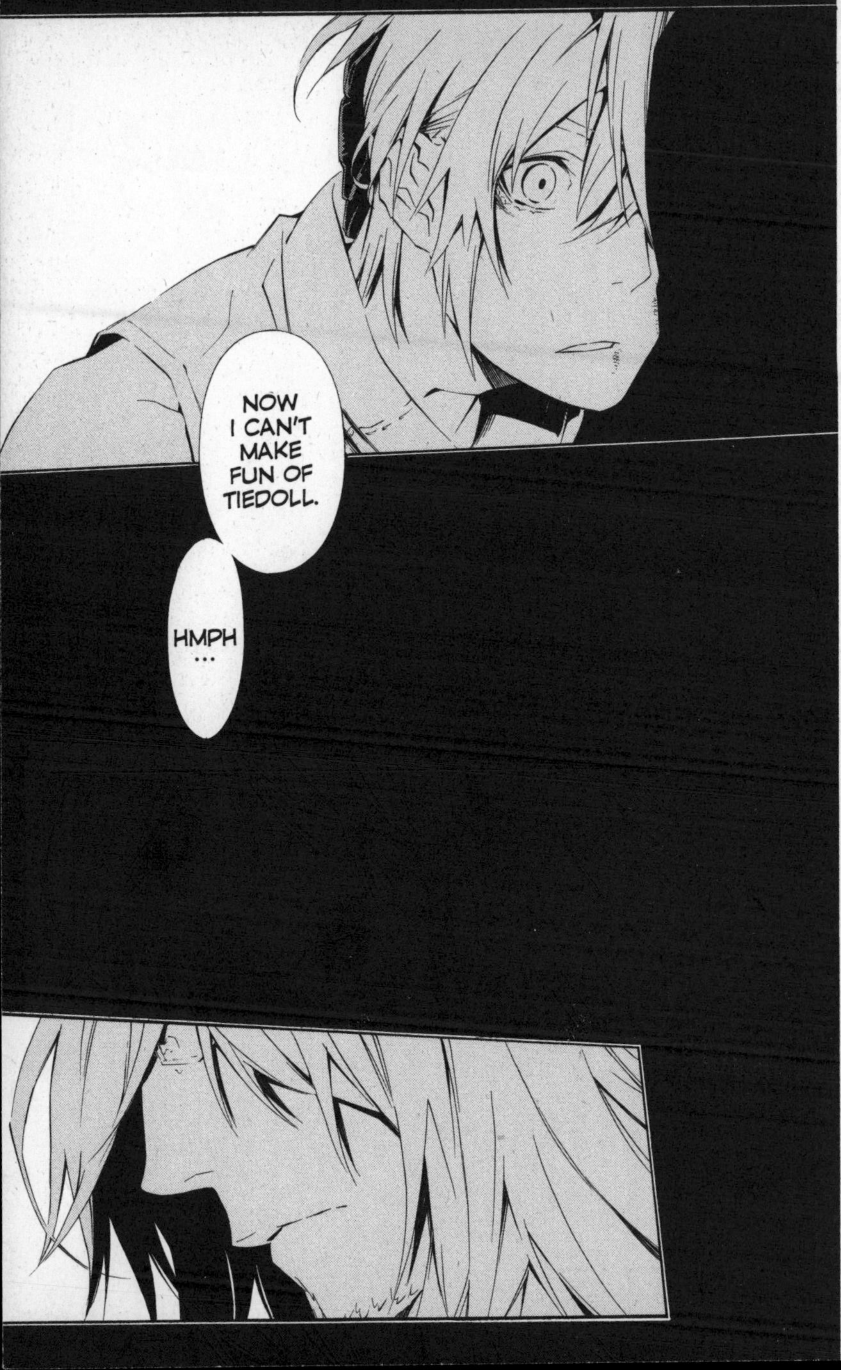
NOW I CAN'T MAKE FUN OF TIEDOLL.
HMPH...

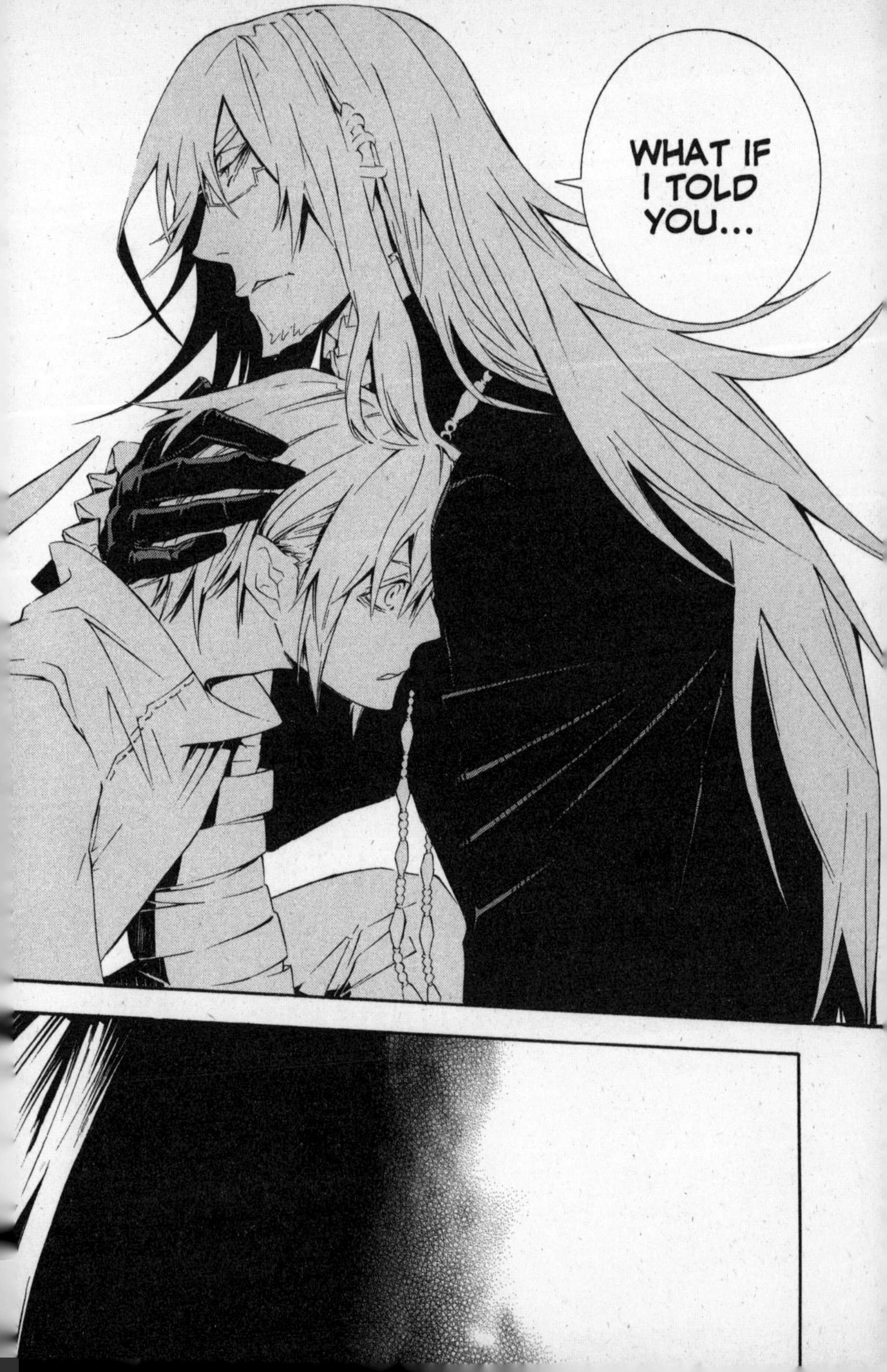
WHAT IF I TOLD YOU...

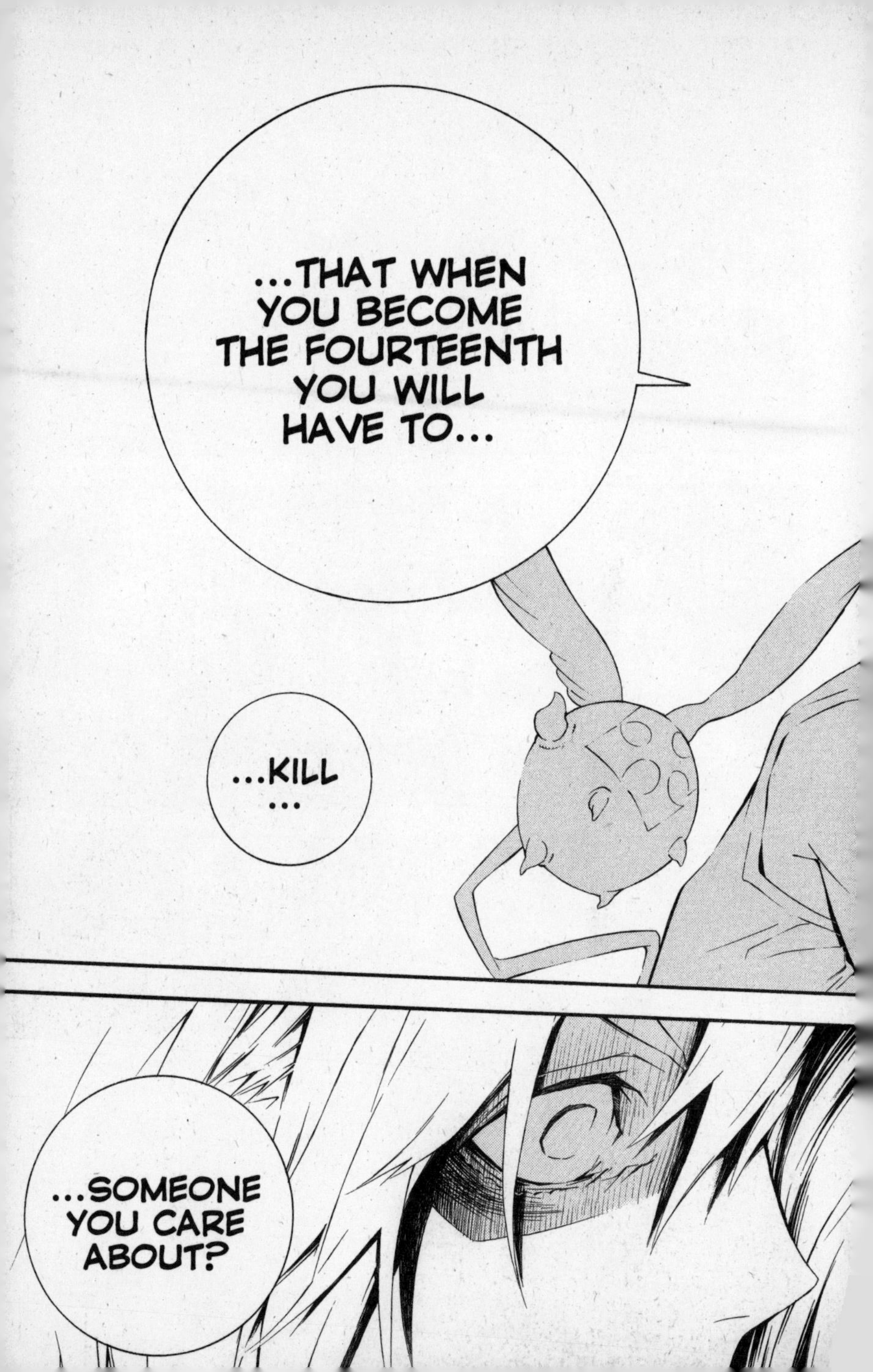
...THAT WHEN YOU BECOME THE FOURTEENTH YOU WILL HAVE TO...
...KILL ...
...SOMEONE YOU CARE ABOUT?

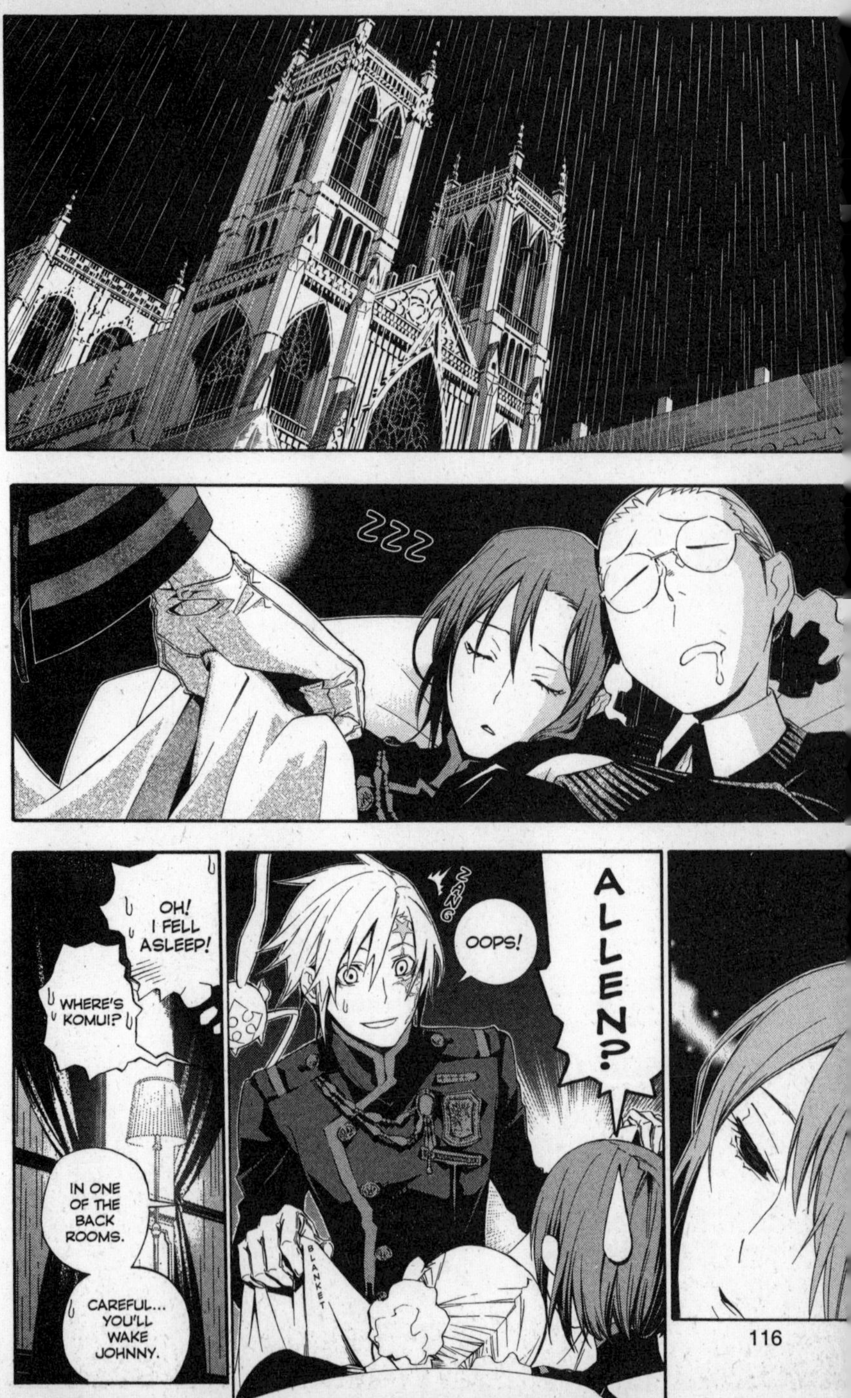
ZZZ
ALLEN?
ZANG
OOPS!
BLANKET
OH! I FELL ASLEEP!
WHERE'S KOMUI?
IN ONE OF THE BACK ROOMS.
CAREFUL... YOU'LL WAKE JOHNNY.

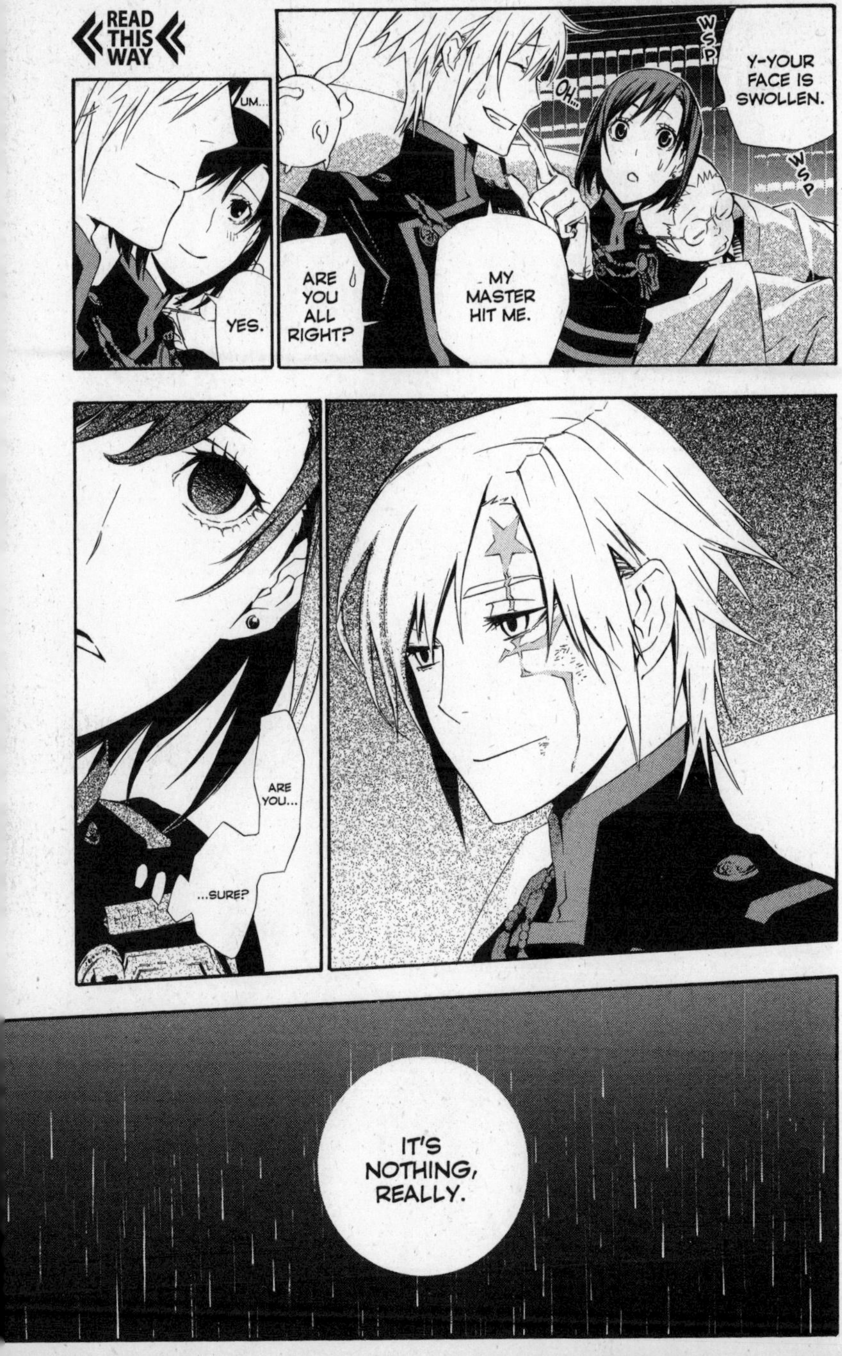
READ THIS WAY
WSP
Y-YOUR FACE IS SWOLLEN.
WSP
OH...
MY MASTER HIT ME.
ARE YOU ALL RIGHT?
UM...
YES.
ARE YOU...
...SURE?
IT'S NOTHING, REALLY.

THE PEOPLE OF D. GRAY-HOUSE

THE ADOPTIVE FATHER RELATES THE HOUSE RULES

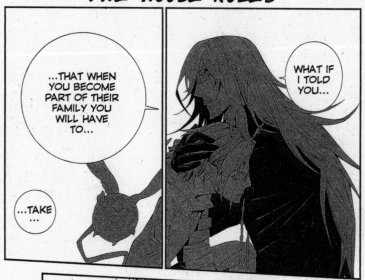

WHAT IF I TOLD YOU...
...THAT WHEN YOU BECOME PART OF THEIR FAMILY YOU WILL HAVE TO...
...TAKE ...
...A BATH WITH HIM?
UGH!

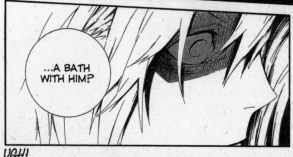

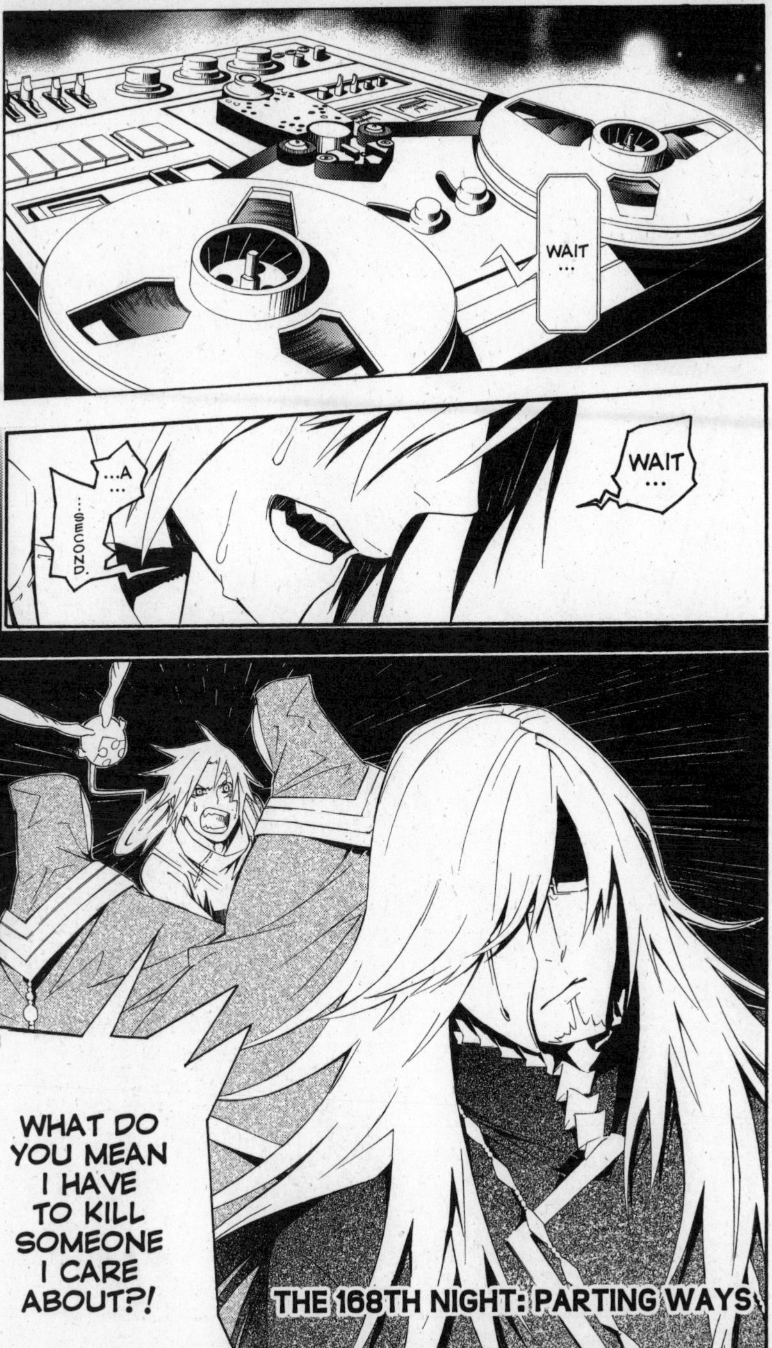
WAIT ...
WAIT ...
...A ... ...SECOND.
WHAT DO YOU MEAN I HAVE TO KILL SOMEONE I CARE ABOUT?!

THE 168TH NIGHT: PARTING WAYS

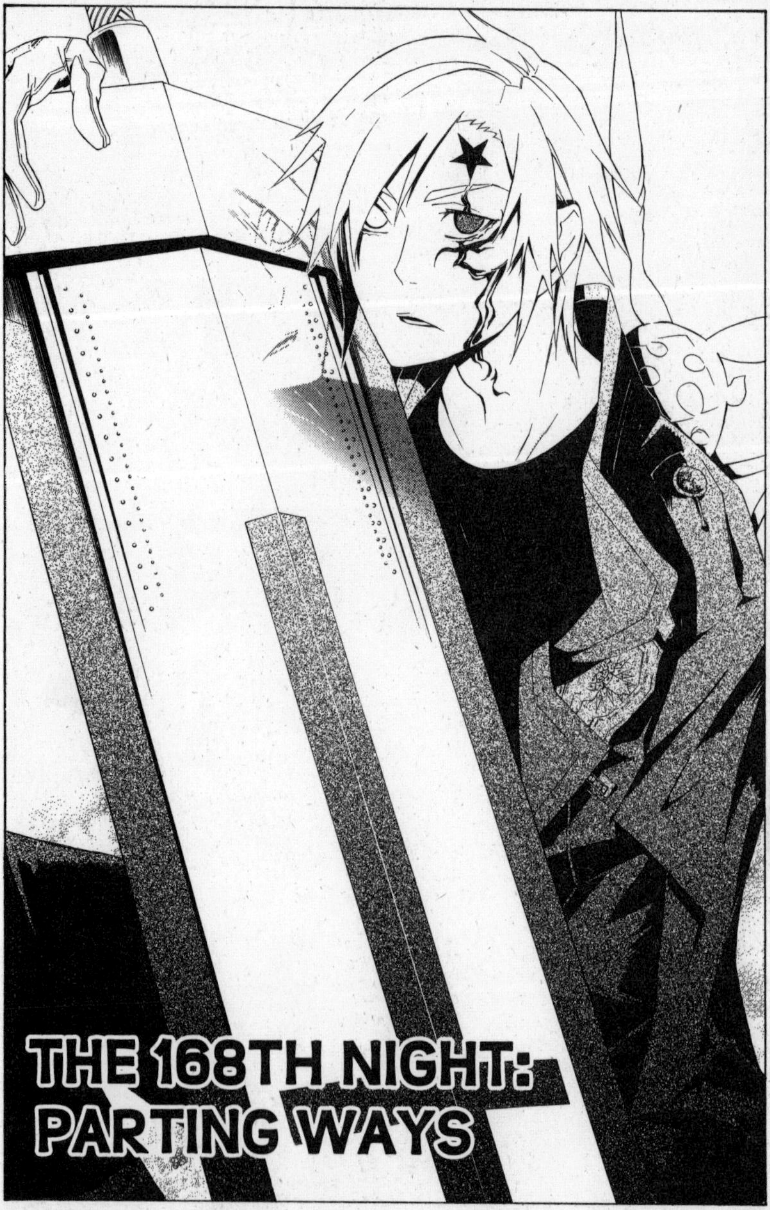
THE 168TH NIGHT:
PARTING WAYS

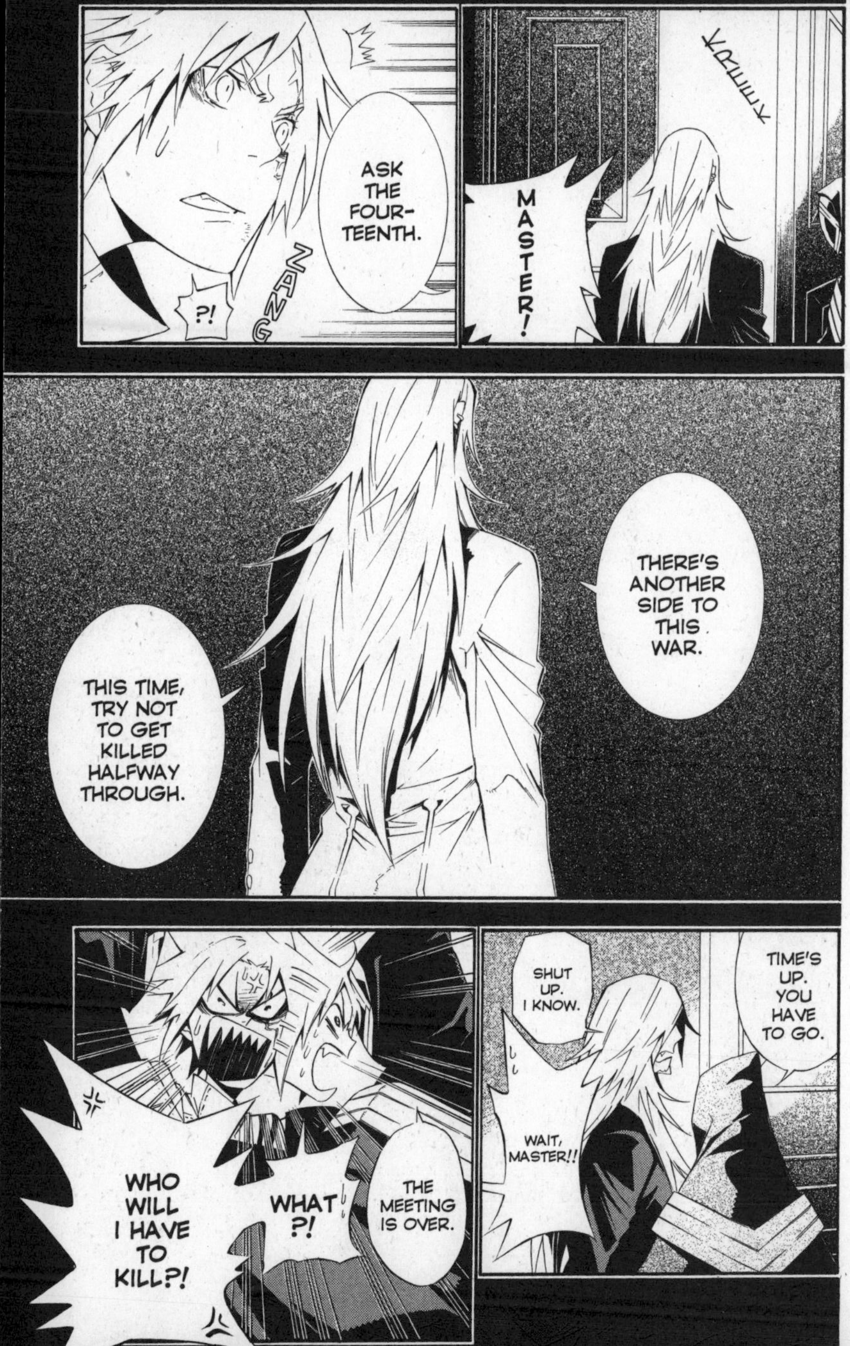
KREEEK
MASTER!
ASK THE FOURTEENTH.
ZANG
?!
THERE'S ANOTHER SIDE TO THIS WAR.
THIS TIME, TRY NOT TO GET KILLED HALFWAY THROUGH.
TIME'S UP. YOU HAVE TO GO.
SHUT UP. I KNOW.
WAIT, MASTER!!
THE MEETING IS OVER.
WHAT?!
WHO WILL I HAVE TO KILL?!

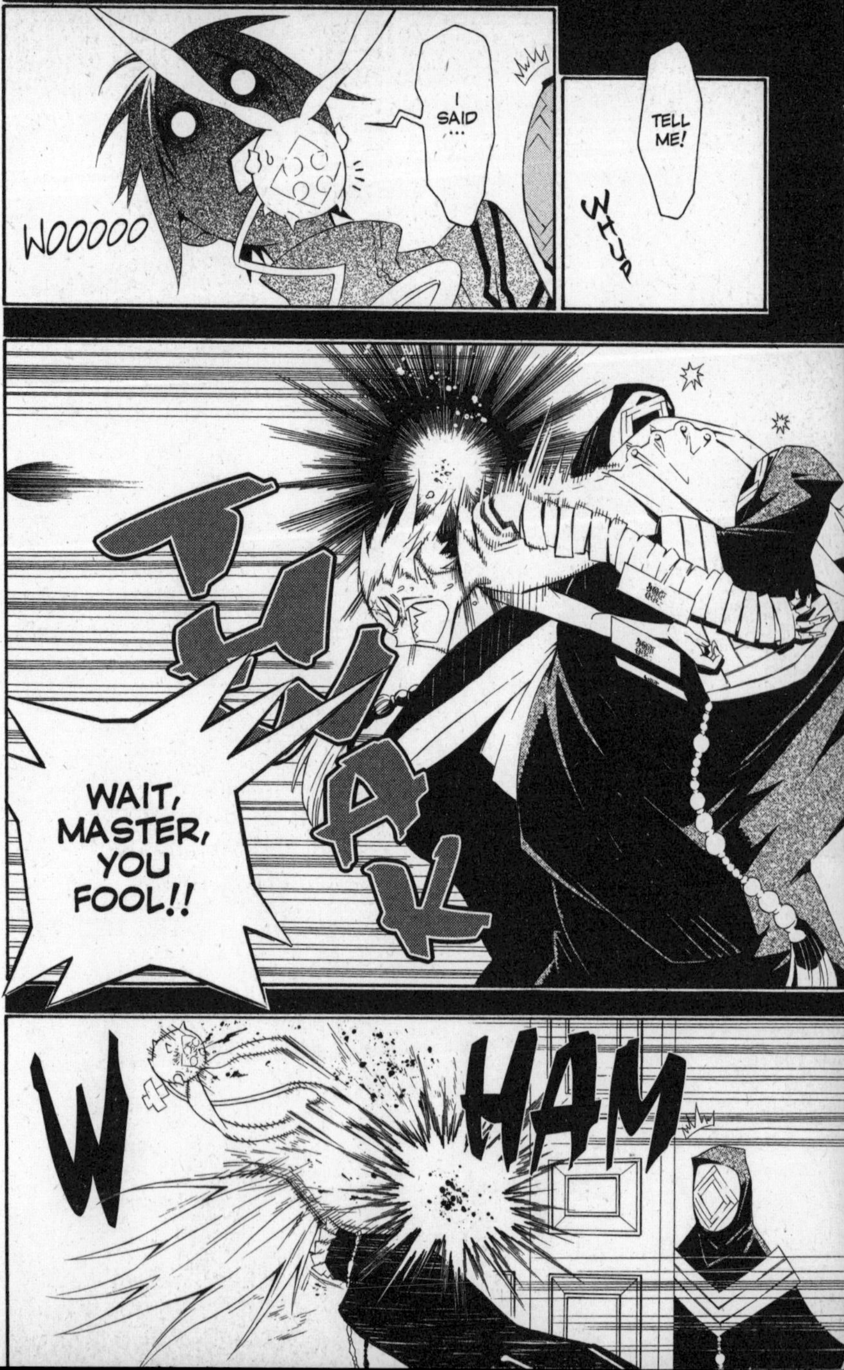
TELL ME!
WHUP
I SAID...
WOOOOO
THWAK
WAIT, MASTER, YOU FOOL!!
WHAM

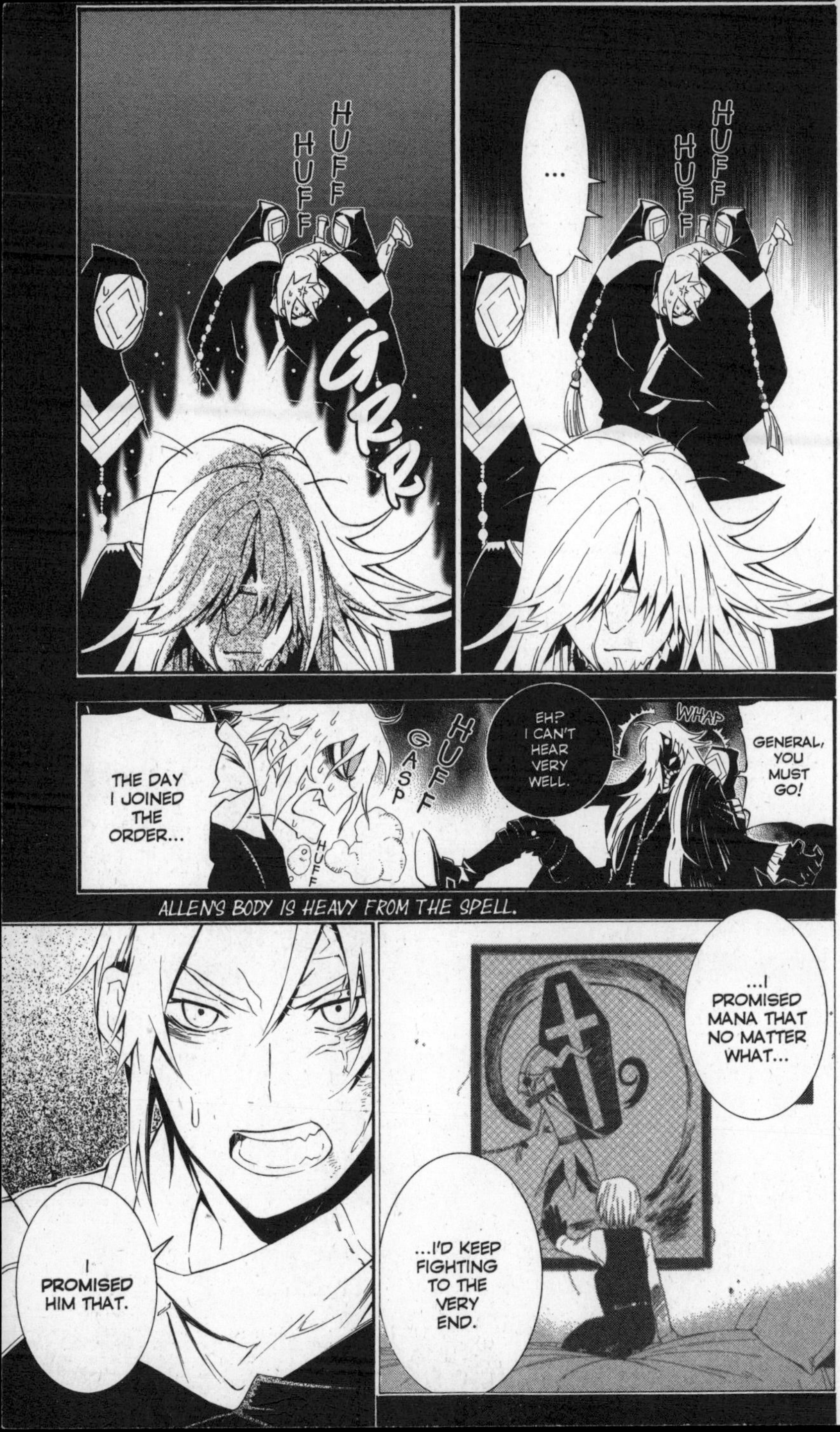
...
HUFF HUFF
HUFF HUFF
GRRR
GENERAL, YOU MUST GO!
WHAP
EH? I CAN'T HEAR VERY WELL.
HUFF
GASP
HUFF
THE DAY I JOINED THE ORDER...
ALLEN'S BODY IS HEAVY FROM THE SPELL.
...I PROMISED MANA THAT NO MATTER WHAT...
...I'D KEEP FIGHTING TO THE VERY END.
I PROMISED HIM THAT.

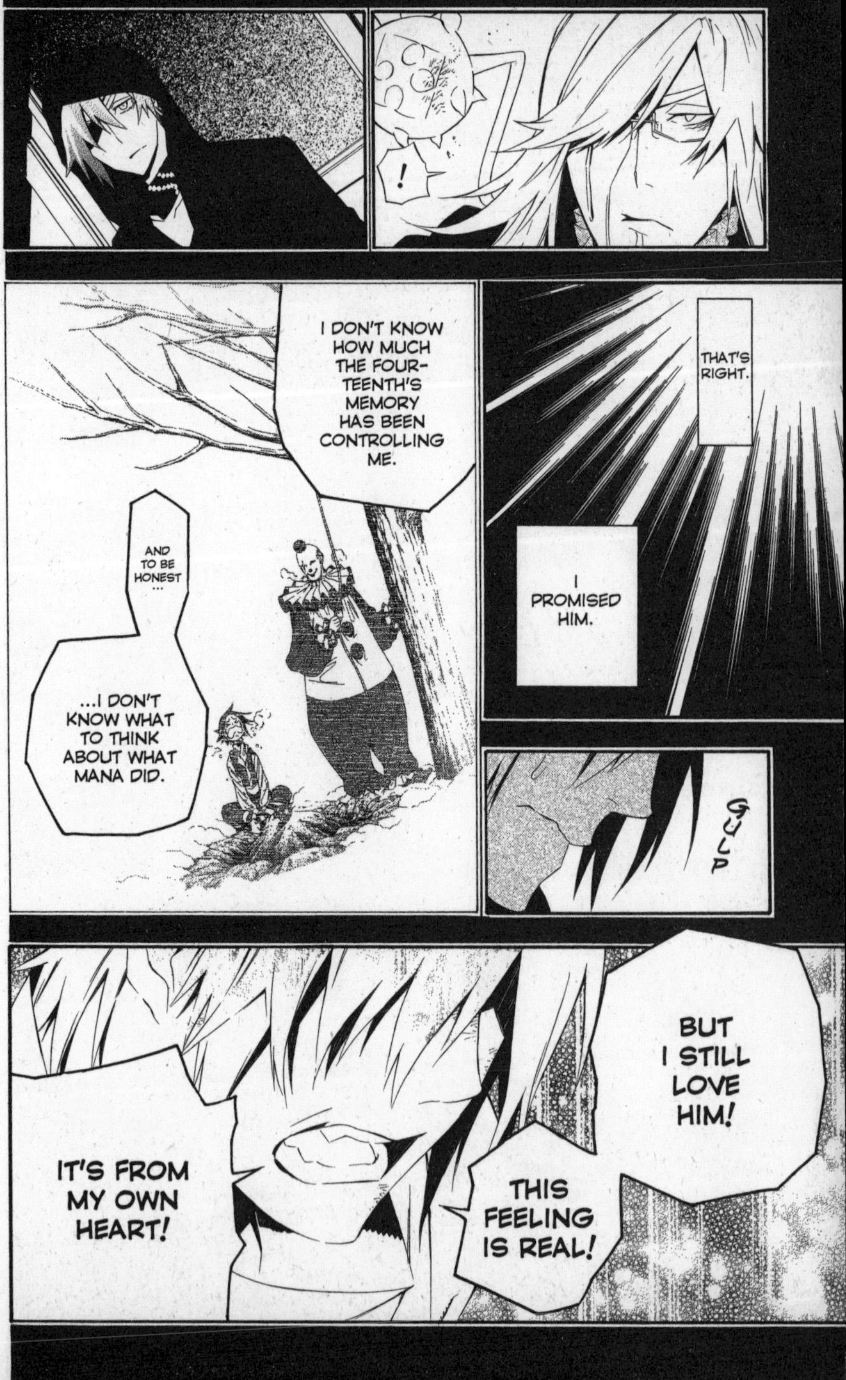
!
THAT'S RIGHT.
I PROMISED HIM.
GULP
I DON'T KNOW HOW MUCH THE FOUR-TEENTH'S MEMORY HAS BEEN CONTROLLING ME.
AND TO BE HONEST...
...I DON'T KNOW WHAT TO THINK ABOUT WHAT MANA DID.
BUT I STILL LOVE HIM!
THIS FEELING IS REAL!
IT'S FROM MY OWN HEART!

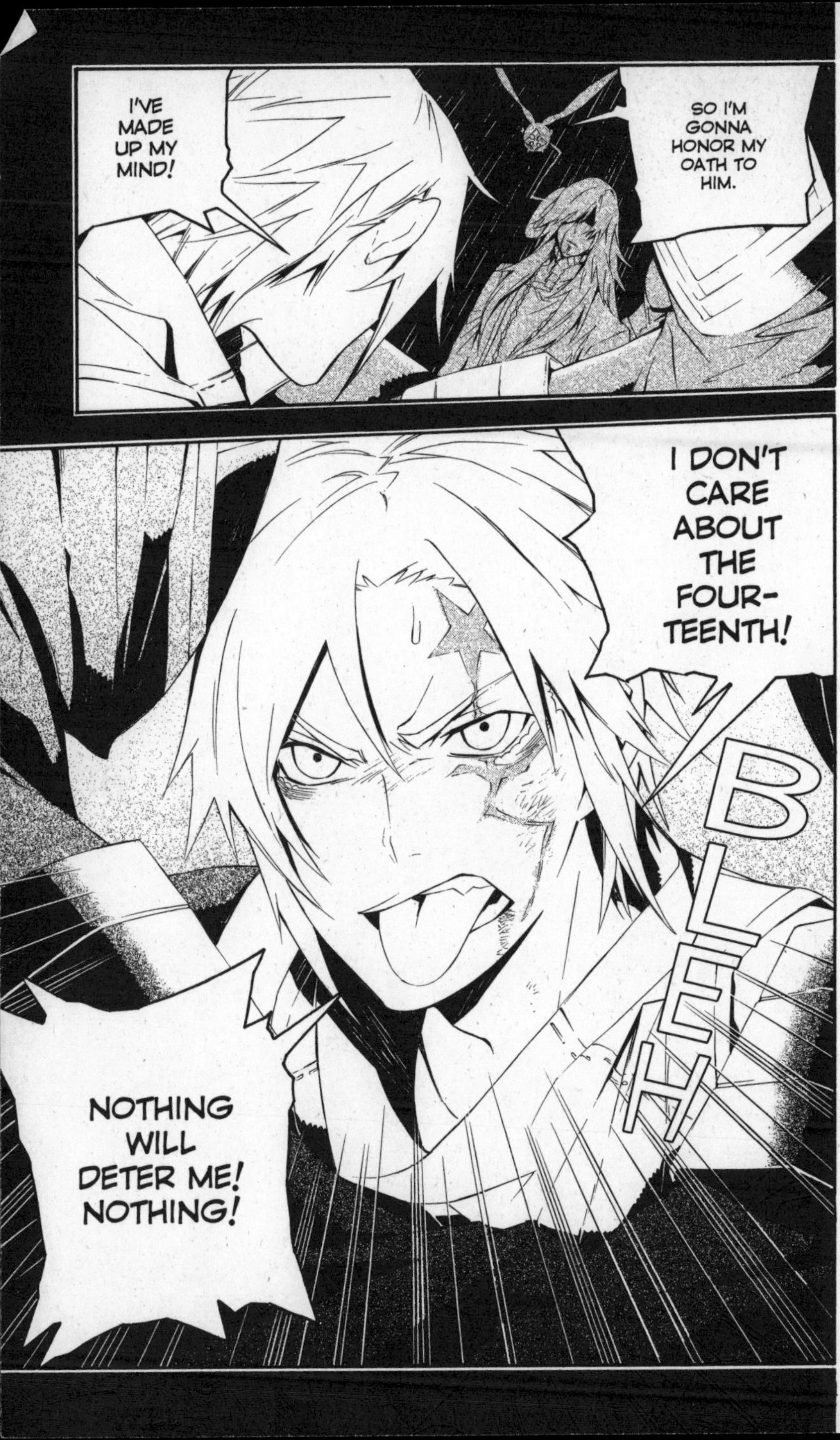
SO I'M GONNA HONOR MY OATH TO HIM.
I'VE MADE UP MY MIND!
I DON'T CARE ABOUT THE FOUR-TEENTH!
BLEH
NOTHING WILL DETER ME! NOTHING!

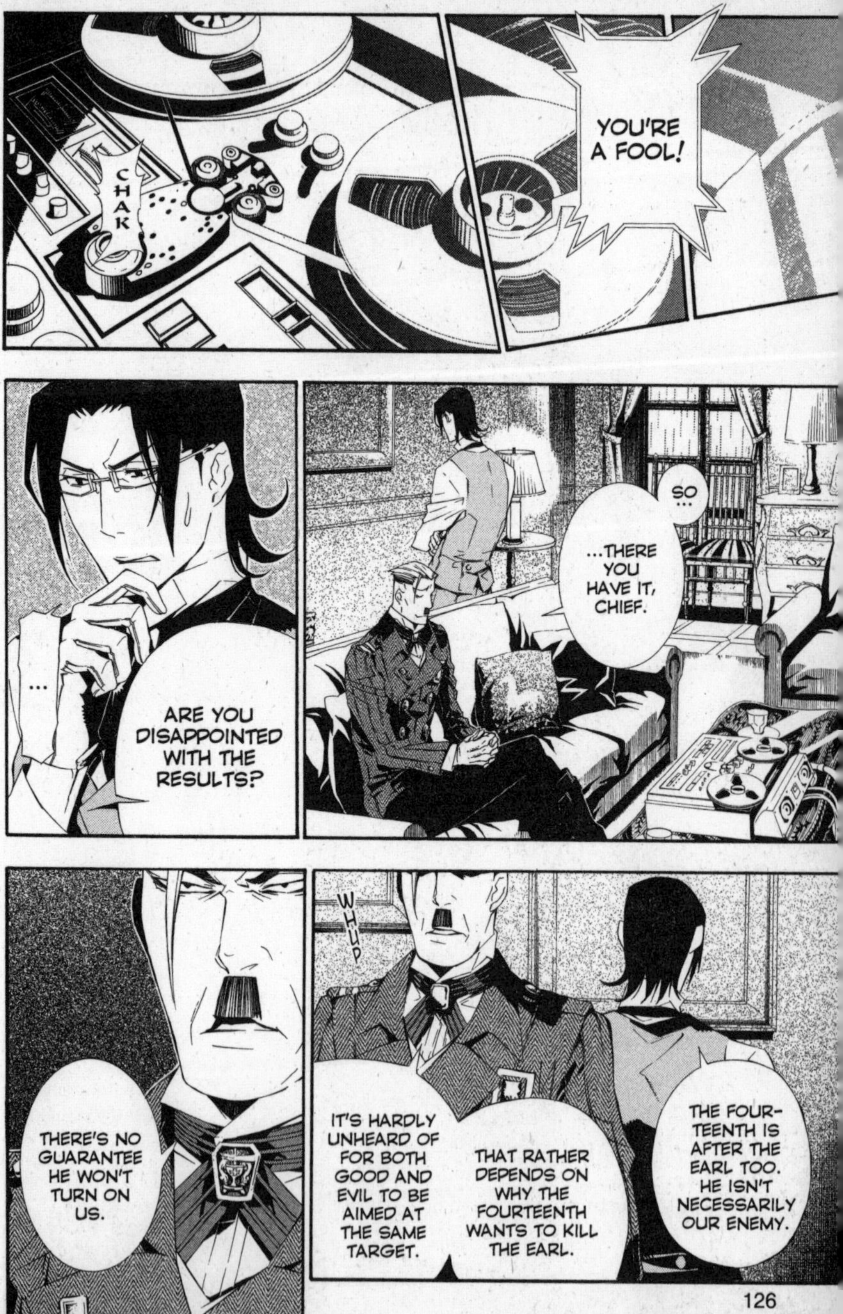
YOU'RE A FOOL!
CHAK
SO...
...THERE YOU HAVE IT, CHIEF.
ARE YOU DISAPPOINTED WITH THE RESULTS?
...
WHUP
THE FOURTEENTH IS AFTER THE EARL TOO. HE ISN'T NECESSARILY OUR ENEMY.
THAT RATHER DEPENDS ON WHY THE FOURTEENTH WANTS TO KILL THE EARL.
IT'S HARDLY UNHEARD OF FOR BOTH GOOD AND EVIL TO BE AIMED AT THE SAME TARGET.
THERE'S NO GUARANTEE HE WON'T TURN ON US.

READ THIS WAY

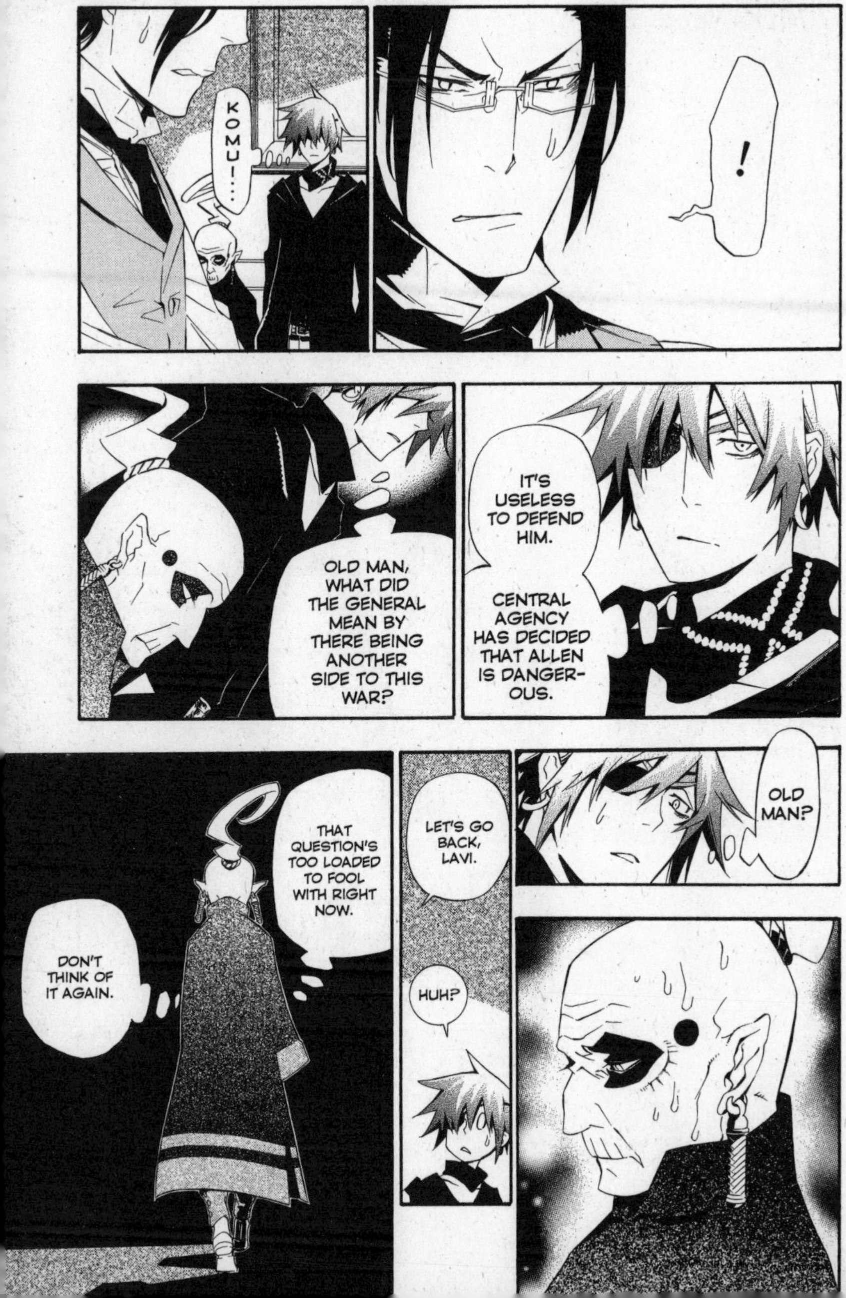
!
KOMUI...
IT'S USELESS TO DEFEND HIM.
CENTRAL AGENCY HAS DECIDED THAT ALLEN IS DANGEROUS.
OLD MAN, WHAT DID THE GENERAL MEAN BY THERE BEING ANOTHER SIDE TO THIS WAR?
OLD MAN?
LET'S GO BACK, LAVI.
HUH?
THAT QUESTION'S TOO LOADED TO FOOL WITH RIGHT NOW.
DON'T THINK OF IT AGAIN.

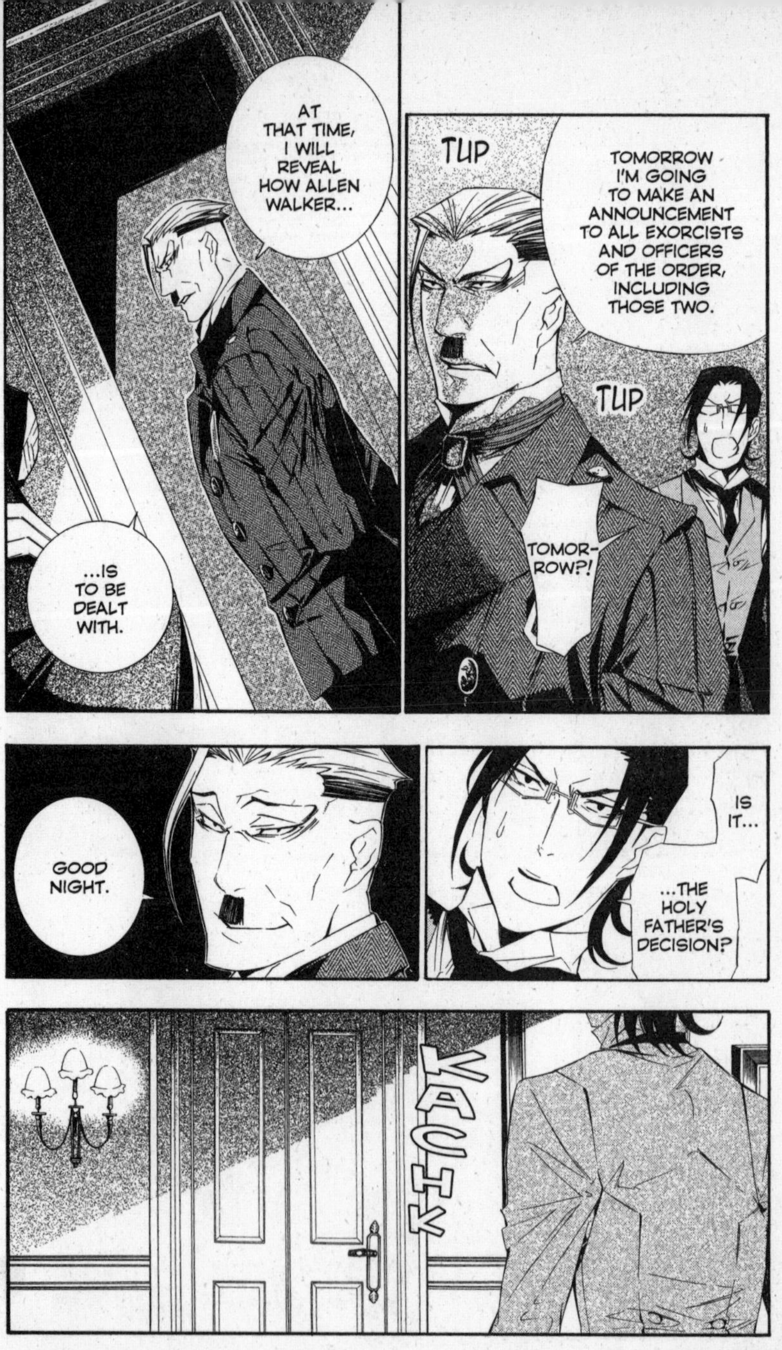
TUP
TOMORROW I'M GOING TO MAKE AN ANNOUNCEMENT TO ALL EXORCISTS AND OFFICERS OF THE ORDER, INCLUDING THOSE TWO.
TUP
TOMOR-ROW?!
AT THAT TIME, I WILL REVEAL HOW ALLEN WALKER...
...IS TO BE DEALT WITH.
IS IT...
...THE HOLY FATHER'S DECISION?
GOOD NIGHT.
KACHK

READ THIS WAY

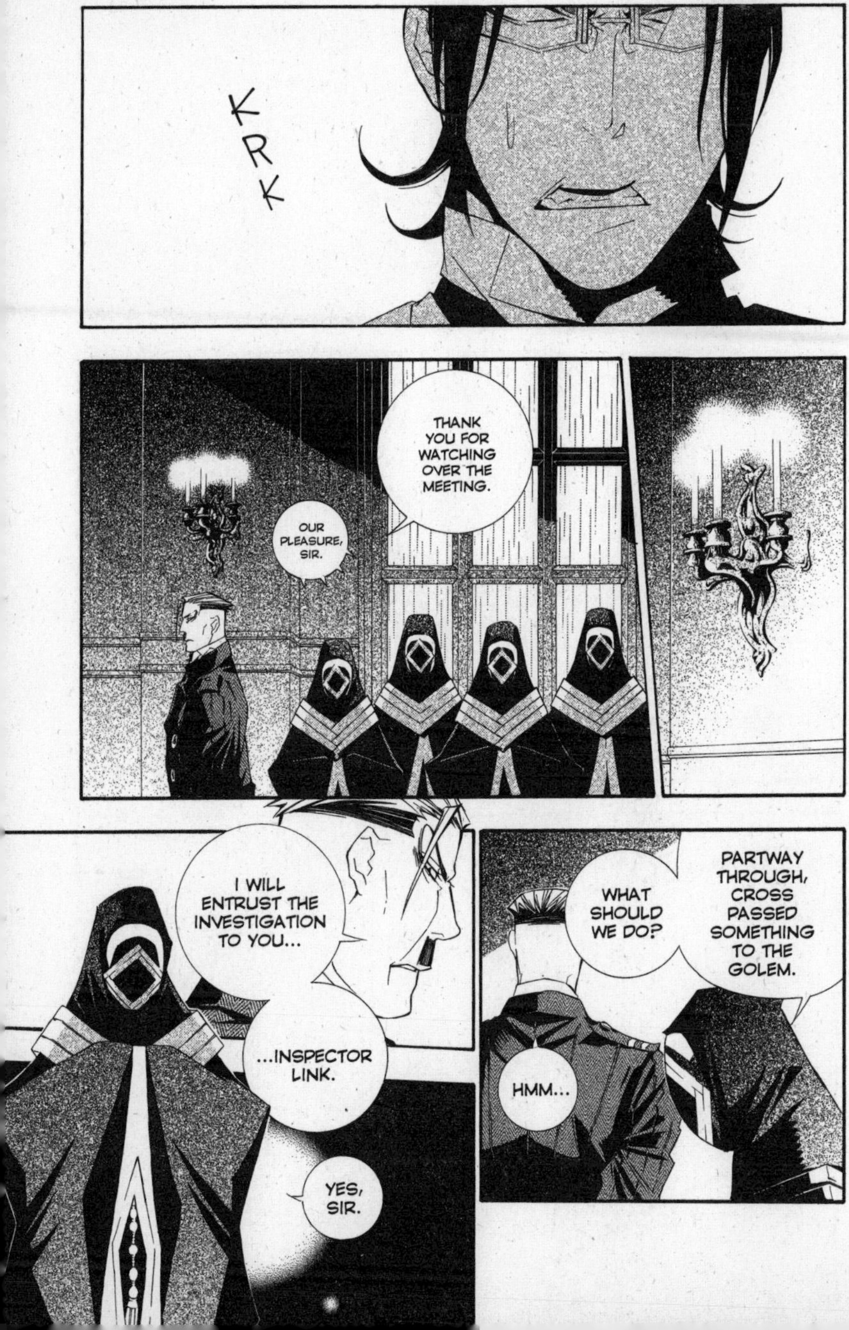
KRK
THANK YOU FOR WATCHING OVER THE MEETING.
OUR PLEASURE, SIR.
PARTWAY THROUGH, CROSS PASSED SOMETHING TO THE GOLEM.
WHAT SHOULD WE DO?
HMM...
I WILL ENTRUST THE INVESTIGATION TO YOU...
...INSPECTOR LINK.
YES, SIR.

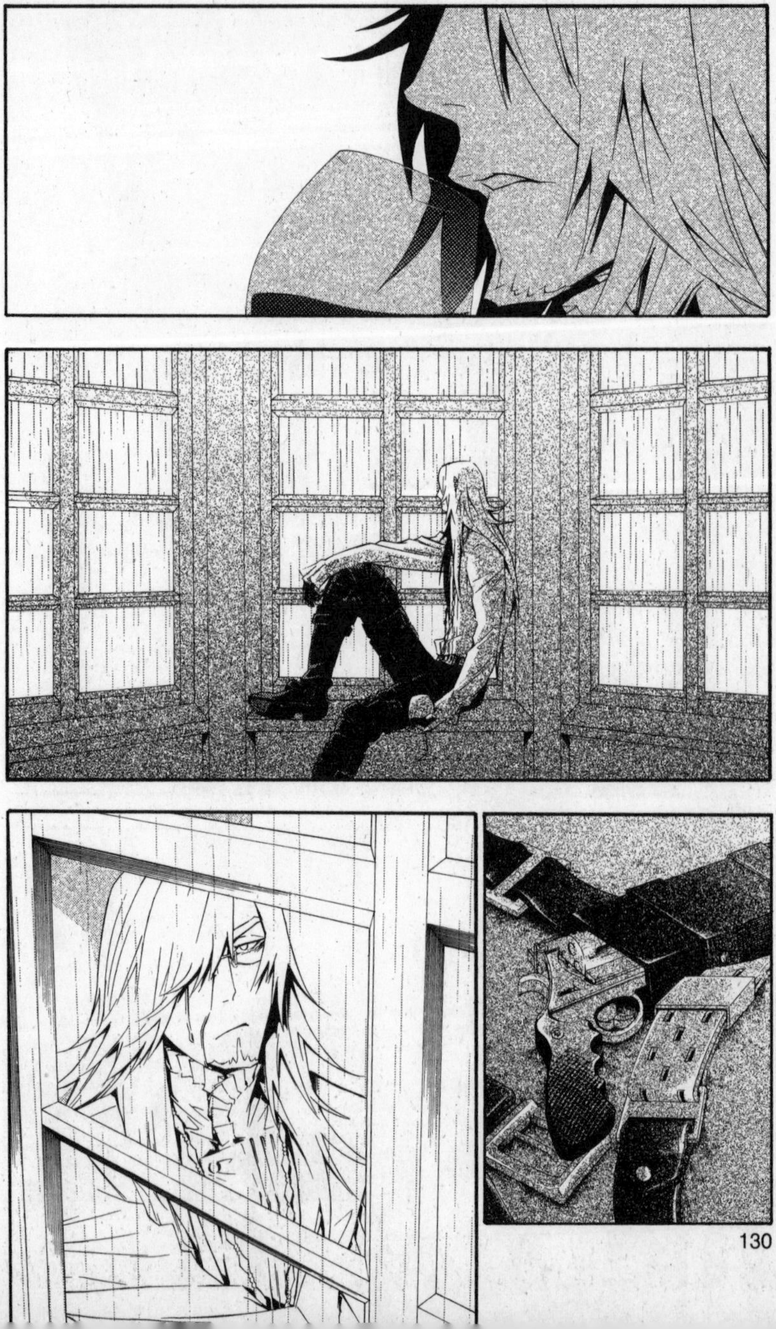

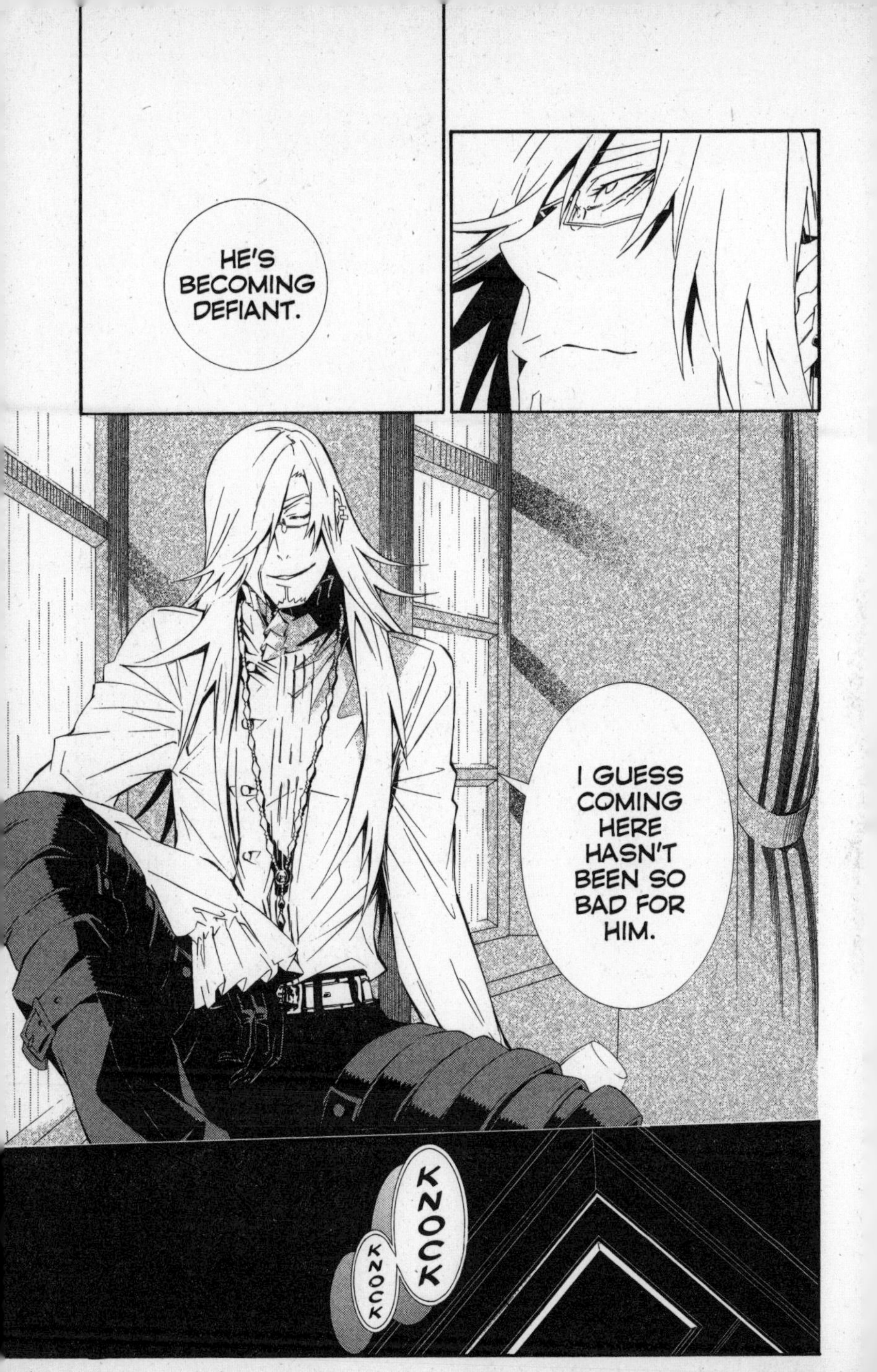
HE'S BECOMING DEFIANT.
I GUESS COMING HERE HASN'T BEEN SO BAD FOR HIM.
KNOCK
KNOCK

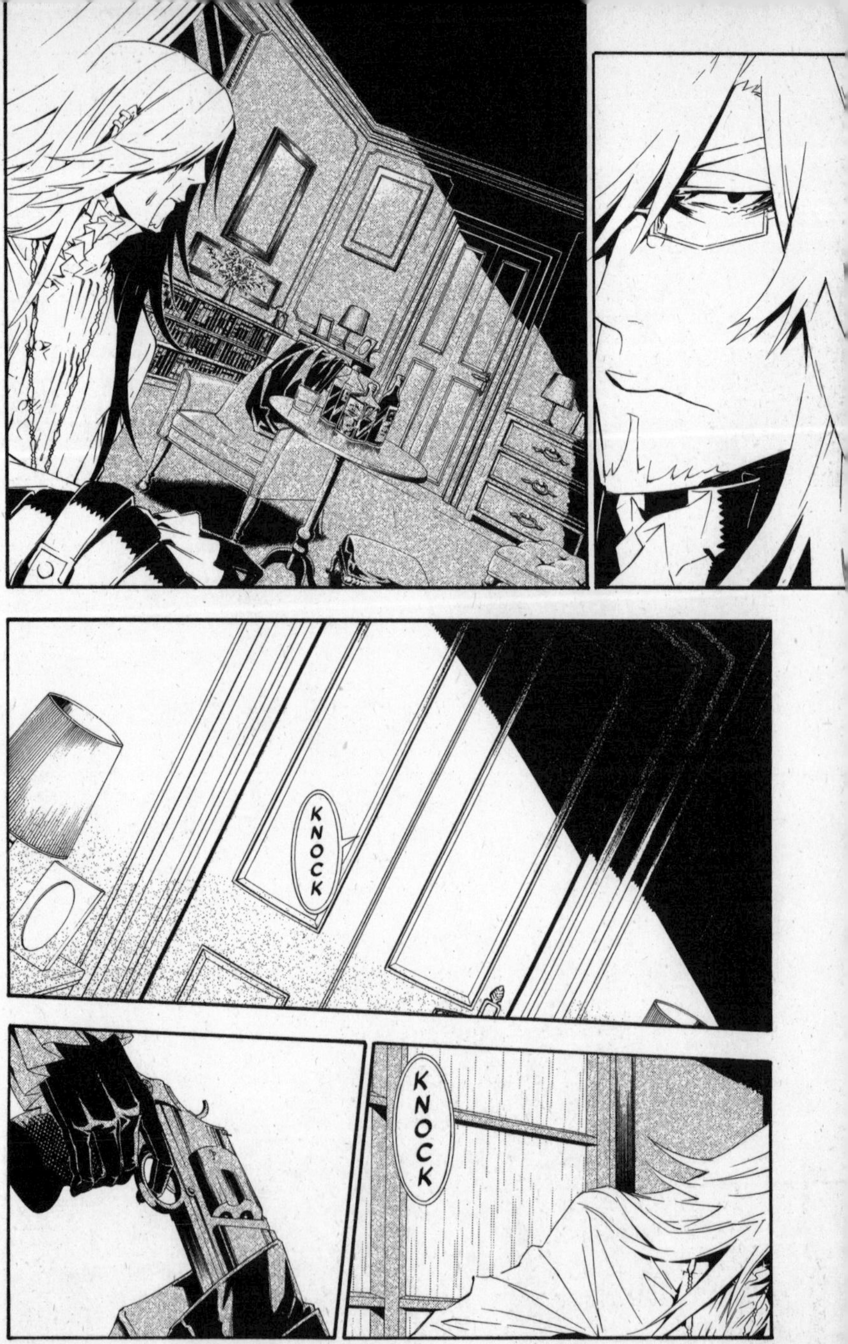
KNOCK
KNOCK

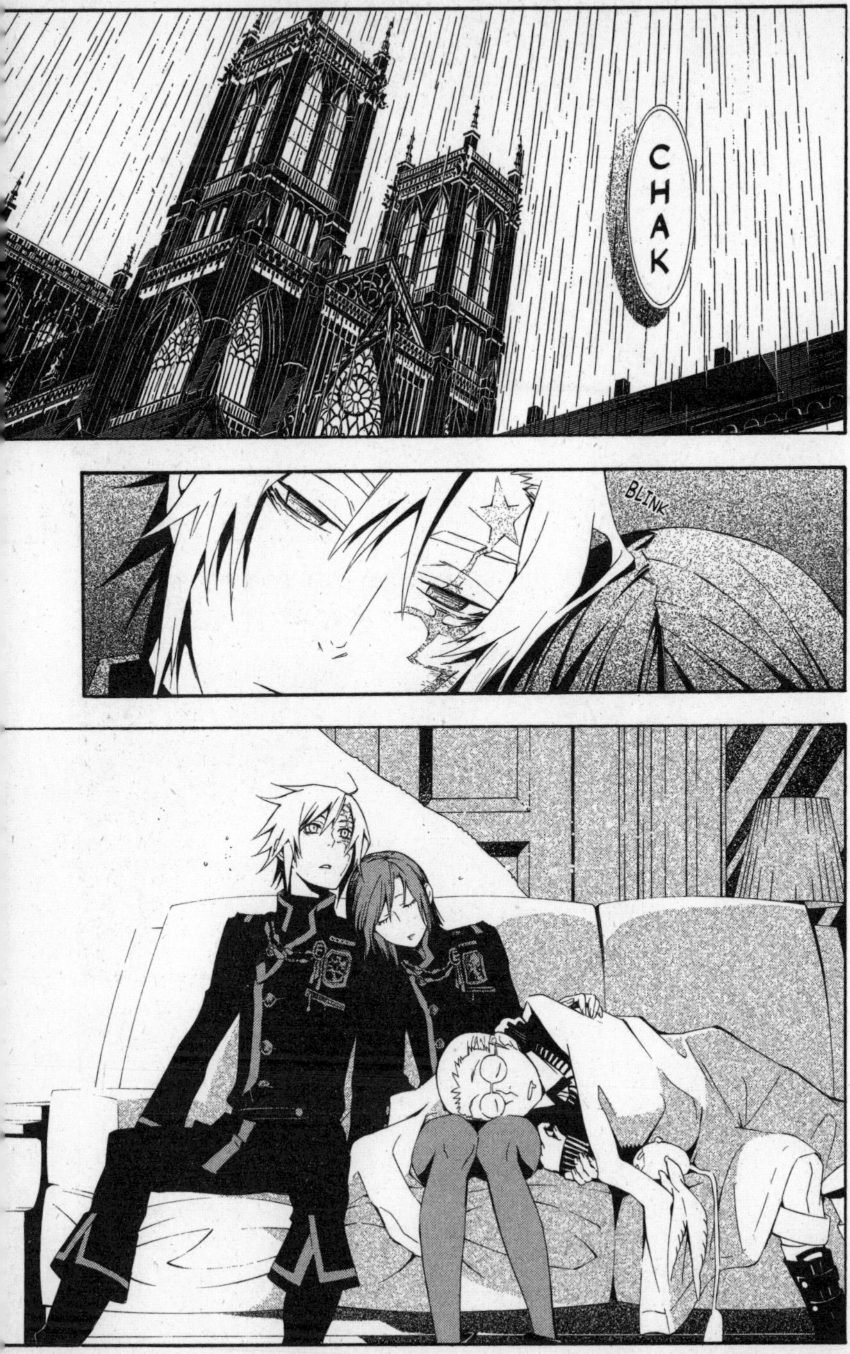
CHAK
BLINK

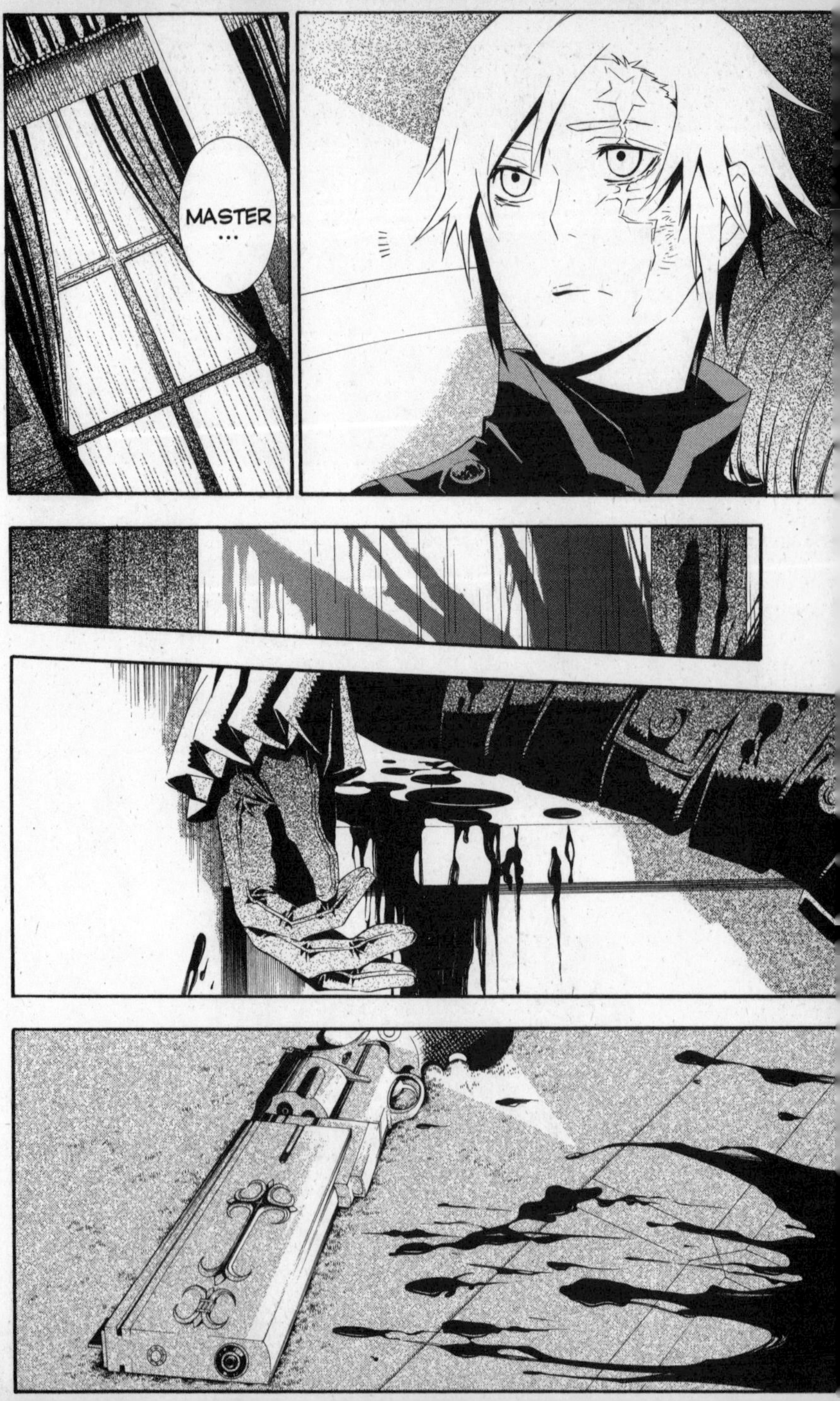
MASTER
...

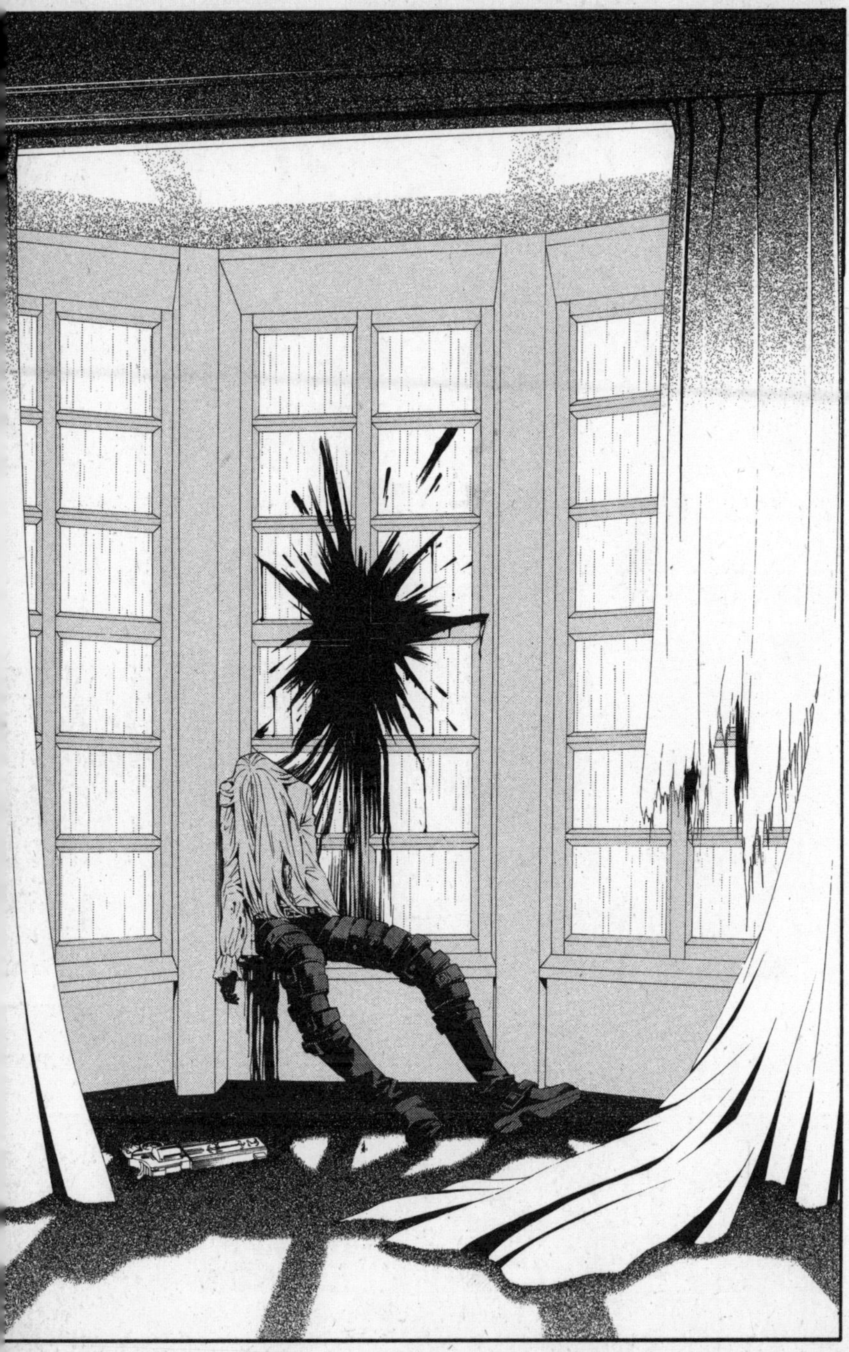

THE PEOPLE OF D.GRAY-HOUSE

THE FATHER'S ELEGY

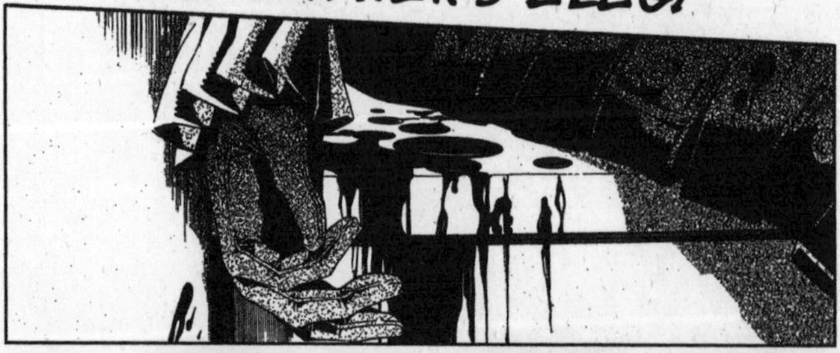

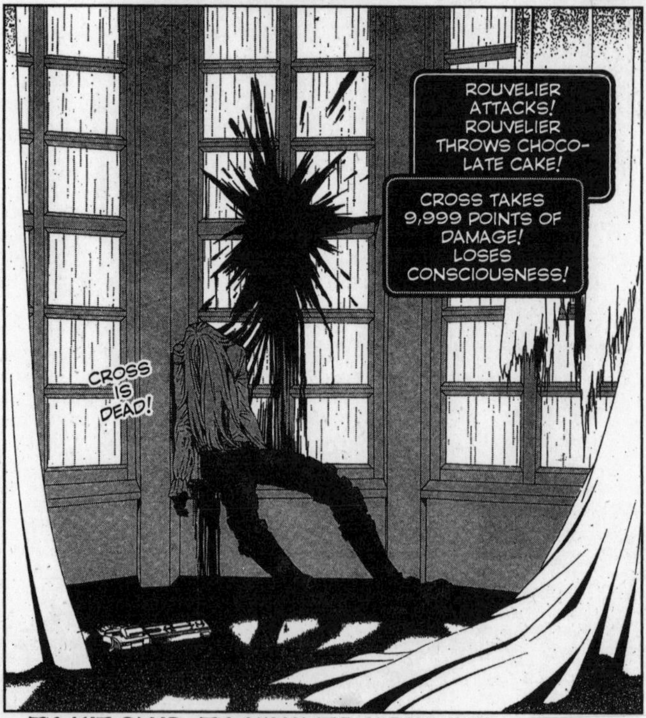
ROUVELIER ATTACKS! ROUVELIER THROWS CHOCO-LATE CAKE!
CROSS TAKES 9,999 POINTS OF DAMAGE! LOSES CONSCIOUSNESS!
CROSS IS DEAD!

IT'S NOT BLOOD. IT'S CHOCOLATE CREAM. (LOL)

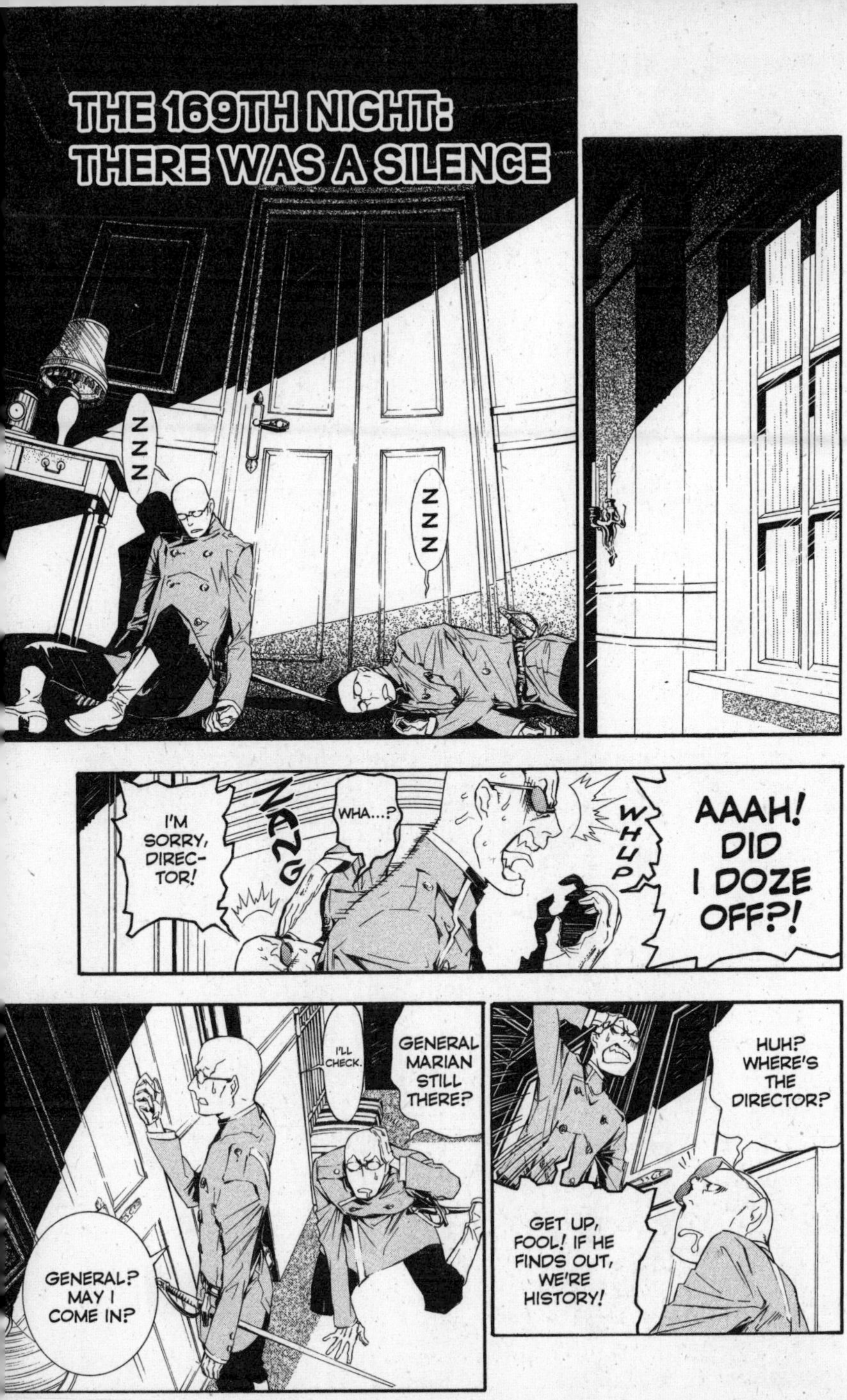
THE 169TH NIGHT: THERE WAS A SILENCE
Z Z Z
Z Z Z
AAAH! DID I DOZE OFF?!
WHUP
WHA...?
NANG
I'M SORRY, DIREC-TOR!
HUH? WHERE'S THE DIRECTOR?
GET UP, FOOL! IF HE FINDS OUT, WE'RE HISTORY!
GENERAL MARIAN STILL THERE?
I'LL CHECK.
GENERAL? MAY I COME IN?

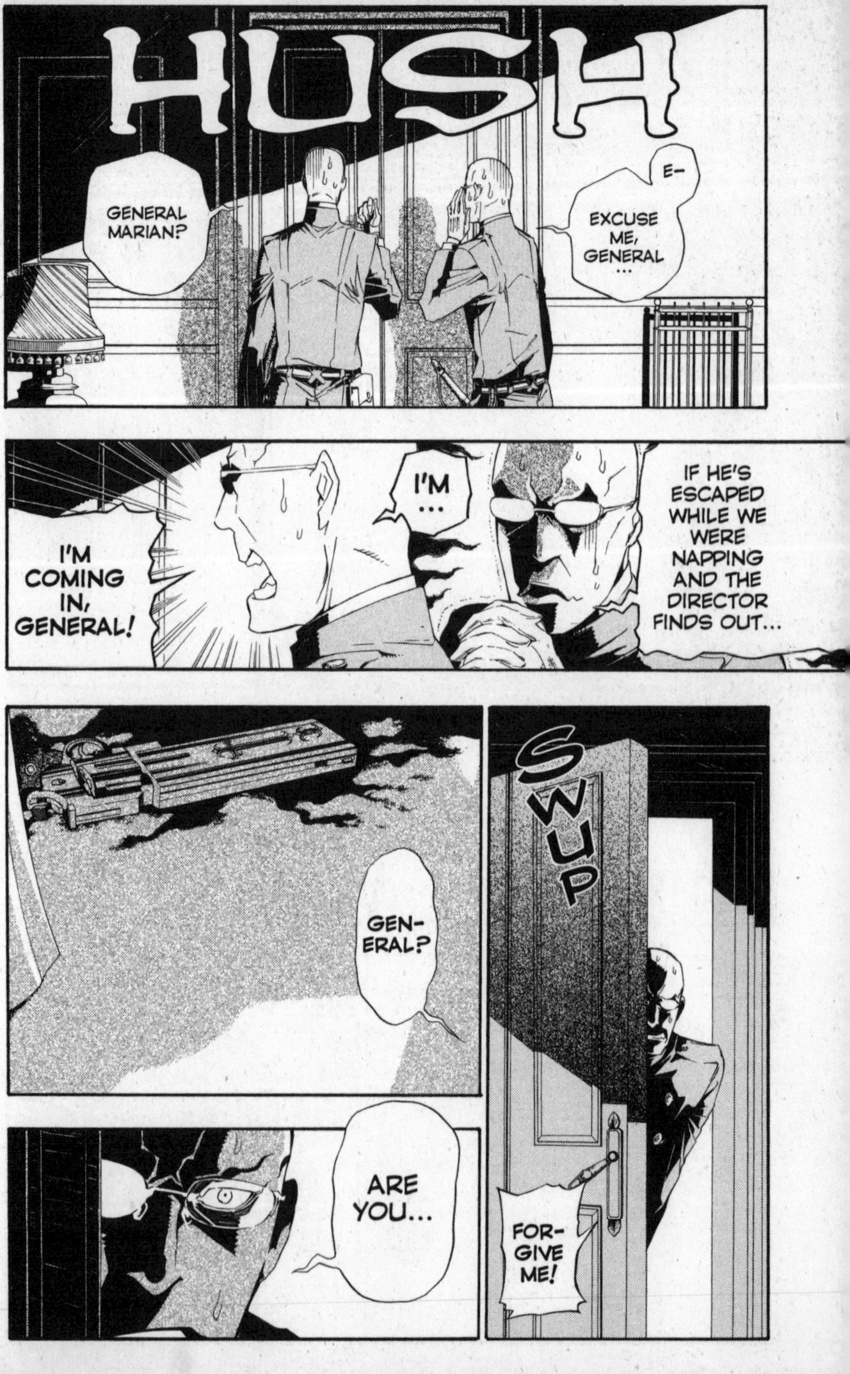
HUSH
E–
EXCUSE ME, GENERAL ...
GENERAL MARIAN?
IF HE'S ESCAPED WHILE WE WERE NAPPING AND THE DIRECTOR FINDS OUT...
I'M ...
I'M COMING IN, GENERAL!
SWUP
FOR-GIVE ME!
GEN-ERAL?
ARE YOU...

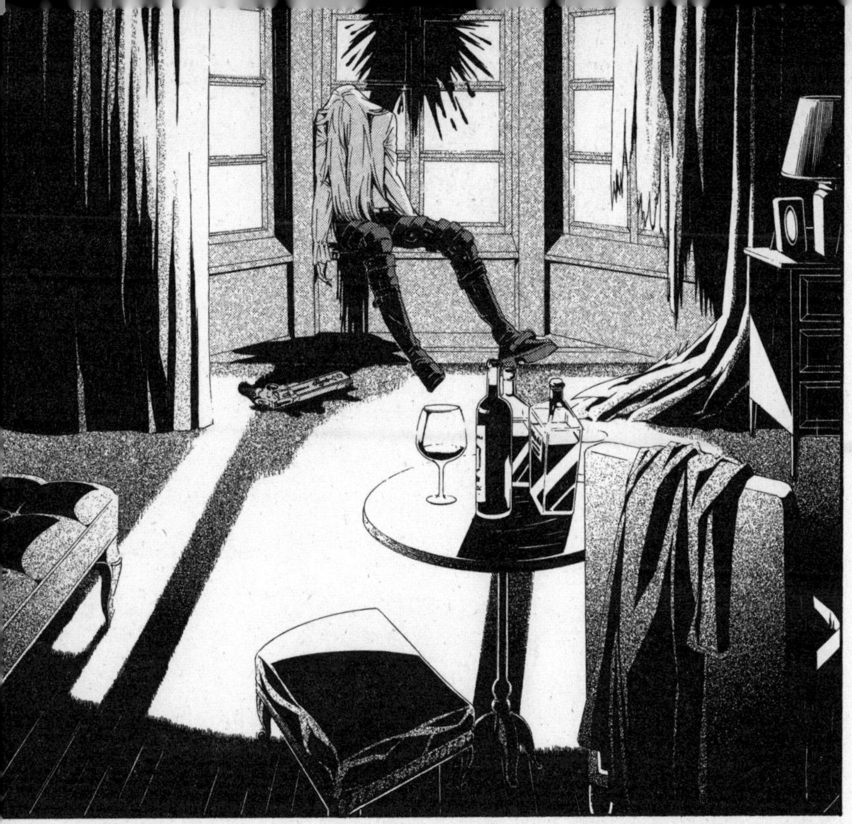

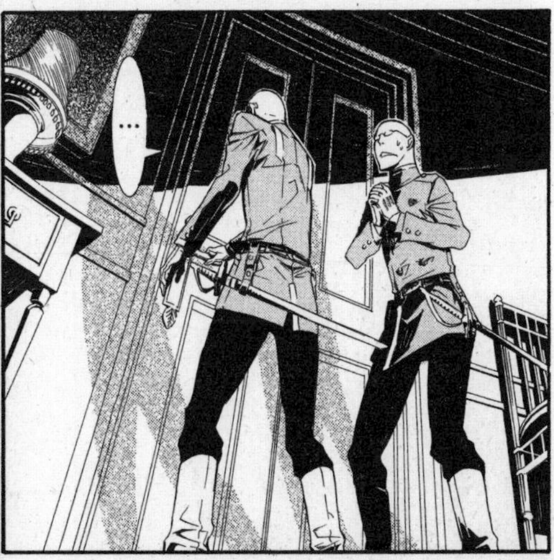
...

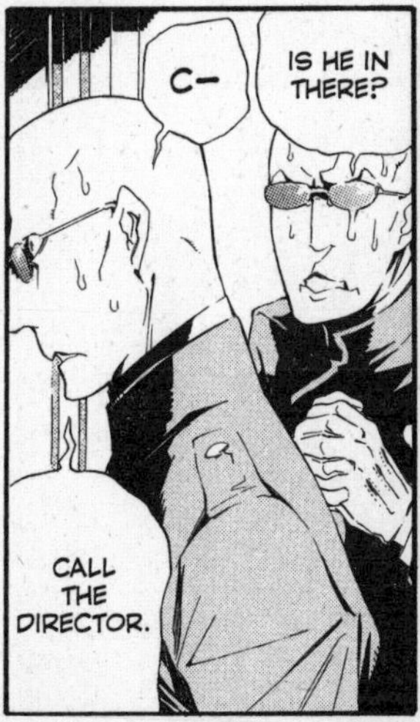
IS HE IN THERE?
C–
CALL THE DIRECTOR.

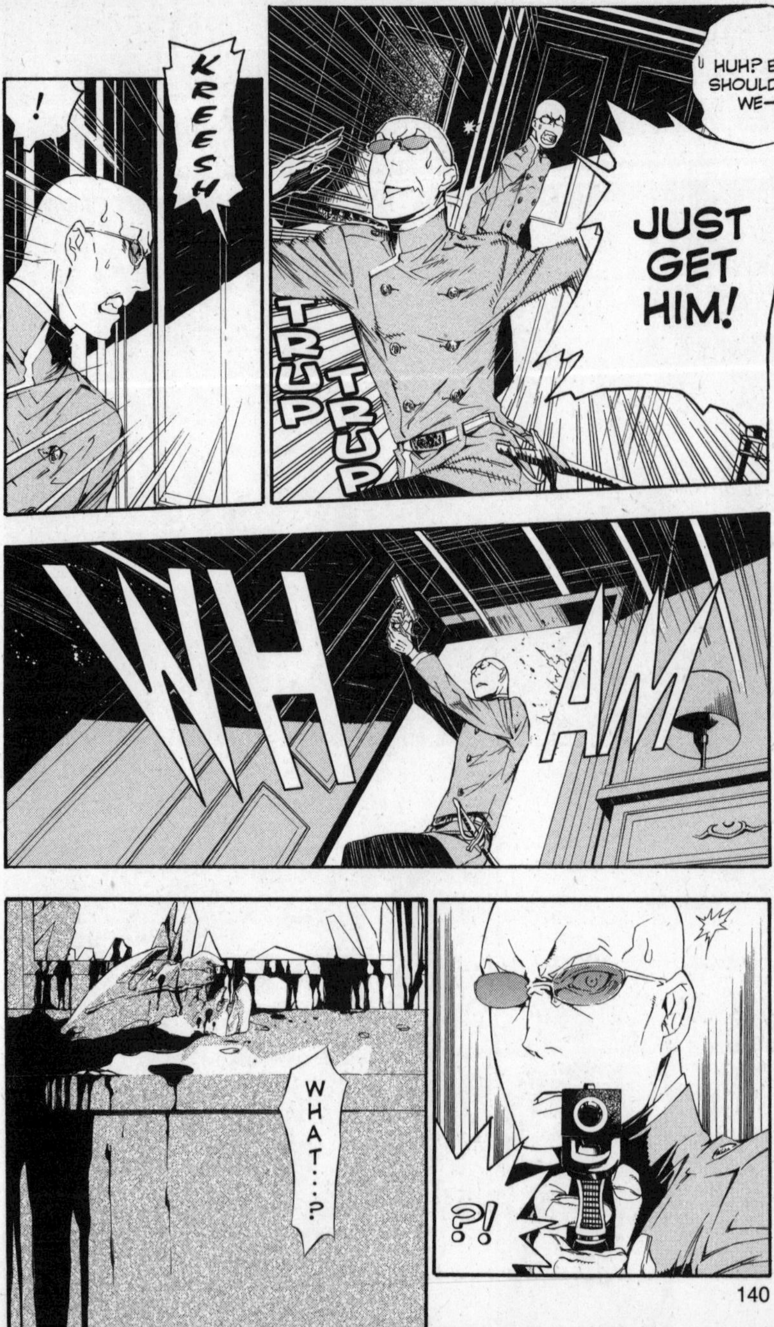
HUH? BUT SHOULDN'T WE–
JUST GET HIM!
TRUP TRUP
KREESH
!
WHAM
?!
WHAT...?

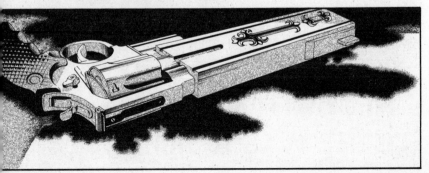

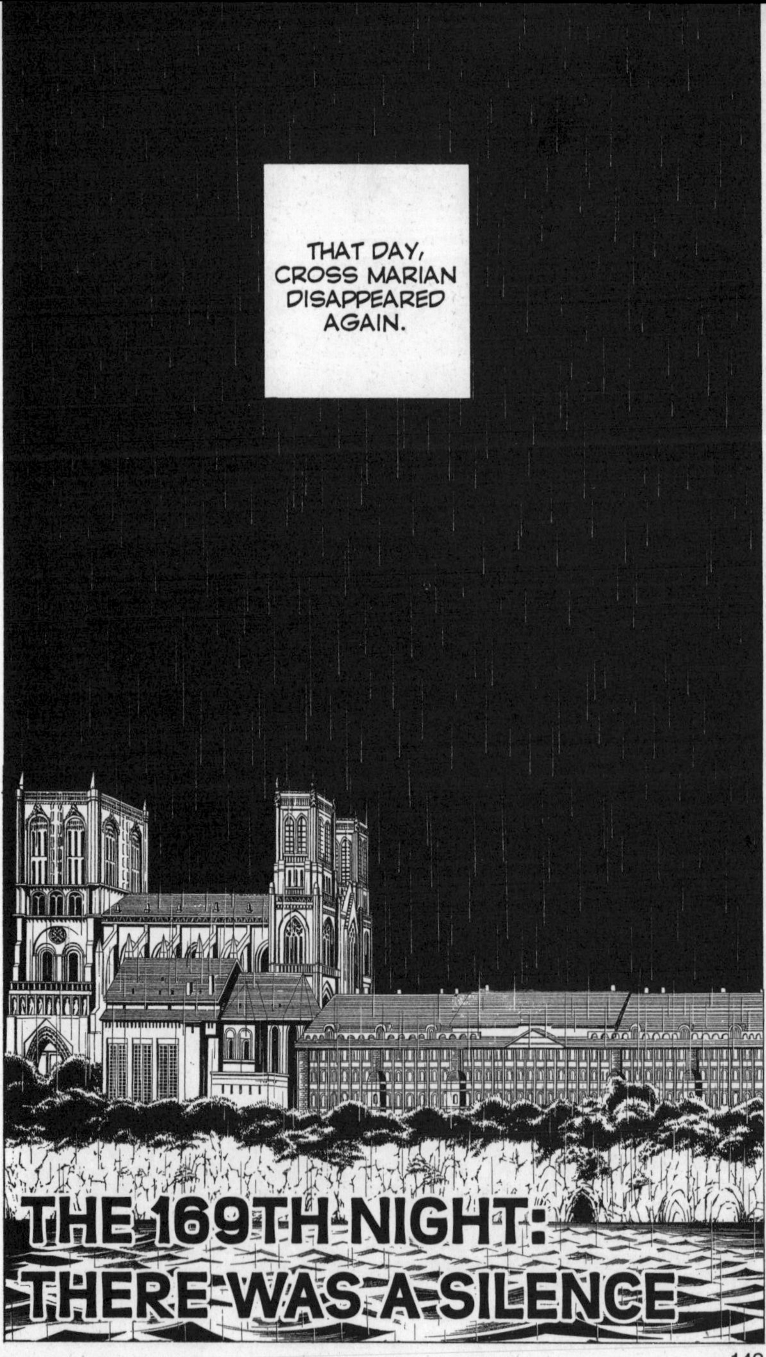
THAT DAY, CROSS MARIAN DISAPPEARED AGAIN.
THE 169TH NIGHT: THERE WAS A SILENCE

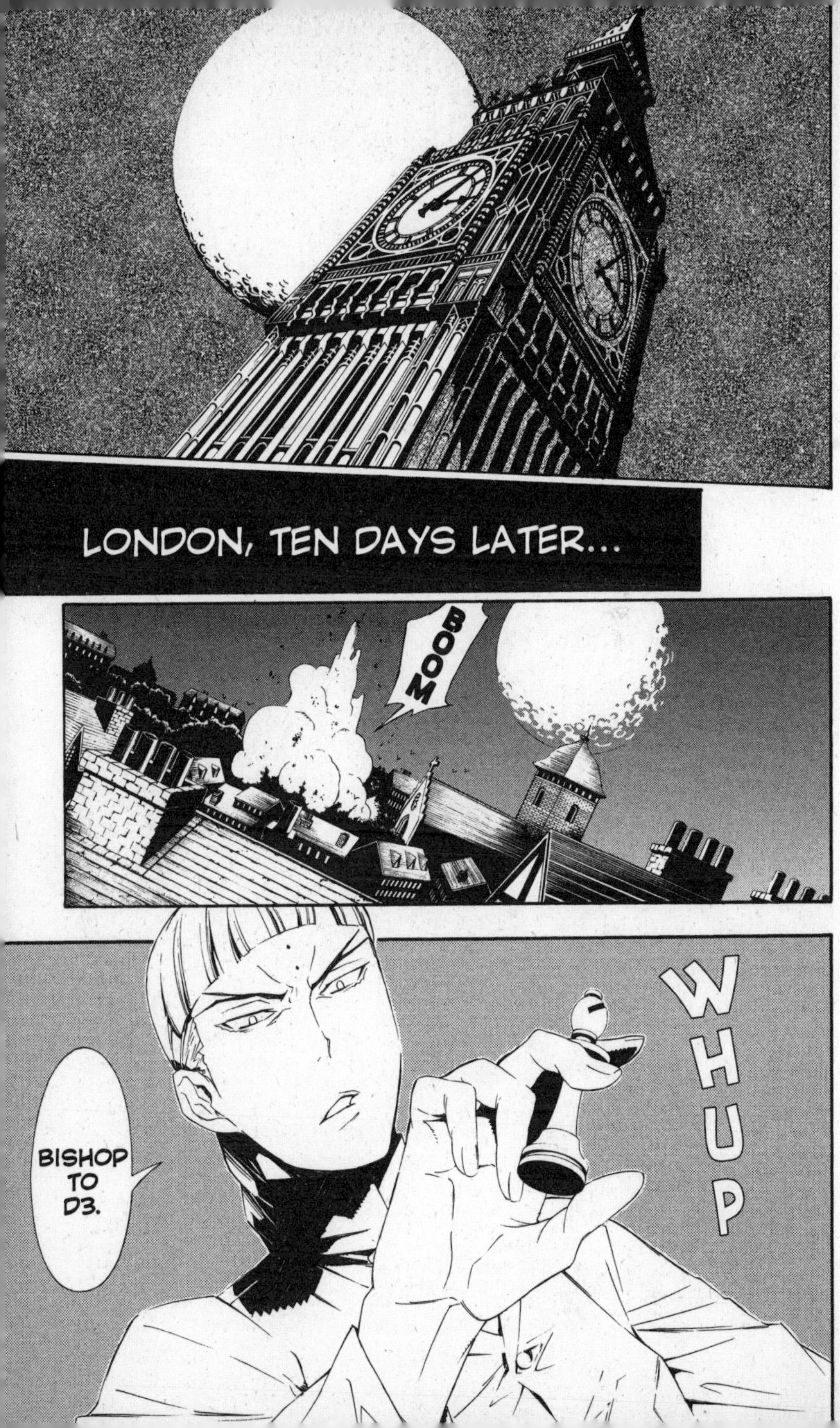
LONDON, TEN DAYS LATER...
BOOM
WHUP
BISHOP TO D3.

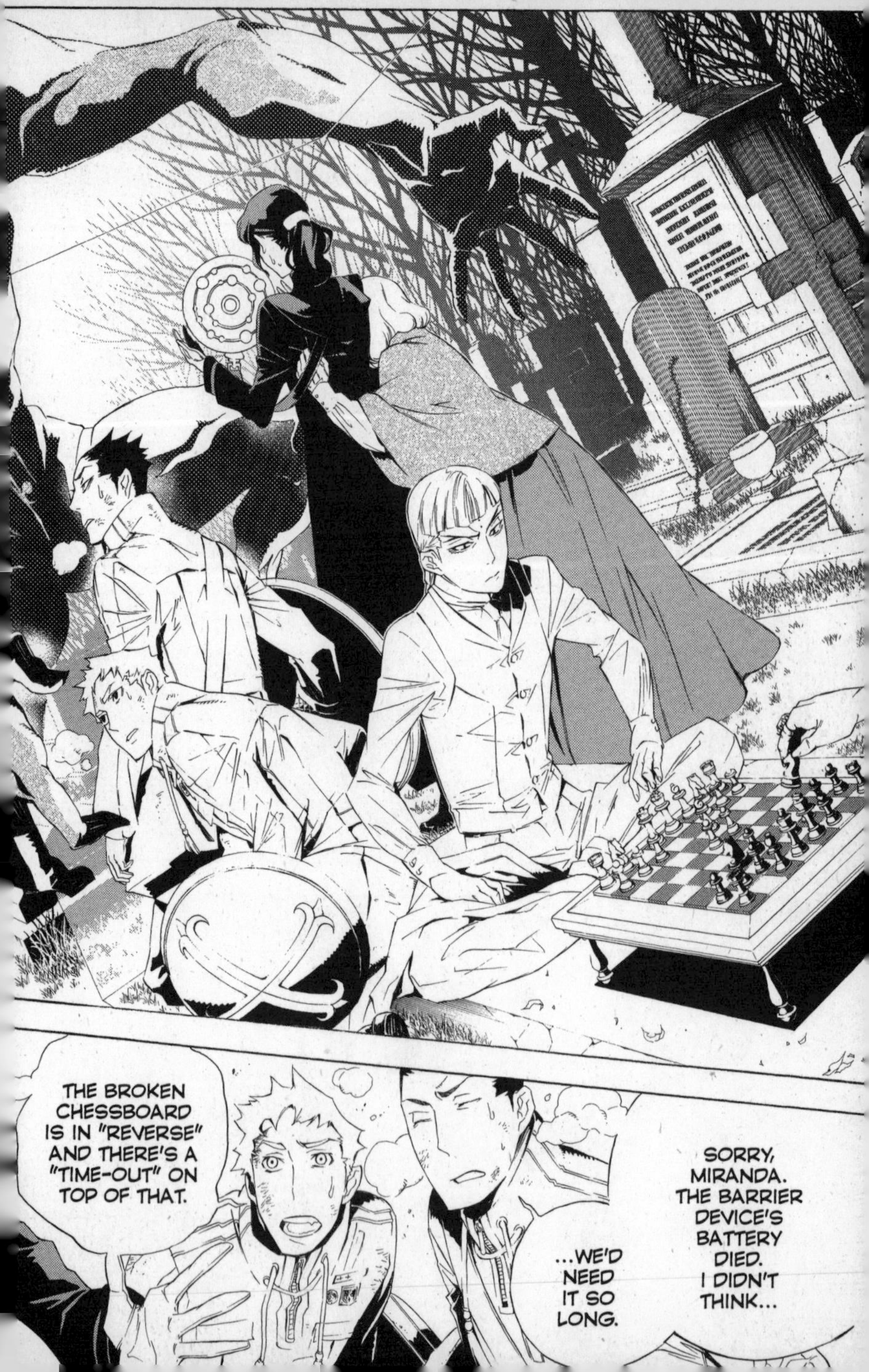
SORRY, MIRANDA. THE BARRIER DEVICE'S BATTERY DIED. I DIDN'T THINK...
...WE'D NEED IT SO LONG.
THE BROKEN CHESSBOARD IS IN "REVERSE" AND THERE'S A "TIME-OUT" ON TOP OF THAT.

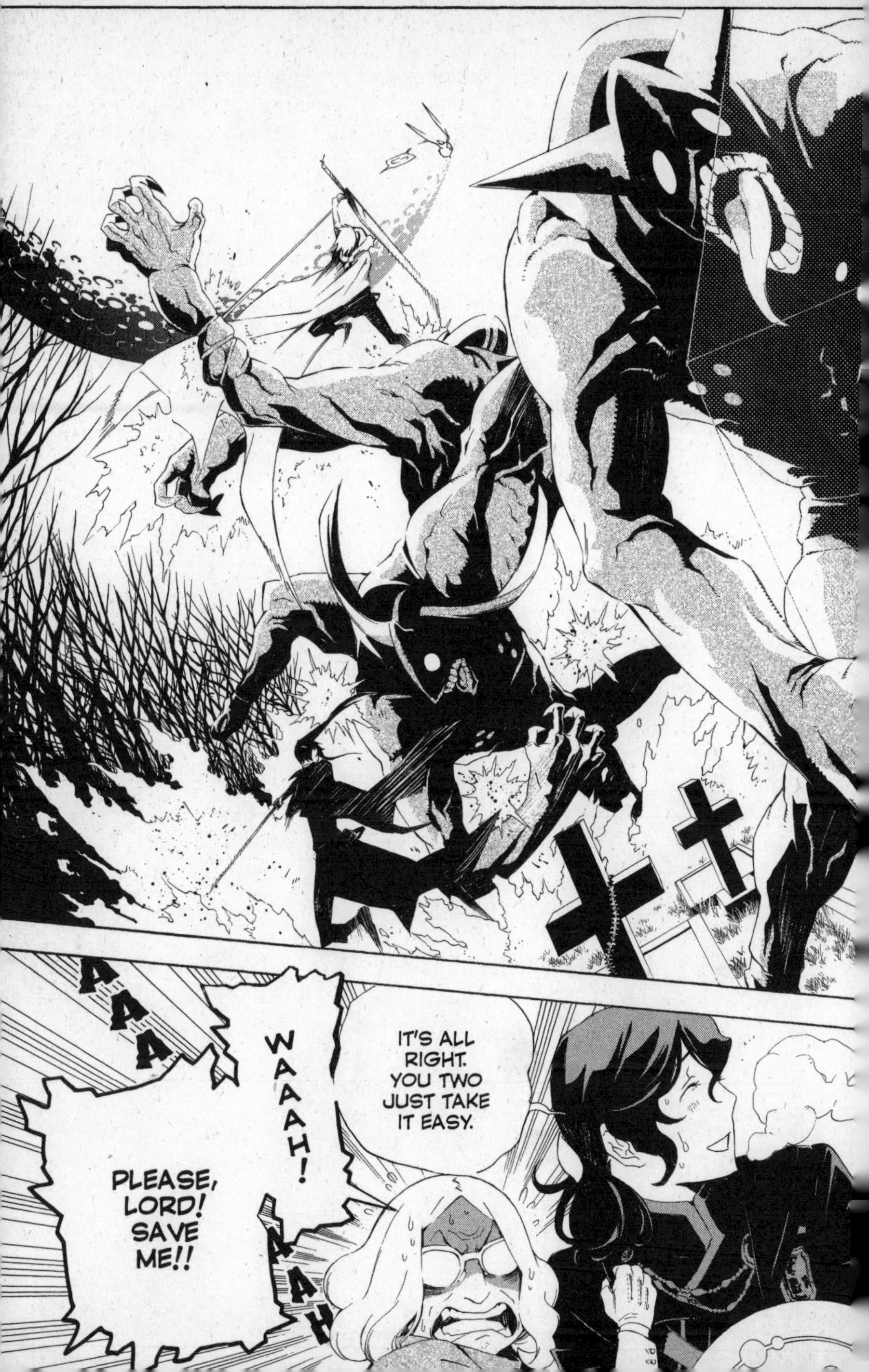
IT'S ALL RIGHT. YOU TWO JUST TAKE IT EASY.
WAAAH!
AAAH
PLEASE, LORD! SAVE ME!!
AAA

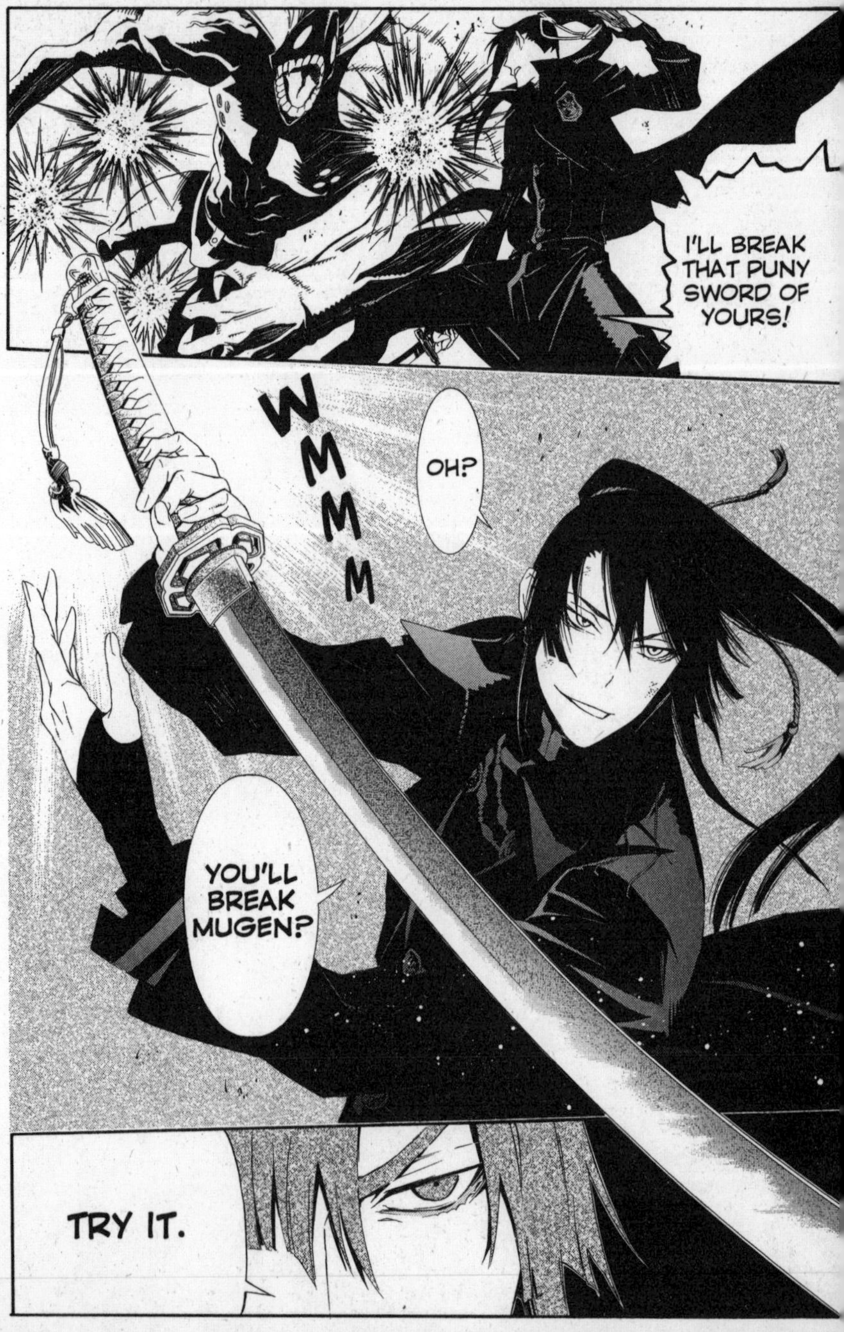
I'LL BREAK THAT PUNY SWORD OF YOURS!
OH?
WMMM
YOU'LL BREAK MUGEN?
TRY IT.

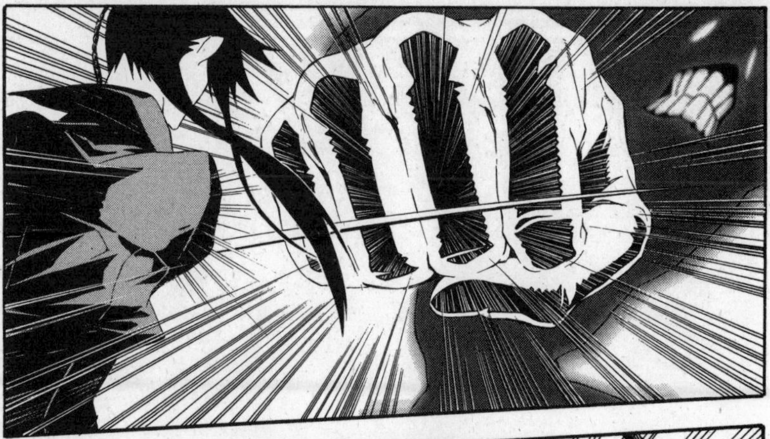
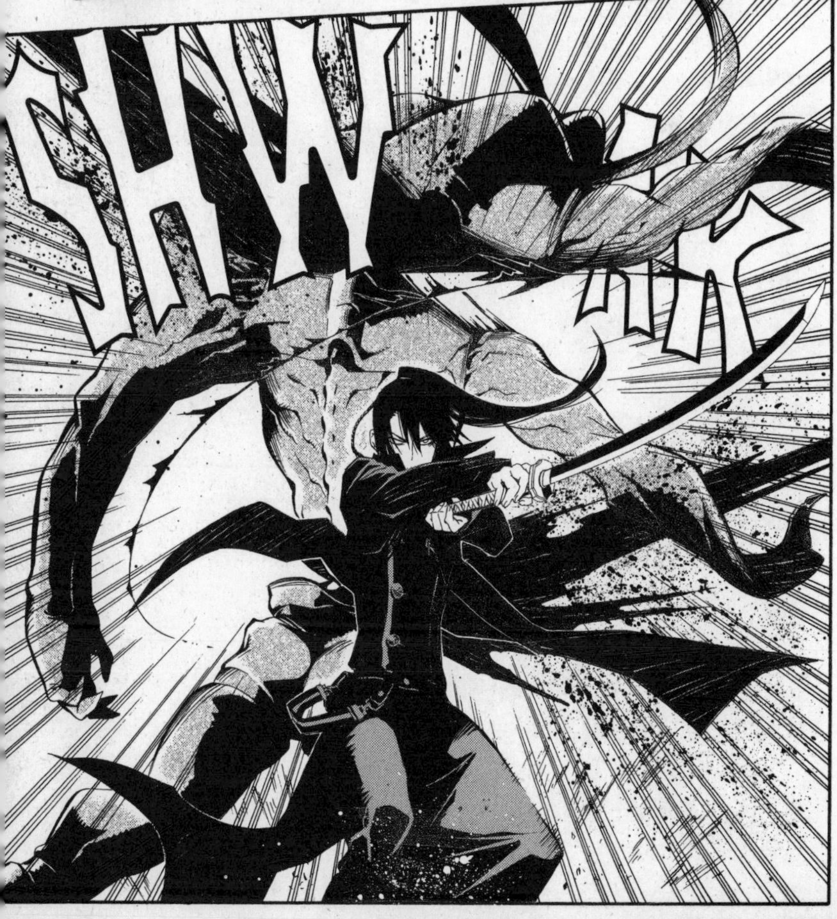
SHWIK

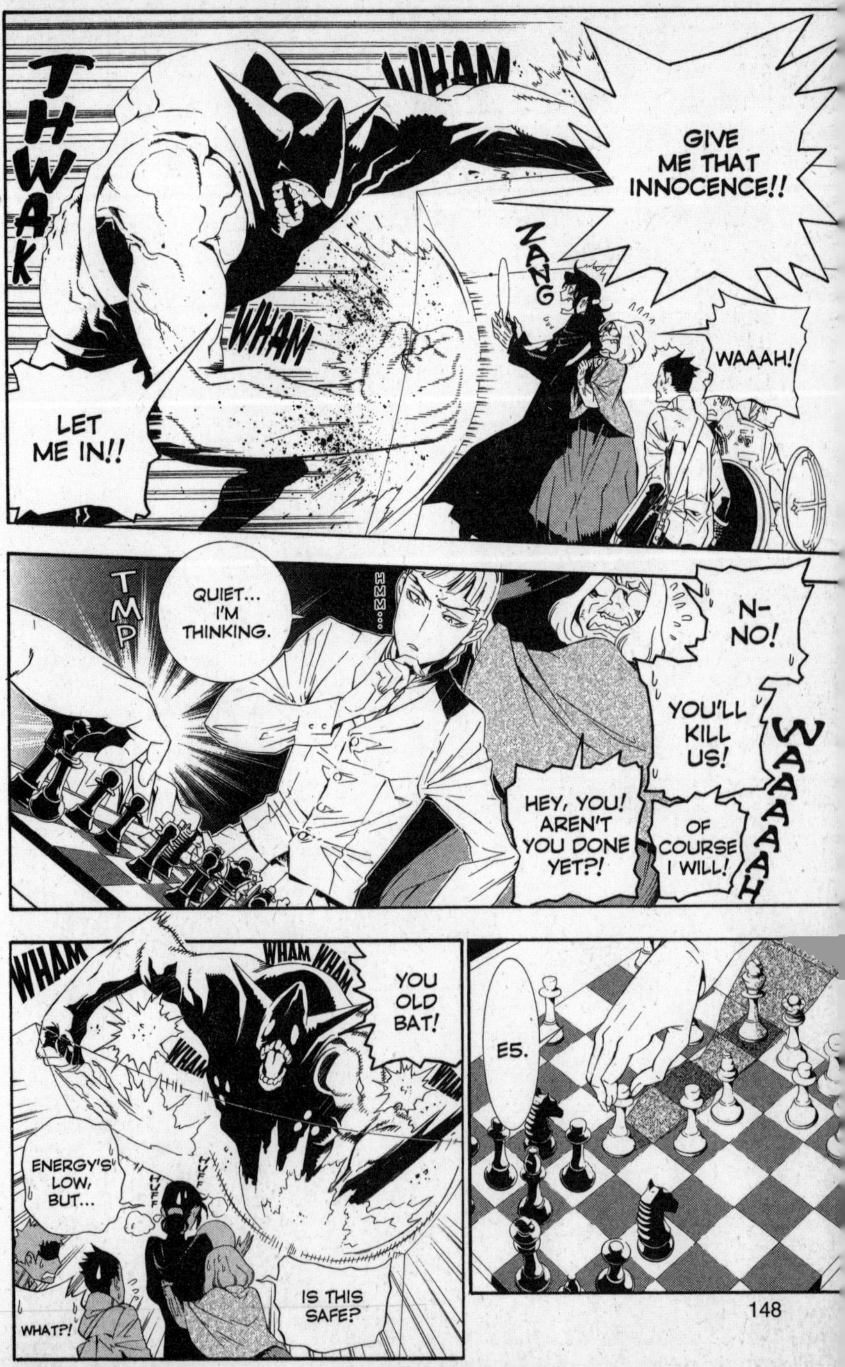
GIVE ME THAT INNOCENCE!!
WHAM
ZANG
WAAAH!
THWAK
WHAM
LET ME IN!!
N-NO!
YOU'LL KILL US!
WAAAAAH
OF COURSE I WILL!
HEY, YOU! AREN'T YOU DONE YET?!
HMM...
QUIET... I'M THINKING.
TMP
E5.
YOU OLD BAT!
WHAM WHAM
WHAM
WHAM
WHAM
ENERGY'S LOW, BUT...
HUFF HUFF
IS THIS SAFE?
WHAT?!

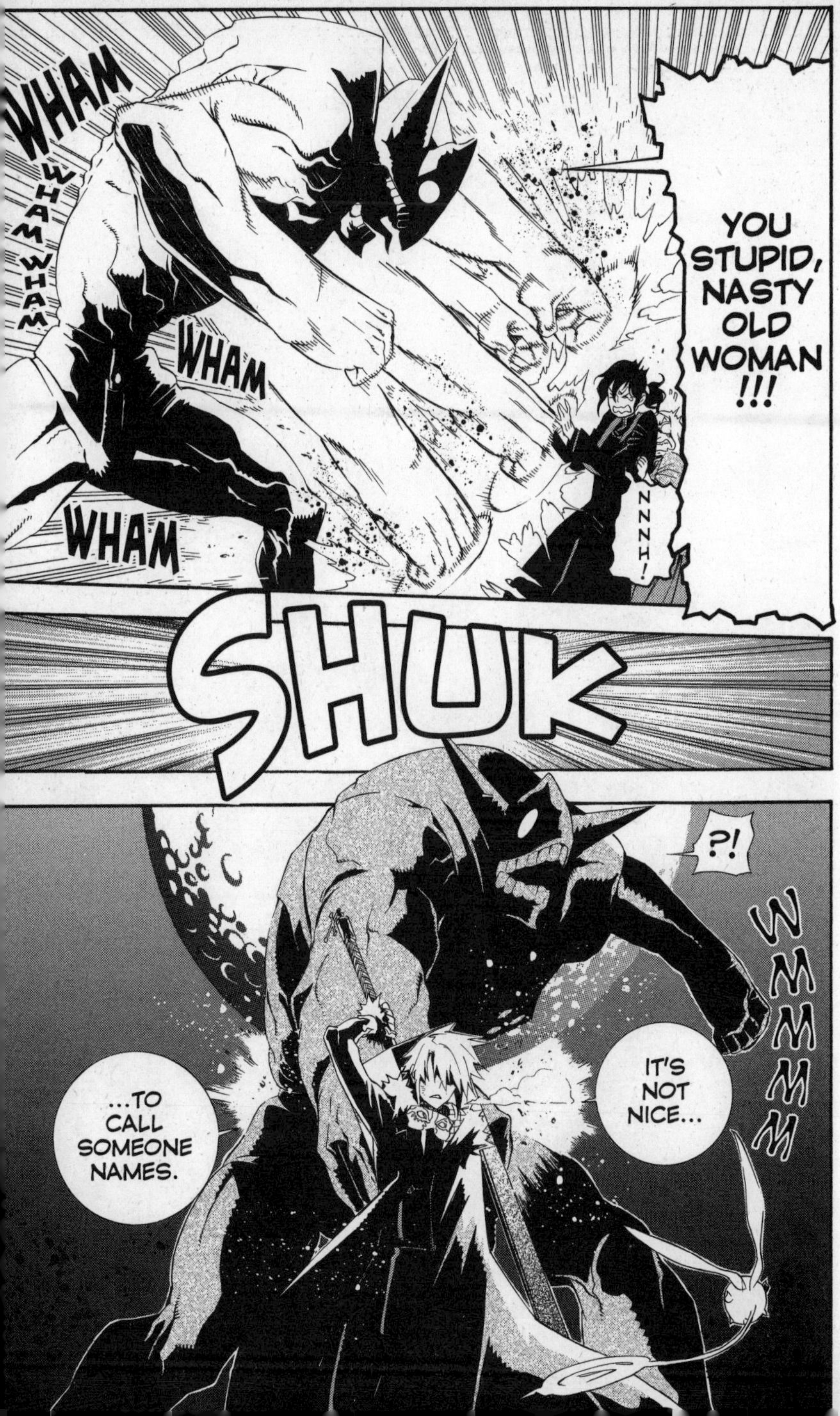
YOU STUPID, NASTY OLD WOMAN!!!
NNNH!
WHAM
WHAM WHAM WHAM
WHAM
WHAM
SHUK
?!
WMMMM
IT'S NOT NICE...
...TO CALL SOMEONE NAMES.

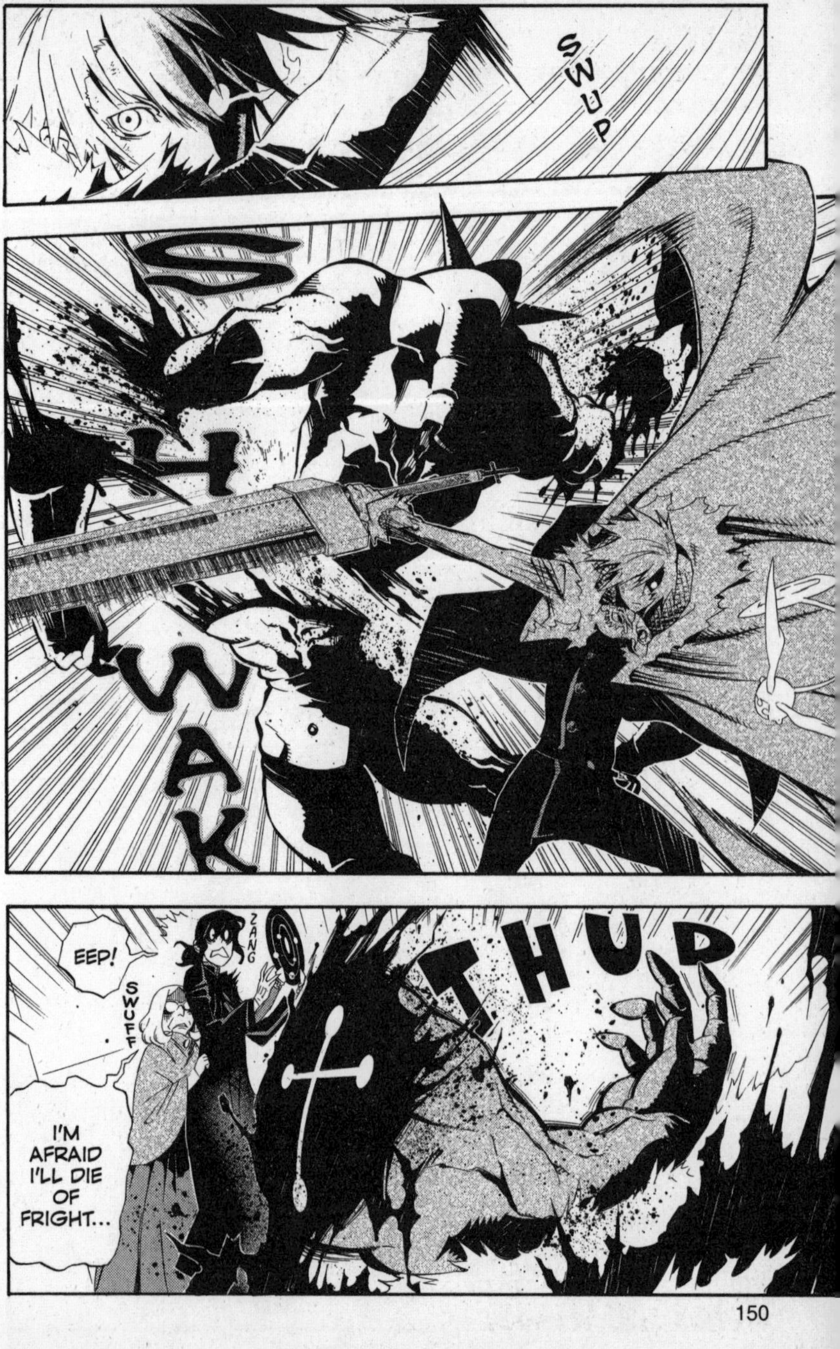
SWUP
SHWAK
THUD
ZANG
EEP!
SWUFF
I'M AFRAID I'LL DIE OF FRIGHT...

READ THIS WAY

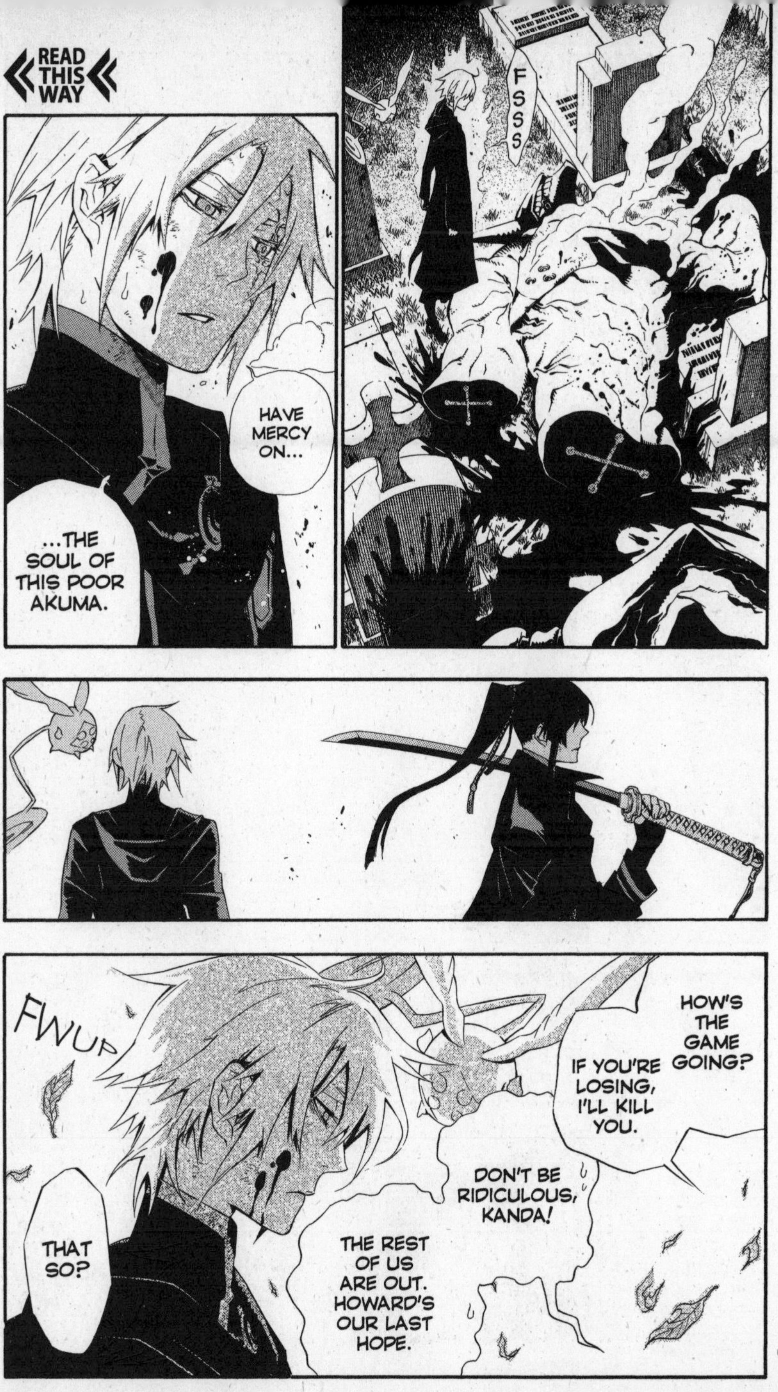

FSSS
HAVE MERCY ON...
...THE SOUL OF THIS POOR AKUMA.
HOW'S THE GAME GOING?
IF YOU'RE LOSING, I'LL KILL YOU.
DON'T BE RIDICULOUS, KANDA!
THE REST OF US ARE OUT. HOWARD'S OUR LAST HOPE.
FWUP
THAT SO?

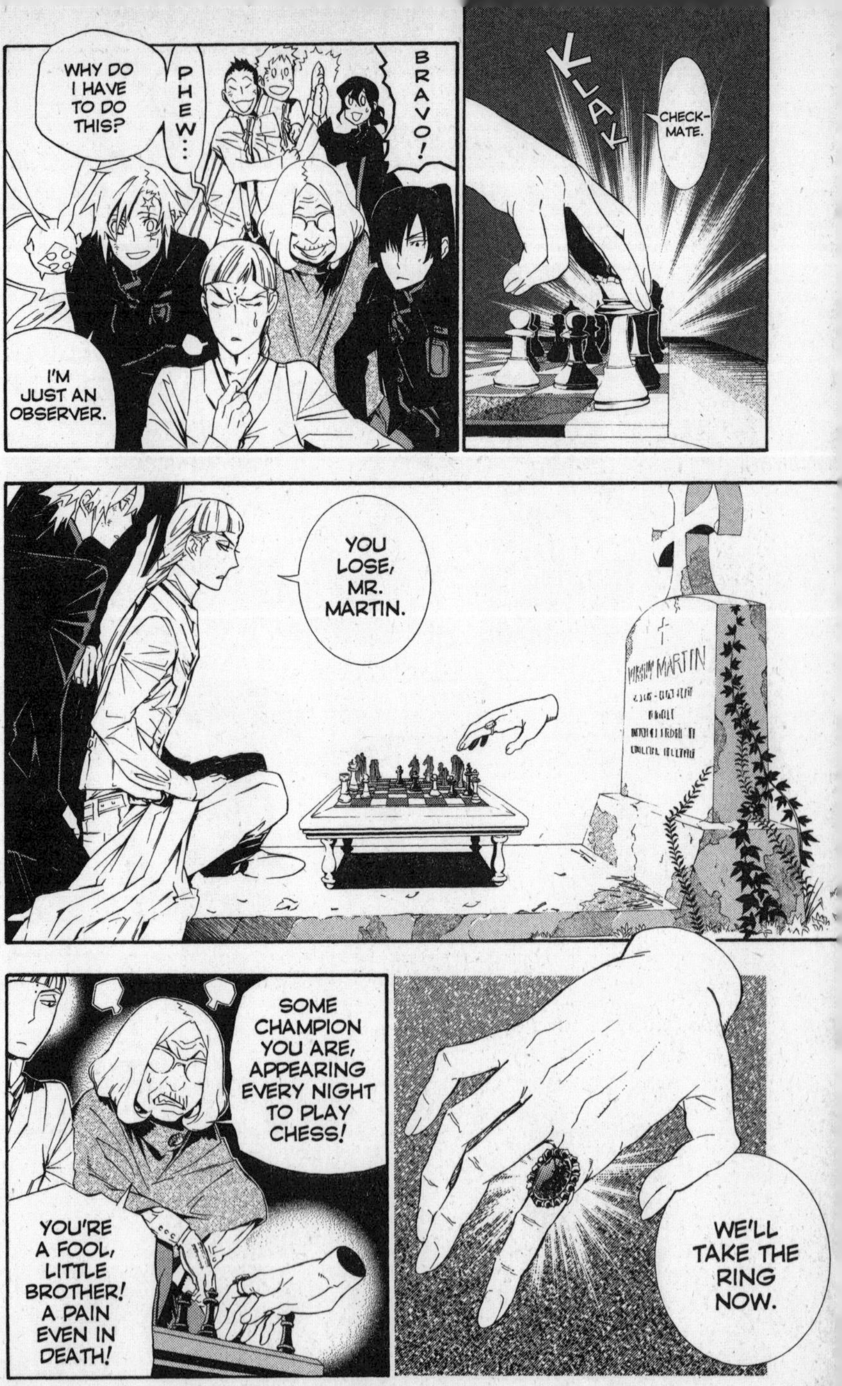
KLAK
CHECK-MATE.
BRAVO!
PHEW...
WHY DO I HAVE TO DO THIS?
I'M JUST AN OBSERVER.
YOU LOSE, MR. MARTIN.
MARTIN
WE'LL TAKE THE RING NOW.
SOME CHAMPION YOU ARE, APPEARING EVERY NIGHT TO PLAY CHESS!
YOU'RE A FOOL, LITTLE BROTHER! A PAIN EVEN IN DEATH!

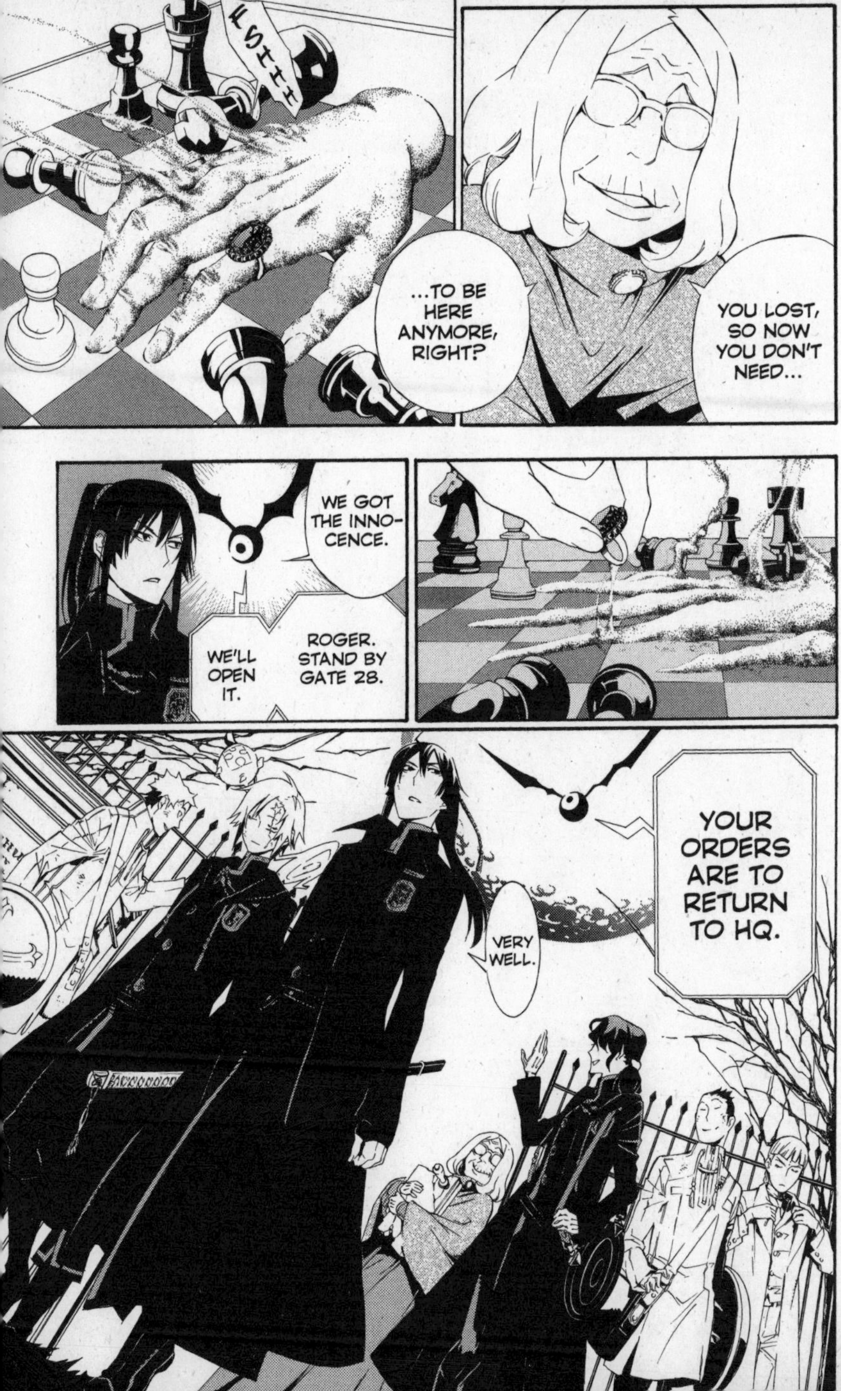
YOU LOST, SO NOW YOU DON'T NEED...
...TO BE HERE ANYMORE, RIGHT?
FSHHH
WE GOT THE INNOCENCE.
ROGER. STAND BY GATE 28.
WE'LL OPEN IT.
YOUR ORDERS ARE TO RETURN TO HQ.
VERY WELL.

THE PEOPLE OF D.GRAY-HOUSE

FATHER AND SON TAKE A BATH

TUP
WE'RE GOING TO TAKE A FATHER-SON BATH TOMORROW.
THAT'S AN ORDER.
TUP
TOMORROW?!
WHEN I'LL ANNOUNCE THAT ALLEN WALKER...
...IS JOINING THE FAMILY.
SO YOU'LL...
...MAKE HIM TAKE A BATH TOO?
GOOD NIGHT.
CHAK
KA

☆ THE PEOPLE OF D.GRAY-HOUSE CAN ONLY READ GRAPHIC NOVELS! CHEER THEM ON!

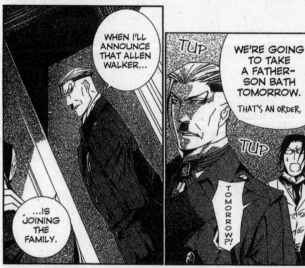

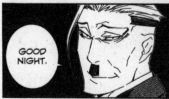

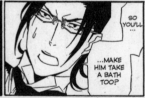

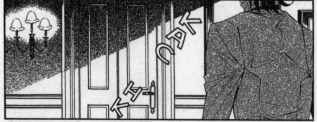

A BATH CRISIS APPROACHES.

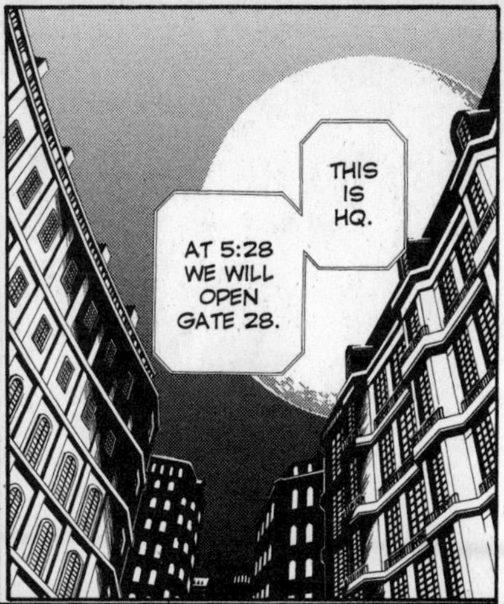
THIS IS HQ.
AT 5:28 WE WILL OPEN GATE 28.

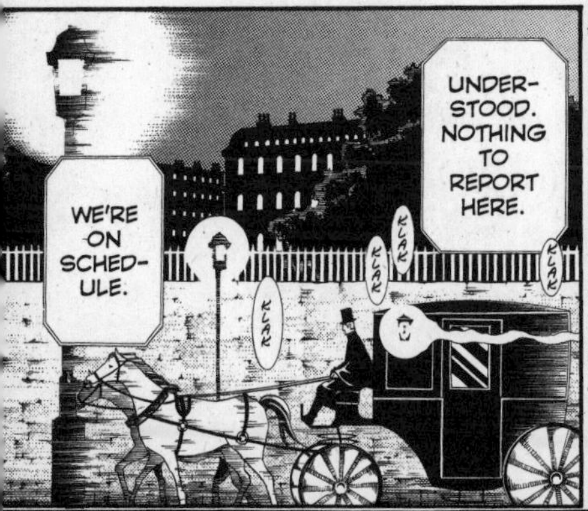
UNDER-STOOD. NOTHING TO REPORT HERE.
KLAK
KLAK
KLAK
KLAK
WE'RE ON SCHED-ULE.

THE 170TH NIGHT: TEN DAYS LATER...

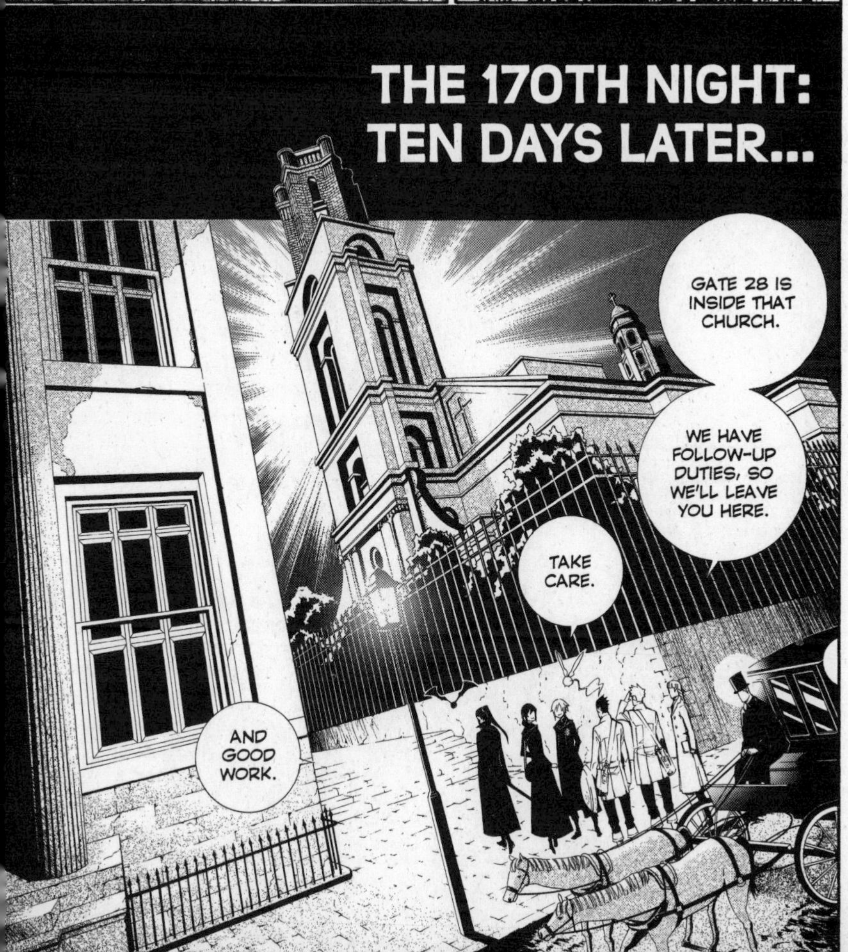
GATE 28 IS INSIDE THAT CHURCH.
WE HAVE FOLLOW-UP DUTIES, SO WE'LL LEAVE YOU HERE.
TAKE CARE.
AND GOOD WORK.

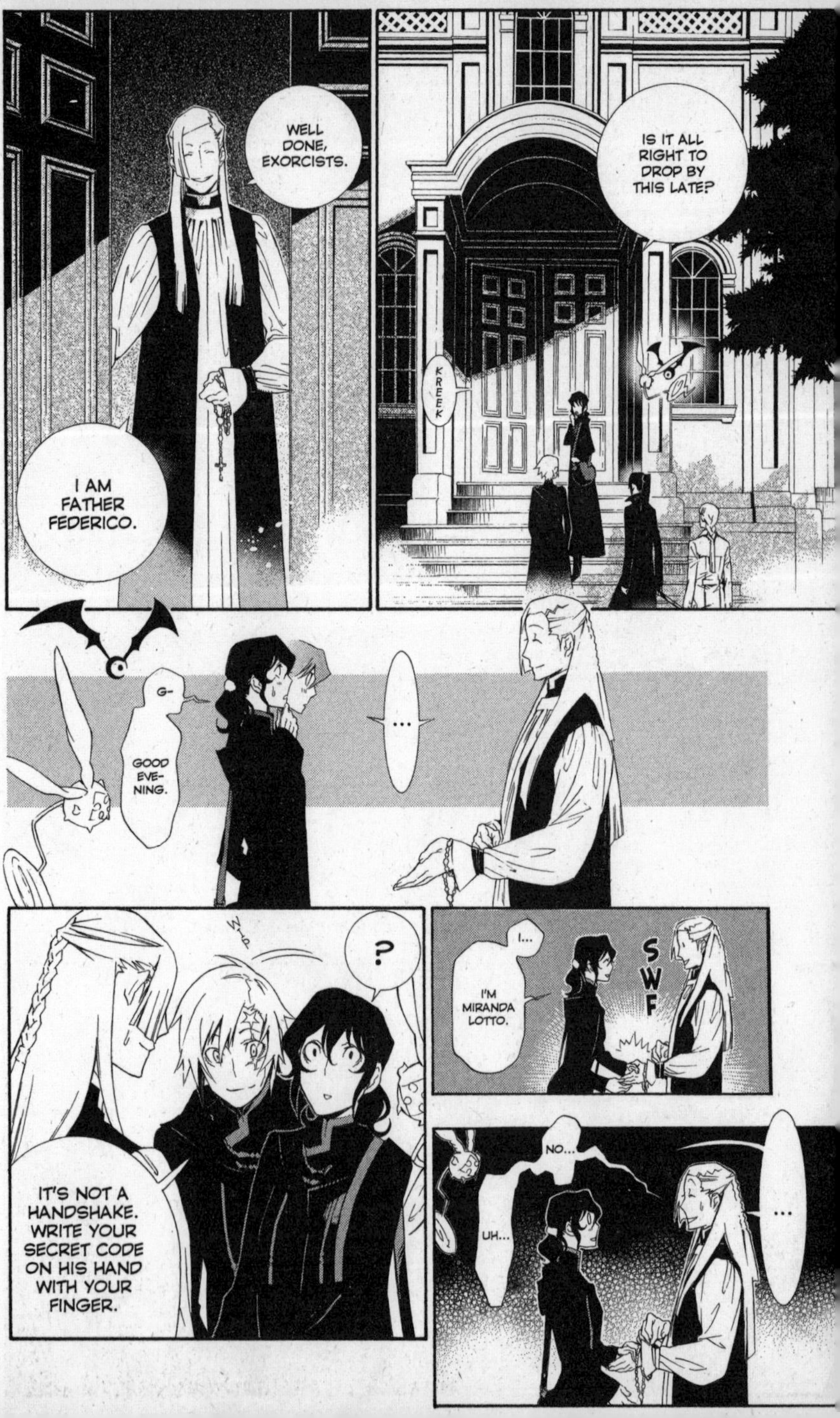
IS IT ALL RIGHT TO DROP BY THIS LATE?
KREEK
WELL DONE, EXORCISTS.
I AM FATHER FEDERICO.
...
G-
GOOD EVE- NING.
I...
SWF
I'M MIRANDA LOTTO.
...
NO...
UH...
?
IT'S NOT A HANDSHAKE. WRITE YOUR SECRET CODE ON HIS HAND WITH YOUR FINGER.

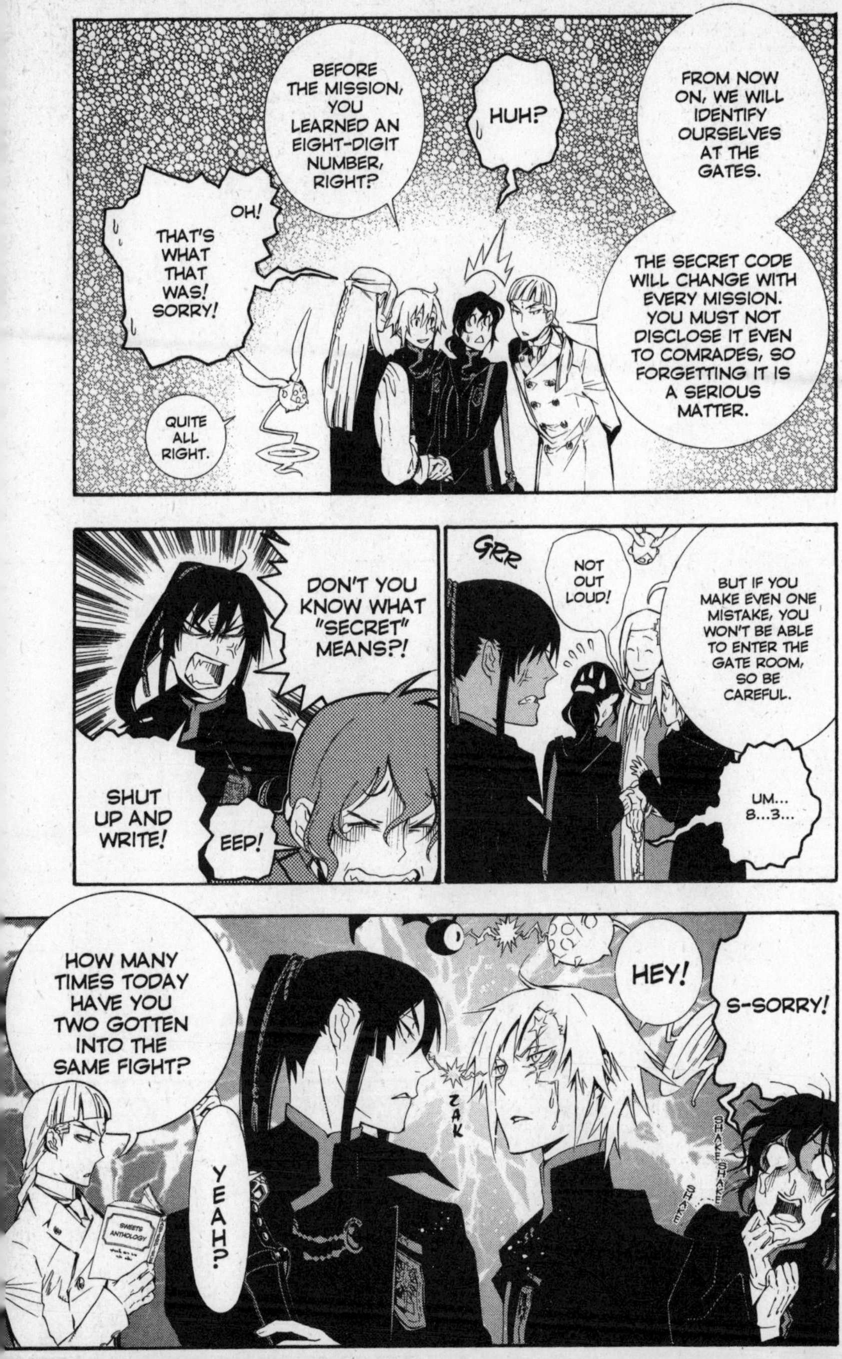
FROM NOW ON, WE WILL IDENTIFY OURSELVES AT THE GATES.
THE SECRET CODE WILL CHANGE WITH EVERY MISSION. YOU MUST NOT DISCLOSE IT EVEN TO COMRADES, SO FORGETTING IT IS A SERIOUS MATTER.
HUH?
BEFORE THE MISSION, YOU LEARNED AN EIGHT-DIGIT NUMBER, RIGHT?
OH!
THAT'S WHAT THAT WAS! SORRY!
QUITE ALL RIGHT.
BUT IF YOU MAKE EVEN ONE MISTAKE, YOU WON'T BE ABLE TO ENTER THE GATE ROOM, SO BE CAREFUL.
NOT OUT LOUD!
GRR
UM... 8...3...
DON'T YOU KNOW WHAT "SECRET" MEANS?!
SHUT UP AND WRITE!
EEP!
S-SORRY!
HEY!
SHAKE SHAKE SHAKE
HOW MANY TIMES TODAY HAVE YOU TWO GOTTEN INTO THE SAME FIGHT?
ZAK
YEAH?
SWEETS ANTHOLOGY

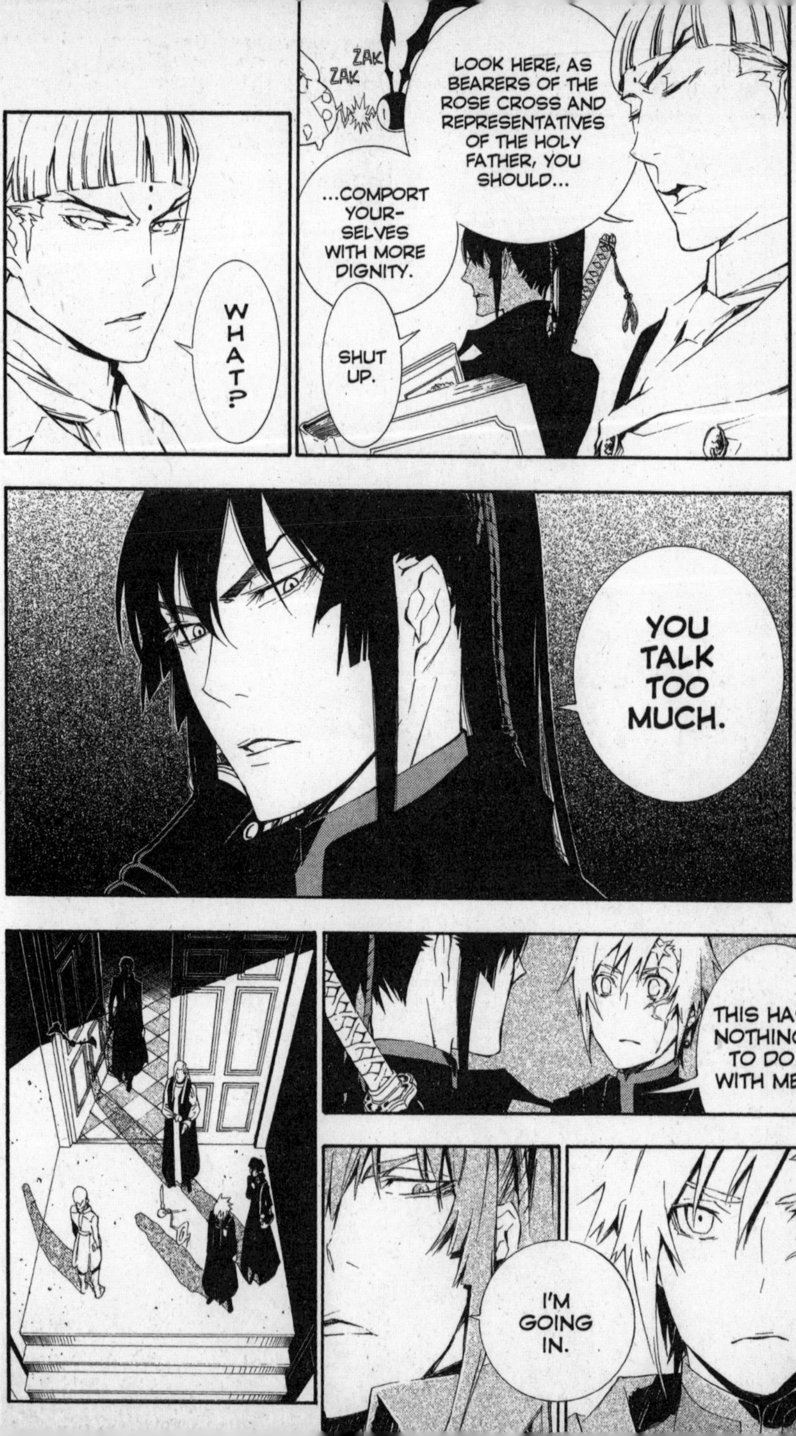
ZAK
ZAK
LOOK HERE, AS BEARERS OF THE ROSE CROSS AND REPRESENTATIVES OF THE HOLY FATHER, YOU SHOULD...
...COMPORT YOUR-SELVES WITH MORE DIGNITY.
SHUT UP.
WHAT?
YOU TALK TOO MUCH.
THIS HAS NOTHING TO DO WITH ME.
I'M GOING IN.

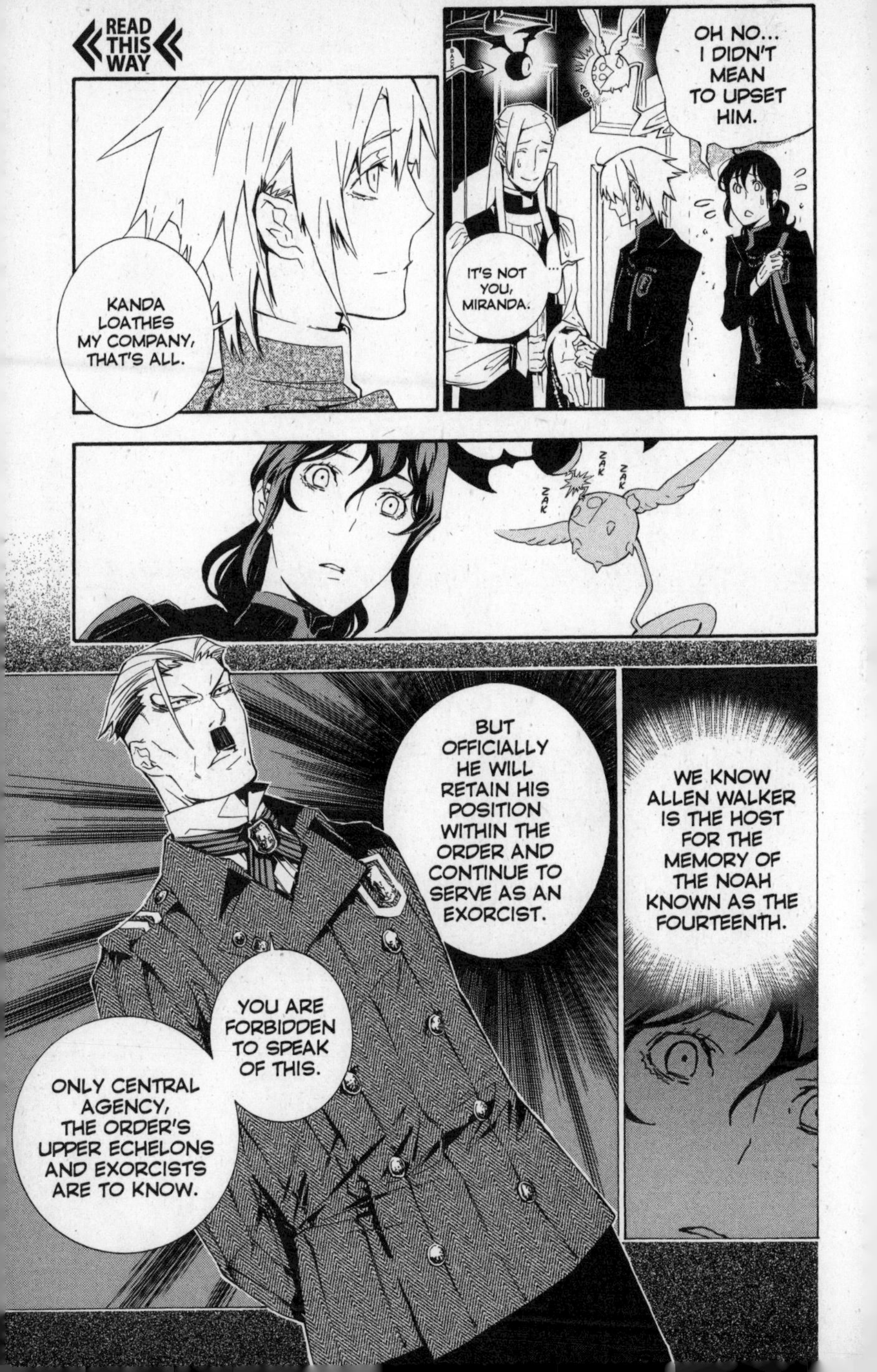
READ THIS WAY
OH NO... I DIDN'T MEAN TO UPSET HIM.
IT'S NOT YOU, MIRANDA.
...
KANDA LOATHES MY COMPANY, THAT'S ALL.
ZAK
ZAK
ZAK
WE KNOW ALLEN WALKER IS THE HOST FOR THE MEMORY OF THE NOAH KNOWN AS THE FOURTEENTH.
BUT OFFICIALLY HE WILL RETAIN HIS POSITION WITHIN THE ORDER AND CONTINUE TO SERVE AS AN EXORCIST.
YOU ARE FORBIDDEN TO SPEAK OF THIS.
ONLY CENTRAL AGENCY, THE ORDER'S UPPER ECHELONS AND EXORCISTS ARE TO KNOW.

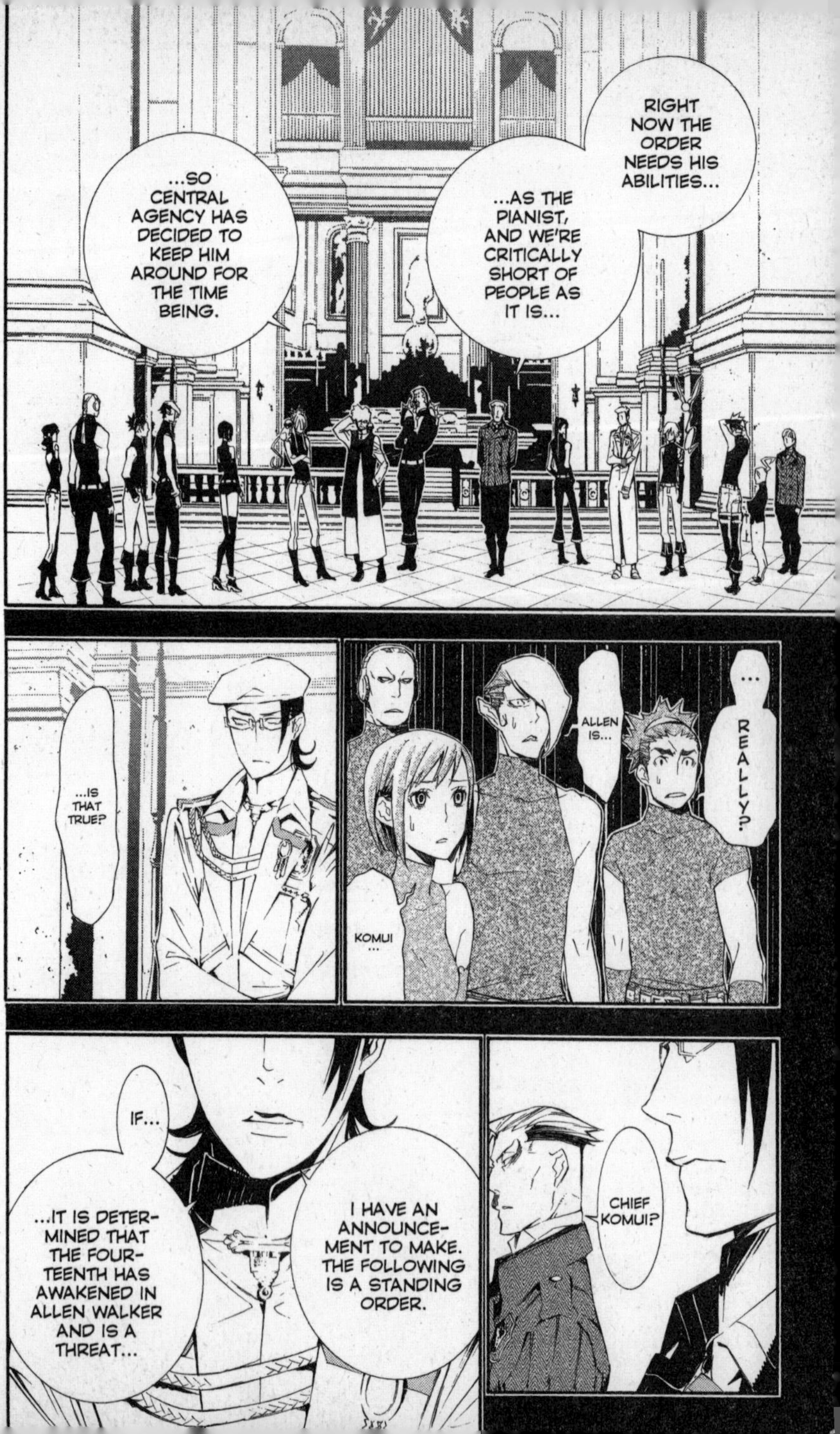
RIGHT NOW THE ORDER NEEDS HIS ABILITIES...
...AS THE PIANIST, AND WE'RE CRITICALLY SHORT OF PEOPLE AS IT IS...
...SO CENTRAL AGENCY HAS DECIDED TO KEEP HIM AROUND FOR THE TIME BEING.
... REALLY?
ALLEN IS...
KOMUI ...
...IS THAT TRUE?
CHIEF KOMUI?
I HAVE AN ANNOUNCE-MENT TO MAKE. THE FOLLOWING IS A STANDING ORDER.
IF...
...IT IS DETER-MINED THAT THE FOUR-TEENTH HAS AWAKENED IN ALLEN WALKER AND IS A THREAT...

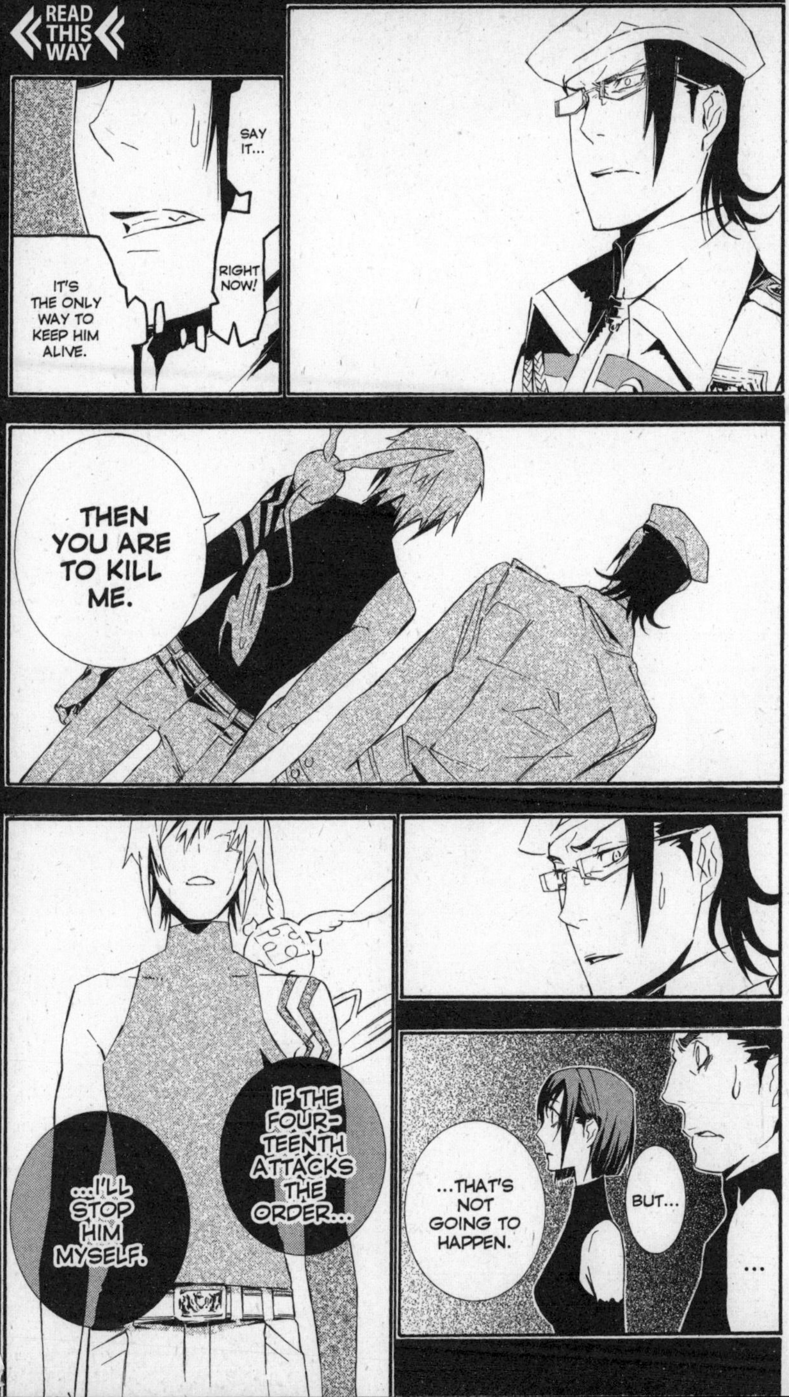
READ THIS WAY
SAY IT...
RIGHT NOW!
IT'S THE ONLY WAY TO KEEP HIM ALIVE.
THEN YOU ARE TO KILL ME.
...THAT'S NOT GOING TO HAPPEN.
BUT...
...
IF THE FOUR-TEENTH ATTACKS THE ORDER...
...I'LL STOP HIM MYSELF.

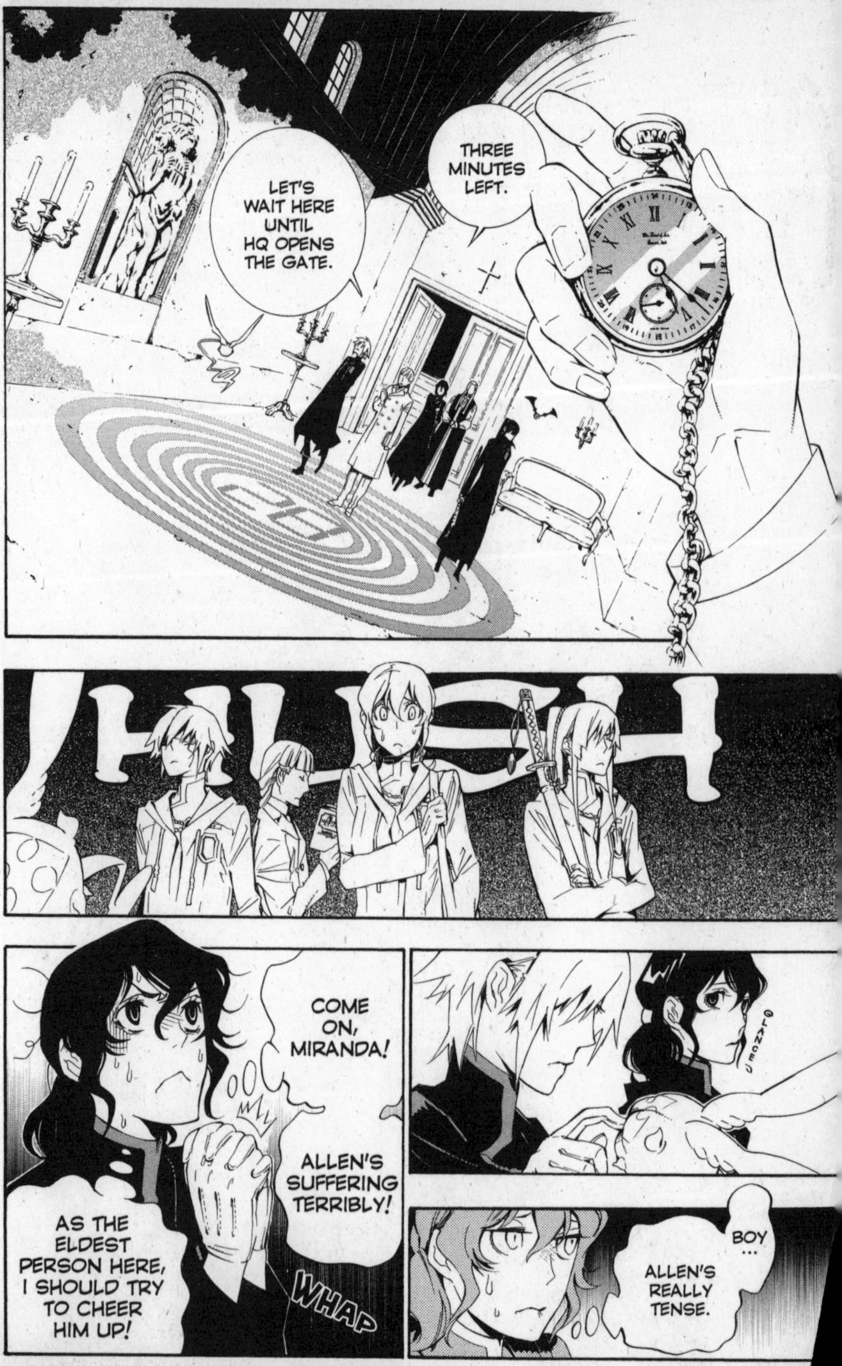
THREE MINUTES LEFT.
LET'S WAIT HERE UNTIL HQ OPENS THE GATE.
GLANCE
BOY...
ALLEN'S REALLY TENSE.
COME ON, MIRANDA!
ALLEN'S SUFFERING TERRIBLY!
AS THE ELDEST PERSON HERE, I SHOULD TRY TO CHEER HIM UP!
WHAP

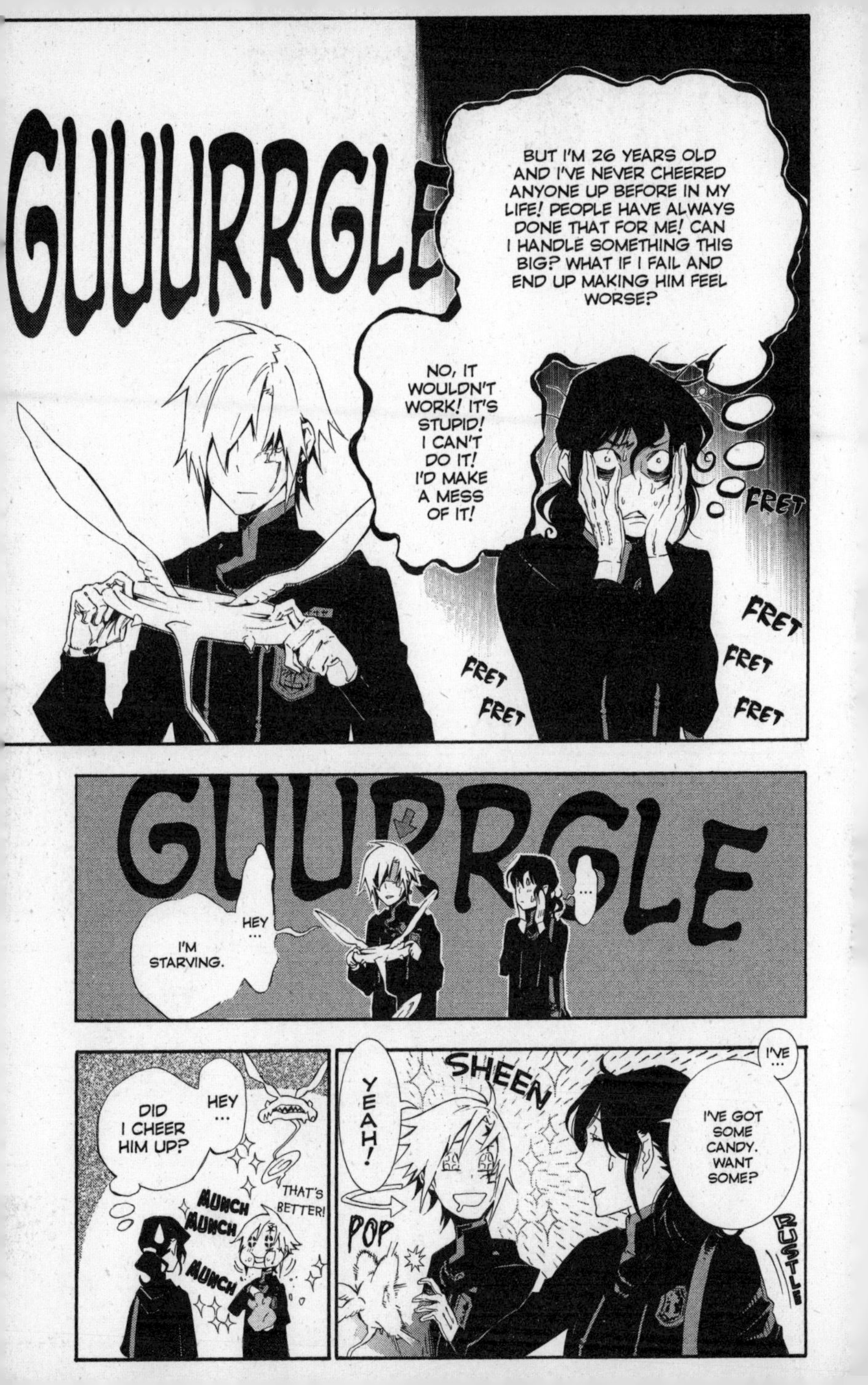
BUT I'M 26 YEARS OLD AND I'VE NEVER CHEERED ANYONE UP BEFORE IN MY LIFE! PEOPLE HAVE ALWAYS DONE THAT FOR ME! CAN I HANDLE SOMETHING THIS BIG? WHAT IF I FAIL AND END UP MAKING HIM FEEL WORSE?
FRET
NO, IT WOULDN'T WORK! IT'S STUPID! I CAN'T DO IT! I'D MAKE A MESS OF IT!
GUUURRGLE
FRET FRET FRET
FRET FRET
GUURRGLE
...
HEY ...
I'M STARVING.
I'VE ...
I'VE GOT SOME CANDY. WANT SOME?
RUSTLE
SHEEN
YEAH!
POP
HEY ...
DID I CHEER HIM UP?
THAT'S BETTER!
MUNCH MUNCH
MUNCH

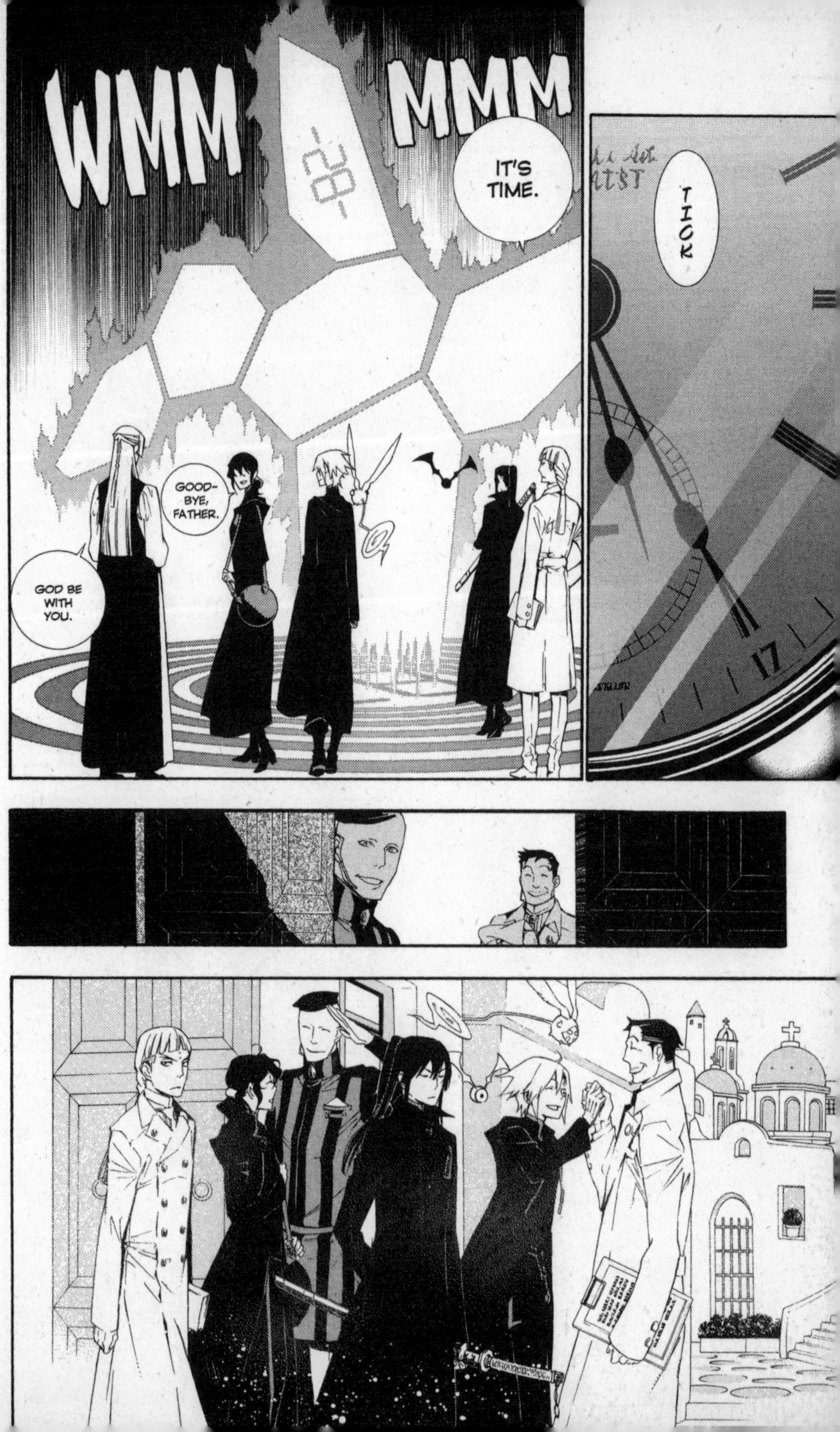
TICK
WMM MMM
IT'S TIME.
GOOD-BYE, FATHER.
GOD BE WITH YOU.

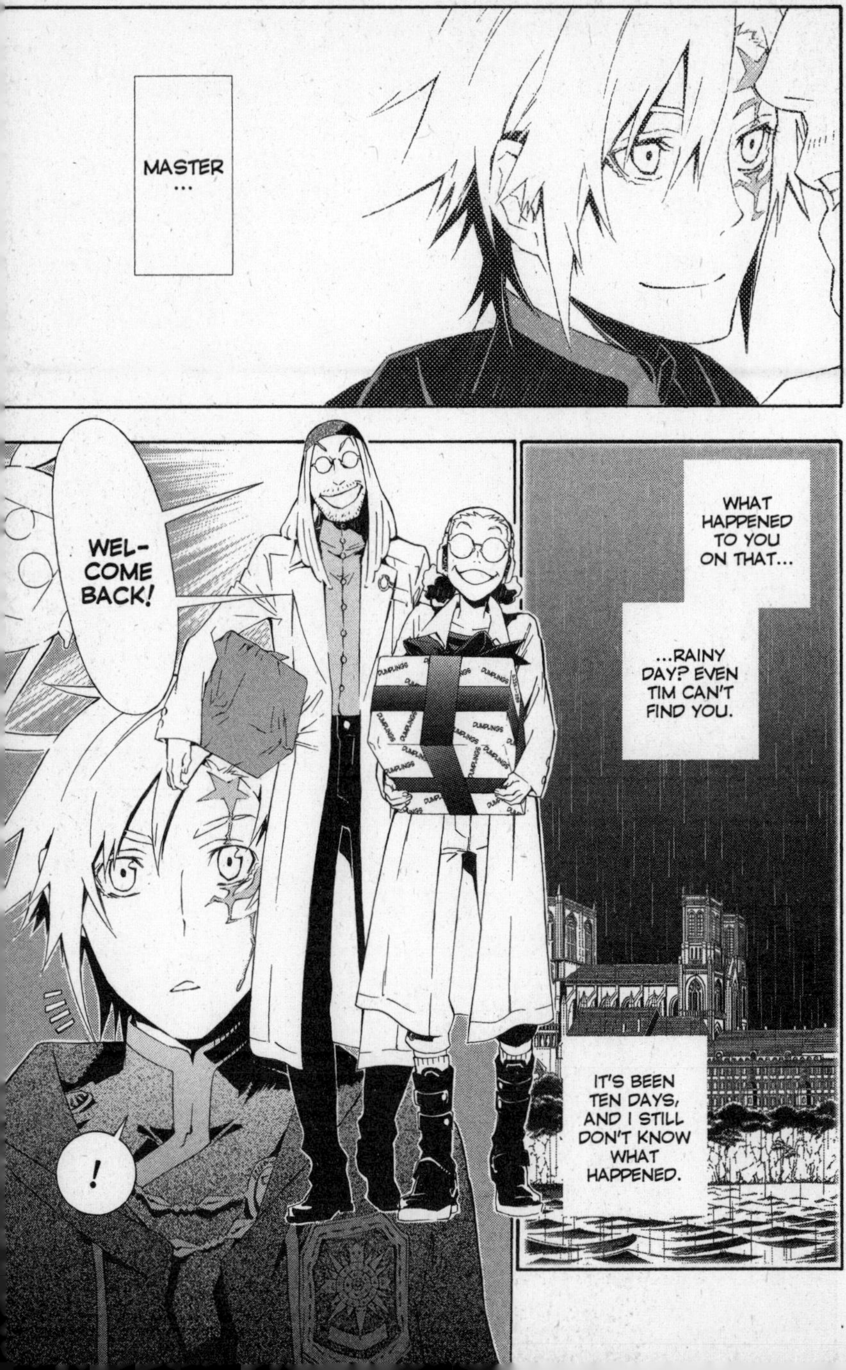
MASTER ...
WHAT HAPPENED TO YOU ON THAT...
...RAINY DAY? EVEN TIM CAN'T FIND YOU.
IT'S BEEN TEN DAYS, AND I STILL DON'T KNOW WHAT HAPPENED.
WEL-COME BACK!
!

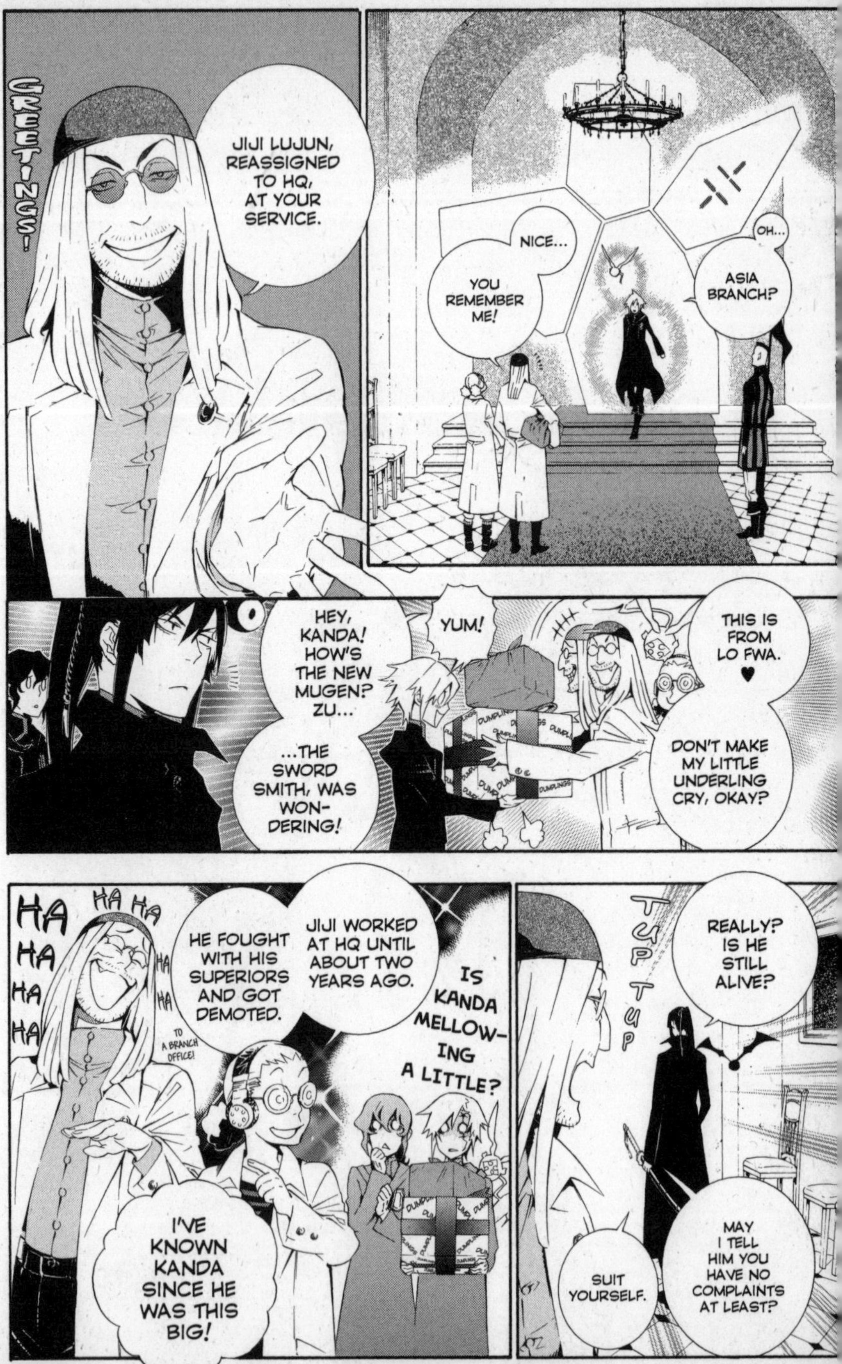
OH...
ASIA BRANCH?
NICE...
YOU REMEMBER ME!
GREETINGS!
JIJI LUJUN, REASSIGNED TO HQ, AT YOUR SERVICE.
THIS IS FROM LO FWA. ♥
DON'T MAKE MY LITTLE UNDERLING CRY, OKAY?
YUM!
HEY, KANDA! HOW'S THE NEW MUGEN? ZU...
...THE SWORD SMITH, WAS WON-DERING!
TUP TUP
REALLY? IS HE STILL ALIVE?
MAY I TELL HIM YOU HAVE NO COMPLAINTS AT LEAST?
SUIT YOURSELF.
IS KANDA MELLOW-ING A LITTLE?
JIJI WORKED AT HQ UNTIL ABOUT TWO YEARS AGO.
HE FOUGHT WITH HIS SUPERIORS AND GOT DEMOTED.
HA HA HA HA HA HA HA HA
TO A BRANCH OFFICE!
I'VE KNOWN KANDA SINCE HE WAS THIS BIG!

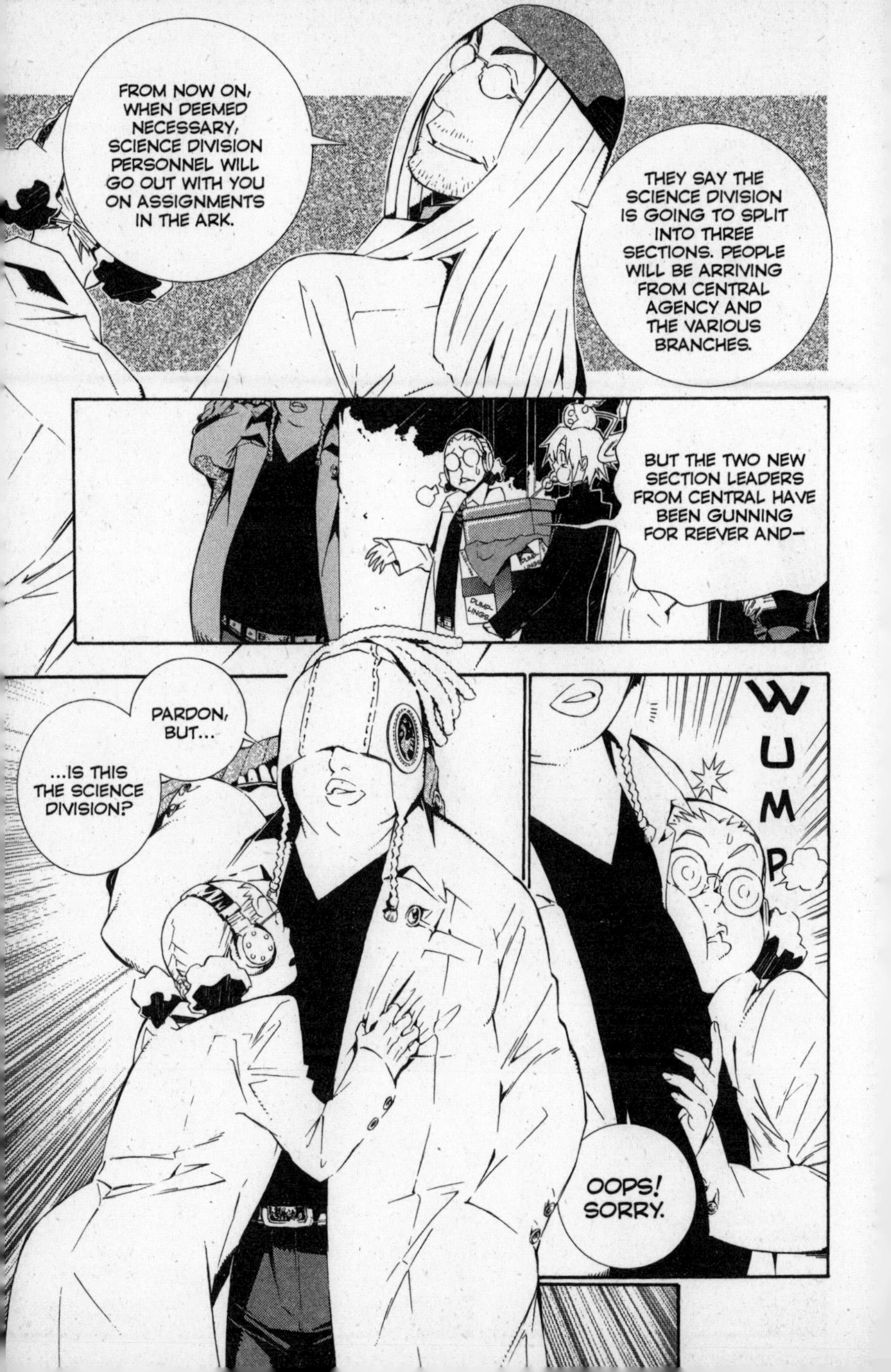
THEY SAY THE SCIENCE DIVISION IS GOING TO SPLIT INTO THREE SECTIONS. PEOPLE WILL BE ARRIVING FROM CENTRAL AGENCY AND THE VARIOUS BRANCHES.
FROM NOW ON, WHEN DEEMED NECESSARY, SCIENCE DIVISION PERSONNEL WILL GO OUT WITH YOU ON ASSIGNMENTS IN THE ARK.
BUT THE TWO NEW SECTION LEADERS FROM CENTRAL HAVE BEEN GUNNING FOR REEVER AND—
DUMP-LINGS
WUMP
OOPS! SORRY.
PARDON, BUT...
...IS THIS THE SCIENCE DIVISION?

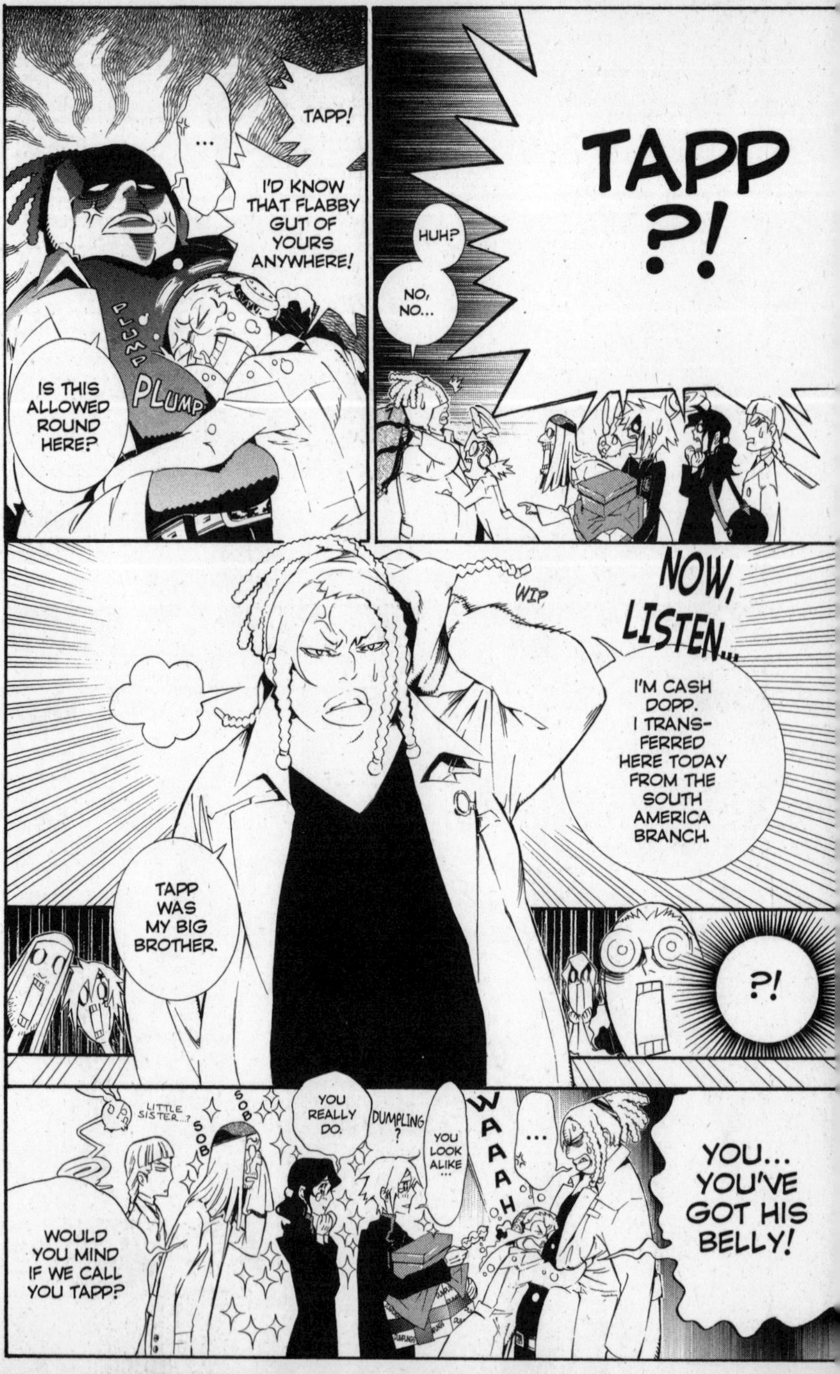
TAPP ?!
HUH?
NO, NO...
TAPP!
...
I'D KNOW THAT FLABBY GUT OF YOURS ANYWHERE!
PLUMP
PLUMP
IS THIS ALLOWED ROUND HERE?
NOW, LISTEN...
WIP
I'M CASH DOPP. I TRANS-FERRED HERE TODAY FROM THE SOUTH AMERICA BRANCH.
TAPP WAS MY BIG BROTHER.
?!
YOU... YOU'VE GOT HIS BELLY!
...
WAAAH
YOU LOOK ALIKE ...
DUMPLING?
YOU REALLY DO.
SOB
SOB
LITTLE SISTER...?
WOULD YOU MIND IF WE CALL YOU TAPP?

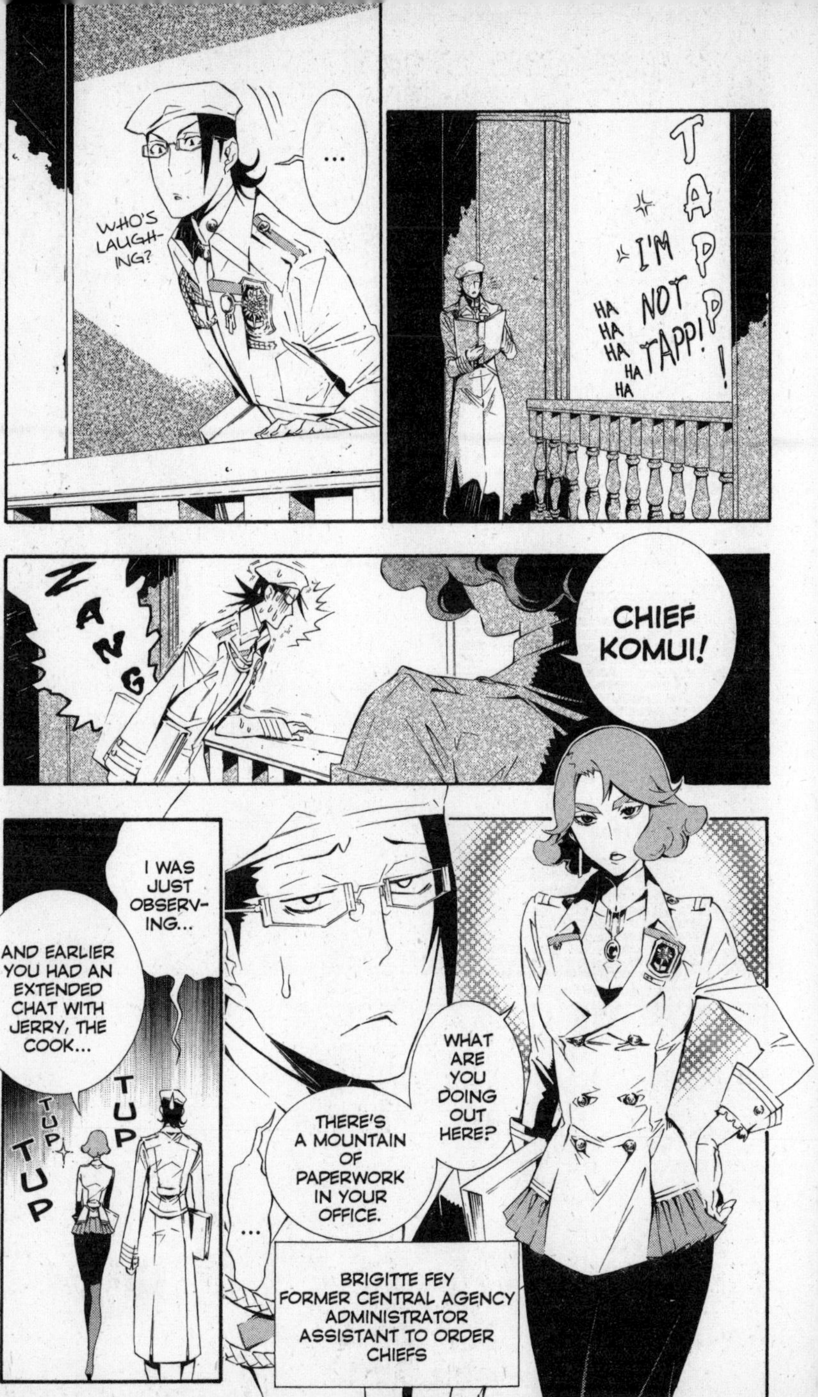
TAPP!
I'M NOT TAPP!
HA HA HA HA HA HA
...
WHO'S LAUGH-ING?
CHIEF KOMUI!
ZANG
WHAT ARE YOU DOING OUT HERE?
THERE'S A MOUNTAIN OF PAPERWORK IN YOUR OFFICE.
BRIGITTE FEY FORMER CENTRAL AGENCY ADMINISTRATOR ASSISTANT TO ORDER CHIEFS
I WAS JUST OBSERV-ING...
...
AND EARLIER YOU HAD AN EXTENDED CHAT WITH JERRY, THE COOK...
TUP TUP
TUP TUP

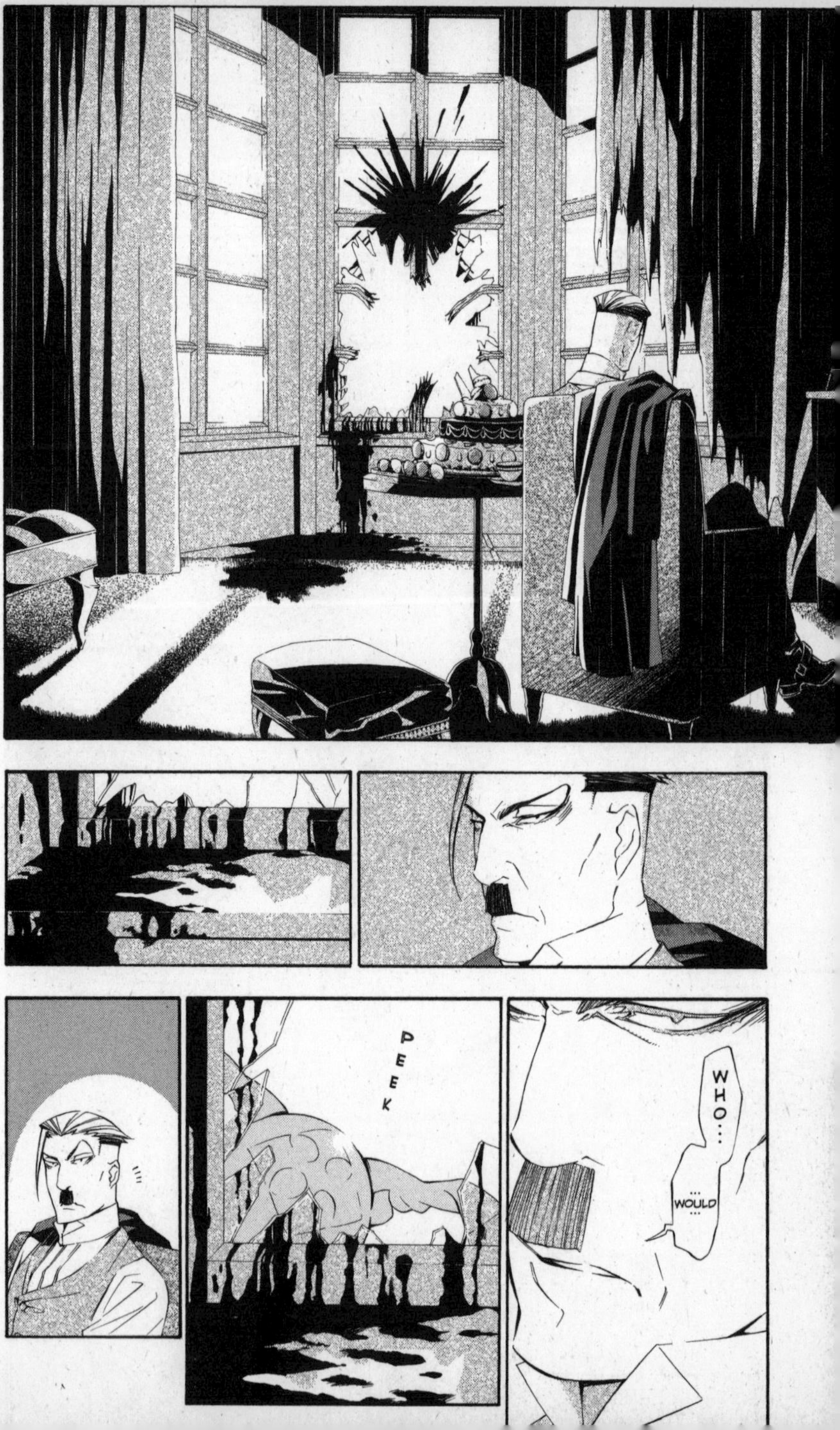
WHO...
...WOULD...
PEEK

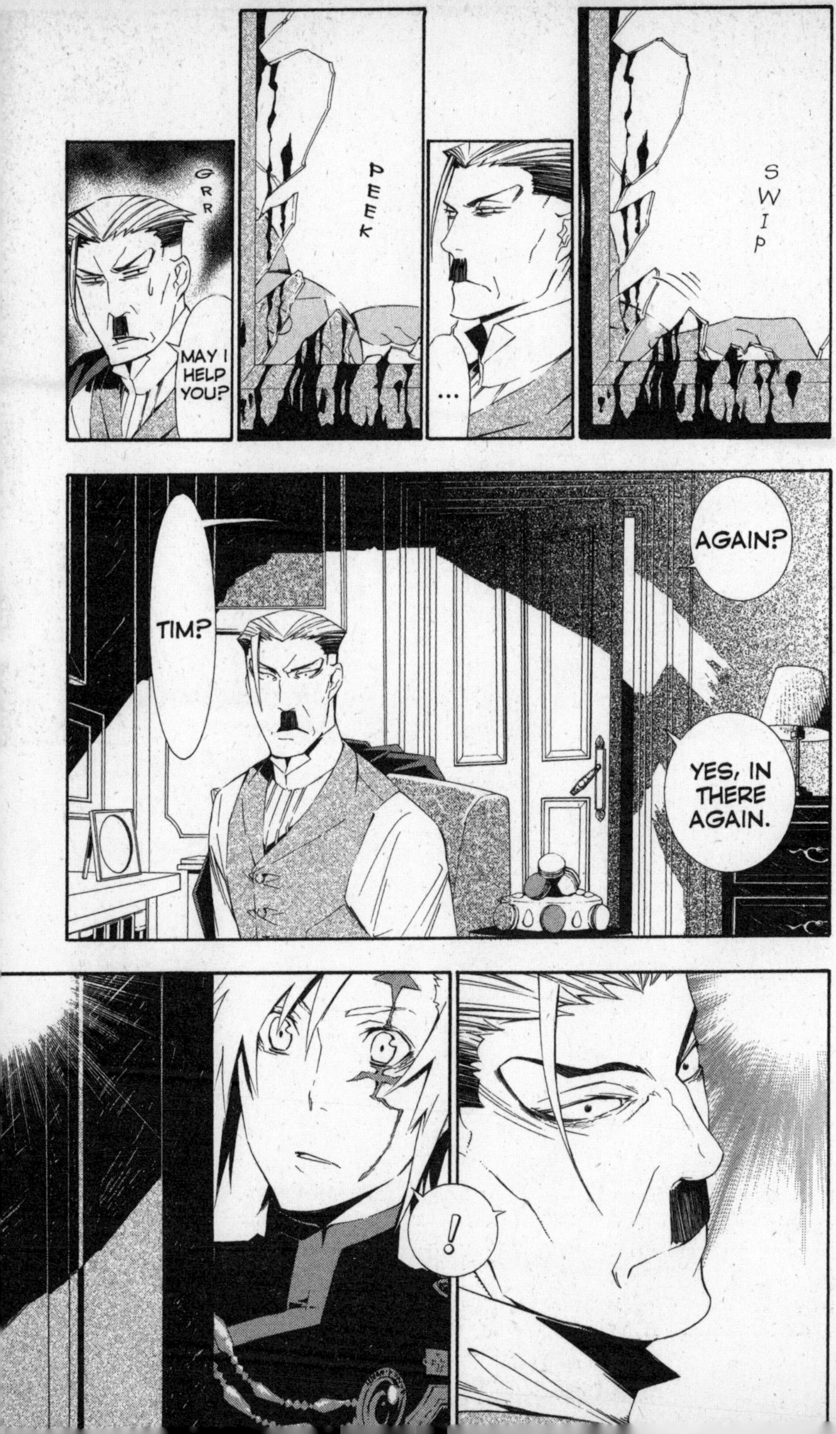
S W I P
...
P E E K
G R R
MAY I HELP YOU?
AGAIN?
TIM?
YES, IN THERE AGAIN.
!

SPECIAL THANKS

CORO

NAKAMURA-SAN

MOM

NAKAJI-SAN

SHIWO

KATAYAMA-SAN

TIIN-CHAN

HOBBIT-KUN

MURAKAMI-KUN

NAO-CHAN

PORK BITS

SHIBUYA

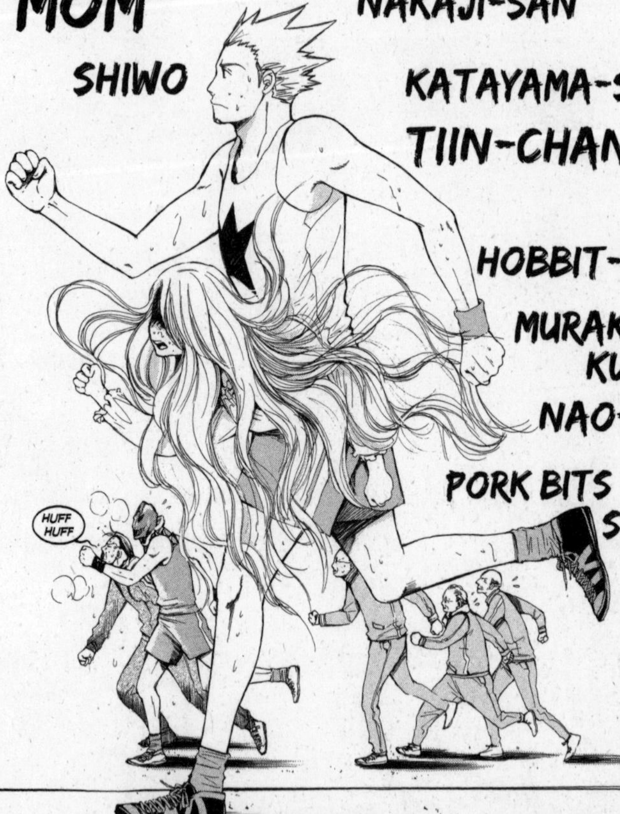
HUFF HUFF

MAMA FROM NICHO-ME

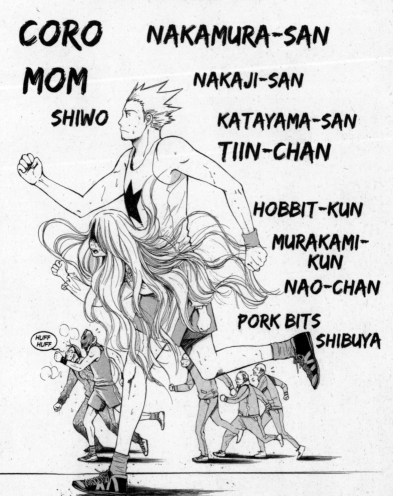

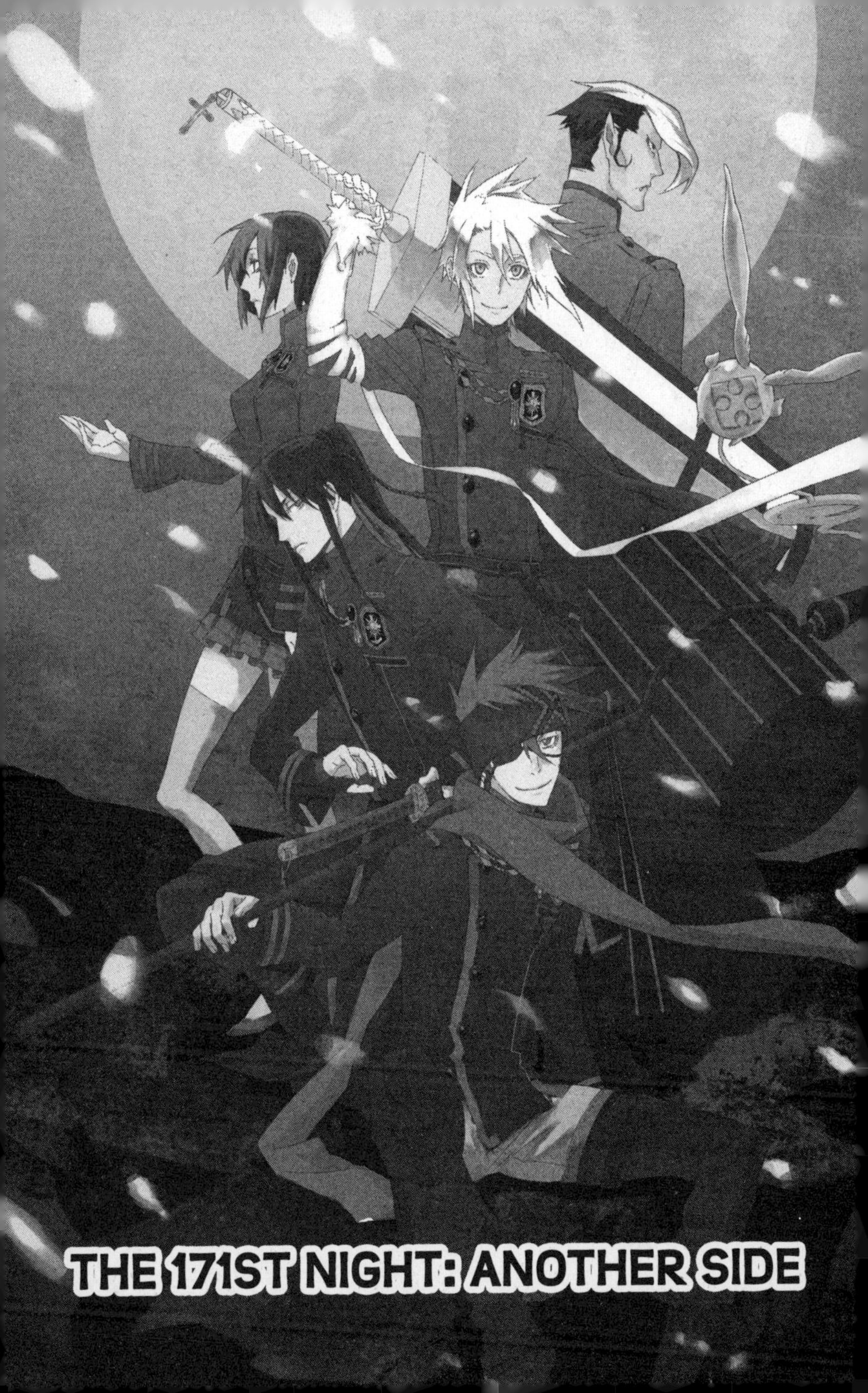

THE 171ST NIGHT: ANOTHER SIDE

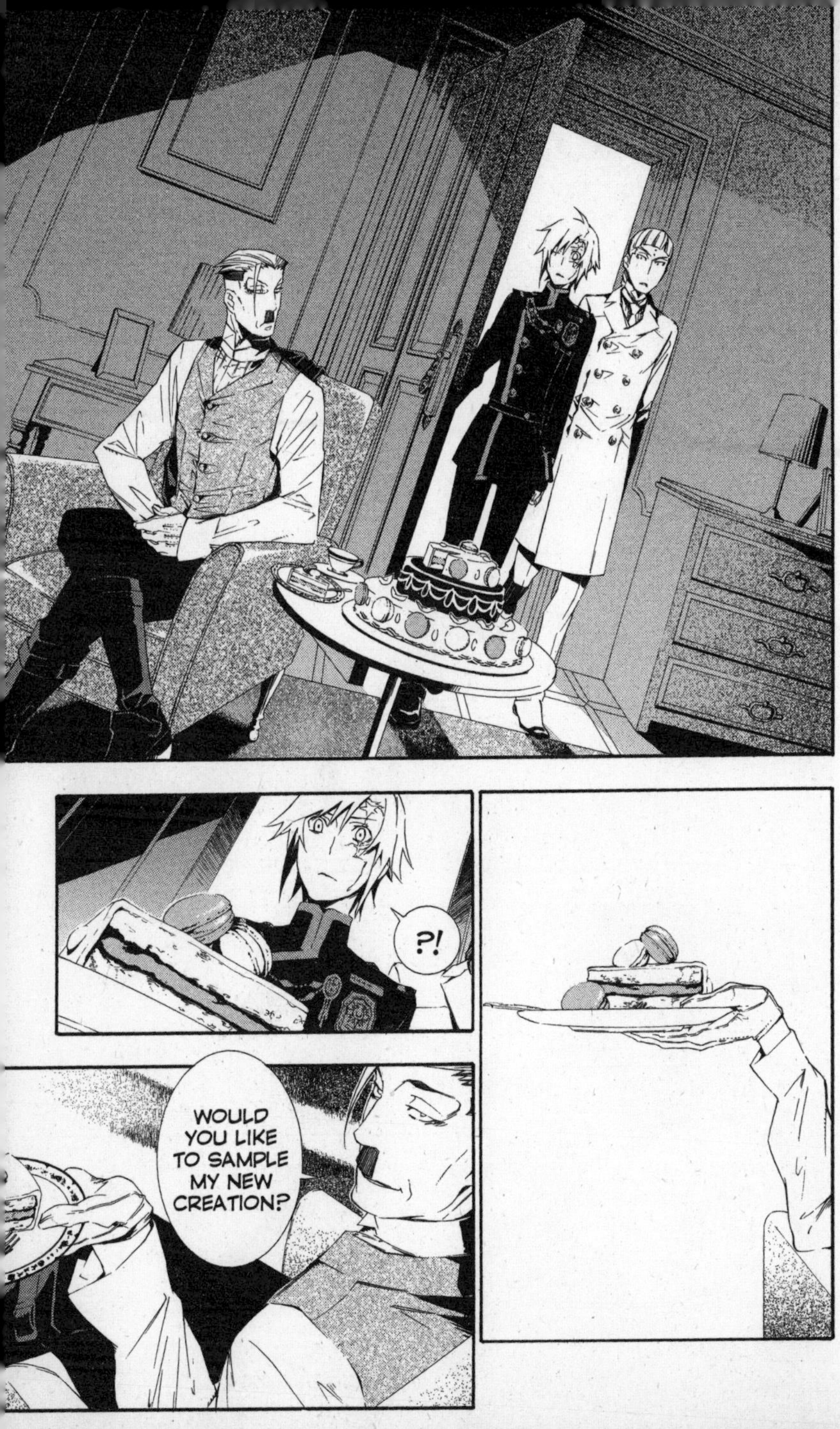
?!
WOULD YOU LIKE TO SAMPLE MY NEW CREATION?

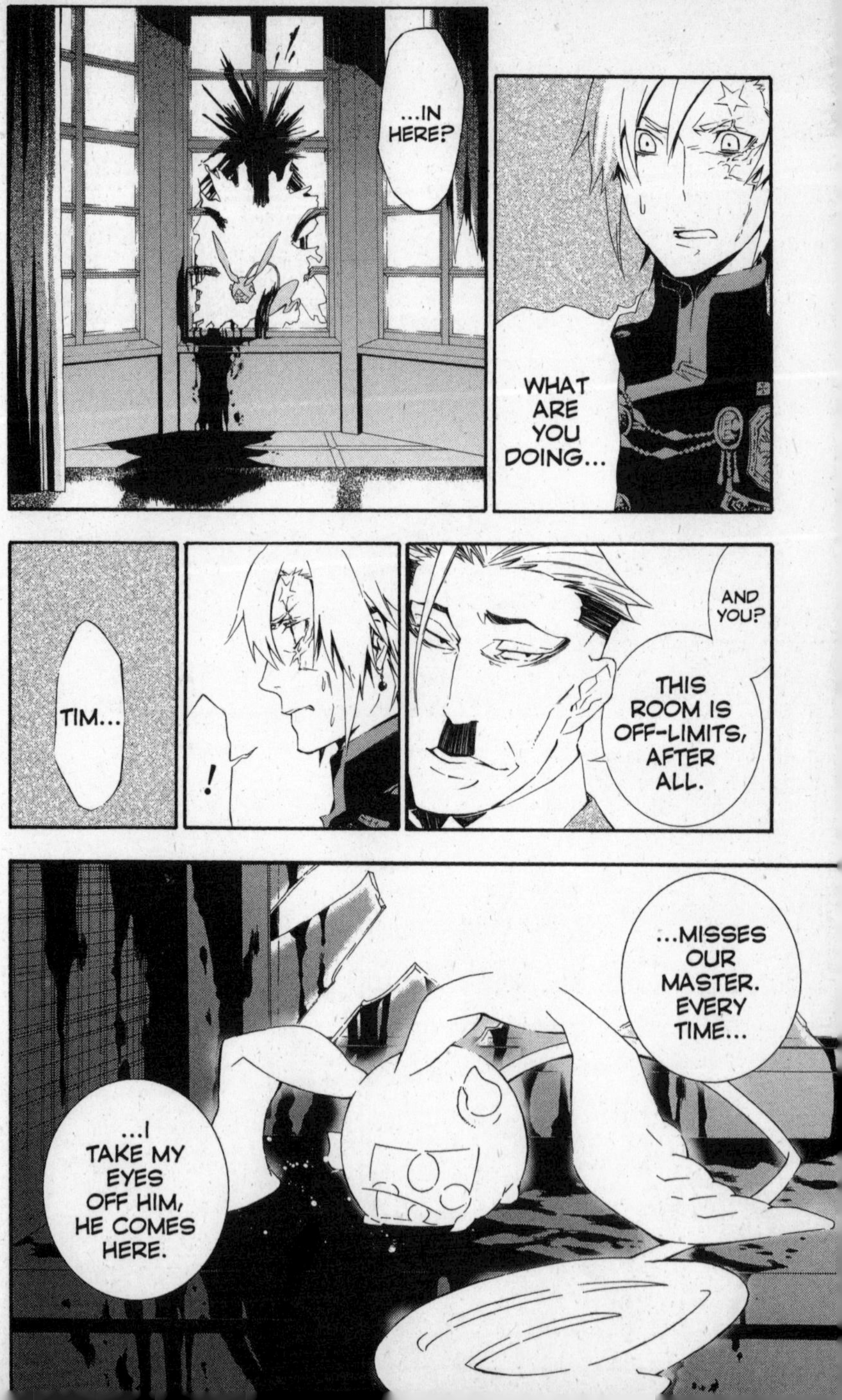
WHAT ARE YOU DOING...
...IN HERE?
AND YOU?
THIS ROOM IS OFF-LIMITS, AFTER ALL.
!
TIM...
...MISSES OUR MASTER. EVERY TIME...
...I TAKE MY EYES OFF HIM, HE COMES HERE.

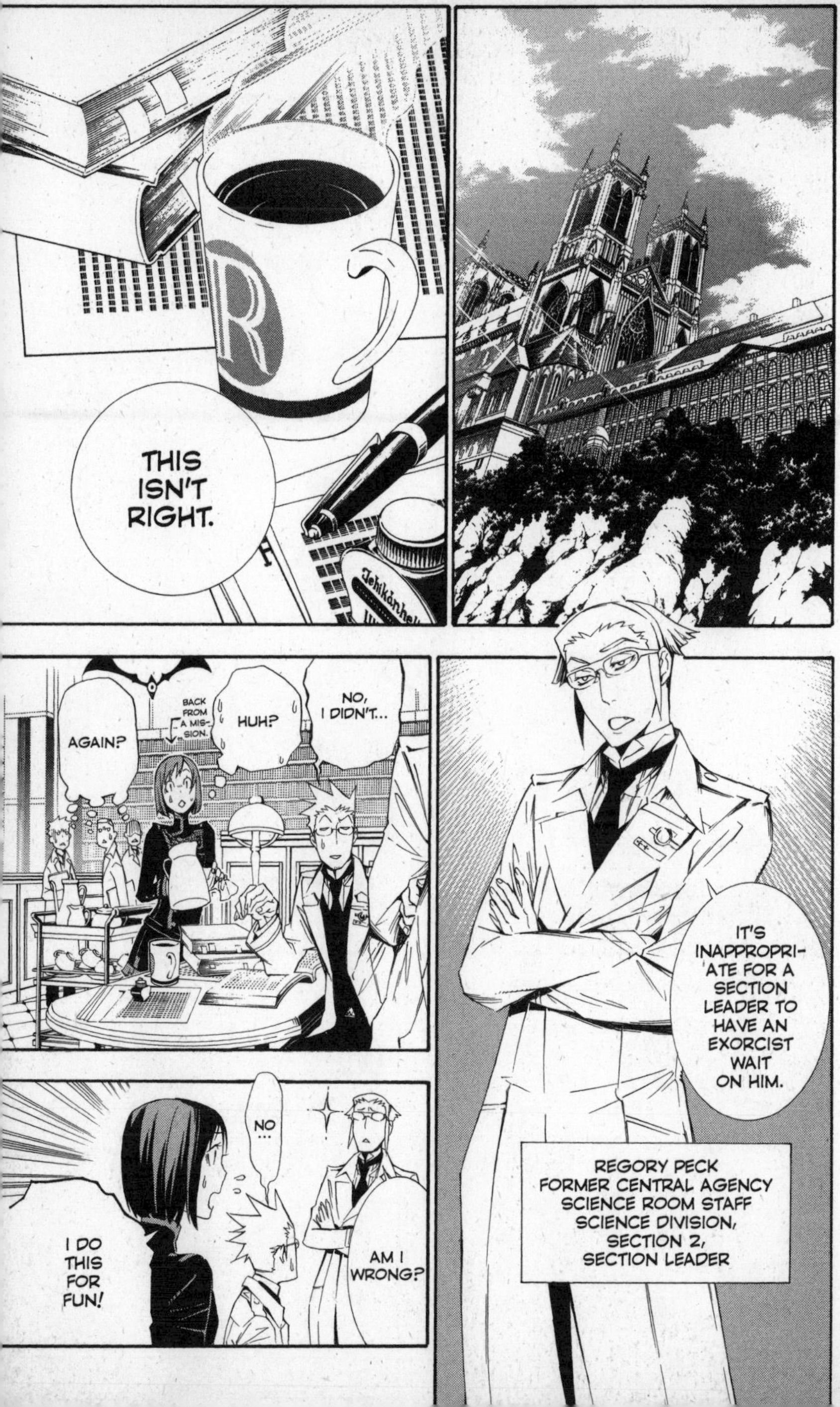
THIS ISN'T RIGHT.
IT'S INAPPROPRIATE FOR A SECTION LEADER TO HAVE AN EXORCIST WAIT ON HIM.
REGORY PECK
FORMER CENTRAL AGENCY SCIENCE ROOM STAFF
SCIENCE DIVISION, SECTION 2, SECTION LEADER
NO, I DIDN'T...
HUH?
BACK FROM A MISSION.
AGAIN?
AM I WRONG?
NO...
I DO THIS FOR FUN!

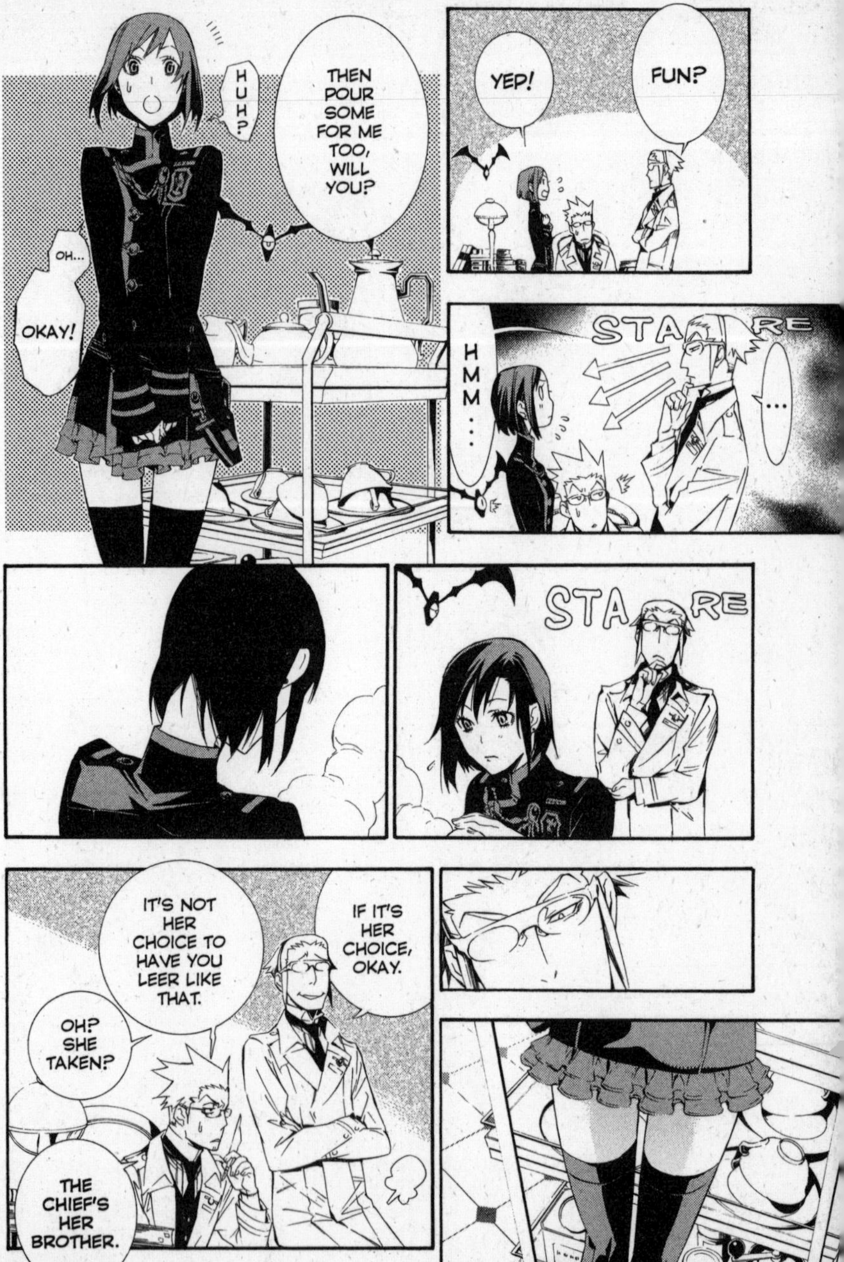
FUN?
YEP!
STARE
...
HMM...
THEN POUR SOME FOR ME TOO, WILL YOU?
HUH?
OH...
OKAY!
STARE
IF IT'S HER CHOICE, OKAY.
IT'S NOT HER CHOICE TO HAVE YOU LEER LIKE THAT.
OH? SHE TAKEN?
THE CHIEF'S HER BROTHER.

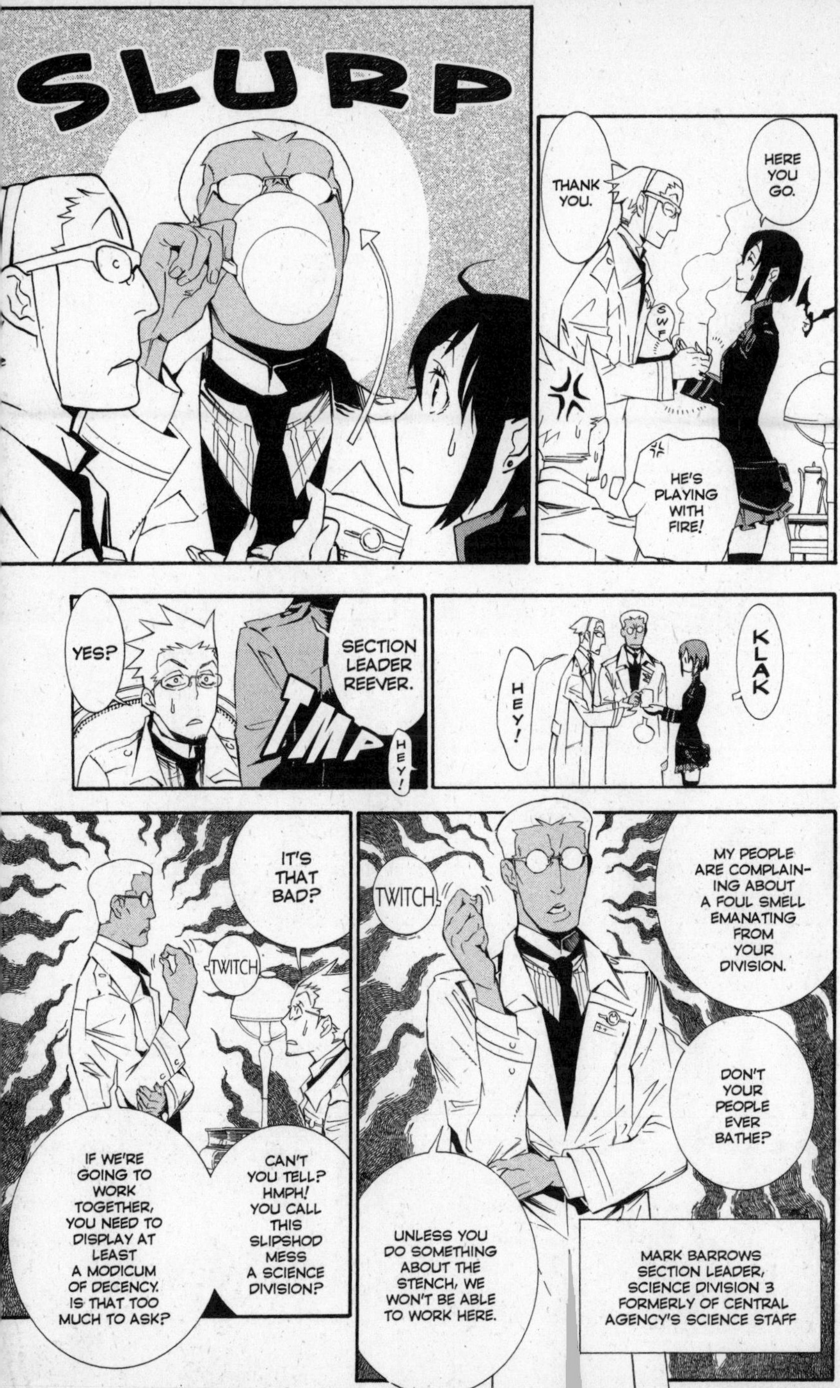
HERE YOU GO.
THANK YOU.
SWF
HE'S PLAYING WITH FIRE!
SLURP
KLAK
HEY!
SECTION LEADER REEVER.
TMP
HEY!
YES?
MY PEOPLE ARE COMPLAINING ABOUT A FOUL SMELL EMANATING FROM YOUR DIVISION.
TWITCH
DON'T YOUR PEOPLE EVER BATHE?
MARK BARROWS SECTION LEADER, SCIENCE DIVISION 3 FORMERLY OF CENTRAL AGENCY'S SCIENCE STAFF
UNLESS YOU DO SOMETHING ABOUT THE STENCH, WE WON'T BE ABLE TO WORK HERE.
IT'S THAT BAD?
TWITCH
CAN'T YOU TELL? HMPH! YOU CALL THIS SLIPSHOD MESS A SCIENCE DIVISION?
IF WE'RE GOING TO WORK TOGETHER, YOU NEED TO DISPLAY AT LEAST A MODICUM OF DECENCY. IS THAT TOO MUCH TO ASK?

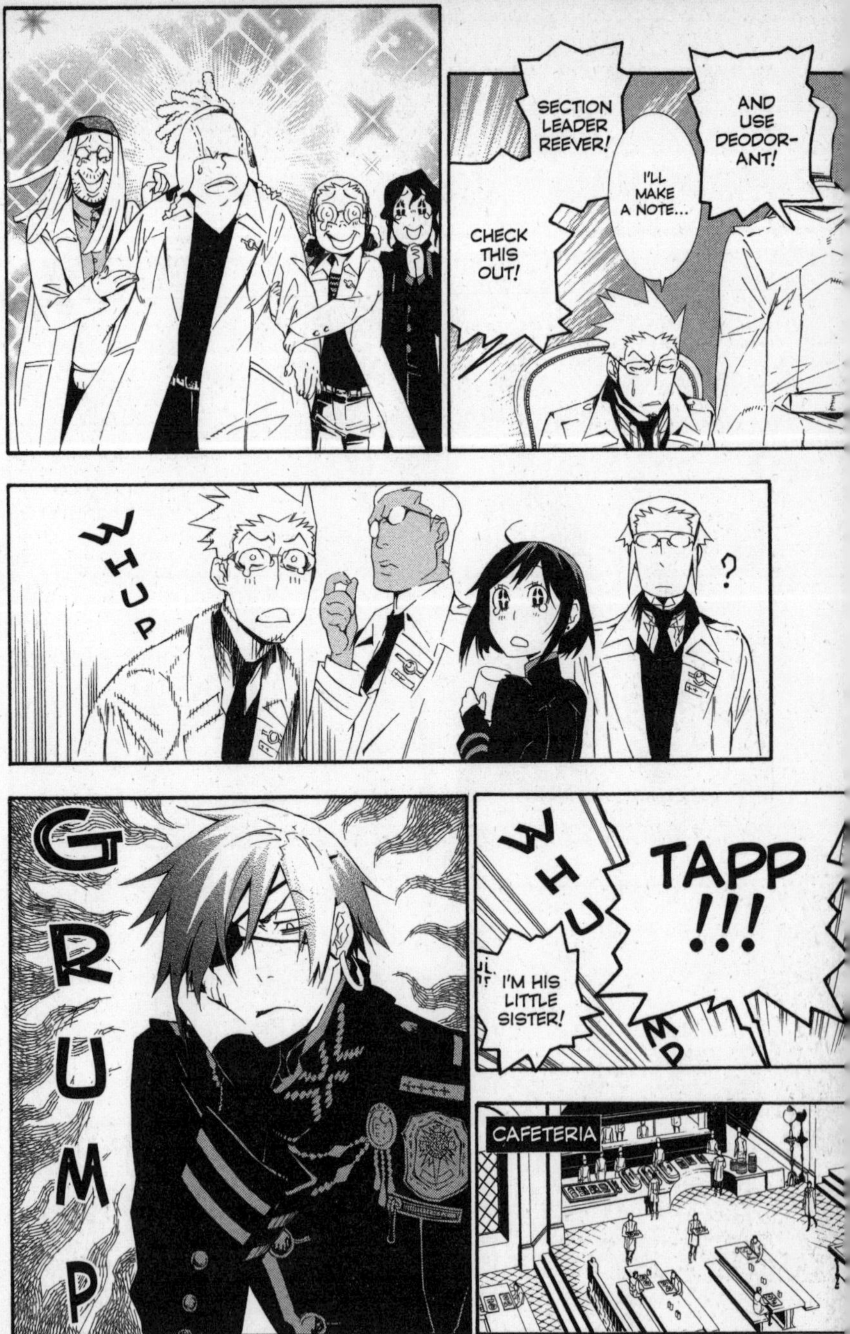
AND USE DEODORANT!
SECTION LEADER REEVER!
I'LL MAKE A NOTE...
CHECK THIS OUT!
?
WHUP
TAPP !!!
WHUMP
I'M HIS LITTLE SISTER!
CAFETERIA
GRUMP

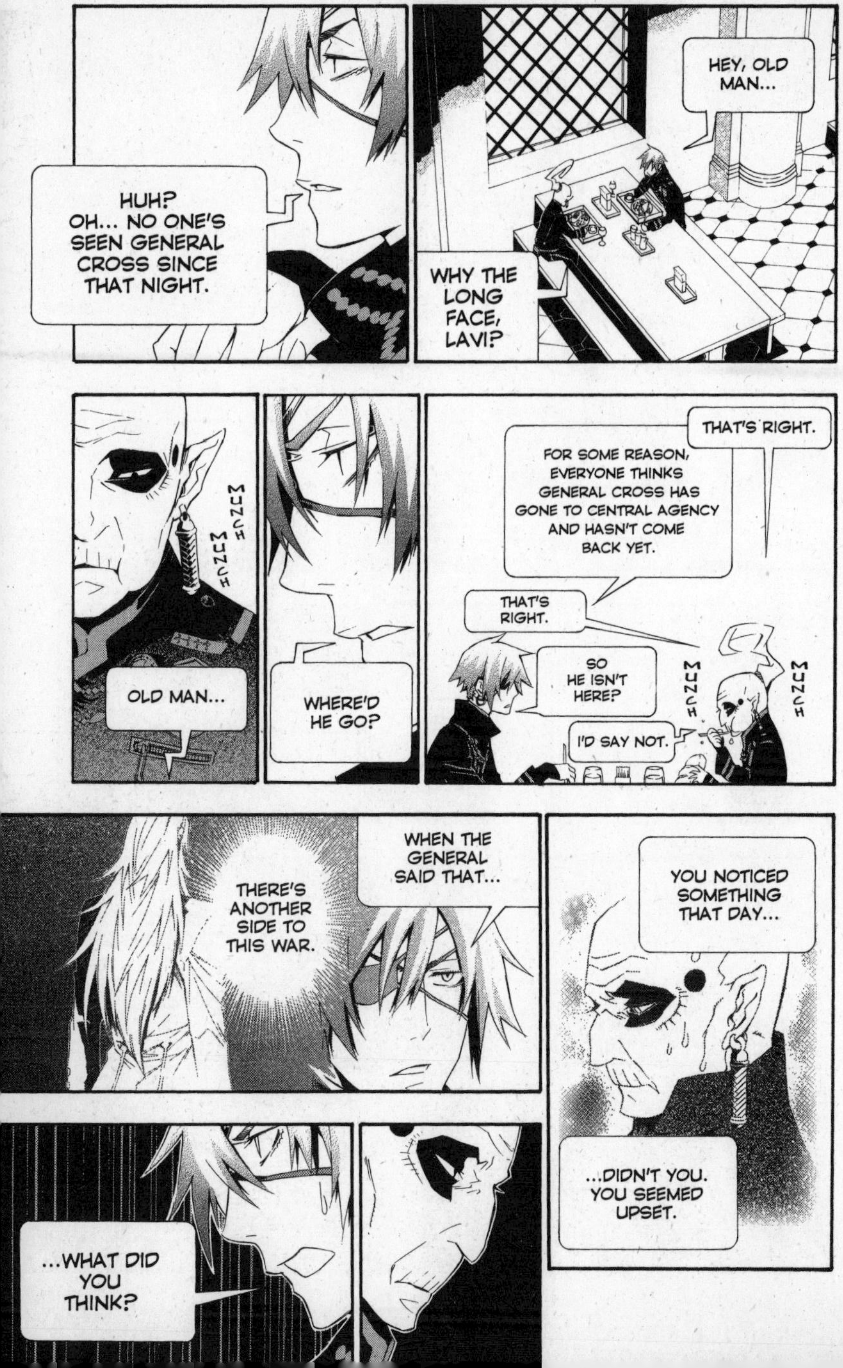
HEY, OLD MAN...
WHY THE LONG FACE, LAVI?
HUH? OH... NO ONE'S SEEN GENERAL CROSS SINCE THAT NIGHT.
THAT'S RIGHT.
FOR SOME REASON, EVERYONE THINKS GENERAL CROSS HAS GONE TO CENTRAL AGENCY AND HASN'T COME BACK YET.
THAT'S RIGHT.
MUNCH
MUNCH
SO HE ISN'T HERE?
I'D SAY NOT.
WHERE'D HE GO?
MUNCH
MUNCH
OLD MAN...
YOU NOTICED SOMETHING THAT DAY...
...DIDN'T YOU. YOU SEEMED UPSET.
WHEN THE GENERAL SAID THAT...
THERE'S ANOTHER SIDE TO THIS WAR.
...WHAT DID YOU THINK?

I DOUBT...

...CROSS MARIAN WILL EVER RETURN TO THE ORDER.

ASSUMING, THAT IS...

...HE ESCAPED WITH HIS LIFE.

?!

...

YOU DON'T MEAN...

ESCAPED?!

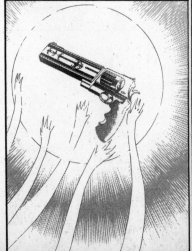

WE MUST BE CAREFUL.

WE WERE THERE WHEN HE SAID IT, SO OUR LIVES ARE IN DANGER TOO.

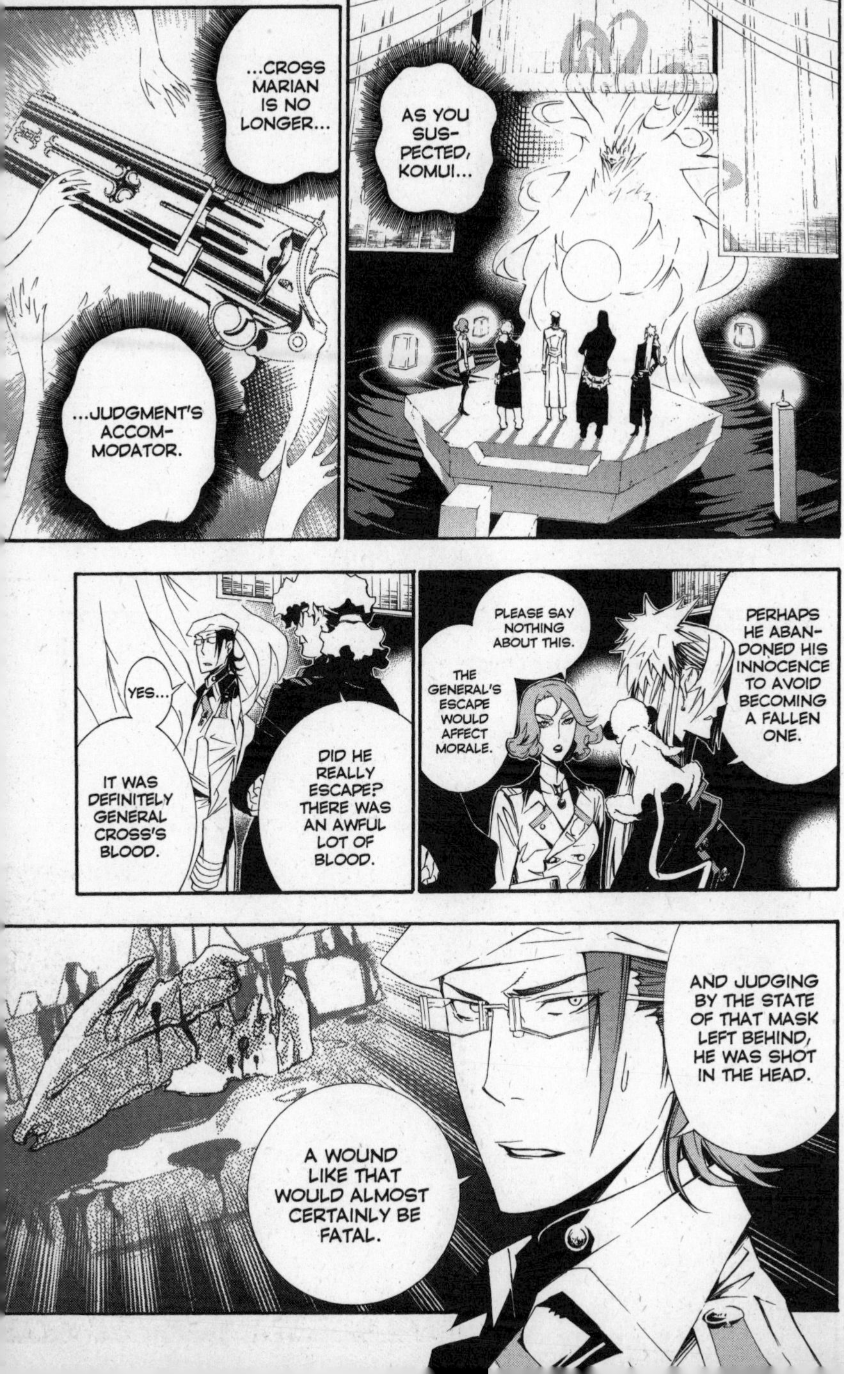
AS YOU SUS-PECTED, KOMUI...
...CROSS MARIAN IS NO LONGER...
...JUDGMENT'S ACCOM-MODATOR.
PERHAPS HE ABAN-DONED HIS INNOCENCE TO AVOID BECOMING A FALLEN ONE.
PLEASE SAY NOTHING ABOUT THIS.
THE GENERAL'S ESCAPE WOULD AFFECT MORALE.
YES...
DID HE REALLY ESCAPE? THERE WAS AN AWFUL LOT OF BLOOD.
IT WAS DEFINITELY GENERAL CROSS'S BLOOD.
AND JUDGING BY THE STATE OF THAT MASK LEFT BEHIND, HE WAS SHOT IN THE HEAD.
A WOUND LIKE THAT WOULD ALMOST CERTAINLY BE FATAL.

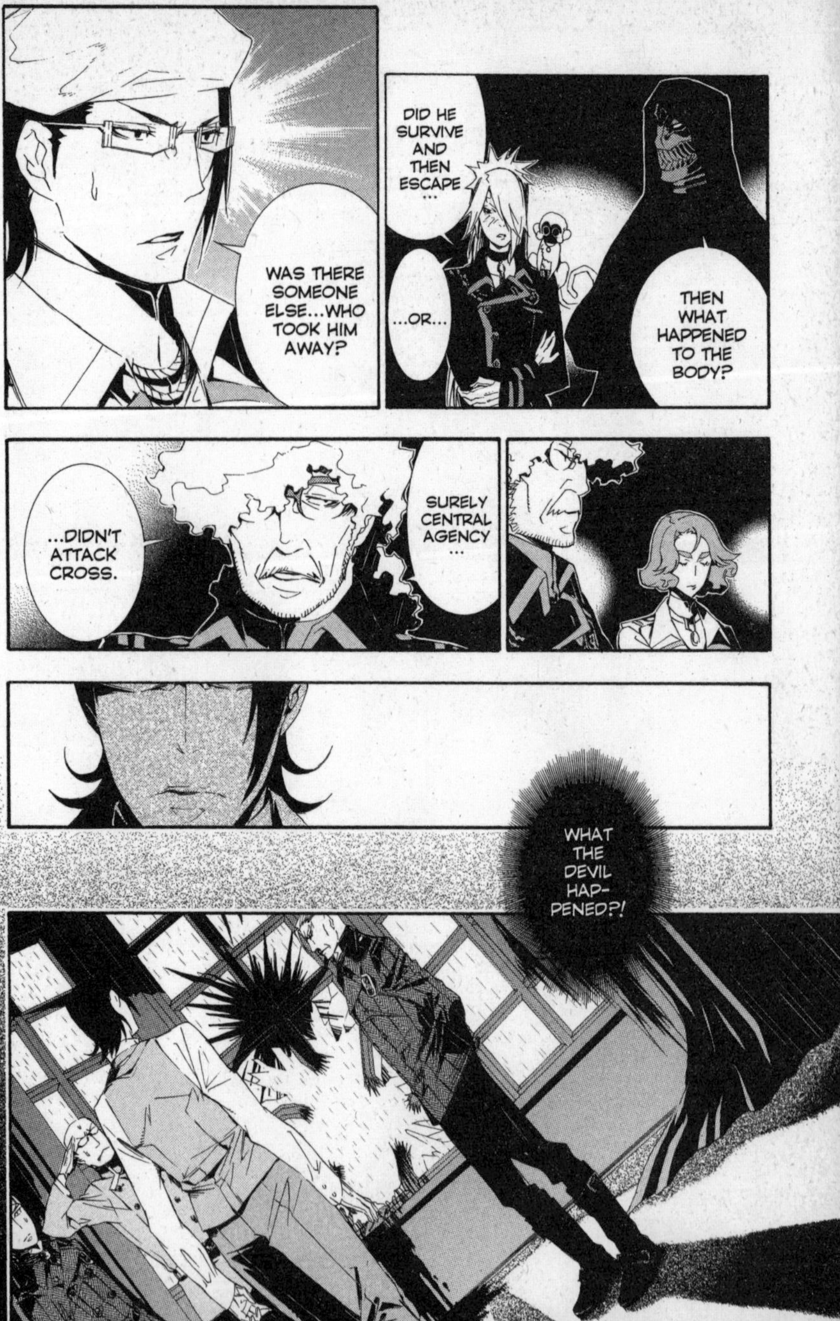
THEN WHAT HAPPENED TO THE BODY?
DID HE SURVIVE AND THEN ESCAPE ...
...OR...
WAS THERE SOMEONE ELSE...WHO TOOK HIM AWAY?
SURELY CENTRAL AGENCY ...
...DIDN'T ATTACK CROSS.
WHAT THE DEVIL HAP-PENED?!

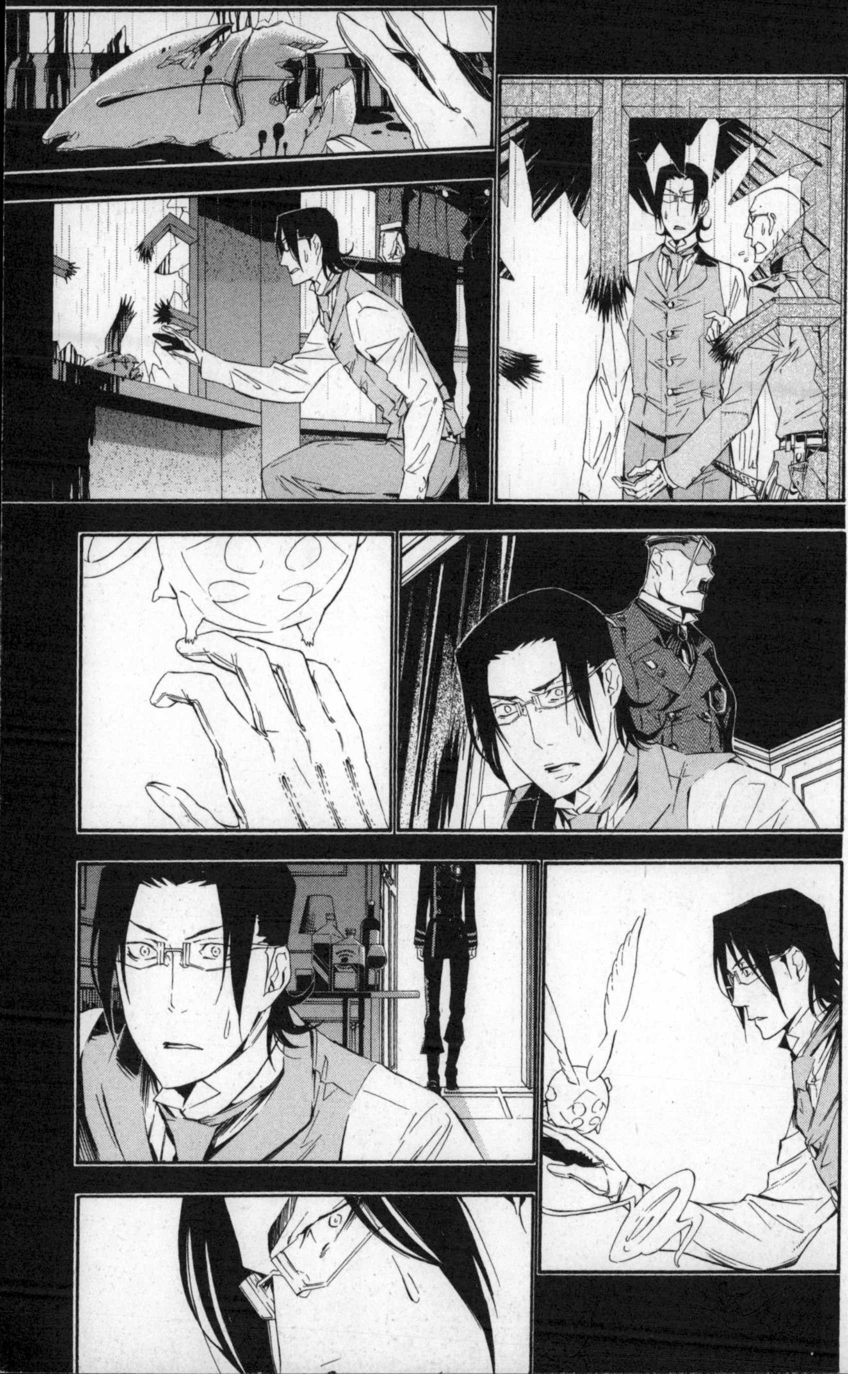

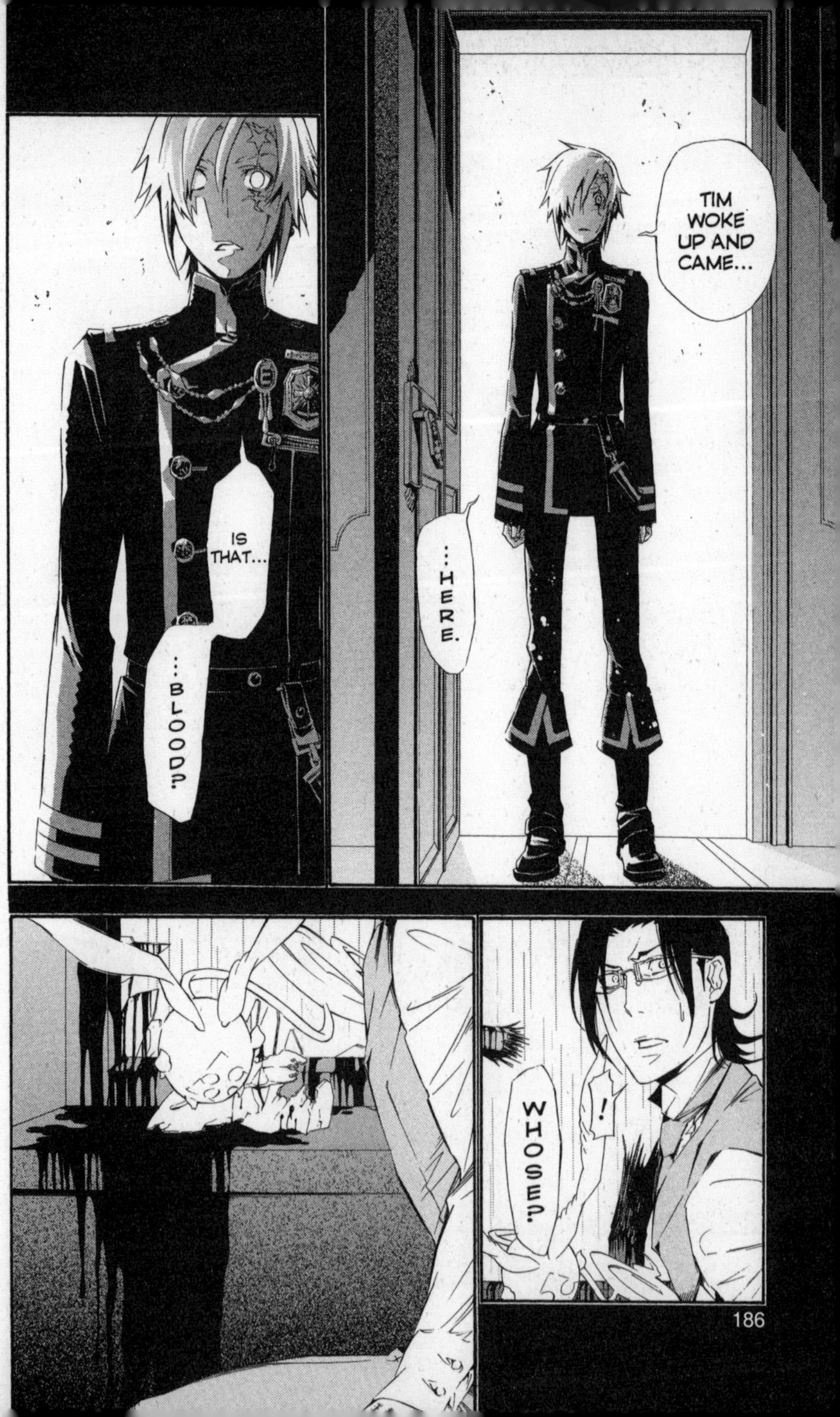
TIM WOKE UP AND CAME...
...HERE.
IS THAT...
...BLOOD?
!
WHOSE?

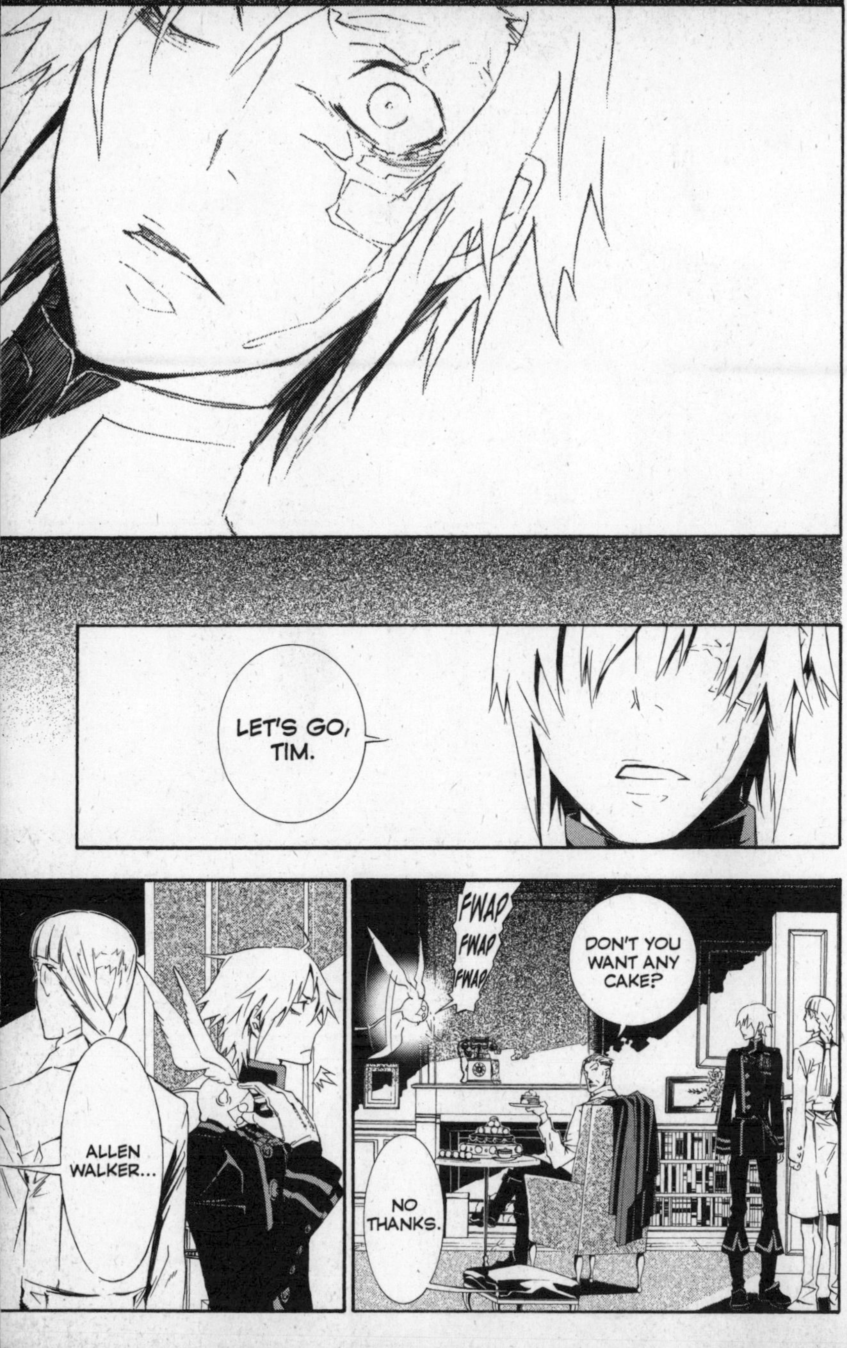
LET'S GO, TIM.
DON'T YOU WANT ANY CAKE?
FWAP FWAP FWAP
NO THANKS.
ALLEN WALKER...

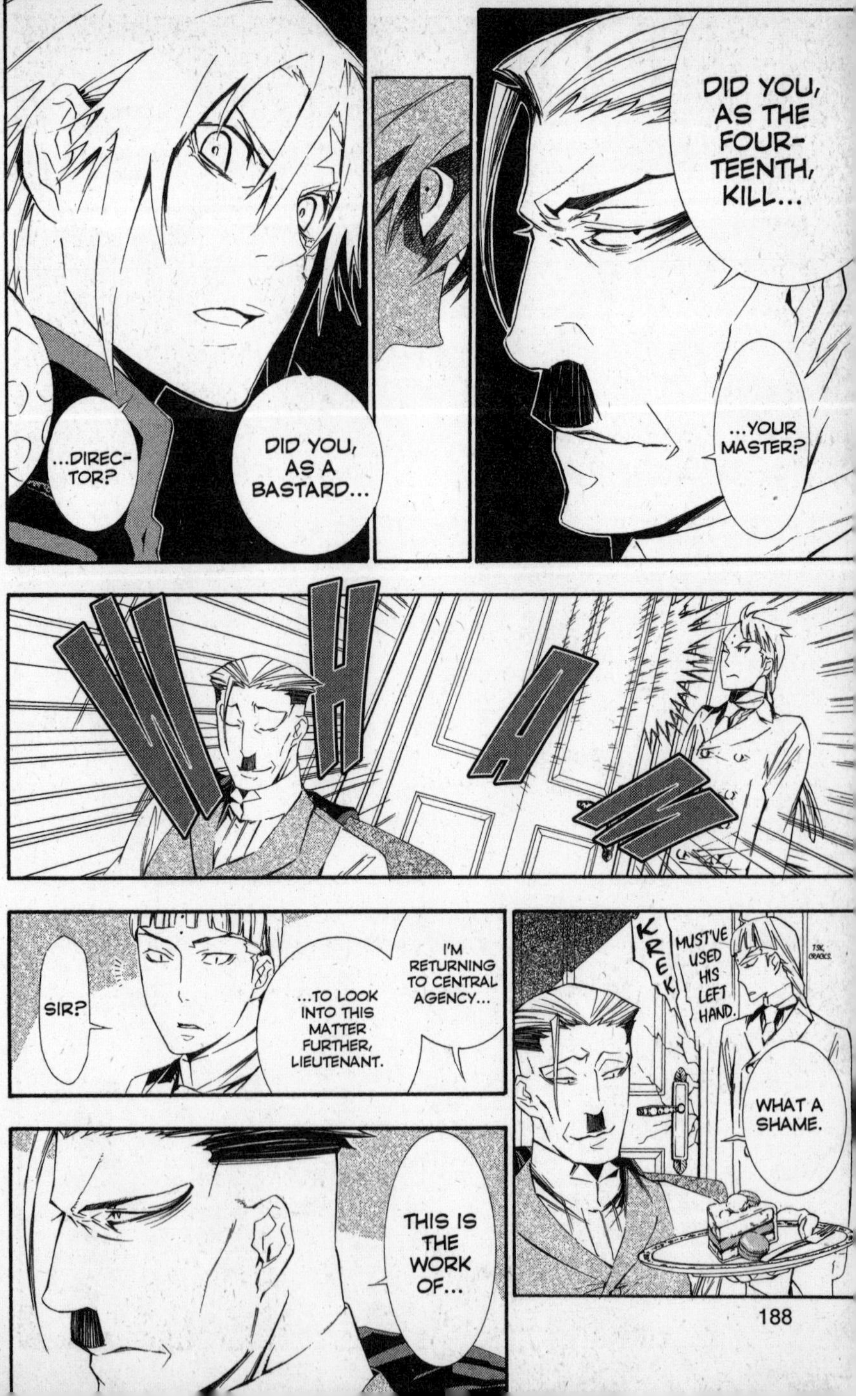
DID YOU, AS THE FOUR-TEENTH, KILL...
...YOUR MASTER?
DID YOU, AS A BASTARD...
...DIRECTOR?
WHAM
KREK
MUST'VE USED HIS LEFT HAND.
TSK CRACKS.
WHAT A SHAME.
I'M RETURNING TO CENTRAL AGENCY...
...TO LOOK INTO THIS MATTER FURTHER, LIEUTENANT.
SIR?
THIS IS THE WORK OF...

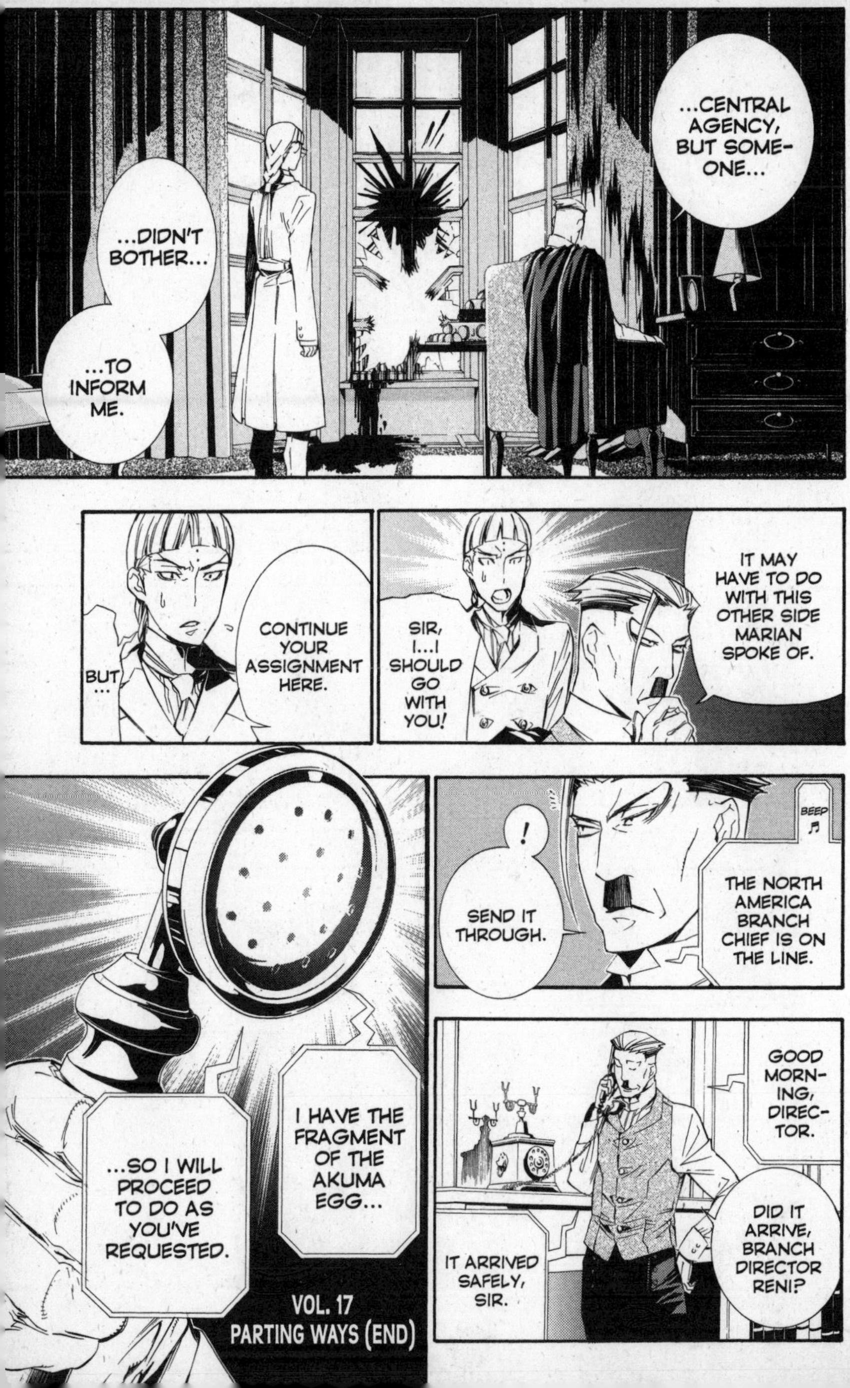
...CENTRAL AGENCY, BUT SOMEONE...
...DIDN'T BOTHER...
...TO INFORM ME.
IT MAY HAVE TO DO WITH THIS OTHER SIDE MARIAN SPOKE OF.
SIR, I...I SHOULD GO WITH YOU!
CONTINUE YOUR ASSIGNMENT HERE.
BUT...
BEEP ♬
THE NORTH AMERICA BRANCH CHIEF IS ON THE LINE.
!
SEND IT THROUGH.
GOOD MORNING, DIRECTOR.
DID IT ARRIVE, BRANCH DIRECTOR RENI?
IT ARRIVED SAFELY, SIR.
I HAVE THE FRAGMENT OF THE AKUMA EGG...
...SO I WILL PROCEED TO DO AS YOU'VE REQUESTED.
VOL. 17 PARTING WAYS (END)

THE PEOPLE OF D.GRAY-HOUSE

THE TRUTH ABOUT FATHER-IN-LAW CROSS MARIAN

I DOUBT...
...THAT CROSS MARIAN WILL EVER RETURN TO THE ORDER.
ASSUMING, THAT IS...
...HE ESCAPED WITH HIS LIFE.
?!
ESCAPED?
...
YOU DON'T MEAN...
HE'S FLEEING HIS DEBTS!
KRK

PLEASE GO INTO DEBT RESPONSIBLY.

THE PEOPLE OF D.GRAY-HOUSE

A STORMY NEW FACE APPEARS!

ARE YOU OUR NEW FAMILY MEMBER ...
...FOURTEENTH?
YES, BUT NO BATHS...
...OLD MAN.
OH, CRACKS.
MUST'VE USED HIS LEFT HAND.
KREK
WHAT A SHAME.
I MUST RETURN TO THE OFFICE.
I BOUGHT A NEW RUBBER DUCKY FOR THE CHILDREN.
SIR...
NOTHING CREEPY ABOUT IT...
DUNNO ABOUT THAT!

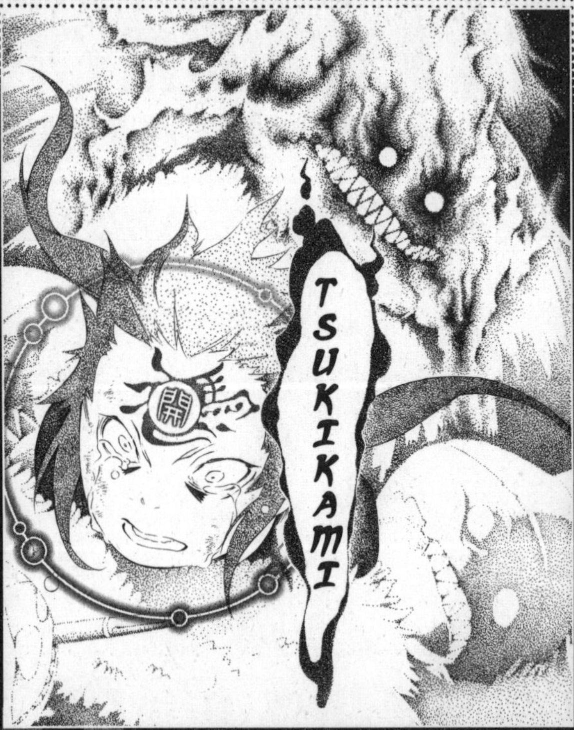
TSUKIKAMI

IN THE NEXT VOLUME...

It's been three months since Cross Marian's disappearance. A detective named Galmar is trying to catch a criminal called G, one of many so called because they all have the same bizarre appearance. Allen and some of his colleagues visit the jail and discover several Black Order Finders being held there as Gs. Then a policeman arrives with the news that G plans to knock over the Louvre!

Available August 2010!